AMERICAN STREAMLINED DESIGN

The World of Tomorrow

AMERICAN STREAMLINED DESIGN

The World of Tomorrow

David A. Hanks and Anne Hoy

Flammarion | The Liliane and David M. Stewart Program for Modern Design

Participating Institutions

Musée des Années 30, Boulogne-Billancourt, France

Georgia Museum of Art, University of Georgia, Athens, Georgia

The Bard Graduate Center for Studies in the Decorative Arts,
    Design and Culture, New York, New York

The Montreal Museum of Fine Arts, Montreal, Canada

Montgomery Museum of Fine Arts, Montgomery, Alabama

Chicago Historical Society, Chicago, Illinois

The Wolfsonian-Florida International University, Miami, Florida

Executive editor
Suzanne Tise-Isoré

**Editor for the Liliane and David M. Stewart
Program for Modern Design**
Anne Hoy

Graphic Design
Bernard Lagacé

Photography
Denis Farley, *photographer*
Nils Herrmann, *art director*

Proofreaders
Christine Schultz-Touge
Nathalie Chapuis

Editorial Assistants
Kate Clark
Frédérique Lagache

Photoengraving
Articrom

Printing
Geca, Milan, Italy

Éditions Flammarion
26 rue Racine 75006 Paris France
www.editions.flammarion.com

Dépôt légal: 05/2005
FC0499
ISBN: 2-0803-0499-2
Printed in Italy

Front cover illustration
Robert Heller, Fan: *Airflow* (cat. 114), c. 1937.
Back cover illustration
Roy Stevens, photograph of nose of Douglas Transport Plane.
From Walter Dorwin Teague, *Design This Day*, 1940.
Page 2
Margaret Bourke-White, photograph of airplane
propellers, c. 1935.
Page 6
Margaret Bourke-White, photograph of tail of Douglas
airplane, c. 1935. From Walter Dorwin Teague, *Design This
Day*, 1940.
Page 7
Anon., detail of a c. 1938 photograph of the *Twentieth Century
Limited*, designed by Henry Dreyfuss. Eric Brill Collection.

TABLE OF CONTENTS

FOREWORD

I t is with heartfelt gratitude that we dedicate this book to Eric Brill. *American Streamlined Design: The World of Tomorrow* presents a groundbreaking selection of industrial products from his recent, most generous donation of over seven hundred and fifty works to The Liliane and David M. Stewart Program for Modern Design. The selection illuminates a particularly American response to the utopian purity of the International Style and the allure of industrial technology, and this publication marks the beginning of a new, public life for Mr. Brill's adventurous collection.

This program, I am happy to write, is the latest incarnation of the Liliane and David M. Stewart Collection, now celebrating a quarter-century of dedication to modern design in all its forms, from mass-produced products and industrial prototypes, as seen here, to one-of-a-kind handicrafts and "functional artworks." The Stewart Collection was the core of the Montreal Museum of Decorative Arts (MMDA), which my late husband and I founded in 1979 and first presented in the Château Dufresne, a Louis XVI-style mansion that we renovated. Canada's first museum of decorative arts, the MMDA was devoted to acquiring and exhibiting outstanding examples of twentieth-century design, and thus it was unique among museums of North America. Its holdings eventually grew to over five thousand objects in all media—furniture, lighting, ceramics, glass, metalwork, jewelry, textiles, and graphic arts. This expansion led us to commission Frank Gehry to design galleries for us in the Jean-Noël Desmarais Pavilion at the Montreal Museum of Fine Arts (MMFA), which opened in 1997. In 2000, the Stewart Collection joined the collections of the MMFA, thus assuring its preservation for today's and future generations.

In 2001, the newly refurbished Liliane and David M. Stewart Pavilion in the MMFA made its debut, presenting both the Stewart Collection and the MMFA's own decorative arts collection in a single continuous space. Together, the two collections span the Renaissance to the present, with a dramatic emphasis on the twentieth century. The union of the two collections is yet another symbol of the acceptance of modern design into art history (a fairly recent phenomenon), as the Stewart Collection joined this eminent museum's sequence of centuries of fine and decorative arts. It ratified our founding belief in the importance of twentieth-century design—a belief that the Stewart Collection itself has helped to promulgate.

But the union of the MMDA and the MMFA has by no means quieted our acquisitive ardor or our curiosity, not only about today's creativity in international design but also about its twentieth-century roots. Quite the contrary. Eric Brill's generosity to the Stewart Program through the American Friends of Canada helps us build on our original mandate, to collect, research, exhibit, and publish the finest possible examples of modern design. Thus *American Streamlined*

Design is intended to be a probing exhibition that contributes both to scholarship and to public appreciation of modern design.

Similarly, its catalogue is in the tradition of publications based on the Stewart Collection, which bear witness to the gradually expanding parameters of its acquisitions. *American Streamlined Design* is published by our trusted ally Flammarion; it is co-authored by the Stewart Collection's longtime curator David A. Hanks and Anne Hoy of New York University and guided by Martin Eidelberg, Professor Emeritus, Rutgers University, all three modern decorative arts connoisseurs and scholars of international repute. Notable among our previous, award-winning publications are *Design 1935-1965: What Modern Was* (1991, reprinted 2001), in which the wealth of American streamlining was highlighted in one of the chapters, and *Designed for Delight: Alternative Aspects of Twentieth-Century Decorative Arts* (1997), which traced certain individualistic currents of modern design within the past century. These and our other books—large and small—have had the goal of presenting the depth of our holdings and encouraging reappraisal of the history of design.

While we have always sought out formative examples of industrial production, the Stewart Collection has not until now been able to boast a representation in depth of such interwar luminaries as Donald Deskey, Henry Dreyfuss, Norman Bel Geddes, Raymond Loewy, and Kem Weber. In addition, the Collection now includes fascinating, lesser-known designers, who are documented for the first time in this book and rightly returned to prominence. Eric Brill's marvelous gift has made all this possible.

It is therefore a signal pleasure to welcome his donation into the company of other impressive gifts to the Stewart Program from collectors, manufacturers, and the designers themselves. And it is pleasing to acknowledge Mr. Brill, both as a friend of long standing to the MMDA and as a fellow collector. His adventurous taste, discerning eye, and keen knowledge are evident in these pages, and will win admiration from all enthusiasts of industrial art. We did not buy our first example of modern design at age thirteen—in his case, a Japanese table radio from the 1930s—nor did we put ourselves through school, in his words, by buying and selling 1940s Wurlitzer *Bubbler* jukeboxes. But we are certainly delighted that he did!

Mrs. David M. Stewart
President
The Liliane and David M. Stewart Program for Modern Design

PREFACE AND ACKNOWLEDGMENTS

This volume is the first book-length examination of American streamlined products of the 1930s and 1940s. It focuses on notable examples from the rich and abundant Brill Collection, which was given to The Liliane and David M. Stewart Program for Modern Design[1] in 2002–2004, and it seeks to illuminate their uses as well as stylistic and functional genesis.[2] Following the straightforward organization of Depression-era publications, this book depicts the spaces of middle-class work and home and how these streamlined items functioned within them.

American Streamlined Design: The World of Tomorrow is indebted to two pioneering studies of streamlining. Donald J. Bush's *The Streamlined Decade* was the first major book on the style; and Jeffrey Meikle's *Twentieth Century Limited: Industrial Design in America, 1925–1939*[3] related design, business, and culture in a thorough exploration, based on the archives of the period's celebrity designers and his readings in 1930s periodicals. Our book has smaller-scale precedents in a few exhibition catalogues,[4] and its subject was given chapters in the book-catalogues *The Machine Age in America, 1918–1941* and *Design 1935–1965: What Modern Was*, which both situate streamlining within modern arts.[5] These are welcome starting points. Yet there is still much to understand about streamlining.

The most recent treatment of the style seems less than ideal. Streamlining is placed under the deluxe umbrella of "Art Deco," the term first given wide circulation by Bevis Hillier in 1968[6] for the looks of the decorative arts at the 1925 Exposition in Paris. *Art Deco, 1910–1939* is the title of a sprawling and synoptic book-catalogue published by the Victoria and Albert Museum in 2003,[7] which elides the formal and sociological differences between streamlining and the various decorative objects of Art Deco. "Art Deco" and "streamlining" are terms most helpfully kept separate. Models for this are provided by the terms "Art Nouveau" and "Secession Style," which are increasingly used by scholars to distinguish Francophone from Austro-German aspects of the decorative arts in 1900. If their distinctions are helpful, those between Art Deco and streamlining are more so. Indeed, streamlining largely spread in one country, the United States, unrelated to French applied arts and separate from them in time. In fact, amid designs of the 1930s, streamlining is more immediately recognizable than is Austrian "straight-line" decoration among *its* contemporary counterparts, seen internationally.

Even critics hostile to streamlining during its heyday identified it with the United States. "Streamlining is the Jazz of the drawing board," quipped Edgar Kaufmann, jr. in 1948. "Both are U.S. phenomena, both are 'popular' in their appeal . . . both are highly commercialized, and use the 'star' system." The "stars" that made streamlining sell, according to Kaufmann, were America's business-wise industrial designers.[8] The positive contribution of the V&A catalogue apropos streamlining is its fresh attention to the decade and to American design in the 1930s. We hope that our own contribution will lead to further, precisely defined research, especially concerning the American designers represented here and streamlined design outside the United States.

———■———

This book and the exhibition it accompanies are the result of the dedicated work of many talented people at the Stewart Program for Modern Design and of many institutions and individuals who have generously supplied information and aid over the past five years.

To the dedicated staff of the Macdonald Stewart Foundation, we owe our gratitude. James Carroll, Director of the Foundation from 1976 until his death in 2004, patiently oversaw arrangements for the publication and exhibition from concept to execution. Angéline Dazé, Registrar of The Lake St. Louis Historical Society, deserves special thanks for her prodigious work, from the first acquisition in the Brill collection to all the registrarial logistics required by a complex project. She also cheerfully oversaw conservation and photography, along with a myriad of other details. Others at the Foundation to whom we owe thanks are Bruce D. Bolton, Lucille Riley, Guy Ducharme, and Doug Ross.

In the office of David A. Hanks & Associates, New York, Kate Clark coordinated the acquisitions published here for the Stewart Program and assisted in their research. She was responsible for numerous aspects of this book, including assisting with the production of the manuscript, researching archival patent and census records, and obtaining the contextual photographs. Those who were particularly helpful in providing the photos are: Lynne Freeman Haque, Canadian Centre for Architecture, Montreal, Quebec; Carolyn Smith, Graphics Director, Bernhardt Design, Lenoir, North Carolina; Leslie Clark, Butler Manufacturing Company, Kansas City, Missouri; Kurt Jensen, Coolstock, Inc., Wimberley, Texas; Jill Bloomer, The Doris and Henry Dreyfuss Study Center Library and Archive, Cooper-Hewitt, National Design Museum, Smithsonian Institution, New York, New York; John Davis, Design Council Slide Collection, Manchester, England; James Hanks and John Kyros, General Motors Media Archives, Detroit, Michigan; Terry Austin, Greyhound Lines, Inc., Dallas, Texas; Richard J. S. Gutman, West Roxbury, Massachusetts; Lynn Catanese and Barbara Hall, Hagley Museum and Library, Wilmington, Delaware; Ford Peatross, Library of Congress, Washington, D.C.; Meghan Mariman and Eric J. Sollinger, Lockheed Martin Corporation, Bethesda, Maryland; Norah Alberto and Natalie Gonzalez, Maidenform, Inc., New York, New York; Lydia Bradshaw, Arts for Transit, Metropolitan Transportation Authority, New York, New York; Linda Kinsey, Michael Graves & Associates, and Brian Revoir, Michael Graves Design, Princeton, New Jersey; Ellen Thomasson, Missouri Historical Society, St. Louis, Missouri; Mikki Carpenter, Museum of Modern Art, New York,

New York; Marybeth Kavanaugh, New-York Historical Society, New York, New York; Marguerite Lavin, Museum of the City of New York, New York; Katy Wood, Motorcycle Hall of Fame Museum, Pickerington, Ohio; Hsu-Han Shang, Queens Museum of Art, Queens, New York; Melody Ennis, Rhode Island School of Design, Providence, Rhode Island; Shirley Manning, Shirley's Hall China Reference Pages, Napa, California; Milena Mussi, Studio Iosa Ghini, Architecture & Design, Milan, Italy; Diane L. Cooter, Syracuse University, Syracuse, New York; Robert Clark, Director of OPLA, United States Patent and Trademark Office, Alexandria, Virginia; Chip Nowacek and Suzy Hertzfeld, The Viktor Schreckengost Foundation, Cleveland Heights, Ohio; and Kevin O'Brien, White & Baldacci, Herndon, Virginia. We would also like to thank Nicolas O. Simon, Long Island University, Brooklyn Campus, New York, who provided patient instruction in the ways of Photoshop. Very special thanks go to Linda-Anne D'Anjou at the Montreal Museum of Fine Arts, Montreal, Quebec, for her helpful advice and assistance with photographs from the museum's collection.

Objects from the Brill collection chosen for the exhibition have frequently required conservation, and we wish to thank Patrick Guigues, of The Lake St. Louis Historical Society, for his skillful work in this regard, and for the able assistance of Robert Sylvestre.

Research for this book was carried out over a three-year period. We were assisted by Jonathan Clancy, who focused on the identification and the biographies of many hitherto unknown designers. At the Library of the Canadian Centre for Architecture, Paul Chénier, Pierre Boisvert, Suzie Quintal, and Francois Roux deserve our warm thanks. In addition, the following individuals and institutions have provided us with research assistance: Dennis Buck, Curator, Aurora Historical Society, Aurora, Illinois; Diane L. Cooter, Reader Services Assistant, Syracuse University Library, Special Collection Research Center, Syracuse, New York; Steve Daily, Curator, Research Collection, Milwaukee County Historical Society, Milwaukee, Wisconsin; Jean Dodenhoff, Curator, Grosse Pointe Historical Society, Grosse Pointe, Michigan; Barry Harwood, Curator of Decorative Arts, Brooklyn Museum; Kurt G. F. Helfrich, Curator, Architecture and Design Collection, University Art Museum, University of California, Santa Barbara; Judy Johnson, Glen Ellyn Historical Society, Glen Ellyn, Illinois; Karen Miller, Reference Librarian, Wilmette Public Library, Wilmette, Illinois; Greg Miller, Librarian, Toledo-Lucas County Public Library, Toledo, Ohio; Mary Mottet, Berwyn Historical Society, Berwyn, Illinois; Marjorie G. McNinch, Reference Archivist, Hagley Museum and Library, Wilmington, Delaware; Joan Swann and Libby Johnson, Co-curators, Westwood Historical Society, Westwood, Massachusetts; Kathy Tassini, Librarian, Historical Society of Haddonfield, Haddonfield, New Jersey; Marsha Wagner, Reference Librarian, Rossford Public Library, Rossford, Ohio; and Ken W. Sayers, Information Consultant, IBM Corporate Archives, Somers, New York.

In addition, relatives of the designers provided enormous assistance with information about them. We thank in particular: William Desser; Sam Hope, introduced to us by the Wauwatosa Historical Society, Wauwatosa, Wisconsin; Laurence Loewy; John Lauve; Robert A. Suomala; Milan Vavrik; and Dorothy Zaiser.

The complex task of producing a publication in French and English editions with a variety of materials has been ably carried out by the staff of Flammarion, Paris, longtime publishing partners for the Stewart Program in its earlier incarnations. Suzanne Tise-Isoré was in charge of the project and its coordination and oversaw its progress from manuscript to book. The handsome design was carried out by Bernard Lagacé, Paris. Anne Hoy edited the manuscript, and copyediting was the responsibility of Christine Schultz-Touge at Flammarion. The French translation was carried out by Jean-François Allain.

Special photography was commissioned for this publication. Denis Farley of Montreal brought great sensitivity to his interpretation of the objects, guided by Bernard Lagacé and Nils Herrmann.

It is also a pleasure to thank the staff of the Montreal Museum of Fine Arts for their cooperation in lending objects from the Stewart Collection to supplement the Brill Collection. To the Director, Guy Cogeval, Chief Curator, Nathalie Bondil, Curators Rosalind Pepall and Diane Charbonneau, as well as Anne-Marie Chevrier and Linda-Anne D'Anjou, we express our deep appreciation.

For their generous donations of contemporary designs to the Program, which are seen here, and for providing assistance in research, special thanks are due to Dr. Michael Sze and his curator, Bernard Paré, of Seattle, Washington.

We would also like to thank Jan L. Spak for her expert guidance and assistance with the project; Jeremiah Gallay for advising us on the exhibition installation; and Anne Edgar, our publicity consultant. Charles Lapointe, Montreal Tourism, gave ongoing encouragement and support to the project.

Above all, we are grateful to Eric Brill for forming this collection and sharing his research, and to Nannette Brill for her enthusiasm and encouragement. Finally, we wish to express our gratitude to Mrs. David M. Stewart for her vision in recognizing the importance of this contribution to the history of design. Her support has been invaluable.

D.A.H./A.H.

Roy Stevens, photograph of nose of Douglas Transport Plane.
From Walter Dorwin Teague, *Design This Day*, 1940.
Margaret Bourke-White, photograph of Goodyear Zeppelin,
United States airship *Akron*, 1931.
Margaret Bourke-White, photograph of Cadillac LaSalle, c. 1935.
Raymond Loewy, S-1 locomotive, Pennsylvania Railroad, 1938.

INTRODUCTION

STREAMLINING: . . . As an aesthetic style mark, and a symbol of twentieth-century machine-age speed, precision, and efficiency, it has been borrowed from the airplane and made to compel the eye anew, with the same flash-and-gleam beauty re-embodied in all travel and transportation machines intended for fast going.[1]

S peed enchanted the United States during the Depression. Not just the fact of machine-powered human flight, which the Wright Brothers had already realized, but the glamorous style of aeronautical design applied to virtually all vehicles in the 1930s: silvery aluminum-skinned aircraft for passenger travel, sleek ocean liners cleaving the sea, long bullet-shaped trains crisscrossing the country, and powerful cars with similar swooping lines. The look of these machines captured the American imagination. The streamlined style originated in them, among other sources, appeared in aspects of modern architecture and interior decoration, and permeated consumer product design in the Depression years and even after World War II. This book and the exhibition it accompanies celebrate the success of this American style in the objects of popular life.

Streamlining evolved from efforts to minimize wind and water resistance in the design of ships in the late eighteenth century, and trains and aircraft from the 1900s on (figs. 2–3).[2] A teardrop or bullet shape meets less resistance and so moves more rapidly. Vehicles with such smooth and continuous surfaces generally perform with greater speed and efficiency, saving time and money while improving the passengers' comfort. This functional reality soon acquired aesthetic merit. "A speeding motor car," claimed the Futurist poet F. T. Marinetti, "is more beautiful than the Victory of Samothrace."

In the 1930s, streamlining epitomized modernity for much of the American populace and for the new profession of industrial design. Whether consumer products had to combat the elements or were stationary, they looked up-to-the-minute with clean and simplified silhouettes, swelling monocoque casings, and gleaming industrial materials. In 1939, the designer Walter Dorwin Teague explained how the style had transcended its origins and was now applied to "things which will never move" and need not "be adapted to the flow of air currents": it "is simply because of the dynamic quality of this line which occurs in streamline forms, and it is characteristic of our age—this line that starts with a parabolic curve and ends in a long backward sweep."[3]

A ceramic pitcher of c. 1938 designed by Paul Schreckengost represents the smart language of streamlining (fig. 4). The smooth sphere of its body is extended to the curve of its spout and the counterbalanced curve of its handle. Accenting its horizontality and graphic profile is its base of speed lines, those repeated horizontal bands derived from chronophotographs of moving objects

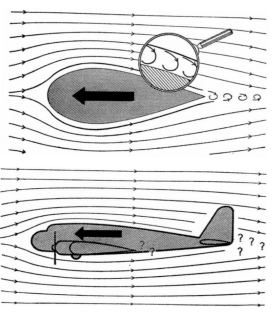

Opp., Fig. 1 Frank Lloyd Wright, exterior of S. C. Johnson Administration Building, Racine, Wisconsin, 1936–39.
Fig. 2 "The boundary layer follows the form of a streamlined body." Illustration from Norman Bel Geddes, "Streamlining," *Atlantic Monthly*, November 1934.
Fig. 3 "Airplane streamlining is very effective. There are few places where the flow pattern is uncertain." Illustration from Norman Bel Geddes, "Streamlining," *Atlantic Monthly*, November 1934.

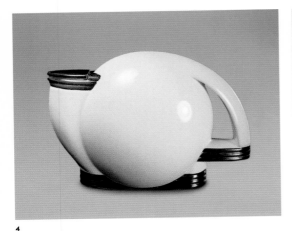

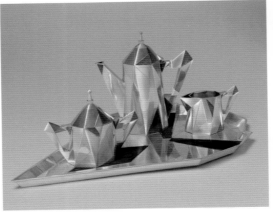

4

5

6

and found in comic books as a shorthand sign for motion. Nothing interrupts the pitcher's flawless, forward-thrusting form, as if drinking its contents promised flight. In its streamlined style, this vessel and the related goods in this book contrast with earlier products that alluded to modern art and machine parts for their chic.

Take Erik Magnussen's *Cubic* coffeepot of 1927, for example (fig. 5). Its type is conventional, but its surface is faceted as if seen through the prism of Analytic Cubism. The varied directions of the jagged planes are accented by contrasting finishes of silver, gilding, and bronze, a treatment whose optical dazzle recalls the ambiguous spatial effects in Picasso's and Braque's early paintings. American critics called such styling "Zig-Zag Moderne" and "modernistic," and associated it with the European luxury designs gathered in Paris at the 1925 *Exposition Internationale des Arts Décoratifs et Industriels Modernes.*[4]

Different from both the Schreckengost and the Magnussen designs is Paul Lobel's 1934 teapot, where a functionalist ethos reigns (fig. 6). The parts of the vessel—body, spout, and handle—are defined as separate and simplified geometric forms. Set at right angles to each other, these spheres and cylinders display their purpose like primer illustrations of "form follows function." They embody the Machine Style seen in the Purist paintings of Fernand Léger and the young Le Corbusier,[5] and objects made at the Bauhaus, the German school of art and design. Americans could design in both the functionalist Machine Style and Streamlining, but it was the latter idiom —with its theatrical evocations of science, modernity, and progress—that won the country's heart.

In streamlined products, in fact, form rarely followed function, but generally concealed it. Svelte welded cowlings and curvy molded housings hid and protected complex working parts and so domesticated machines, from locomotives to power drills, suggesting their performance was simple and speedy. Such works did not look threatening—like the cogs and wheels that devoured Charlie Chaplin in his 1936 film *Modern Times*—but dynamic and futuristic, even sexy. The extended parabola of streamlining, wrote Teague, "occurs constantly throughout our bodies—a muscular male body or a beautifully formed female body."[6] Streamlined styling romanticized technology; it gave new or updated tools and utensils expressive personalities and helped make them user-friendly. For the designer Harold Van Doren, streamlining was

> . . . a phenomenon no designer can ignore and no modern book on design can afford
> not to discuss. . . . The manufacturer who wants his laundry tubs . . . streamlined is in
> reality asking you to modernize them, to find the means for substituting curvilinear

Fig. 4 Paul Schreckengost, Pitcher, ceramic, c. 1938. New York, Collection of Paul Schreckengost.
Fig. 5 Erik Magnussen, *Cubic* Coffee Service, silver and bronze, partially gilt and oxidized, 1927. Collection of the Museum of Art, Rhode Island School of Design. Gift of Textron, Inc.
Fig. 6 Paul A. Lobel, Tea Service, 1934, silver plate, wood, for International Silver Company. The Metropolitan Museum of Art. Gift of M. H. Lobel and C. H. Lobel.

forms for rectilinear forms. . . . He expects, too, that unnecessary exposure of mechanical parts will be eliminated, that buttons will be substituted for levers, and control panels and dials will be organized into simple and easily read groups. . . . [7]

By the early 1930s the Cubo-Futurist fracturing of forms in Magnussen's coffee pot looked discordant and alien to both streamlining designers and Machine Style proponents in the United States. Yet the two camps exaggerated their differences as they fought to support native modern design. In 1932 the young architect Philip Johnson and the architectural historian Henry-Russell Hitchcock mounted their "International Style" exhibition at The Museum of Modern Art, documenting their espousal of the austere language and utopian social goals of Bauhaus and Russian architecture and design. Two years later, in *Machine Art*, another exhibition at MoMA (fig. 7), Johnson defined the museum's principles for applied arts, displaying machine parts like abstract sculpture together with similarly functionalist mass-produced objects. "The machine process itself," he wrote, "contain[s] the elements of a new beauty. . . ."

> A polished ball bearing is beautiful. The motors of Gar Wood's speedboat are beautiful. Analogous is the beauty of pure engineering in factories, in grain silos, in suspension bridges; the beauty of these designs consists of their simple geometric relations: the catenary curve and straight posts of the bridge, the interlocking cylinders of the silo, the spherical perfection of the ball bearing.[8]

The teapot by Lobel could illustrate this text (fig. 6).

Both Johnson and Lobel were appealing to the same aesthetic of platonically pure shapes in shining metal that had already captured the imaginations of modernist photographers like Paul

Fig. 7 Installation of *Machine Art* exhibition. The Museum of Modern Art, 1934.

Strand and such Precisionist painters as Charles Sheeler in the 1920s. Johnson's juxtapositions were intended to ennoble functionalist design in America and elsewhere, while distancing it from what he termed the " 'Modernistic' French machine-age aesthetic" and from objects with "neo-classical trappings and bizarre ornament."[9] (He was referring to two decorative currents at the Paris Exposition of 1925.) Yet despite the museum's influence, the machine and its parts as product design sources were embraced by relatively few U.S. consumers. Instead, the bravado of the streamlined style was appealing in an era of emotional as well as economic depression.[10]

The products surveyed here were aimed at the breadth of the middle class. Low-slung, back-swept chairs in tubular steel; rocket-like soda siphons; vacuum cleaners, scooters, and outboard motors with teardrop-shaped cowlings; staplers and tape dispensers with horizontal "speed whiskers": they all offered performance and panache at a reasonable price. For a deposit of just a few dollars, most people could take home a shiny new General Electric refrigerator and share in the dream of progress and a better, modernized future that President Franklin D. Roosevelt called the promise of the New Deal. Even without credit or installment buying, a modest outlay could update a kitchen with a chromium-plated Westinghouse toaster, an office with a Bakelite desk lamp by Polaroid, a home workroom with a *Craftsman* power drill from Sears, Roebuck, and a "clubroom" with electric drink mixers and a portable RCA phonograph. Such purchases would help businesses and homes update their appearance and improve their functioning. While they encouraged consumption and thus offered a way out of the Depression, they vowed through their air-smoothed styling to contribute to a unified and modish environment. To some critics and many consumers, they looked both contemporary and American. In the depth of the Depression, the glossy products could be identified with country, modernity, and progress—indeed, with recovery.

Statistics put American unemployment at 24.9 percent in 1933 and 26.7 percent in 1934,[11] but forces for economic revival were present and had been in place since the 1920s. Certain industries, such as automobile manufacturing, had reached overcapacity in the twenties, and began seeking new ways of stimulating demand.[12] At the same time, mass production at low cost was increasingly possible in the gamut of consumer products, encouraging high-volume output and frequent styling changes and mechanical improvements to stimulate sales. Relatively new appliances, such as radios, justified new forms. With the growth of automobile travel and the popularity of movies and illustrated magazines beginning in the 1920s, interest in a national culture burgeoned, while consumer appetites sharpened for the goods of the good life. All this aided Roosevelt when he became president in 1933, and he mobilized the engine of government spending, creating jobs and new purchasing power. The steady recovery from 1934 on was spurred by encouragements to production and consumption; an ever-higher living standard was viewed not as a fantasy but as a right for all Americans.

The consumer economy of the 1920s had generated the new field of industrial design. Between 1926 and 1929, four influential industrial designers had opened offices in New York City—Walter Dorwin Teague, Norman Bel Geddes, Raymond Loewy, and Henry Dreyfuss—and by the early 1930s they were joined by Harold Van Doren and Russel Wright. In 1934 the National Alliance of Art & Industry (founded with support from John D. Rockefeller, Jr., and the Carnegie Corporation) opened its first exhibition of "the wonders of industrial design," products by a hundred designers, from a prefabricated house to washing machines. The Alliance chose works by Dreyfuss, Lurelle Guild, Donald Deskey, Gustav Jensen, and others for its show in New York's RCA

Fig. 8 Advertisement for a streamlined bra, *Allo* by Maiden Form, c. 1937.
Fig. 9 Advertisement for streamlined men's underwear from *Saturday Evening Post*, May 1, 1937.

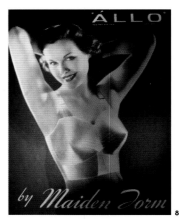

Fig. 10 Advertisement for a streamlined casket from *Advertising and Selling,* August 26, 1937.

Building. The Alliance was dedicated to "the union of art and industry for the benefit of the consumer" and to "good design"[13]: these men identified it with streamlining, as their products in this book demonstrate. They recognized the broad appeal of the style and transferred it from mass-transportation vehicles to heavy appliances and the humblest office equipment. Harnessing the growing power of advertising and public relations, they assured the wide market penetration of the streamlined style.

Their recognition of its sales power produced some surprising, even humorous results. A streamlined bra was advertised in 1937, shining like stainless steel and stitched with speed lines (fig. 8), forecasting Jean Paul Gaultier's costumes for Madonna. In 1937 an ad trumpeted, "Yes—'streamlining' in men's underwear!" (fig. 9), and explained: "One-piece. Smooth-fitting all over. No gaping, no unsightly bunching at the back. No excess cloth anywhere. . . ." Even a casket was streamlined with rounded corners and speed line grooves in yet another example of the style's commercialism, for this item was designed, ironically, for someone no longer in a hurry (fig. 10).

Streamlining continued into the postwar period, giving jukeboxes and handheld mixers voluptuous sheaths. It was rediscovered in the 1960s by Pop artists seeking their popular culture roots and revived in the 1970s by Postmodern designers and architects, as well as architectural preservationists (notably in Miami's North Beach). Today it is both fondly quoted, as seen in this book's last chapter, and unconsciously paraphrased; it is identified with *Airstream* mobile homes and the *Broadway Limited* locomotive, with the futuristically styled consumer goods seen here, and the U.S. World's Fairs of 1933 and 1939 with their happy faith in the World of Tomorrow. Streamlining was, and is, for everyone.

The Emerging Profession of Industrial Design

Not surprisingly, some of the most celebrated American industrial designers of the period migrated from advertising—Raymond Loewy, Walter Dorwin Teague, and Donald Deskey among them.[14] They grasped that new packaging and product designs would work together with advertising and promotion to spark consumption. Design was "the silent salesman" and a key marketing tool, according to Earnest Elmo Calkins, who established the first styling and design department at his Manhattan advertising agency, Calkins & Holden, and made Egmont Arens its director.[15] Arens saw the industrial designer as a "consumer engineer," operating at the nexus of mechanical inventors and manufacturers on the one hand, and advertising executives on the other. He had near-magical abilities to increase sales. In *Consumer Engineering: A New Technique for Prosperity,* Arens framed his ideas on consumer psychology as tools for economic recovery. What some later critics would see as consumer manipulation with products of "planned obsolescence" was Arens's recipe for a capitalist renaissance.

"Streamlining has captured American imagination to mean modern, efficient, well-organized, sweet, clean and beautiful," Arens claimed in a telegram to President Roosevelt in 1934. He offered to speak on "Streamlining for Recovery" and appealed to the federal government and to businesses to accept streamlining as a word.[16]

New packaging and new designs were viewed as tonics for the Depression's disease—underconsumption. Fresh design and presentation would help distinguish a given product in an increasingly crowded field; they might attract impulse spenders at the store; and they could identify their manufacturers with stylishness and modernity and foster brand loyalty even if this year's model were replaced by next year's.[17] America's manufacturers, who had contributed to the doubling of advertising revenues between 1920 and 1927,[18] got the point.

Theater was also a field that nurtured the industrial designers who created their own profession at the end of the 1920s. Norman Bel Geddes, John Vassos, Henry Dreyfuss, and Rolph Scarlett had all designed theater sets, and their fancies would fly for industry with design possibilities ignored by those who had only architectural or engineering backgrounds. Bel Geddes also conceived sweeping, banded sets for dramatic windows for fashionable department stores (fig. 11), while Vassos and Donald Deskey were among those who created striking store windows on their road to becoming industrial designers. When these men turned from product to showroom and even factory design, their touchstone was "eye appeal" rather than engineering. They recognized the importance of image in an economy that was shifting from production to consumption. Design could be generated by the need for brand identity, rather than the logic of function or construction.

This accounts for the industrial designer's easy assumption of the sequence of tasks from a product's blueprints to its packaging, advertising, and presentation. To meet the demands of large and growing corporations, the offices of the streamlined designers enlarged the services they offered. From a one-person business in 1928, Raymond Loewy's Manhattan-based firm, for example, expanded to around fifty with an office in London by 1936, and by the 1950s it boasted a staff of two hundred, with additional offices in Chicago, South Bend, and São Paulo, and a client list of about one hundred domestic and foreign companies.[19] By the mid-1930s the Dreyfuss office was offering all the services possible.

> The organization known as Henry Dreyfuss was formed with the idea of serving the manufacturer in all phases of his business in which eye value was of importance. Mr. Dreyfuss is interested in following the job through from beginning to end which, on occasion, includes not only designing the product itself but the package in which it is sold, the display with which it is merchandised, the display case in which it is shown, and the showroom which is its background.[20]

Not every observer approved this development, however. While admitting that these U.S. industrial designers were "pioneers" who soon aimed "at professional ethics and responsibilities (including education of young designers)," Edgar Kaufmann, jr. implied from the perspective of 1957 that they lacked aesthetics or that necessity had overwhelmed them in the 1930s.

> Economically realistic as perhaps only a generation arriving in a depression could be, market-conscious on a scale and at a level incomprehensible to most Europeans whose biggest sales were traditionally to underdeveloped colonies, the American industrial designers of the 1930s faced facts first and paid little attention to the traditions, experiences and ideals the modern movement had accumulated since the middle of the previous century.[21]

In fact, the designers of the 1930s included many cultivated émigrés. Loewy was born and reared in Paris; John Vassos emigrated from Bucharest; Kem Weber and Peter Müller-Munk from Berlin; Paul T. Frankl from Geneva; Paul Lobel from Bakou, Romania; William Lescaze from Geneva; and Dr. Peter Schlumbohm from Kiel, Germany. All of these men were familiar with the work of designers in the 1925 Paris Exposition and the architectural and artistic languages of modernism. These and many other designers brought their training in European schools and their apprenticeships to skilled European masters to the U.S. market.

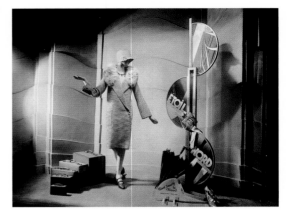

Fig. 11 Norman Bel Geddes, display window for Franklin Simon department store, New York City, c. 1927.

Kem Weber, for example, entered the Academy of Applied Arts in Berlin in 1908 and began master classes with the modernist Bruno Paul, the director of the school. In 1914, Paul sent Weber to the United States to design the German section of the Panama-Pacific Exposition in San Francisco. When the outbreak of World War I prevented his return, Weber decided to remain in the United States. His education made him a conduit between the German modernists and his American colleagues and clients.[22]

Streamlining in Architecture

In the 1930s streamlining pervaded most areas of American life, especially the built environment. It marked several pavilions at the Chicago *Century of Progress Exposition* of 1933–34 and it reached its apogee at the 1939 New York World's Fair. Though contemporaries hailed it as uniquely American, elements of Expressionist design and French and Dutch modernism contributed to U.S. streamlined architecture. The "International Style" exhibition of 1932 at MoMA included buildings by Le Corbusier and J. J. P. Oud that relied on sweeping curves in smooth reinforced concrete and rhyming ribbon windows. The work of c. 1910–20 of the German architect Eric Mendelsohn also proved influential, and through his visits to the United States, publications and exhibitions of his designs, and eventually his immigration to the U.S., he offered an eloquent precedent for sculptural designs with emphatic horizontals, continuous silhouettes, and repeated banding around teardrop shapes. Writing in 1930, Sheldon Cheney praised Mendelsohn for conceiving "new characteristic building forms out of concrete, metal, and glass," and he illustrated the German's Expressionist sketches of the period around World War I (fig. 12). His "sketches of hangars, factories, and railway stations [were] without precedent and intriguingly powerful," Cheney went on. "There is no question about the originality, vitality, and machine-massiveness of the designs."[23]

In 1924 Bel Geddes met Mendelsohn, who gave him a sketch of his Einstein Tower in Potsdam. This remarkable building of 1921, a precedent for streamlined architecture, was a symbol of progress and faith in science: it celebrated the genius who conceived the theory of relativity. Bel Geddes was convinced that new architectural forms would come from such advances and the achievements of technology and engineering. Mendelsohn's architecture, which included the dramatic Petersdorff Department Store in Breslau, Germany, 1928 (fig. 13), would influence Bel Geddes's own designs in the streamlined style.[24]

Mendelsohn's example also reached American design via Frank Lloyd Wright, whom he met in November 1924. The two were impressed with each other, and Wright asked the visiting architect for sketches. Mendelsohn recalled that Wright described his work as "Original, powerful—the future" and said that he was more a sculptor than an architect, more a modeler than a builder.[25] These plastic qualities typify streamlined design. The style marks Wright's S. C. Johnson Administration Building, Racine, Wisconsin, 1936–39 (fig. 1), whose broad, curving, horizontal forms strongly suggest the impact of Mendelsohn's early sketches. Meanwhile Wright sneered at cubic International Style buildings as "flat-chested" design.[26]

"Streamlined modern" was a style chosen for certain public architectural projects of the 1930s, which appeared from coast to coast. The sheer physical scale of these striking buildings and the publicity they generated familiarized the public with the hallmarks of streamlining and encouraged the appearance of those marks in mass-market products. A powerful example is seen in the Mendelsohn-like warehouse built for the Hecht Company in Washington, D.C., designed in 1937 by

Fig. 12 Eric Mendelsohn, sketches for industrial buildings, c. 1915–1920, with streamlined forms. From Sheldon Cheney, *The New World Architecture*, 1930.

Fig. 13 Eric Mendelsohn, Petersdorff Department Store, Breslau, Germany, 1928.

Abbott, Merkt & Company, engineers and architects (fig. 14). Six stories high, it was built of reinforced concrete in slab construction, with an exterior of horizontal bands. These alternate between masonry, glass, and terra-cotta and buff-colored brick, stating the theme of massive horizontality.[27] On the West Coast, the Pan-Pacific Auditorium of 1935 in Hollywood (fig. 17), built for the National Housing Exposition, was a superb example of streamlining. Designed by Charles F. Plummer, Walter Wurdeman, and Welton Becket,[28] the building (now destroyed) was low, with horizontal banding added to emphasize its streamlining. Particularly memorable were the piers that rose above the entrance and metamorphosed into playful streamlined lighting and flagpoles. They looked like aerodynamic structures but were in fact mere decorations.[29]

Streamlining sometimes invaded the sacrosanct realm of German-based modernism, as seen in the Richard H. Mandel house by Edward Durell Stone (see figs. 48, 50). William Lescaze also admitted using streamlining as an "enriching variation in his straight-line Functionalism."[30] In the Philadelphia Savings Fund Society Building of 1919–32 in Philadelphia (figs. 15–16), which he designed with George Howe, the entrance and first floors are united as a horizontal base with a canopy sweeping around the corner site. This rounded base provides a dynamic launching pad for the upward thrust of the skyscraper, a bold contrast recalling that found in some of Mendelsohn's aerodynamic sketches. Inside the PSFS Building, echoes of the canopy's continuous line are visible on the balcony of the double-height banking floor, the banking counters, and the tubular steel railings around certain desks.

Streamlining was also used for marketing architectural elements, as illustrated in a 1935 advertisement for extra-strong flooring (fig. 18). Here fantasy streamlined architecture suggests a future city, in the exuberant mode of the comic books' Buck Rogers. In fact, a testament to the popularity of streamlining appears in the comic books, movies (fig. 19), and mass magazines of the 1930s, such as *Popular Mechanics* (fig. 20). This completes the circle of stylistic influence, for streamlining was enriched by earlier examples of science fiction and visionary expression. The science fiction writer H. G. Wells had described a "vision of the city of the future, with its glass, curves and controlled

Fig. 17 Charles F. Plummer, Walter Wurdeman, and Welton Becket, Pan-Pacific Auditorium, Hollywood, California, 1935.

Fig. 18 Detail from advertisement for
H. H. Robertson Company, Pittsburgh,
Pennsylvania, "The Floor of the Future."
From *The Architectural Forum*, August 1935.
Fig. 19 Still from film RKO's *Shall We Dance*,
starring Fred Astaire and Ginger Rogers, 1937.

environment free from rain, cold, disease, chaos and squalor."[31] An attempt at realizing the vision was made in the 1935 film, *Things to Come*, based on Wells's writing. It was a taste of what New York's 1939 *World of Tomorrow* fair would achieve.

New Materials and Manufacturing Techniques

It is ironic that functionalist critics dismissed streamlined design as window dressing. They upheld "truth to materials" as a quality of valued design, perhaps unaware that streamlining was in fact well suited to the new materials developed in the early twentieth century. These new materials lent themselves to new production techniques. Plastics including Bakelite were cast in multiples in molds where the fluid material could be poured or injected. The rounded corners of streamlined objects were particularly receptive to this molding process. Stress during the cooling process was also reduced with the surfaces of curved shapes. For streamlined forms of steel or aluminum, the rounded edges could be pressed out of a single sheet, whereas rectilinear forms required more time and hence larger expenditures as the edges had to be welded manually. Though mass-production techniques lent themselves to various styles, including the neo-classicizing current in Art Deco, they went hand in hand with streamlining.

Harold Van Doren, who is credited with introducing industrial design to the Midwest, illustrated various curved and simplified forms that could be incorporated into streamlined products in his classic textbook *Industrial Design*, 1940 (fig. 21). Following normal custom, industrial design objects were always produced first in clay models, which fostered their sculptural quality. Van Doren advised his design pupils: "the student will do well to practice modeling such form in clay, in the abstract. Paper work will do him little good. As he proceeds, many fascinating shapes will develop, each new one leading to others and each suggesting many product design applications."[32]

Aluminum was another of the new materials to have great impact on design in the 1930s. It was light, flexible, yet as strong as iron, and resistant to corrosion, and it had high thermal and electrical conductivity. Such firms as Kensington Inc., a division of the Aluminum Company of America, capitalized on this, boasting about such wares designed by Lurelle Guild as the bowl and vase seen in cat. 96 and 97 (reproduced here) that it was "proud of the non-tarnishing characteristic, of the fact that finger marks mysteriously disappear and that it is a hard metal although it looks soft. . . ."[33] At the other end of the scale in terms of size, aluminum was employed as a brilliant cowling on trains, aircraft, and other vehicles. Like a new dress, it was slipped over unchanged locomotive motors, increasing their speed through its lighter weight (fig. 22). Through a series of futuristic advertisements in the 1940s, the Bohn Aluminum and Brass Corporation promoted the use of its material to stimulate postwar sales. Fig. 23 illustrates a speeding airplane, train, and automobile, all streamlined and all made speedier by the lightness of the alloy.

Another "miracle" alloy was Monel, made of nickel, which the International Nickel Company developed in 1905, but diverted to wartime use during World War I to build battleships. After the war the company needed to find new domestic uses for Monel, and behold, kitchens helped it get over the slump in the battleship business. A "streamlined sink" was designed for International Nickel by the Danish-born Gustav Jensen (unrelated to the silversmith), who streamlined it with horizontal banding and curved edges. The Jensen design was introduced in 1931 through advertisements in various shelter magazines.[34] It was the only streamlined object included in the 1934 *Machine Art* exhibition at MoMA (fig. 24).[35]

Fig. 20 Cover of *Popular Mechanics* 61, no. 3 (March 1934), cover story, "Secrets of Super-Speed!" The Liliane and David M. Stewart Collection.

The greatest advances in new materials took place in plastics. These new synthetic materials included Bakelite, Plexiglas, vinyl, and polystyrene. According to the Cheneys, Van Doren was the first American designer to experiment extensively with synthetics and their color possibilities,[36] while Teague described the necessity of adapting the form to the material, and insisted that "only through study of the material do we discover its possibility of beauty."[37] Formless in themselves, plastics could be molded, extruded, and stamped in the early technology of the medium, and so they easily lent themselves to the fluid form language of streamlining. As an inexpensive and completely malleable substitute for metals, they were unequalled. Streamlined consumer goods in Bakelite and other synthetics would contribute to the acceptance of plastics during World War II and their wide use thereafter.

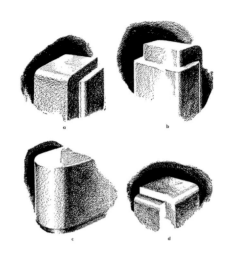

Functionalist merit, however, was second to metaphoric power in the popularity of streamlining. Its strength as a style lay in its far-reaching command of allusions. These covered every aspect of travel in the first third of the century, a century that had already conceived the space-time continuum and cheered Charles Lindbergh's transatlantic flight in 1927. The streamlining designers took their inspiration from planes—as well as ships and trains.

Metaphors for a Fast Society

Streamlining began on trains, according to the architectural historian Siegfried Giedion: a tubular form was given to railroad cars as early as 1887.[38] But the first modern streamliner, a diesel-driven train with a steel skeleton and corrugated aluminum skin, was the 1934 Burlington *Zephyr*. As Raymond Loewy's chart of the evolution of locomotives shows (fig. 27), the design of trains evolved from the boxlike cars of the nineteenth century to the more sweeping and harmonious forms of the 1930s.

Loewy designed one of the two best-known trains of the streamlined era, the Pennsylvania Railroad's *Broadway Limited*, 1937 (fig. 25), while Henry Dreyfuss was the creator of New York

Fig. 21 "Corner Treatments." From Harold Van Doren, *Industrial Design*, 1940.
Fig. 22 Right: Henry Dreyfuss, *Mercury* locomotive; left: Designer unknown, J-1c Hudson locomotive, both New York Central System, 1936.
Fig. 23 Advertisement for Bohn Aluminum and Brass Corporation, c. 1945. The Liliane and David M. Stewart Collection.
Fig. 24 "Streamline Monel metal sink," designed by Gustav Jensen for the International Nickel Co., Inc. From *Machine Art*, The Museum of Modern Art, 1934.

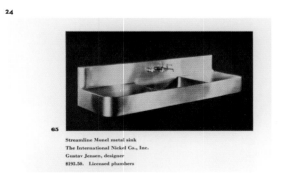

28

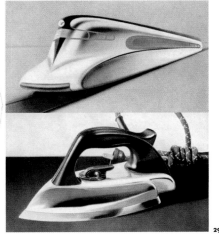

29

Wright, but in an aircraft developed in Germany by Count Ferdinand von Zeppelin. It was tested in 1897, and in 1900 the *Zeppelin* made an eighteen-minute voyage. Airship service took off with successful international flights for passengers and mail. In 1931 Margaret Bourke-White photographed the streamlined form of a Goodyear Zeppelin (p. 14); and another Goodyear craft was prominently featured in the 1933 *Century of Progress Exposition* in Chicago. The public love affair with Zeppelins ended only after the disastrous explosion and burning of the *Hindenburg* in 1937 in Lakehurst, New Jersey.

The airplane quickly became the most important source of form for the new aesthetic of streamlining, and its evolution was also drawn by Loewy (fig. 36), implicitly supporting his preference for streamlining in all products, whether airborne or stationary. A benchmark of aerodynamic styling was the Douglas Commercial or DC-3. With its rounded nose, sleekly contoured body, tapering wings, smooth engine cowls, and parabolic tail, it became one of the most successful of the streamlined passenger airplanes (fig. 33). In service by 1936, it influenced the design of trains, cars, and objects alike.[43] In 1935, Le Corbusier had proclaimed, "the airplane is the symbol of the new age," and he celebrated the beauty of the vehicle and the functional spareness of its parts.[44] That a renowned French architect praised the inventions of Americans gave nationalistic critics a sense of pride.

Ships were also streamlined for primarily functional reasons: to cut the resistance of the wind and water. As outlined in another of Loewy's charts (fig. 34), they became still more streamlined in the 1930s. Bel Geddes was early in praising the looks of the modern craft, and he designed a streamlined ocean liner in 1932 (fig. 31) whose overall form resembled the aerodynamic shape of a Zeppelin. The smokestacks and pilot's bridge were the only protuberances in the otherwise pure form, ready for flight across the Atlantic. The usually awkward forms of the lifeboats were concealed in the body and would slide out horizontally as needed. About another Bel Geddes nautical design, for a diesel yacht, a contemporary critic raved: "Streamlined principles, hitherto confined for the most part in ship design to the hulk alone, have here been used throughout, promising

Fig. 27 Raymond Loewy, evolution charts of locomotives and passenger cars. From Cheney and Cheney, *Art and the Machine*, 1936.

Fig. 28 Raymond Loewy, bar in the *Broadway Limited*, Pennsylvania Railroad, 1937. From *The Architectural Forum*, September 1938.

Fig. 29 Raymond Loewy, "Fast Commuter" railway car and Westinghouse electric iron. From Cheney and Cheney, *Art and the Machine*, 1936.

Fig. 30 Walter Dorwin Teague, high-speed monorail, c. 1937. From *Pencil Points*, September 1937.

30

greater seaworthiness, comfort, and efficiency. In stormy, cold, or rainy weather, all decks are to be closed in, shedding water easily and providing complete protection for passengers."[45] (Sadly, none of Geddes's designs for transportation were realized.)

Loewy also designed streamlined ships, as well as ferryboats (fig. 32). The Bohn Aluminum and Brass Corporation used the fanciful image of a streamlined ship—"one of the transatlantic liners of the future"—to identify its metals with this romantic mode of luxury transportation (cat. 161). Ocean liners were floating hotels, a source of patriotic pride and competition, and a locus for alluring design. These traits typified them from the late nineteenth century, but in the interwar period streamlining enhanced their stylishness and the allure they embodied of both greater speed and comfort. Whether the vehicles illustrated here were constructed or not, they spoke to the yearnings of Americans and helped inspire the product designers who tried to satisfy them.

Rapid Mass Transit, Practical and Poetic

As for cars, they began to be streamlined early in the twentieth century, and by the early 1930s such styling was widely if not uniformly accepted. Loewy's chronology of design progress is again prophetic as it insists on the inevitability of stylistic change (fig. 35). Many of his models were developed in the United States by Detroit manufacturers, and fewer European cars were streamlined. An advertisement for the new Chrysler *Airflow* gushed: "Old mother nature has always designed her creatures for the function they are to perform. She has streamlined her fastest fish . . . her swiftest

Fig. 31 Norman Bel Geddes, model of ocean liner, 1932. From Bel Geddes, *Horizons*, 1932.

Fig. 32 Raymond Loewy, *Princess Anne* ferryboat, 1933.

Fig. 33 Douglas Aircraft, American Airlines Flagship DC-3, 1935. From advertisement in *Time*, November 9, 1936.

Fig. 34 Raymond Loewy, evolution chart of power ships. From Cheney and Cheney, *Art and the Machine*, 1936.

Fig. 35 Raymond Loewy, evolution chart of automobiles. From Cheney and Cheney, *Art and the Machine*, 1936.

Fig. 36 Raymond Loewy, evolution chart of airplanes. From Cheney and Cheney, *Art and the Machine*, 1936.

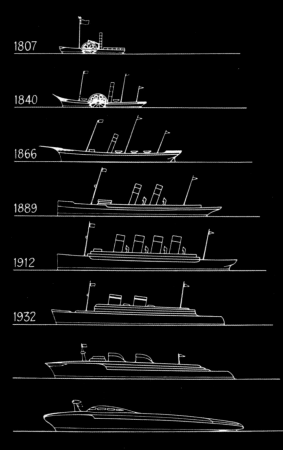

1807

1840

1866

1889

1912

1932

34

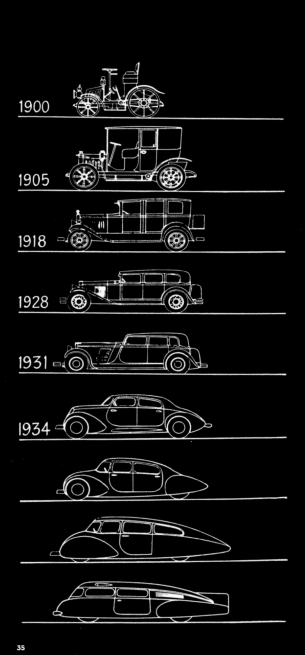

1900

1905

1918

1928

1931

1934

35

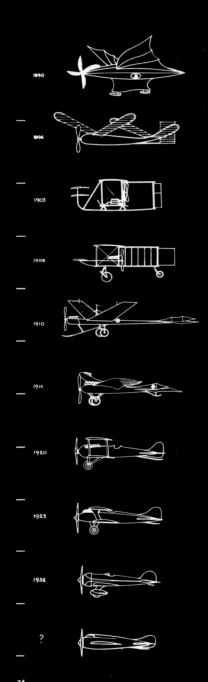

1890

1894

1903

1906

1910

1914

1920

1923

1932

?

36

birds . . . her fleetest animals that move on land. . . . You have only to look at a dolphin, a gull, or a greyhound to appreciate the rightness of the tapering, flowing contour of the new Airflow Chrysler" (fig. 37).[46] Automobiles of the future were also envisioned: Buckminster Fuller developed three experimental prototypes for his *Dymaxion* car (fig. 38) in 1933–34, each of which relied on a streamlined form and the principles of aerodynamics for its economies. The three-wheeled vehicle was powered by a Ford V-8 motor in the rear and it achieved high speeds with low fuel consumption. The first reexamination of the automobile form since the Model T, it had teardrop streamlining for scientific reasons. Streamlining for Fuller was no passing fancy of the stylist, but the optimum form in industrial design.[47]

Streamlining also appeared in all the other forms of mass transportation: buses, bicycles, motorcycles, and the iconic *Airstream* trailer or mobile home. The Greyhound Bus Company, for example, in competition with trains and cars for Middle-American travelers, hired Loewy to update the looks of its rolling stock. With maximum economy, his redesign of the Greyhound bus in c. 1937 used a streamlined paint job alone to convey speed and efficiency (fig. 39). Schwinn had already introduced the streamlined bike it called *Aerocycle* in 1934, and advertised its "new welded frame— built like an aeroplane fuselage."[48] One of the most remarkable American designs for a streamlined bike came from John Vassos, who designed a dramatic aerodynamic example in c. 1938, seen in the patent drawing (fig. 40).[49] With its teardrop casing and swooping handle bars and seat, it appears to have emerged from a successful wind tunnel test.

37

Fig. 37 Carl Breer and the Chrysler Engineering Staff, Chrysler *Airflow* automobile, as seen in a 1934 advertisement.
Fig. 38 Buckminster Fuller, *Dymaxion* Car no. 3, 1933. From Cheney and Cheney, *Art and the Machine*, 1936.
Fig. 39 Raymond Loewy, Greyhound bus, 1937.

38

39

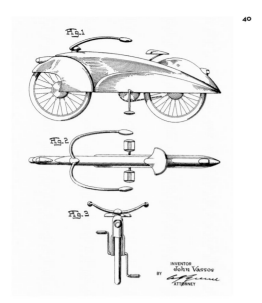

40

41

42

Fig. 40. Patent drawing for bicycle, designed by
John Vassos c. 1938.
Fig. 41. Motorcycle, *Indian Chief,* Indian Motorcycle
Company, 1940.
Fig. 42. *Airstream Clipper* trailer, pulled by the bicyclist
Jean Latourneau, 1947.

The motorcycle had elements of streamlining in earlier twentieth-century versions, but the impact of American streamlining is best seen in 1930s designs by the Indian Motorcycle Company of Springfield, Massachusetts. The firm had started to manufacture motorcycles in 1902, and in 1922 introduced the *Indian Chief*. During the 1930s the *Chief* became more streamlined, as seen in the example in fig. 41 with its emphatic parabolic and teardrop fenders covering the wheels.

The most familiar American streamlined vehicle may still be the *Airstream* motor home trailer. Its inventor Wallace Merle Byam began making trailers in the 1920s with the prefabricated kits of wood he designed; in 1930 he founded a company to build them. At mid-decade, he began to experiment with techniques from the aircraft industry to decrease wind resistance and increase speed. In 1936 his Airstream Trailer Company introduced the *Airstream Clipper*, seen here in a 1947 photograph of the French bicycle racer Jean Latourneau pulling it in order to demonstrate the lightness of the vehicle (fig. 42). Named for the Pan American plane, the *Airstream Clipper* had a monocoque body of riveted aluminum derived from airplane design. It could sleep four, as its tubular steel framed dinette table could convert to a bed; it was equipped with electric lights and even offered air conditioning using dry ice.

Planes, trains, buses, cars, bikes, even mobile homes—as seen here, examples of all of them were streamlined in the 1930s, and the style was identified with their speed, efficiency, glamour, and service to the broad population. As Loewy's evolutionary charts implied, streamlining was the latest expression of a logical development in all vehicles. It would be applied with equal logic to new and improved consumer goods, for their buyers saw themselves favorably in the metaphor of the style. As Egmont Arens put it, streamlining expressed "this peculiar genius of the American people to be going places—and be going there fast."[50]

World's Fairs in America

In the United States the 1930s were capped at either end by major world's fairs, which contributed to defining and popularizing streamlining. The Chicago *Century of Progress Exposition,* which celebrated the city's centennial over a two-year period, 1933–34, demonstrated that streamlining had arrived. A room by Walter Dorwin Teague for the Ford Building (fig. 43) demonstrates streamlining in the horizontal banding of the walls. The classically inspired furniture is reminiscent of chairs by the French designer Jacques-Emile Ruhlmann, suggesting how well the American style meshed with more conservative European imports.

Although the fair was held during the Depression, its admission price did not deter middle-class visitors. They basked in the fair's dream of a promising future. It included Buckminster Fuller's three-wheeled *Dymaxion* Car no. 3, the Burlington *Zephyr,* completed in April 1934 as the first streamlined train, the Chrysler *Airflow* automobile, and the Goodyear blimp floating over futuristic architecture. On May 26, 1934, the opening day of the fair's second season, the *Zephyr* arrived after a lightning trip from Denver to Chicago: it took only fourteen hours, cutting twelve hours from the time of scheduled trains.[51] At the same time a Lincoln log cabin and a replica of how Fort Dearborn looked in 1833 were displayed, suggesting that progress in the next century would be as dramatic, continuous, and inevitable as it had been in the last.

The New York World's Fair of 1939 was dedicated to "building the world of tomorrow with the tools of today": it was the ultimate endorsement for streamlining. This fair featured streamlining everywhere, in its architecture, products, and exhibition displays (figs. 44–47). Rather than showcasing

43

Fig. 43 Walter Dorwin Teague, foyer for the Executive Lounge of the Ford Building, *Century of Progress Exposition,* Chicago, 1933–34. From *Pencil Points,* September 1937.
Opp., Fig. 44 James Gambrel Rogers, Pylon of the Chrysler Motors Building, New York World's Fair, 1939.

Fig. 45. Cover of brochure for *Futurama*, The General Motors "Highways and Horizons" Exhibition, New York World's Fair, 1939. The Liliane and David M. Stewart Collection.

American architects, the fair was shaped by the celebrity industrial designers, including Bel Geddes, Deskey, Dreyfuss, Teague, and Vassos. They presented exhibits on such themes as transportation and communication, and they designed impressive structures, inside and out, for America's major corporations. In the General Motors "Highways and Horizons" pavilion, *Futurama* by Bel Geddes was the most popular attraction at the fair. Seated in a row of moving armchairs, visitors viewed the greenbelts, highways, and towers of the future metropolis. The towers, intended to be a quarter of a mile high, were streamlined homages to Le Corbusier; the fourteen-lane highways, with lanes for different speeds, were a prototype meant to persuade the federal government to sponsor a national highway system. Here, in coherent visual form, was an exciting yet comforting vision on the eve of World War II: the problems of yesterday and today could be ignored, thanks to the progress of American industry; tomorrow held every possibility, eased by rapid transportation and instantaneous communication. The designers of subsequent decades, as seen in our last chapter here, quote the formal elements of streamlining, but they have never recaptured such optimism.

Fig. 46 Raymond Loewy, *Rocketport*, Chrysler Motors Building, New York World's Fair, 1939.
Fig. 47 View of New York World's Fair, 1939.

THE BRILL COLLECTION
AND THE RICHARD H. MANDEL HOUSE

American Streamlined Design: The World of Tomorrow is drawn in large measure from the collection of American industrial design assembled by Eric Brill. For the last thirty-five years, this former oil products trader and blender has been acquiring design prototypes and mass-produced industrial objects made between 1930 and 1950, and on this occasion we applaud not only his generosity in sharing his collection with the public, but also the triumph of the splendid streamlined design of that era.

Although born on Long Island, New York, Brill grew up in Asia and Europe because of his father's position at Pepsi-Cola, which caused the family to live in many parts of the world. At age thirteen, while his family was in Tokyo, he bought his first modernist product, a Japanese table-model radio of the 1930s. He recalls early boyhood trips on Boeing-made, Pan American double-decker *Stratocruiser* propeller airplanes, and he credits his fascination with streamlining and speed to his exposure to such airplanes and airports. As a teenager in the late 1960s, Brill began to collect classic motorcycles and racing bikes. Then, while in college at the University of Wisconsin-Madison, he started reading design magazines from the 1930s and collecting industrial design in a more systematic fashion. He helped earn his way through school by buying and selling vintage Wurlitzer jukeboxes, such as the *Bubbler* model 1015.[1] A decade later he began collecting modern industrial designs from the 1930s. His collection was well under way, and he would be able to share it with his wife, Nannette, and their growing family.

Over time, Brill's aesthetic preference has emerged for simple, powerful works in which the aesthetics of art, architecture, and the functionalism of industrial design come together. Of the more than seven hundred and fifty examples of American industrial design in the Brill Collection, most are bold, modernist objects in a language epitomized for him by a Kasimir Malevich painting he owns,[2] an elemental abstraction of c. 1920 (fig. 49). His delight in it is more than formalist. Brill's father was a navigator during World War II, and when his B-17 was shot down in France, he joined and fought with the French Underground. As Brill wrote:

> Reading about, hearing about, and seeing some of the battlefields of WWII, as well as realizing the pivotal role the USSR played in saving the world from Hitler . . . all influenced me to a distinctly leftist perspective, which went hand in hand with my love of machine design and production, and the possibility of beautiful, efficient goods for all people. This is probably why I

49

Opp., Fig. 48 View of Edward Durell Stone's Richard H. Mandel house, 1933–35, Bedford Hills, New York. From *The Architectural Forum*, August 1935.
Fig. 49 Kasimir Malevich, *Untitled* (Black Circle), undated, c. 1922. Gouache on paper board, 27.9 x 27.9 cm. Eric Brill Collection, Bedford Hills, New York.

get so excited about the Malevich painting . . . it's not only that it is a revelation that a simple

circle floating within a square can look so incredibly beautiful, but also that art can function at

its highest level using simple, accessible forms and techniques.[3]

The Malevich painting and the Brill Collection are totally in accord with the interiors of the Richard H. Mandel house, a property that the Brills purchased in 1992. Although then in dilapidated condition, this house, built in 1933–35 for a wealthy designer, was a perfect match for the Brills' passionate interest in design from that period, and they began the long process of restoring it to its original condition.

Located on what were originally ninety acres overlooking the Croton Reservoir in Bedford Hills, New York, the Mandel house (figs. 48, 50) was designed by Edward Durell Stone (1902–1978), while Donald Deskey (1894–1989) was responsible for the interior architecture and Kurt Versen (1901–1997) designed the lighting.[4] The landscaping was executed by Michael Rapuano, who extended the lines of the building, especially to the north, with plantings and terraces.

Stone probably met Deskey, eight years his senior, through his work for the various architects of Rockefeller Center (Reinhard & Hofmeister, Corbett, Harrison & MacMurray, Hood and Fouilhoux). Deskey had the commission for some forty lobby and lounge areas for Radio City Music Hall, and the architects had appointed Stone to be chief designer of the interiors of the Radio City theater and the Center Theater.[5] Because Stone and Mandel worked for Deskey, the Mandel commission developed as a joint project in Deskey's office. This commission launched Stone's career, as he later wrote: "In 1933 I became, in my own right, an architect." He credited Deskey with introducing him to Mandel, "who asked me to design a house for him. He was interested in a good business arrangement and I was interested in undertaking my first modern house, so I worked for $40 a week and as I was also teaching interior design in the evenings, between the two jobs I managed to survive."[6]

Deskey was then thirty-eight, and at the top of his career with his suave and witty interiors for Radio City Music Hall.[7] He had trained as an artist, studying painting part-time in Los Angeles and in San Francisco. Like other industrial designers of the 1920s, he began his career in advertising, first in Chicago and then in New York, where he moved in 1921. Deskey visited Paris in 1923, and again in 1925, to pursue painting further, and on the latter trip he had gone to the *Exposition Internationale des Arts Décoratifs et Industriels Modernes* in Paris, and he also recalled visiting the Bauhaus in Dessau. Returning to New York, he began his career as an industrial designer in 1926 and was soon known for his furniture, lamps, and interiors. He skillfully integrated Bakelite, tubular steel, and other new industrial materials with exotic veneers, leather upholstery, and natural fibers. By about 1930, Deskey's designs had evolved from his earlier use of a decorative, Cubist-oriented style to a simpler, modernist idiom with streamlined silhouettes.[8]

Mandel had studied design in Paris in the 1920s, and worked for the fashionable design firm of Dominique,[9] although his position as an heir to the Mandel Brothers department store in Chicago must have saved him from financial need. After he returned to the United States, he joined Deskey's firm in 1931, and provided Deskey with furniture designs and probably financial backing as well.[10]

For the Mandel house, the associations between patron, interior designer, and architect were propitious, and so were the times. Stone and Deskey received the Bedford Hills commission no more than a year after the landmark 1932 Museum of Modern Art exhibition gathered important

Fig. 50 Model of Mandel house, Donald Deskey Collection, Cooper-Hewitt, National Design Museum, Smithsonian Institution.

new architecture under the rubric "the International Style." In the highly influential book by Henry-Russell Hitchcock and Philip Johnson based on the exhibition, MoMA's director Alfred H. Barr, Jr. defined the style by three distinguishing aesthetic principles: "emphasis on volume—spaces enclosed by thin planes or surfaces as opposed to the suggestion of mass and solidity; regularity as opposed to symmetry or other kinds of obvious balance; and, lastly, dependence upon the intrinsic elegance of materials, technical perfection, and fine proportions, as opposed to orna-ment."[11] The Mandel house illustrates these principles with an aplomb that seems well beyond Stone's years.[12] It is an International Style house, adapted to American taste and the New York State landscape, with a streamlined bay that would later harmonize with the Brills' collection.

The vast, flat-roofed, thirty-eight-room residence is unified by the expansive horizontals of its three stories. Constructed of concrete blocks sheathed in white-painted stucco, and by bands of windows fitted flush with the wall surfaces, casting no shadows, the Mandel house eloquently speaks the language of modernism. Approached from the long driveway (fig. 48), the house appears lightly anchored on the hillcrest by its low parapet wall with clipped hedges and by its most strik-ing feature, a semicircular dining room.[13] A motif of welcome and prospect, this pavilion of floor-to-ceiling glass bricks and plate glass turns the corner from the living-room wing to the entry and the wing of children's and service quarters. The interpenetrating planes with a curved element at a key

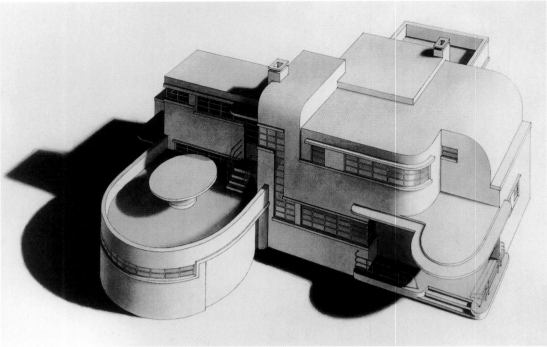

junction are Cubist ingredients, displaying Stone's cultural sophistication. Seen from the southwest (fig. 48), the jutting second-floor terrace seems almost airborne, extended from the master bedroom on three slender, recessed Lally columns. From all vantage points, the home's asymmetrical composition of intersecting low-slung rectangles appears dynamic and varied. Its cost, not including the furnishings, was $60,000, a considerable sum in the Depression years. No wonder that twelve periodicals featured the Mandel house within months of its completion, in January 1935, and the house continued to be recognized in design magazines throughout the decade. The October 1940 issue of *The Architectural Forum* cited it as one of the outstanding designs of the past decade.

Almost all observers recognized Stone's accomplished rendition of the International Style, and the acclaim for the house did much to confirm American acceptance of the idiom in the late 1930s. Here and later, Stone displayed his skills at adapting advanced form languages for specific patrons and regions. The house also reflected the low horizontal thrusts of Frank Lloyd Wright's Prairie houses and his structures at Taliesin in Spring Green, Wisconsin, with their echoing lines of terraces and plantings. And Richard Neutra's and Le Corbusier's ribbon windows and taut white walls, widened to form parapets for roof terraces above, are recalled too, possibly from the representation of their work in MoMA's 1932 exhibition.[14] Stone's proportions are long, low, and horizontal, however, and his extended lines generally accent the ground plane with subtle reassurance.

Most remarkable is Stone's curving bay containing the dining room above the bar/recreation room, the circular element protruding so dramatically on the exterior (fig. 51). An elegant example of streamlining, this can be compared to the more thoroughgoing use of the language in 1931–32 by such American architects as George Howe, William Lescaze, and Norman Bel Geddes (fig. 52), all of whom were encouraged by some of the same models that inspired Stone. All three designs illustrated here use a vocabulary of curves and right angles, with spherical elements generally set at

Fig. 51 View of semicircular bay at Mandel house with bar/recreation room on the ground level, dining room on the first floor level, and sun deck on the second floor level. From *The Architectural Forum*, August 1935.
Fig. 52 Norman Bel Geddes, *The House of Tomorrow* (never executed), 1931, drawing, Norman Bel Geddes Collection, Hoblitzelle Theatre Arts Library, The Humanities Research Center, University of Texas, Austin.
Fig. 53 J. J. P. Oud, Hook of Holland, store, workers' housing project, 1924–29. From Sheldon Cheney, *The New World Architecture*, New York, 1930.

the conjunction of two rectangular units. But Stone's design is simpler, more restrained, and more obviously functional. In his use of the curved element, Stone's design recalls a long vanguard tradition of rounded forms, including the swooping lines of Eric Mendelsohn's drawings of the 1910s and buildings of the 1930s (fig. 12), and the cylindrical shapes in J. J. P. Oud's Hook of Holland workers' housing project, 1924–29, with its termination in a pavilion-like shop (fig. 53). Contemporary modernists and conservatives alike applauded Stone's use of the rounded form at the Mandel house. There it announces the owner's hospitality and lets them command the view of lush woods and water. From the exterior it suggests the observation deck of an airport or the cockpit of a plane or dirigible. Summoning up the preeminent emblem of modernity, *The Architectural Forum* of August 1935 saw the house as "a giant airplane [that] seems to partake of the openness of the landscape and sky."[15]

Inside, the stairways leading from the ground floor to the hall, dining and living rooms above, and thence to the second-floor terrace, boast generously scaled aluminum rails and cork floors. They present visually energetic spaces that are distantly reminiscent of Le Corbusier's interiors at the 1928–30 Villa Savoye in Poissy, just outside Paris. The Mandel stairs, in particular, so enchanted Edward Steichen, then Condé Nast's artistic director, that he staged fashion shoots there for *Vogue* (fig. 54).[16] Extending the nautical allusion, the bedrooms and halls are illuminated by Kurt Versen's chrome-ringed, porthole-like lights, which are flush-mounted to the ceilings.

Dominating the first floor is the thirty-by-fifty-foot living room (fig. 56), whose continuous plate-glass windows embrace the panoramic landscape. Glass double doors facing onto the north terrace expand the sense of space further. In this vastness, the furniture designed and supplied by Deskey, especially his baby grand piano, serve as room dividers, defining spaces within the open plan (fig. 55).

Sweeping, sparsely furnished rectangles, these and most of the rooms of the Mandel house are modernist but not streamlined. However, the semi-circular bay of the dining area and bar (figs. 57–58) celebrates streamlined styling in its low, horizontal emphasis, smooth surfaces, and rounded forms. Above, in the dining room, the vista west is breathtaking, and the changing light at sunset plays off the artificial lighting, especially as it glows through the frosted glass inset in the Bakelite surfaces of Deskey's dining table and sideboard (fig. 57). Stone has recreated the visual drama of a control tower, that symbol of modern travel and expanded horizons. Below, in the bar/recreation room (fig. 58), the nautical/aviation theme continues. A built-in leather banquette nestles against the curved wall, echoed by the low curved backs of Deskey's chairs. Additional curves are offered by the white Bakelite bar, alluringly lit from below, and its conforming chromium foot rail and mirror back. Tubular steel furniture, similar to that created by Marcel Breuer at the Bauhaus, completes the aura of a luxury liner's lounge. The mural above the banquette, by Witold Gordon (who had painted two murals for Radio City Music Hall), amusingly combines world-spanning liquor motifs, from the Johnny Walker Scotsman and the Dubonnet man to a mermaid holding rum and a sugar cane. With its color and charm, it is far from the extreme strictures of functionalism.

The bar mural represents a graceful American acquisition of the more decorative, sophisticated side of European modernism. In their restoration of the house, the Brills commissioned a replica of the mural which was painstakingly copied by the Montreal painter Réjean Tétreault from a color photograph in the May 1935 *House & Garden* (fig. 59). Sixty-some pieces that Deskey designed or selected for the house were purchased with it or found in the storage room, and they, along with

53

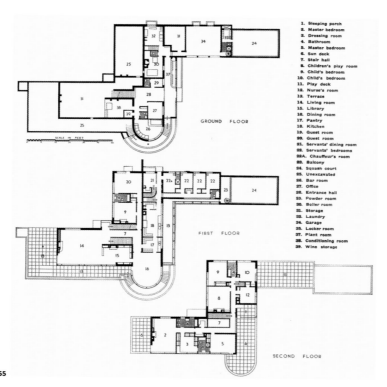

1.	Sleeping porch
2.	Master bedroom
3.	Dressing room
4.	Bathroom
5.	Master bedroom
6.	Sun deck
7.	Stair hall
8.	Children's play room
9.	Child's bedroom
10.	Child's bedroom
11.	Play deck
12.	Nurse's room
13.	Terrace
14.	Living room
15.	Library
16.	Dining room
17.	Pantry
18.	Kitchen
19.	Guest room
20.	Guest room
21.	Servants' dining room
22.	Servants' bedrooms
22A.	Chauffeur's room
23.	Balcony
24.	Squash court
25.	Unexcavated
26.	Bar room
27.	Office
28.	Entrance hall
29.	Powder room
30.	Boiler room
31.	Storage
32.	Laundry
34.	Garage
35.	Locker room
37.	Plant room
38.	Conditioning room
39.	Wine storage

Fig. 54 Edward Steichen, "Washable Dinner-Dresses."
From *Vogue*, May 15, 1935.
Fig. 55 Ground plans of Mandel house.
From *The Architectural Forum*, August 1935.
Fig. 56 Living room of Mandel house, interiors and furnishings by Donald Deskey. Donald Deskey Collection, Cooper-Hewitt, National Design Museum, Smithsonian Institution.
Fig. 57 Dining room of Mandel house.
From *The Architectural Forum*, August 1935.

the Brills' own collection of his work, allowed a comprehensive recreation of the Mandels' environment. The Brills' restoration of the total—including replastering and painting 11,000 square feet of rooms, refurbishing two hundred casement window frames, and replacing five roofs and numerous decks—required more than ten years.[17]

In 1995, the Mandel house was named to the National Register of Historic Places. It was six decades after the residence was finished in 1935, the same year that *The Architectural Forum* wrote that "it was developed slowly and carefully through the collaboration of owner, architect, and designer who were equally interested in every problem from the orientation of the house on the property to the disposition of coffee tables and ash trays. Modern architecture, perhaps more than other style[s], demands this collaboration."[18] That collaboration has been richly enlarged by Eric and Nannette Brill, reflecting their dual passions for collecting and preservation. From their perspective, Stone's Mandel house and the extraordinary promise of the "World of Tomorrow" in their collection are being preserved to be shared with still future generations.

58

Fig. 58 Bar/recreation room of Mandel house. From *Fortune*, October 1935.
Opp., Fig. 59 Mural and banquette in bar room, Mandel house. From *House & Garden*, May 1935.

"TO GRACE
THE FINEST DESK"

Streamlining the Commercial World

1

"Invest in the future" and "Time is money," two of the mottoes of American business, encouraged streamlining in all aspects of industry in the 1930s—from the layouts of offices, showrooms, and gas stations to the design and packaging of new products. Streamlining connoted modernity, speed, efficiency, and therefore higher profits. The styling attracted customers to department stores and diners and appealed to the users of office machines. In an economy increasingly defined by consumption, it appealed to shoppers, especially as financial recovery began in 1933, and to white-collar workers alike. Streamlining, in a word, meant sales.

It is no coincidence that one of the most famous icons among streamlined commercial interiors of the 1930s was the "Model Office and Studio for an Industrial Designer" by Raymond Loewy and theater set designer Lee Simonson (fig. 60).[1] Promoting the style and the industrial designer as its artist, this interior was designed for the exhibition *Contemporary American Industrial Art,* held at The Metropolitan Museum of Art in 1934. Virtually devoid of right angles, the room was curved in its corners, windows, table tops, continuous display shelves, and all its furnishings. The walls were of ivory-colored plastic laminate panels outlined in horizontal bands of blue gunmetal, and these horizontal lines and curves of the streamlined style were enhanced by the tubular steel furniture. Without filing cabinets or closets, this was more a showroom than an office or studio; here Loewy's models for his 1934 *Hupmobile* and his designs for the 1933 *Princess Anne* ferryboat were displayed to advantage.[2]

Real showrooms were recognized as presenting particular design problems. An article of 1938 on the subject asserted that "sales efficiency" required that the setting must exploit the appearance of the product and its functional properties.[3] In the showrooms of progressive companies, dramatic streamlined settings for its goods created a unified, alluring image for the manufacturer. Often the same industrial designer was responsible for both the products and the interior architecture. In c. 1935, Walter Dorwin Teague designed the exterior and interior of the A. B. Dick Company's office and showroom in Chicago (figs. 61–62), and he also designed some of its leading products, all illustrating the streamlined aesthetic at its best. Office equipment, in this case a streamlined mimeograph machine, was presented in a dramatic setting, a setting announced on an entrance façade of black glass with aluminum trim contrasting with the broad plate glass of the show window and door. Interior plaster walls were painted white, and "Flexwood," a thin wood

Fig. 60 Raymond Loewy and Lee Simonson, "Model Office and Studio for an Industrial Designer," designed for the exhibition *Contemporary American Industrial Art,* The Metropolitan Museum of Art, 1934.

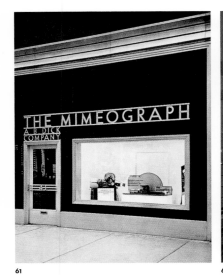

61   62   63

veneer popular in the 1930s, was applied to the wainscot, with chromium-plated "snap-on" moldings throughout, emphasizing the streamlined effect. Typical of a progressive public space in the period, the flooring was rubber-tile linoleum. The total looked clean and elegant, with rounded corners and horizontal lines, all attributes associated with streamlining.[4] Teague's New York showroom for the Ford Motor Company, c. 1938 (fig. 63), was another glamorous interior, which a contemporary account praised for its simplicity and restrained style.[5] Its double height allowed customers to admire the cars from a balcony above them. (The sole decoration, its huge mural was a photomontage of happy Ford workers, mostly at their famed assembly lines. Its subtext was that car sales supported jobs.)

In Lurelle Guild's showrooms for Alcoa, which opened in 1934 in New York's RCA building (figs. 64–65), the material was the message. Aluminum consumer goods and industrial machines appeared like jewelry within rounded vitrines edged in aluminum. Curved lines articulating the walls and floors were intended to draw the viewer from display to display. The palette was silvery, underscoring a selling point of aluminum: it offered the beauty of the old precious metal, according to its promoters, and the economy and performance required by modern life.

Department stores are simply multiple showrooms, sheltering a panoply of products under one roof, and in the 1930s they were often streamlined modern designs from roof to sidewalk. A

Fig. 61 Walter Dorwin Teague, exterior of the A. B. Dick Company office and showroom, Chicago, c. 1935.
Fig. 62 Walter Dorwin Teague, A. B. Dick Company office and showroom.
Fig. 63 Walter Dorwin Teague, designer, and Gavin Hadden, engineer, Ford Motor Company showroom, New York, c. 1938.

64   65

Fig. 64 Lurelle Guild, Alcoa showroom, RCA building, New York, 1934.
Fig. 65 Lurelle Guild, Alcoa showroom, RCA building, New York, 1934.

66

stylized interior of a department store was depicted by John Vassos (fig. 66) for the book of his futuristic images called *Contempo*, which he co-authored with his wife, Ruth.[6] Seen from two stories above, perhaps from an escalator, the curvilinear counters with their smooth surfaces and repeated columns create an aura of grandeur. A streamlined setting—chic and easy to maintain— would help sell products. In their planar simplicity, such designs made effective backdrops.

The architecture and layouts of gasoline stations were often streamlined to enhance their association with streamlined automobiles and their thrilling speed and to improve their access. For Socony, Norman Bel Geddes prepared twenty-four charts and a model to analyze the functional requirements of gas stations: such thorough practicality was expected to guarantee the usefulness of this model to Socony's entire national chain.[7] The Socony service station seen in a postcard (fig. 67) appears to be the result of Bel Geddes's study. Speedier service is implied by the design, with easy routes in and out, and the curving end of the building is echoed by the pavement bending around it. A rounded canopy extends invitingly from the entrance over one set of gas pumps, and above this the large "Socony" logo appears on a curved vertical fin. Surfaces are smooth, light, and bright; the aura of cleanliness and efficiency was intended to help sell the services offered—from full repairs to gas and restrooms.

Restaurants were part of the commercial world that often employed streamlining for interiors as well as furnishings. The Automat, a Swiss invention, was introduced to Philadelphia in 1902 and then New York in 1912. In the 1930s the Automat was sometimes streamlined, as seen in Scharf's Automatique Cafeteria in Brooklyn designed by Ralph Pomerance and Simon Breines in 1938 (fig. 68), which provided complete food service in a relatively narrow space. Food preparation and presentation were vertically organized, connected by dumbwaiters, allowing for circulation on the main floor and departmentalized food service in the basement. The automatic machines from

67

NORTHLAND MOTORS, INC.
LAKE PLACID GARAGE
Lake Placid, N. Y.

Fig. 66 John Vassos, interior of a department store. From John and Ruth Vassos, *Contempo: The American Tempo*, 1929, Brill Collection.
Fig. 67 Postcard, "Northland Motors, Inc., Lake Placid Garage, Lake Placid, N.Y." Coolstock.com Collection.

which the restaurant takes its name were banked on one wall.[8] When the customer put in the coins, the glass door framing the dish flipped open. Behind the wall of doors was a narrow corridor for attendants to keep the shelves filled.[9]

Many American diners were streamlined, as seen in the example in fig. 69, and modeled on railroad dining cars. These long, low, sleek structures with their glistening stainless steel and porcelain tiling were efficient, clean, and streamlined in their look and spatial organization.[10] The diner was associated with Americans on the road; here was an early instance of fast food for workers at lunch or for travelers.

Clustered in America's largest cities, the skyscraper was the home for most offices, office equipment, and information systems. By necessity, given their vertical orientation, few skyscrapers were streamlined in their overall design, but rather in their parts. Consider the Philadelphia Savings Fund Society building in Philadelphia and the McGraw-Hill building in New York (see figs. 15, 16, and 166). Both have streamlined bases, for example, and the banking floor of the former choreographs public movement with continuous counters while its ribbon-like balconies dramatize its two-story height.

On the office floors of business America, however, streamlining was primarily seen in the organization of human and work flow patterns to save steps. This additional meaning of "streamlining," as making work more efficient, originated in the early twentieth century in the factory studies of Frederick W. Taylor (1865–1915), the so-called father of scientific management. Taylor decried the inefficiency caused by poorly designed equipment and wasted movements. Through time-motion studies of workers and tasks, he sought to increase productivity by "eliminating unnecessary motions and substituting fast for slow and inefficient motions." His goal was to introduce "one method and one implement which is quicker and better than any of the rest. . . ."[11]

Fig. 68 Exterior of Scharf's Automatique Cafeteria, Brooklyn, New York, designed by Ralph Pomerance and Simon Breines, c. 1938. From *Architectural Record*, April 1938.
Fig. 69 Interior of diner, manufactured by Paramount Diner Company, Haledon, New Jersey, c. 1935–45.

Taylor's concepts were realized most importantly in the assembly line, but also in office designs with large open spaces punctuated by desks facing the same direction. This allowed for work to flow from desk to desk and for staff supervision. Frank Lloyd Wright's Larkin Building of 1904 in Buffalo, New York, one of the great workspaces of the twentieth century, illustrates this open plan (fig. 70). Although the Larkin Building was not streamlined, it introduced the plan and technology that would typify the modern office of the 1930s and would demonstrate the practical meaning of streamlining. The six-story structure was organized around a large open atrium where the employees of this mail-order business processed huge volumes of sales. The space beneath the windows of each story was used for built-in steel filing cabinets, which were among the earliest vertical file systems.[12] Located in an odorous factory district, the building was designed to be a self-contained and clean environment for the workers. To bring in daylight and fresh air, it was equipped with an early form of air-conditioning and with skylights.

Taylor's principles were to be influential in the 1930s as well, as typified by an article of 1939 stating that planning a modern office required a knowledge of the equipment available and consideration of all factors affecting the efficiency of the office—the type of work, filing systems, relationship to departments, and flow of activity. "While it was common practice a few years ago for the executive to have a massive desk with a multitude of pigeon holes and drawers, for the safekeeping of confidential data, the tendency today is toward streamlining, with nothing in the desk except current work, reports and the like."[13] This definition of "streamlining" not as styling but as the separation and simplification of tasks and storage would continue to be applied throughout the century.

Thirty years after the Larkin Building, Wright designed another revolutionary office structure—streamlined in its architecture, interior and exterior, and its furnishings, which were integral to the design (fig. 71). In contrast to the rectilinear Larkin, Wright's S. C. Johnson Administration Building of 1936–39 in Racine, Wisconsin, presents a streamlined open plan on its main floor. The "Great Workroom,"[14] a spacious interior ringed by a balcony and illuminated by skylights, is a dazzling, soaring space. It is vaulted by a forest of giant piers, which grow like mushrooms each from a very small base to a large circular top, serving aesthetic as well as structural purposes. Like the Larkin, the Johnson Building was intended to be an ideal working environment as envisioned by a benignly paternalistic company. It also shielded the worker from the unpleasant noise and odors of its industrial location. Strips of translucent Pyrex tubing were used as partitions and circular skylights throughout the building, embodying its streamlined style (fig. 72).[15] The circle motif is extended in Wright's custom furnishings, which include desks with oval cantilevered work surfaces and drawers that swivel out rather than slide, as well as three-legged chairs, all works of tubular steel. Streamlined in function and appearance, the Johnson Building and its furnishings embody efficiency and high theater—both meanings of "streamlining."

Stylistically streamlined office interiors such as Wright's were relatively rare, probably because the typical office was not open to the public and did not require the expense of a space designed to impress potential buyers. But new office equipment was invariably streamlined in the 1930s. The country's economy had shifted from farms and local crafts to national industries and sales in the early twentieth century, and the office reflected these business trends, which included the development of a middle management. The goal of managers was to implement marketing strategies, coordinate distribution networks, and track sales performance.[16] All this required

Fig. 70 Frank Lloyd Wright, interior of the Larkin Building, Buffalo, New York, 1904.

71

records. The improved business products described in this section were marketed to managers—and their secretaries, accountants, and clerks—and they served mostly as aids in generating and keeping track of paperwork.

For the workplace, many functional streamlined objects were designed that have survived, and they make up the majority of the works in this section.[17] Most of the machines described here, such as the typewriter, were invented long before the 1930s, but now previously cumbersome designs were streamlined to please the consumer and the office worker. Other machines were, as stated in patent specifications, "new and improved." Some inventions—such as the *Autodex* (a forerunner of the *Rolodex*)—made their debut in the 1930s. Although the widespread use of the personal computer was not to occur until the 1980s, the computer itself was firmly established in the 1930s with pioneering work by International Business Machines Corporation (IBM). IBM's Accounting Machine (407), introduced in 1949, indicates the survival of streamlining in the postwar period; it boasts rounded corners and speed-line trim at its base and near its top (fig. 73).

Characteristic of streamlining, such a casing was designed to protect sensitive or potentially dangerous interior mechanisms and to cover what would have been viewed as unsightly working parts. This is seen in an array of office machines and in particular in evolutionary sequences of photographs in period magazines intended to illustrate progress in modern design (fig. 74).

Such streamlined objects not only *looked* modern in styling but *were* modern in technology: as patent documentation indicates, they were inventions designed to make offices more productive—a requirement for highly competitive companies in a capitalist society. In these tools, the foremost designers of the 1930s envisioned the business world of today.

Fig. 71 Frank Lloyd Wright, lobby, S. C. Johnson Administration Building, Racine, Wisconsin, 1936.
Fig. 72 Frank Lloyd Wright, office, S. C. Johnson Administration Building.
Fig. 73 IBM Corporation, Accounting Machine (407), designed c. 1949.
Fig. 74 Evolution of typewriters from 1930 to 1940. From "Design Decade," *The Architectural Forum*, October 1940.

1. John E. Alcott

DESK LAMP: MODEL NO. 112

Designed c. 1938[1]

Bakelite, aluminum, cellulose film

22.9 x 19.1 x 21.6 cm

Produced by Polaroid Corporation,
Cambridge, Massachusetts

B021

2. Walter Dorwin Teague

DESK LAMP: MODEL NO. 114, *EXECUTIVE*

Designed 1939

Bakelite, aluminum, cellulose film

33.3 x 25.6 x 23.1 cm

Produced by Polaroid Corporation,
Cambridge, Massachusetts, 1939–1941;[2]
Mitchell Manufacturing Company, c. 1941

The Montreal Museum of Fine Arts,
The Liliane and David M. Stewart Collection

D82.113.1

Edwin H. Land's invention of polarizing materials, patented in 1933, revolutionized the control of light in products from sunglasses to cameras to lamps.[3] But several years of work were needed to make the early designs using Land's materials look equally revolutionary. Both of these lamps control the glare of 100-watt bulbs by shielding them under hoods and behind light-diffusing polarized celluloid film. Alcott's earthbound model of 1938, resembling a coach or miner's lamp, was "the first lamp to provide light free from reflected glare," and it sold for $16.50.[4] According to an advertisement in *Fortune* (fig. 75), visibility was doubled.[5]

Alcott used streamlining in his squat and blocklike lamp, but only in details, such as the rounded corners, the triple grooving on some edges and the back, and the parabolic profile of the hood. Teague's lamp, on the other hand, designed a year later, foreshadows the space age. His streamlining is integral: base, shaft, and hood are all smooth rounded forms set in dynamic counterpoint. Though both lamps are of Bakelite and aluminum, Teague's contrasts the dark plastic of hood and base with the sheen of the metal shaft. Alcott's is square in section and looks heavy, while Teague's appears gravity-defying, and the backswept shaft and cantilevered hood, both with cooling vents, seem ready for launching.

Teague's design, his first for Polaroid, achieved more than daring grace: his lamp cost less than Alcott's, retailing for $9.75; it illuminated a larger area, covering an entire newspaper evenly; it was simpler to operate; and although taller, it was less bulky.[6] Sales shot up, as was typical of products by the businessman "whose business was design," according to Sheldon and Martha Cheney. Stating his goals as "improved appearance, greater ease of service, and economy of manufacture," Teague generally analyzed each object's function and structure and its manufacturer's production, sales, and advertising methods before he designed a product.[7] This thoroughness benefited Polaroid, which retained Teague though the early 1960s, and his other client companies.

Fig. 75 Advertisement for Polaroid lamp. From *Fortune*, November 1938.

Cat. 1

Cat. 2

Fig. 76 Eliot Noyes, IBM *Selectric* typewriter, 1961. Somers, New York, IBM Corporation Archives.

3. John Adam Zellers
Herbert E. Bridgewater
PORTABLE TYPEWRITER: *STREAMLINER*
Designed c. 1935[8]
Enameled and chromium-plated steel, rubber, plastic
11.5 x 27 x 30.5 cm
Produced by Remington Rand Inc., Buffalo, New York
B196

Sleek, low-slung, continuously curved, this portable typewriter is a far cry from the first machine that made typing significantly faster than writing. That machine, invented by Sholes & Glidden, was introduced in 1874 by Remington, which also manufactured the *Streamliner*, but the two typewriters look as different as the horse-drawn buggy and the Chrysler *Airflow* car. Late nineteenth-century typewriters resemble their eighteenth-century prototypes: they are boxy and sharp-edged, more vertical than horizontal in overall

composition, and their basic parts—keyboard, keys, and carriage—remain visually separate. The 1874 Sholes & Glidden machine was mounted on a sewing machine stand, and a foot treadle was used to operate its carriage return; it typed only capital letters, and the operator could not see what was typed without stopping and swinging the carriage upward.[9] Nonetheless, typing was still faster than the pen, even though nineteenth-century typists normally used only two fingers of each hand. This changed at some point during the end of that century to "touch typing," or the use of all ten fingers, assisted by the Sholes & Glidden "QWERTY" keyboard layout. This arrangement, named for the sequence of letters at the upper left of the keyboard, reflects how frequently letters are thought to occur in English spelling. The system, used today, was intended to increase the typist's speed and to limit mistakes.

The *Streamliner* has a shift key, allowing each individual key to produce upper-case and lower-case letters, an improvement that Remington made

in 1878. And it is a "front strike" machine—an innovation of 1893—which lets the typist see the typing as the keys strike the platen. It is not this typewriter's machinery that Remington patented, however, but its "ornamental design," including its "convexly carved cover plate," in the words of the patent application. This aerodynamic housing forecasts the styling of the 1961 IBM *Selectric*, designed under the direction of Eliot Noyes (fig. 76): every element is low and curved, from the paper rest to the space bar, and the base sweeps up to the cover to form a rounded frame for the keys. The sans serif letters of the model name "STREAMLINER" lean forward, trailing speed lines, recalling the generic name given to the high-speed locomotives that thrilled visitors at the 1933–34 Chicago *Century of Progress* fair. This typewriter design likewise promises speed, the speed required of typists in the modern office. As a portable typewriter,[10] it is also capable of producing businesslike documents almost anywhere. The 24/7 work week and the home office are not far away.

4. William B. Petzold
STENOTYPE MACHINE
Designed c. 1939[11]
Bakelite, enameled steel, aluminum,
paper, rubber, paint
12.5 x 28.5 x 22 cm
Produced by The Stenotype Company,
Chicago, Illinois
B240

Court reporters supply word-for-word transcriptions of testimony to help judge or jury reach a verdict. But how can their writing match the speed of speech? The first American shorthand machine, invented in 1879 by Miles M. Bartholomew, was built on both the manual shorthand writing systems developed in the nineteenth century and the typewriters of the period. "Word-at-a-stroke" machines were introduced around the turn of the century and soon began to serve journalists and business people more widely than handwritten transcripts. In 1912 the Universal Stenotype Company, manufacturer of this machine,[12] entered the competition. Its founder, the reporter and inventor Ward Stone Ireland, reduced the machine's weight from fifty-four to around eight pounds and simplified the keyboard to exact the fullest results from the fewest strokes. Business schools hailed

the invention and speed championship records were set by inexperienced "stenos." At this moment, court reporters are still operating machines with Ireland's keyboard.[13]

Because all stenotype machines take rolls of narrow paper and have fewer keys than typewriters, they can be smaller and more compact. Even among shorthand machines, however, this model looks simplified and extra-efficient. Its modified teardrop shape and shiny black housing make it resemble a car's gas pedal. Its symmetry and elongation are enhanced by the ivory lines

that run from the front of its base to its top, incorporating the word "STENOTYPE" in stylized, recessed capital letters. Ridges like speed lines appear on both sides, and access to the paper supply is from a drawer at the rear. Like the Remington portable typewriter of 1935 (cat. 3), this machine is curved in almost every element, including its keys. Such styling was part of sales appeal: as early as 1930 a *Business Week* article, "The Eyes Have It," described five hundred businessmen who had hired artists to improve the appearance of their wares.[14]

5. Willis A. Kropp
ADDING MACHINE
Designed c. 1939[15]
Bakelite, aluminum, enameled
and chromium-plated steel, rubber, paper
13.5 x 23 x 34 cm (with paper roll)
Produced by Victor Adding Machine Company,
Chicago, Illinois
B271

This gleaming adding machine, ready to calculate six-figure sums, looks far different from its progenitor—a wooden macaroni box that Dorr E. Felt fitted with meat skewers, twine, string, and staples in 1885[16]—and even its 1920s counterpart by the Victor Company. Its slanted, parabolic, jet-black Bakelite form is animated by the rounded, rectangular aluminum recess for the rows of differently toned plastic keys, and this elegant color scheme of ebony and silver continues in the handle and the sans serif letters spelling out "VICTOR" on the black body beneath the tape. (Users could not fail to note this name every time they checked their work.) A contemporary advertisement by the company claimed that this model was "engineered like an airplane . . . [with] a trim streamlined beauty."[17] The claim reflects the magic of streamlining and its evocation of the speed of flight, for beyond the smoothly curved housing of the adding machine, it bears no resemblance to the elements of a plane.

Today, this manual machine has been outmoded twice, by the introduction of electronic calculators in 1961 and by their replacement with microchip power in the 1980s. Nevertheless, the necessity for a record tape has continued, assuring the survival of adding machines distantly resembling this as office accessories. The slang "number crunching" for accounting may come from the sounds of machines like this Victor adding up.

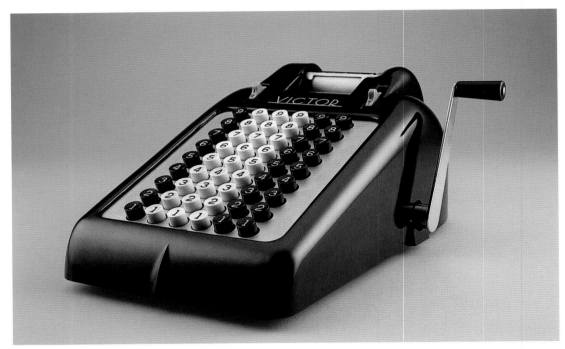

6. Henry Dreyfuss
Walter B. Payne
CHECK WRITING MACHINE:
MODEL NO. 60, *PROTECTOGRAPH*
Designed c. 1940[18]
Painted and enameled steel, aluminum,
Bakelite, rubber, painted wood
25.5 x 23 x 28 cm
Produced by The Todd Company, Inc.,
Rochester, New York
B376

Businesses with more than a few employees drawing paychecks and companies paying dividends were among the consumers of check writers. Their stamping was supposed to make forgery difficult, if not impossible, thus protecting the company's funds. How to make devices such as these, with dozens of working parts within, look fast, dependable, and easy to use?

This machine and a predecessor (fig. 77) manufactured by The Todd Company illustrate the evolution to streamlined styling from the 1910s to 1940. Like the different lamps made for Polaroid by John Alcott and Walter Dorwin Teague (cat. 1–2), they suggest why companies invested in the services of celebrity industrial designers. The anonymously designed *Protectograph* of c. 1915 bristles with different chrome-plated handles and parts projecting from its long heavy body.

Fig. 77 Designer unknown, *Protectograph*, enameled and chromium-plated steel, manufactured by The Todd Company, c. 1915, Rochester, New York. Eric Brill Collection.

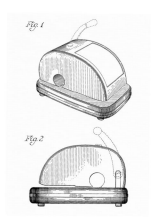

Fig. 78 Henry Dreyfuss and Walter B. Payne, detail of a patent drawing for "Casing for a Check Writing Machine or Similar Article."

Yet in that rounded-off cylinder with its tapering base, numbers plaque on top, and manufacturer's name on its front, it resembles an early locomotive.

By 1940, however, the metaphor of speed and power could be read in a mere parabola. This is the shape of Henry Dreyfuss and Walter B. Payne's check writer, a compact device half as long as the c. 1925 model. The task of punching out checks looks simple—and indeed it is simpler than before because individual levers can be set for numbers up to 99,999,999, while the earlier device required setting large sums and then lining up a sliding part placed at right angles to the machine body. The slots for the levers are brightly outlined in the Dreyfuss and Payne machine, producing the equivalent of speed lines, and the colors of the levers change at 100 and 100,000, on the example of adding machine keys, to make setting the numbers easier. Even the handle, a continuous tapering parabola, is an improvement in simplification over those of its forebears. The form of the 1940 machine makes its operation plain.

According to the Cheneys in *Art and the Machine*, the designer Henry Dreyfuss, in styling a version of this check writing machine, had "to devise a distinctive and unusual appearance and yet one in keeping with conservative bank and business-office interiors."[19] Any housing would shield the working parts, but Dreyfuss's smooth parabolic form is simplicity itself. The curved handle conforms in shape to the body, as does the broad base with its rounded corners and terra-cotta-colored metal banding recessed around it. This is seen most clearly in the patent drawing (fig. 78). The stippled gray of the body was doubtless intended to add sobriety to the *Protectograph*, and to minimize fingerprints. The label on the bottom warns that only authorized Todd representatives should service or repair the machine.

That label records fifteen patents, including the utility patent for the works (2,092,852), submitted September 14, 1937, by Walter B. Payne, and claiming he had invented a machine "light, compact, and of neat appearance." Because Dreyfuss's name does not appear on this application (but does on that for the specifications for the casing), it is evident that Payne's contribution was technological while Dreyfuss's was aesthetic. This division of labors suggests a growing phenomenon of the 1930s, that the design process was becoming a more collaborative effort, reflecting the complexities of both technology and marketing in the twentieth century.

Cat. 6

7. William B. Petzold

DUPLICATOR: *DUPLICARD*

Designed c. 1940[20]
Bakelite, rubber, painted wood,
flannel, steel
13 x 26.5 x 19.2 cm
Produced by Pac Manufacturing Corporation,
Terre Haute, Indiana
B008

A bold teardrop shape in glistening black Bakelite, this machine appears monumental, though it is about the size of a small man's shoe. With its smooth graduated bands and rounded top, it recalls the locomotive Raymond Loewy designed for the Pennsylvania Railroad with much fanfare in 1937 (fig. 25). Petzold's streamlined housing gives

unexpected glamour to an everyday function: this machine addresses postcards.

In the middle of the top, the model name "DUPLICARD" forms an elongated logo of raised letters[21] on a red ground and a trailing red line extends to the roller, pointing out where the card to be duplicated should be inserted. On the bottom of the machine, the instructions for operation from the retailer direct you to "brush ink evenly on the flannel pad" inside and to place the prepared stencil facing down on the cylinder. After moving the cylinder back into printing position, "Place card in gravity feed chute and turn the crank counter-clockwise one revolution."

Though the *Duplicard* requires manual operation, it was still more efficient than hand-addressing correspondence. Indeed, it looks more

advanced than the technology it contains, which dates from the 1870s. By that decade, the principles of transfer printing were in wide use in the United States. Remington's typewriter was broadly marketed, as was greaseless carbon paper coated only on one side: the combination enabled a typist to generate up to ten copies at the same time as the original. These time-saving business conveniences built on inventions made as early as 1780—the date that James Watt, innovator of the steam engine, patented a letter copying press—and 1806, when Ralph Wedgwood (second cousin of Josiah, of ceramic fame) patented an early form of carbon paper.[22] This history suggests that the modern office was technically in the making during the American Revolution. It remained for designers of the 1930s to give a modern style to modern business machines.

8. Albert E. Pollock

ADDRESS BOOK:
MODEL NO. P-642A, *AUTODEX*
Designed c. 1938[23]
Bakelite, plastic, felt
2.5 x 11.5 x 19.8 cm
Produced by Zephyr American Corporation,
New York, New York
B249

Finding names, addresses, and phone numbers quickly is essential in a fast-paced office, and the *Autodex* address book was invented to answer that need. You move the arrow on its top to the alphabet letter wanted, then press the band at the bottom of the list, and the lid pops open to the name group in question. The designer's patent drawing (fig. 79) shows both the interior and exterior of the *Autodex* and the device—the spring and notched index cards held by the arrow—that makes the book open to the desired letter.

The slim, symmetrical, streamlined form of the index is enhanced by the raised center banding with its white painted alphabet letters.

According to the description on the *Autodex*'s first stiff page, it was "made in several models and, with your message on the cover, makes the perfect business gift." The pages inside are loose-leaf "and can be easily removed for typing." The button to press is shaped like a pair of airplane wings with central speed lines. These simple elements suggest how rapidly the *Autodex* can serve the harried professional. It looks and is efficient: one wastes no time riffling through conventional lists of names.

The family resemblance between the *Autodex* and other desktop machines in this chapter (cf. cat. 11 and 12) suggests the success of the streamlined style rather than designers' lack of imagination. The visual harmony of an office full of such devices would have been reassuring. Though economic prospects might have been uncertain, an environment of similar futuristically shaped devices would have conveyed optimism about that future.

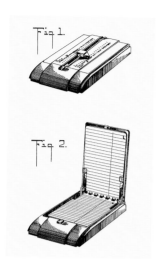

Fig. 79 Albert E. Pollock, detail of a patent drawing for a "List Finder."

9. Robert Davol Budlong

RECEIPT PRINTER: *ACCU-RITE*

Designed c. 1934[24]
Enameled and chromium-plated steel,
aluminum, plastic, rubber
15 x 43.5 x 22.5 cm
Produced by United Autographic Register
Company (Uarco), Chicago, Illinois
B403

10. Russell Katz

RECEIPT PRINTER

Designed c. 1938[25]
Bakelite, steel, enameled steel, rubber
8 x 33 x 17 cm
Manufacturer unknown
B518

11. Walter Dorwin Teague

RECEIPT PRINTER

Designed c. 1946[26]
Enameled and chromium-plated steel, paint
7 x 29.5 x 16 cm
Produced by Moore Business Forms, Inc.,
Oneonta, New York
B231

The desire for receipts may have originated with the first consumer's first purchase. As late nineteenth-century businesses grew, to move from the handmade copy to the mechanical duplicate or facsimile was the challenge, and then to limit the time spent on recording repeated transactions, as in stores, banks, and accounting departments. The earliest carbon paper, invented in the first decade of the nineteenth century, allowed for a few exact copies, and, in the same years, resourceful publishers began answering the demand for standard business documents. Sandwiches of printed forms and carbon paper speeded the production of receipts. The containers for them were known as "copywriters" and "autographic registers" between the world wars.

These three receipt printers show some of the variables of the streamlined style. The 1934 *Accu-rite*, the earliest of the three machines, betrays its date by its relatively rectilinear form. Twice as tall as Teague's model, it is rounded at the front and back rather than all sides. Nevertheless, it has aspects of the modern style. Like the other printers, its receipt window is rounded, the contrast between its chromium-plated and enameled surfaces is snappy, and its overall horizontality is enhanced by the graduated banding along its sides. Its interior can be locked to allow safe storage of the owner's copies of receipts, and a mechanism allows receipts to be processed by odd or even number.

Much more streamlined and sleek is the Katz register, cat. 10. Resembling a racing car, it is seen to advantage in its patent drawing (fig. 80). The black Bakelite of its case contrasts with the red lever, used to advance the receipts out of the short end of the machine, where they can be torn off. Only that lever projects beyond its unified form. Speed

Fig. 80 Russell Katz, detail of patent drawing for a "Casing for an Autographic Register."

lines swoop up one side to the top, and a hinged section provides storage of completed receipts.

Also low and sleek is the machine by Teague, which he apparently based on his design for a sales slip register of ten years earlier. Both have smooth casings with rounded corners, and, on one side, repeated grooves suggesting speed lines. In the receipt printer, the grooves are chromium-plated and extend from the window down the front of the machine, incorporating the manufacturer's name, "MOORE," on a red ground. The rest of the device is enameled a light gray, for a look that is both businesslike and chic.

Moore was founded in Toronto, Canada, by Samuel J. Moore, who is considered the inventor of the modern business form.[27] In 1936 the company developed the "Formaliner," a device to control the alignment and vertical spacing of marginally punched, continuous forms. Teague's printer contains this mechanism, but his casing design does not reveal it. Like the other streamlined designers, he assumed that consumers did not need to see how things worked in order to buy them. Instead, the smooth lines of their designs seemed to assure smooth performance.

Cat. 9

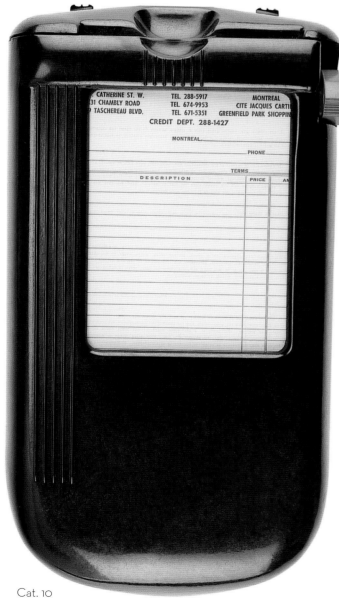

Cat. 10

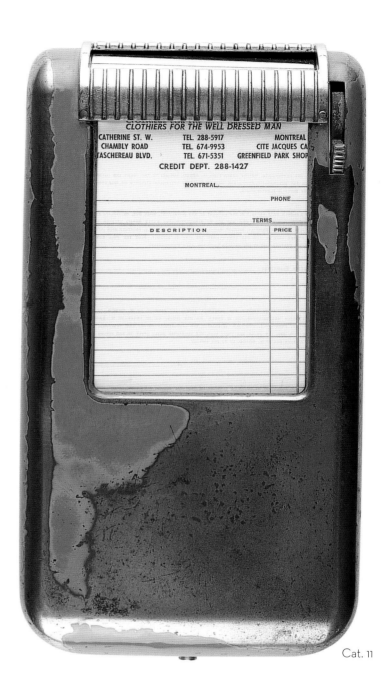

Cat. 11

12. William B. Petzold

Calendar Desk Pad Unit: *Autopoint*

Designed c. 1940[28]
Bakelite, plastic, enameled steel
4.7 x 19 x 12 cm
Produced by Autopoint Company,
Chicago, Illinois
B577

13. William B. Petzold

**Calendar, Thermometer,
and Humidity Indicator:** *Calendaire*

Designed c. 1940[29]
Bakelite, plastic, enameled steel
6 x 11.5 x 17 cm
Produced by Autopoint Company,
Chicago, Illinois
B466

The association of time and speed is implicit in the styling of these two desktop calendars. Like the fenders of fast-moving cars, their parabolic bodies curve forward, with tiers of banding on their sides. The openings for their dates are smoothly inset like car windows; only the white knobs to change the dates interrupt the sweep of their continuous bases. As a resourceful manufacturer, Autopoint distinguished these models, conceived by the same designer apparently the same year, by "extra features": the calendar desk pad unit has space for a note pad, while the calendar, thermometer, and humidity indicator monitor the office climate as well as the day. The latter, with its rounded top tapering down to its body, resembles the 1936 Cord sedan, then the most advanced front-engine automobile (fig. 81). The executive who could only afford the calendar at least bought some of the cachet of the car.

That both these products are made of Bakelite is no coincidence. By the late 1930s the Bakelite company owned Autopoint and was obviously motivated to use the manufacturer to widen the market for its plastic and to diversify its products, especially for small items in the office and home.[30] As the American economy improved over the decade, small purchases became more widely possible, and items such as these were good candidates: they combined utility and allure.

Fig. 81 *Cord* sedan, 1936 model, from Cheney and Cheney, *Art and the Machine*, 1936.

Cat. 12

Cat. 13

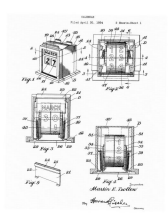

14. Designer unknown

CALENDAR

Designed c. 1936[31]

Bakelite, brass, enameled steel

6 x 7.5 x 11 cm

Produced by Brown & Bigelow, St. Paul, Minnesota

B184

The power of the streamlined style is demonstrated by the differences between this cheeky little desk calendar and its utility patent drawing (fig. 82). Without a base, the calendar is a simple parabolic shape whose forward-canted contours are inflected at the front by its date window, the raised brass bar on its top, and the rounded fin behind. Press the bar and it engages and rotates the cylinders inside printed with the months and numbers. The tail fin lets the owner pick up and move the smooth-surfaced device easily, and it adds a stylistic fillip: such flanges originated in the aerodynamic tail fins of aircraft, which in turn inspired racing car designs as early as the 1920s. From Norman Bel Geddes's model family car of 1934 (fig. 83) through Detroit's designs of the 1950s, tail fins were meant to conjure up excitingly high speeds—speeds beyond the limits allowed on American highways. By comparison, the patent drawing shows a housing that looks house-like. Time marches on, this boxy upright calendar seems to say, while the manufactured version seeks to conjure up the speed of light.

The item's manufacturer, Brown & Bigelow, continues in business today as one of the world's largest makers and distributors of promotional products, including advertising calendars. Here its early marketing astuteness is visible in the custom-printing of a business's name on the top bar of the calendar. The Overton Foundry, South Gate, California, may have given the calendar to clients or its own sales people or executives. For its part, Brown & Bigelow was content to have its name stamped on the bottom of the device.

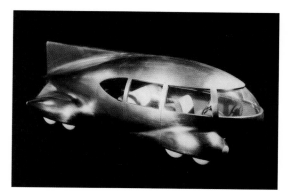

Fig. 83 Norman Bel Geddes, model of automobile, 1934. From *Pencil Points*, January 1937.

15. Stephen A. Crosby

STAPLER: MODEL NO. 3C

Designed c. 1937[32]

Enameled steel, painted wood, Bakelite

15.2 x 10 x 4 cm

Produced by Parrot Speed Fastener Corporation, Long Island City, New York

B007

16. Henry Ruskin

STAPLER: DE LUXE MODEL, *PRESTO STREAMLINED*

Designed c. 1940[33]

Enameled steel, steel, rubber

4 x 15 x 5 cm

Produced by Metal Specialties Manufacturing Company, Chicago, Illinois

B473

The box for the c. 1940 stapler (fig. 84) sums up its selling points: "Presto Streamlined Stapler: To Grace the finest desk. Saves time!" With this stapler the humblest secretary or filing clerk could quickly gather and organize documents while taking pride in the elegance of the latest design. Inside the base is a container for four hundred staples, and the magazine holds a hundred, making reloading faster. The product is rounded, long, and low, from the arm to the base, which is graduated down to a set of parallel grooves. Streamlines articulate the sides, and the name plate and staple magazine of the arm are silvery steel accents contrasting with the dark enamel of the machine. The design embodies both beauty and efficiency, the essence of streamlining in products small and large.

The achievement of *Presto*'s designer, Henry Ruskin, is more stylistic than technical, as seen by comparison with an earlier stapler, cat. 15, by Stephen A. Crosby. Crosby's device was mechanically advanced for its time and it is streamlined, but it looks two-dimensional rather than sculptured, and its parts remain visually separate. The arm springs forward from hinges in what resemble car fenders, and the punch, with its teardrop shape and speed lines, suggests a car's accelerator pedal. But if this all-black stapler evokes an automobile, the *Presto* recalls a train. Its design completely conceals its works in a smooth flowing form. The superior design signals that with this device the office work flow will be similarly smooth.

The contribution to time-saving of Parrot Speed Fastener Corporation, manufacturer of Crosby's device, lay in its invention of a stapler that opened at the top so that the office worker could drop in a strip of preformed wire staples glued together. The first stapling machine with a magazine for staplers that fed automatically was patented in 1875. Until then, the desktop devices to fasten papers with metal staples secured only one U-shaped wire at a time and had to be reloaded with each use. Earlier methods were even more laborious: pins, stitching, tapes, or ribbons strung through punched holes and tied, and sometimes secured further with wax seals.[34] The electric staplers invented in the late 1950s, which can secure a dozen pages with a second's touch, seem light years away. They are technically indebted to Parrot Speed, yet their styling closely resembles that of the *Presto*.

Cat. 15

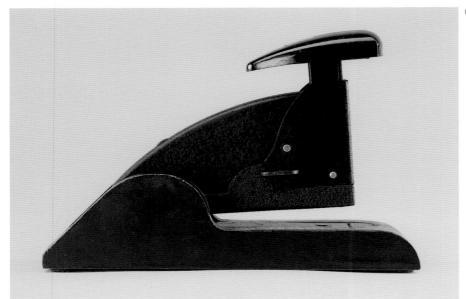

Cat. 16

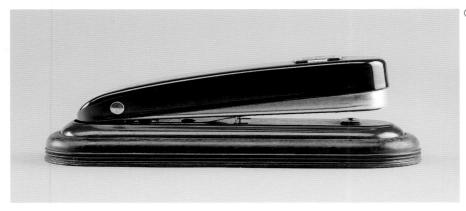

Fig. 84 Box for *Presto Streamlined* stapler.

17. Designer unknown

COMPUTER CARD HOLE PUNCH

Designed c. 1945–50
Painted steel, aluminum, rubber
6.5 x 20.5 x 4.5 cm
Produced by International Business Machines
Corporation (IBM), New York, New York
B149

The long curling silhouette of this computer card punch, accented in polished aluminum, is an emblem of streamlining. As in the *Twentieth Century Limited* locomotive, the marquee of the *Automat*, or the *Presto* stapler (cat. 16), the single swoosh of silver dominates the styling of this product and epitomizes modern speed and efficiency. On the bottom of the rubber base is a handsome impressed graphic design with speed lines and sans serif capitals spelling out the company's full name. That the punch was apparently designed around 1945–50 witnesses the continued popularity of streamlining.

There is no record of this stunning design in the IBM archives, nor were any patent applications for it found. Its approximate dating is based on its stylistic similarity to other IBM products of the same period. The use of the company's full name on the bottom provides a terminal date, for IBM initials predominate in its graphics from the mid-1950s on.[35] Was this punch a gift design for record-breaking marketers or a company anniversary memento? Certainly a computer card hole punch would have been a proper symbol of IBM in the early 1950s. Sturdy punch cards, the key element of information processing at its inception, were still used and still corrected by hand. IBM could also trace its history to the cards' inventor, for Herman Hollerith's company was one of several that merged in 1924 to become International Business Machines.

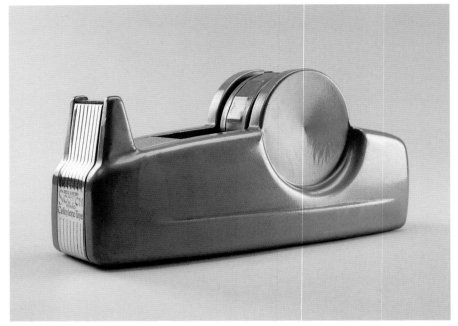

Cat. 18

Cat. 19

18. Jean Otis Reinecke

Tape Dispenser: *Scotch Cellulose*

Designed c. 1938[36]

Painted cast iron, chromium-plated steel, rubber

11.5 x 22.1 x 10.2 cm

Produced by Minnesota Mining & Manufacturing

Company (3M), St. Paul, Minnesota

B108

19. Jean Otis Reinecke

Tape Dispenser: *Scotch*

Designed c. 1952[37]

Enameled and chromium-plated steel, rubber

11.5 x 24 x 8 cm

Produced by Minnesota Mining & Manufacturing

Company (3M), St. Paul, Minnesota

B444

20. Egmont Arens

Tape Dispenser: Model No. 208, *National*

Designed c. 1942[38]

Steel, chromium-plated steel, plastic,

painted metal, rubber

17 x 31 x 12.5 cm

Produced by Nashua Package Sealing Division

of Nashua Corporation, Nashua, New Hampshire

The Liliane and David M. Stewart Collection

SHLSL 2002.16

The first transparent adhesive tape, marketed as *Scotch Cellulose Tape*, was invented in 1930 by Richard G. Drew, a technical director at Minnesota Mining & Manufacturing Company. He had invented *Scotch* masking tape for 3M five years before. The 1930 invention was so successful that "Scotch tape" has become synonymous for the material, like "Kleenex" for disposable tissues.

The challenge for 3M was selling not the tape but its most desirable dispenser. It had to be heavy enough to remain stationary when a length of tape was pulled off, safe in the position of its cutting blade, and sufficiently stylish to look modern and efficient. Successive designs recall the sequences of aeronautical designs by Raymond Loewy and Le Corbusier illustrating the evolution in streamlined forms from complex and relatively upright to simple and low-slung. The dispenser of c. 1925 in fig. 85 is all sharp angles, from its stepped base to its name plate. But later designs are pleasingly plump. The Reinecke dispenser of c. 1938, painted a stippled forest green, was for a much wider tape than is commonly manufactured today. The axle of the tape roll is covered with a bulbous extrusion from the swelling body, and the cutter, accented by speed lines, extends smoothly from the base. Like its predecessors, it has a metal housing with a "wrinkle finish" to conceal imperfections in manufacturing and fingerprints when in use.

About Reinecke's 1952 model, a contemporary writer announced, "Although this is a heavy-duty model, its use spread from the shipping platform to the wrapping counters of exclusive shops, and the need for pleasing appearance has constantly increased."[39] In contrast to the c. 1938 dispenser, 3M's later version is much lighter in weight. Rather than submerging the tape in the streamlined case, the axle on which the tape unrolls is functionally identified by the indented design, a characteristic of postwar streamlining. Subtle grooving around the base and the chromium-plated banding are remnants of streamlining.

Fig. 85 Designer unknown, *Scotch* tape dispenser, c. 1925. From *U.S. Industrial Design*, 1951.

Whereas both 3M tape dispensers displayed the transparent tape product, Egmont Arens's design for the Nashua Corporation (cat. 20), for a gummed paper tape, encases it and all of the mechanism in a sleek form resembling a high-speed train engine. The handle, designed to dispense the tape in a quick stroke, is shaped to conform to the streamlined curves of the body. The gray enameled body contrasts with the bright chromium-plated steel top, where "NATIONAL" appears in red letters in a vertical white band. This bold logo points to the slot where the tape emerges. Inside, the tape passes over sponges that moisten it for use. Arens's design controls and conceals this potentially messy function. An early champion of streamlining, he created a form that is both utilitarian and attractive.

With step-by-step images, a contemporary account described Arens's redesign of the Nashua tape dispenser: "First the clay models were made, then plaster models, and finally a wooden model, complete in every detail, which the die makers reproduced exactly." [40] The results were smooth and streamlined so the dispenser could be easily wiped clean. "Old style tape dispensers have usually been kept in the back room, but this new model, owing to its good style, is finding a place right on the counter of retail stores." [41]

Cat. 20

21. Edward C. Hoffmann

PENCIL SHARPENER: *ELECTRO-POINTER XI*

Designed c. 1939[42]

Plaskon, plastic, rubber

14.5 x 21 x 9.5 cm

Produced by Swingline, Inc.,

Long Island City, New York

B314

How much faster than a manual pencil sharpener is an electric model? Does the latter offer more control? Perhaps, in the modern, electrified office of the 1930s and 1940s, perception was more important than reality, and the secretary, like the domestic, had to be wooed with gadgets sold as labor-saving devices. In any case, the *Electro-Pointer XI* is modern in both form and materials. A manually adjustable ring allows for small, medium, and large pencils. Inserting the pencil activates the sharpening device hidden inside. A drawer of clear plastic below catches the wood shavings.

The *Electro-Pointer* is made of a plastic invented around 1931 called Plaskon, a substance that experienced little shrinkage or expansion in manufacture, resisted cracking and chipping, and insulated against noise—a desirable quality in a machine for high-speed grinding. Plaskon replaced heavy metal housings, reduced manufacturing costs, and allowed designs of continuous curves, as seen here. This automatic pencil sharpener won an award in 1941 sponsored by *Modern Plastics* magazine and was featured in advertisements for the Plaskon Company of Toledo.[43] In shape, it resembles a propeller cowling, and with a pencil in it, it might suggest a rocket launcher. If clerical work was necessary, at least it could take place in the office of the future. The *Electro-Pointer* pencil sharpener was first produced by Triple "E" Products Company, St. Louis, Missouri, which operated from 1940 to 1951, and so the stamp "Swingline" on this object indicates that it was produced after 1951. That it was designed in 1939, twelve years earlier, indicates the continued attraction of its streamlined style.

22. Joseph Palma, Jr.

INTERCOM: MODEL NO. 210B, *AMPLICALL*

Designed c. 1947[44]

Bakelite, brass, glass

15.5 x 26.5 x 15 cm

Produced by Rauland-Borg Corporation,

Chicago, Illinois

B660

The resemblance between this smoothly rounded intercom and Raymond Loewy's radio for Emerson Electric Company (cat. 127) is not coincidental: both symmetrical Bakelite cases contain speakers and amplifiers for sound projection. Loewy's light-hued semicircular dial face, like a rising sun, becomes a shallow cone of nested graduated rings in Joseph Palma's "Interoffice Communication Cabinet." The metaphor of the form is a loudspeaker, and the name *Amplicall* combines the notions of calling and amplification. Bosses could raise help without raising their voices, or doctors could call nurses. Today the Rauland firm specializes in hospital communications systems.[45]

23. Attributed to Lurelle van Arsdale Guild[46]
WALL CUP DISPENSER:
MODEL NO. 1404, *DIXIE CUPS*
Designed c. 1935–45
Painted steel, aluminum, plastic
43 x 8 x 8 cm
Produced by Dixie Cup Company, Easton,
Pennsylvania
B103

24. Samuel N. Hope
CUP DISPENSING CABINET: *LILY*
Designed c. 1940[47]
Enameled and chromium-plated steel, rubber
25 x 11.5 x 10.2 cm
Produced by Lily-Tulip Cup Corporation,
New York, New York
B047

The germ theory of disease contagion, which
became widely accepted in the late nineteenth
century, gave rise to civic health projects as vast
as public bath building in cities and as small as
state laws abolishing shared drinking glasses
and tin dippers at public water sources. Fountains
designed to allow drinking without glasses were
one replacement, but the disposable paper cup
proved to be the cheapest, longest-lived, and most
widely applicable solution to public thirst. In c. 1908,
Lawrence Luellen invented the first such cup—
made of a circle of paper pleated into a cone
shape[48] and held with paraffin. He first called it
the "Health Kup" and then, in 1919, exploiting the
popularity of a line of dolls, the "Dixie Cup."[49]

    The Dixie dispenser, attached to a water cooler,
allowed one to obtain a new, clean, individual paper
cup for a cool drink of water. You simply pull the
hanging cup from the bottom: inside, a projecting
rim, which supports the stack of nested cups,
releases one at a time. The same screw-on rim is
removable to allow loading of a new stack of cups.
This interior design in Dixie and other dispensers
also permits a simple, unitary housing, which was
easier to manufacture. The tall cylinder of this
model probably accommodates the tallest stack
of cups that could be conveniently boxed and
shipped, reducing the labor of refilling. The
dispenser's verticality also functions aesthetically:
with its glistening, grooved aluminum band

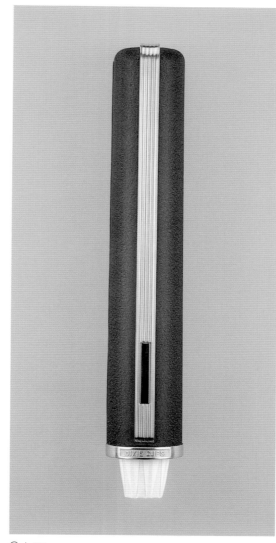

Cat. 23

Cat. 24

extended from top to bottom, it resembles
a skyscraper, associating the office it serves
with that acme of modernity.

    Lily-Tulip was a rival manufacturer, and like Dixie,
it produced the cups in several sizes and dispensers
for them. A modified teardrop in plan, the *Lily*
dispenser has a shaped handle whose verticality
is accented by vertical grooving continued from
front to back. The hinged front opens easily for
access to the cups, and the glistening chromium-
plated steel base indicates that the dispenser
can stand on a flat surface. Overall, the container
looks like a bullet or rocket. Yet its stippled brown
shell would match the sober palette of metal
machines in the offices and institutions of the late
1930s and early 1940s.

25. Henry Dreyfuss

THERMOS PITCHER: MODEL NO. 549

Designed 1935
Enameled steel, aluminum, glass, rubber
19.5 x 20.5 x 13.3 cm
Produced by The American Thermos Bottle
Company, Norwich, Connecticut
B016

26. Henry Dreyfuss

THERMOS PITCHER AND TRAY:
MODEL NO. 549

Designed 1935
Enameled steel, aluminum, glass, rubber
Pitcher: 19.5 x 20.5 x 13.3 cm
Tray: 19.5 x 26.2 cm
Produced by The American Thermos Bottle
Company, Norwich, Connecticut
B544

Thermos bottles originated with the practical goal of keeping beverages hot or cold, and they were (and still are) associated with picnics, camping, and lunch boxes. In the 1930s The American Thermos Bottle Company wanted to broaden and upgrade their use to enlarge sales: it sought a design for a jug that could serve in either office or home.[50] It would retain the heat or cold of liquids with the usual vacuum lining; but a stylish and serviceable vessel, harmonizing with the aesthetics of both the desk and the dining-room table, would open markets while saving manufacturing costs. The company turned to Dreyfuss, who had already produced best-selling designs for a rainbow of products. Between designing the epochal General

Fig. 86 View of Thermos pitcher base, showing impressed signature of Henry Dreyfuss.

Electric *Flatop* refrigerator of 1933 and the 1938 *Twentieth Century Limited* train (fig. 26, p. 29), he created this compact Thermos pitcher. It has streamlined elements of both those designs.

Like the refrigerator, the Thermos pitcher is simplified to a few rounded parts of aluminum and enameled steel. Dreyfuss conceived the base and body as one molded sphere, unified the lid and neck as one oval form, and gave the handle the body's curve, extending it from the neckband to meet the horizontally grooved banding at the bottom. In shape the vessel forecasts his locomotive's bulbous front, but it retains conservative elements, or what Dreyfuss called "survival forms." The band on the base, he wrote, "is, for instance, a modern version of an older molding. . . . By embodying a familiar pattern in an otherwise wholly new and possibly radical form, we can make the unusual acceptable to many people

who would otherwise reject it."[51] At the same time, the pitcher is easy to use, reflecting the Dreyfuss firm's ergonomic research. "We know that . . . handles under half an inch in diameter are likely to cut into the hand under heavy loading, and handles more than one and one quarter inches in diameter feel fat and give a feeling of insecurity."[52] This handle is an aluminum strip one inch wide. To assure buyers of their good taste, the matching aluminum on the bottom bears Dreyfuss's signature in facsimile script, like a signed work of art (fig. 86), indicating the growing status of the industrial designer whose celebrity was used to market products.[53] Obviously American Thermos thought that a "designer item" would be more saleable than its usual line. Available in several colors and two sizes, the pitcher was accompanied by either an oval or trefoil-shaped tray, which allowed space for the user's choice of glass.

Cat. 25

Cat. 26

"POWER AT YOUR FINGERTIPS"

Streamlining Manual Labor

2

For the average American, joblessness was the nightmare of the Depression, but there was no lack of work at home. In fact, the middle-class housewife faced more labor, given the diminishing pool of servants and her own thinner wallet. And the middle-class husband was encouraged to be a handyman, not only to save money on hired help but to benefit from federally secured low-cost loans for home ownership and home improvement. Through the National Housing Act of 1934, home owners could borrow up to $2,000 for as many as five years and home buyers could get mortgages—both at low interest. Whether they bought old houses that needed renovation or the new houses designed as starters or shells to be completed according to need and available cash, families benefited by knowing "how to." About one in eight eligible U.S. families took home modernization loans in 1934–37.[1]

For their part, manufacturers of home appliances, from vacuum cleaners to sanders, saw sales opportunities in the domestic market: it was far from saturated, unlike car ownership, and the relatively low price of products, vis-à-vis that for large durable goods like refrigerators, meant they might achieve wide consumption. Advertising sprang into action, underlining the gender stereotypes of domestic goddess and Mr. Fix-It that would survive for the family into the 1950s. Streamlining was everywhere.

While the appearance of the public world changed most drastically in the 1930s, thanks to the New Deal's massive construction projects, the private domestic interior changed as well with the introduction of new spaces or the conversion of old ones into rooms devoted to work. The 1930s saw the gradual substitution of electrical refrigerators for ice boxes, thus outmoding the pantry. This room and others near the kitchen or in the cellar were prime candidates for laundry rooms. Efficiently arranged for the laundry routine, they could be equipped with modern appliances, including a sink, tub, washing machine, clothes dryer, electric iron and roller-type ironer, and ironing board. Writing in 1936, Sheldon and Martha Cheney proclaimed that the laundry room "has, even more widely than the playroom, engaged the attention of interior designers, and its efficiency has been furthered by the ingenious provision of unit washing-and-ironing equipment by at least a half-dozen industrial designers. . . . Eleven million homes now make use of this particular kind of equipment."[2]

The machines for executing household chores, such as washing, ironing, sewing, and vacuuming in any of the rooms of the domestic interior, were often encased in streamlined shells to make what was considered "woman's work" appear more attractive and easier to do. These appliances, both large and small, were crucial to the "clean and honest" middle class and especially to the housewife. A spotless home and immaculately dressed family in crisply pressed clothes were her responsibility. At the lower edge of the middle class, maintaining appearances was especially important in retaining bourgeois status; and as the economy plummeted between 1929 and 1932 the homemaker was even more pressured to uphold her class standards. Advertisers encouraged her to handle all washing, drying, and pressing at home and to buy the tools of her upper-class sisters, who had purchased them to benefit their servants. More was expected of Mrs. America and thus she had less time, but new and improved appliances were supposed to do her work in a jiffy.[3] Did American manufacturers encourage middle-class housework collaboratives, in which neighbors shared ownership of appliances? Of course not.

Rather, consumer goods makers responded to the New Deal's cheaper electrical power by lowering prices and redesigning appliances. Following the example of the Ford Model T, cheaper washers were produced in bulk to blanket the broad middle-class market. "The easy, luxury market may be approaching saturation," wrote a *Business Week* author in 1934, and "may eventually depend (like automobiles again) on replacement sales, but the balance of the 20 million wired homes in the country . . . makes a far bigger market."[4] Designs such as Henry Dreyfuss's washer for Apex Electrical Manufacturing Company (fig. 87) were also powerfully attractive: this smooth canister-like appliance, adorned only with central speed lines, resembles an industrial turbine, well-equipped to handle the heaviest laundry load.

In addition to the laundry room, middle-class homes had rooms or spaces devoted to work in general—some built into existing rooms: "Special equipment and work space are needed behind the scenes in every household. . . . These maintenance jobs . . . can all be handled in one carefully planned . . . very compact work space . . . fitted into the end wall of a bedroom or study. . . ."[5] The "Work Center" became a new design goal: "It used to be possible to talk about the kitchen without dragging in such fancy titles as 'work center.' And if the word were used in its old sense it would still be acceptable; but 'kitchen' today means a minimum space where cooking is done and where eating would be if there were room. The space described as a work center, on the other hand, covers not only cooking, but laundry, heating, storage and dining."[6] Full of appliances, such a space was technically possible as increasing numbers of homes could invest in electric wiring upgrades (allowed in the 1934 National Housing Act loans for home rehabilitation). And the appliances themselves were more affordable as New Deal projects such as the Tennessee Valley Authority Act of 1933 guaranteed low-cost power.

In the 1930s and thereafter, a room for what was considered "man's work" could be found in the basement, garage, or a separate structure in the spirit of the old-fashioned tool shed, built for this purpose. Indeed, in 1942, a basement workshop was described as doubling for an air-raid shelter (fig. 88) in an article profiling ten hobbyists.[7] Mail-order catalogue companies such as Sears, Roebuck and Company made tools and equipment available to a mass market. Both the Sears *Craftsman* catalogue and magazines such as *Popular Mechanics* and *Popular Science Monthly* advertised a large array of workshop machinery for such rooms, from hand tools to large equipment for building furniture or even entire houses. The husband as handyman was economical because he saved the cost of hired labor, and the role was promoted as creative and satisfying to those families striving for the good life.

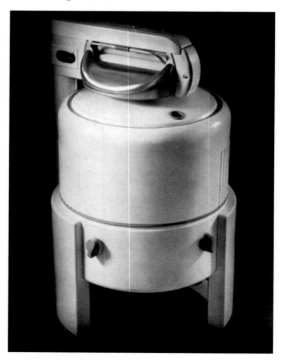

Fig. 87 Henry Dreyfuss, washing machine for Apex Electrical Manufacturing Co., c. 1940.

Like appliances for women—irons, vacuums, and so on—men's woodworking tools were also streamlined to suggest the speed and efficiency of their functioning, as seen in the designs in this section. Styling became an important element in selling these useful items. At the same time, hand tools had to be rugged and dependable, hence the thrust of Sears, Roebuck's design and marketing under the *Craftsman* label. The look of industrial might lent an aura of dependability to the company's products.

At home in the 1930s, hand tools—if heavy in appearance—became literally lighter and therefore easier to use with the introduction of new materials such as aluminum. Mowing the lawn, for instance, traditionally the man's responsibility, was no longer sweated labor and it was pitched to all members of the family. According to a shelter magazine, "The day of the heavy lawn mower is definitely past. Trimming lawns has become one of the gentler forms of exercise. This is due to the light-weight mower equipped with pneumatic tires and made of metal just as tough as that we used to have in the old days. . . ."[8] When the Bohn Aluminum and Brass Corporation envisioned exciting uses for aluminum after the war, it illustrated a power lawn mower (cat. 164) with space-age styling. Judging by its distance from the modern home behind it, it flies over miles of lawn without human hands, so light and powerful are its design and material.

Meanwhile, in high schools vocational training was felt essential because the "fundamental concept of American education . . . in a democratic social organization is to aid individuals in adapting themselves to harmonious living and to recognize and teach the means for development of the individual."[9] While girls studied "home economics"—nutritious meal planning, cooking, sewing, and so on—boys took "shop" in American public schools, and learned carpentry, machine tooling, repair,

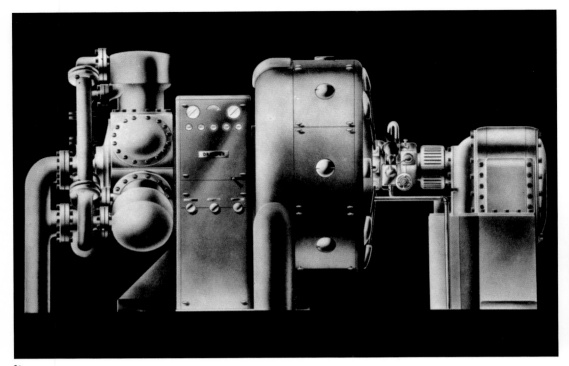

and the like. Similar classes might be offered to adults in the evening in high schools or colleges. Whether or not such training led to jobs, it helped familiarize household members with new tools and methods as homes economized with do-it-yourself approaches to chores and improvements. Both the training of the professional industrial designer and the training of the student and future homeowner were of concern to critics in the field during the 1930s. The Cheneys wrote:

> Ultimately all grammar- and high-school students in America will certainly be given what is known in the Soviet system as "polytechnical" training; that is, the student will learn by direct contact the feel and special capabilities of all basic materials—wood, metals, plastics, stone, glass, textiles, paper—and of all common tools and type of machines and the simpler productive processes. . . . This polytechnical preparation, basic to any true knowledge of the modern machine-implemented world, will mean experience of the arts and industries in a sense unknown in our present intellectual-ized curriculum.[10]

If streamlined tools found pride of place in American houses, they were also adopted in factories, farms, and food-service businesses. Manufacturers learned from the automotive industry how to use sheet steel, and also how to benefit by employing industrial designers. Raymond Loewy designed tractors for International Harvester (fig. 91) and, not to be outdone, Henry Dreyfuss designed them for John Deere. Stressing a look of power and simplicity of use, the new tractors gained bold housings with wrap-around speed lines and ergonomically shaped seats. As the federal Farm Security Administration helped farmers to purchase land and improve their farms (FSA, 1937–1946), such tractors were intended to appeal to them as one of the rewards of recovery. Durable goods such as these could be bought on time, and when in 1938 the federal government lengthened the payback period to nearly two years on the credit it underwrote, the market widened for those and other modernized goods.[11]

Fig. 89 Walter Dorwin Teague, 600 H.P. radial motor, Dresser Manufacturing Co., as redesigned. From Walter Dorwin Teague, *Design This Day*, 1940.
Fig. 90 Designer unknown, 600 H.P. radial motor, Dresser Manufacturing Co., as first built. From *Design This Day*.

As the recovery picked up steam in the late 1930s, manufacturers of less visible products saw the benefits of industrial design. Raymond Loewy, for example, designed a cream separator (cat. 53) and despite wartime rationings of metals, Egmont Arens created the voluptuously sculptural *Streamliner* meat slicer (cat. 51) for use in restaurants, markets, and delicatessens. Though everyday consumers would see such machines rarely, if at all, their manufacturers credited streamlined styling with distinguishing their products from the competition, with lifting the user's morale and easing his work, and with giving their sales personnel new marketing material.[12]

In the 1930s the interiors of factories were likely to be rectilinear, but the large machines themselves were often streamlined. In *Design This Day*, Walter Dorwin Teague contrasted an earlier radial motor (fig. 90) to his own redesigned example (fig. 89) and proclaimed: "We feel a necessity to organize the complex things we make into an obvious unity."[13] Teague's streamlined form is unified in a design that was thought to appeal to the factory worker: the machine was psychologically less threatening; it was even user-friendly. "No loss of limbs could be feared, and the visual ordering of the parts made the functioning and maintenance of the machines easier. The encased parts could be more easily wiped clean." For the factory machine, as well as the machine in office or home, the encasing of complex mechanisms in smooth streamlined sheaths was not only more pleasing but more efficient. Man and machine appeared to function better together, in smooth harmony.

Fig. 91 Raymond Loewy, tractors for International Harvester. From *The Architectural Forum*, October 1940.

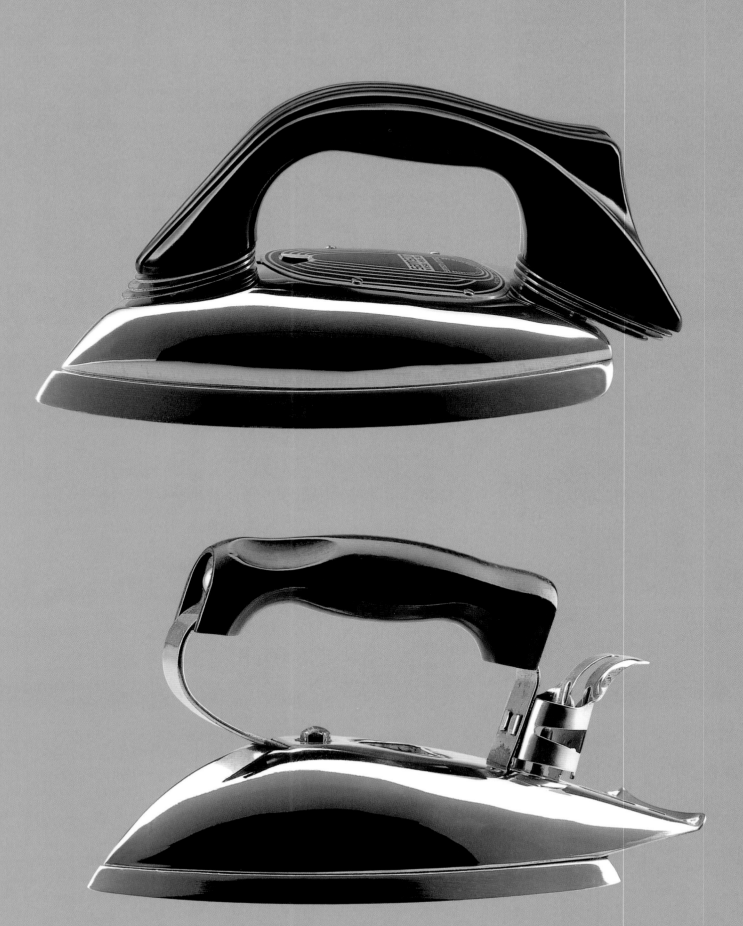

27. Abe O. Samuels

IRON: *VISU-HEAT*
Designed c. 1936[1]
Chromium-plated steel, Bakelite, partially enameled
11.5 x 23.5 x 12.7 cm
Produced by Samson-United, Rochester,
New York, and Toronto, Canada
B073

28. Designer unknown

IRON: MODEL NO. SA-4344,
STERLING STREAMLINE
Designed 1930–40
Steel, enameled and chromium-plated steel,
Bakelite, lacquered wood
13 x 22 x 11 cm
Produced by Chicago Electric Manufacturing
Company, Chicago, Illinois
B420

29. Clifford Brooks Stevens
Edward P. Schreyer

IRON: MODEL NO. W410, *PETIPOINT*
Designed c. 1941[2]
Chromium-plated steel, steel, Bakelite
12.8 x 26 x 12.5 cm
Produced by Waverly Tool Company,
Sandusky, Ohio[3]
B191

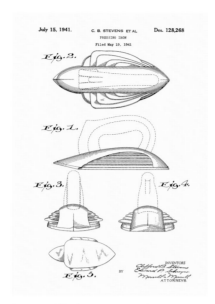

Fig. 92 Clifford B. Stevens et al., patent drawing for "Pressing Iron."

These irons illustrate some of the design possibilities for modernized irons. All use streamlining to conjure up visions of speedy, easy execution of the hot, onerous, seemingly eternal chore of pressing wrinkled fabrics.

Irons in their late eighteenth-century inception were made of weighty iron (hence their name) and used in pairs, one heating on a stove while the other was employed. Though made of steel and electrified by the turn of the century,[4] irons still had to compete with one another and appeal to the housewife, her servant, and the commercial launderer alike. To the plump triangle of the steel body and the heat-proof Bakelite handle were added a heat control and an electrical cord, as well as finish and detailing to attract the buyer. Chromium plating was *de rigueur* here, as in other steel kitchen appliances, for its easy care and alluring shine. Aerodynamic styling came naturally, given the repeated forward gesture of the user. Sheldon and Martha Cheney compared a Westinghouse iron to Raymond Loewy's *Fast Commuter* locomotive (see fig. 29): both illustrated "simplification, plastic order, and functional expression"[5] as their designs minimized the resistance of cloth or wind.

The utmost in streamlining, the *Petipoint* iron (cat. 29) has an aerodynamically styled body and ergonomically shaped handle, to conform to one's grip. But its design transcends functionalism. The graduated fins on its sides, which have slits to modulate the heat, extend beyond the plane of the cowl, resembling wings or the wake of a ship surging through water, and the flight theme is echoed in the ducktail at the end. Yet these elements are practical: the fins allow the iron to rest on its side, and the little duck tail—or *petite point*—can be used to press fine details, like tucked sleeves. Speed lines appear on the front and back of the handle, and the handle's large size relative to the base suggests the user's easy control of the appliance. In the patent drawing (fig. 92), presenting five beautiful perspectives, the iron resembles a futuristic spaceship or a study of the force lines of an airborne missile.[6]

In the *Visu-Heat* iron (cat. 27), the separation of handle from base is dramatized by three shaped metal plates at either end, which conceal the bolt attachments while stressing the curvaceous lines of the appliance. In enameled metal, the Samson nameplate repeats these ovals, which accent a little window where the iron's changing temperature is made "*Visu*-al." According to the original instructions, you thus run no risk of "ironing clothes at the wrong temperature." Nonetheless, you should "Allow your iron to heat up until the pointer on the dial indicates the correct temperature for the fabric. . . . If the handle becomes too hot, it may be due to placing it on a flat stand while not in use, instead of the scientifically designed heel rest. . . ."[7]

In the simpler *Sterling Streamline* iron (cat. 28), which has a thumb guard, the heart-shaped thermostat control is emphasized beneath the handle. This feature allowed the heat to be adjusted according to the type of fabric being ironed. The control was especially important for the many new synthetic fabrics, such as nylon and rayon, which were becoming popular in the 1930s. They had to be pressed at much lower temperatures than wool, cotton, and silk. The name *Sterling Streamline* plays on the traditional and modern values supposedly embodied by the iron: its chromium is as bright as silver, and its teardrop shape with forward-leaning handle suggests it can move through any mass of fabric full speed ahead.

30. John Richard Morgan
SEWING MACHINE: MODEL NO. 117.59,[8]
KENMORE IMPERIAL ROTARY
Designed c. 1935[9]
Enameled cast iron, steel, chromium-plated
and enameled steel, rubber, brass, glass
32.5 x 45.6 x 19.2 cm
Produced for Sears, Roebuck and Company,
Chicago, Illinois
B433

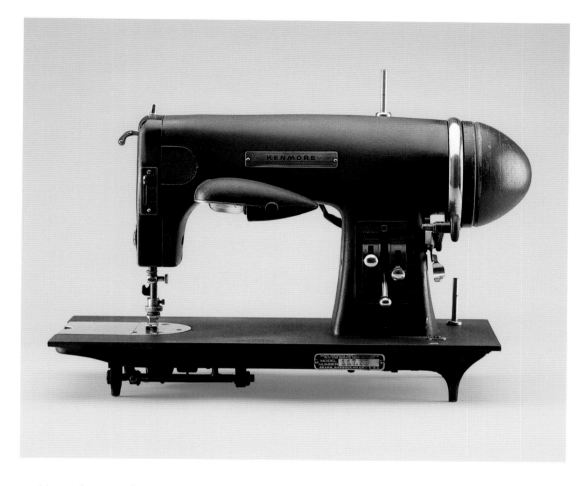

As an invention, the sewing machine was eighty-four years old when Sears, Roebuck introduced this streamlined version around 1936. What is new here is the smooth continuous cowling of the standard C-shaped body, which conceals the dozens upon dozens of parts that revolutionized garment manufacture. Seen from above, the arm of the *Imperial Rotary* has an elongated teardrop form, while its flywheel is hidden within a half-sphere, accented by the chromium-plated, ring-like hand wheel. Echoing these curves, a hooded light bulb nestles in the arc of the arm and illuminates the sewing. In pleasing counterpoint are the flat faces of the needle head and the pedestal. In the 1930s the domestic seamstress may have needed to sew to save money, but Sears—"The World's Largest Store," according to the thirty-eight-page operating manual—suggested through the machine's styling that the task would be swift and simple.

The inventions combined to mechanize sewing were in fact far from simple. And the achievements that made the United States the unchallenged world manufacturer of sewing machines until the 1940s lay not only in mechanics but in marketing. Walter Hunt invented the first lock-stitch machine in 1833; Elias Howe invented and patented the prototype of the modern sewing machine in 1846; and Isaac Merritt Singer combined the preceding inventions with a treadle and the ability to sew a straight or curved line and began selling his product to a skeptical public in 1852. By convincing women they could operate the machines and by overcoming price resistance with installment-plan sales and generous trade-in terms, the Singer Sewing Machine Company proved so successful that it became one of the country's first multinational firms. At the Philadelphia Centennial, 1876, Singer had its own pavilion to broadcast its production of over 800,000 machines a year. Women were freed of the drudgery of hand sewing their families' clothes, while clothing manufacture was industrialized with the same machines in heavy-duty form, giving jobs to thousands of manual workers, mostly women. Ready-to-wear garments became cheaper, an estimated one-sixth of the price of handmade clothes,[10] and soon they were valued not for their durability but for their chic. No wonder sewing machine styling was up-to-the-minute: while the early Singer machine mirrored Victorian furbelows with its gilded filigree, this Sears model echoed 1930s dress with its bold silhouette.

31. Henry Dreyfuss

VACUUM CLEANER: MODEL NO. 150

Designed c. 1935[11]
Steel, enameled steel, aluminum, canvas,
rubber, Bakelite
122 x 32.5 x 36.5 cm
Produced by The Hoover Company,
North Canton, Ohio
B138

32. John R. Morgan

VACUUM CLEANER: MODEL NO. 116,9815-1,
KENMORE

Designed c. 1937[12]
Plastic, steel
125 x 35.5 x 35.5 cm.
Produced for Sears, Roebuck and Company,
Chicago, Illinois
B435

33. Malcolm S. Park

VACUUM CLEANER: MODEL NO. RD4

Designed c. 1938[13]
Aluminum, steel, rubber
127 x 38 x 51 cm
Produced by Singer Manufacturing Company,
New York, New York
B378

Electric vacuum cleaners were not always standard equipment in American homes. Early nineteenth-century wives or their servants fought dust and grime with brooms and carpet beaters; and their daughters used hand-pumped contraptions of wood with canvas bags. The first electric "suction sweeper" appeared in 1907, invented by a janitor with a dust allergy at Hoover Harness and Leather Goods. The company retooled to improve the janitor's combination of electric fan, feed sack, and box, and was so successful that, for many Americans, "to Hoover" meant "to vacuum" into the 1940s, and the term is still used in Great Britain.

Cat. 31

Cat. 32

Some critics mocked Dreyfuss's styling of this Hoover vacuum cleaner (cat. 31) like one of his locomotives (see fig. 26): "What is the speed of housework?" they asked. But the housewife welcomed the latest weapons in the eternal war against domestic dirt. This trim machine looked as if it not only cleaned quickly but stayed clean itself. Its low, flaring body with rubber bumpers fit under the lowest-slung furniture, while its hemispheric motor housing suggested it packed the power of an army tank. A band of chromium stressed the separation of those parts and announced the Hoover brand name, which was repeated on the cloth bag. Faced with such forceful simplicity, subsequent designers chose to elaborate on the machine's working elements.

Cat. 33

John Morgan exaggerated the motor's military associations by shaping his housing like a helmet or a tank's machine-gun turret, accented with grooves sweeping back from its air vent (cat. 32). He widened the body with wing-like extensions, as did Malcolm Park, who united the body and housing in a banded S-curve of metal (cat. 33). In Park's design for Singer, the company logo looms over the machine in a disk on the handle. This vacuum's curvilinear styling, enhanced by speed lines, suggests the rolling power within.

34. Lurelle Guild

VACUUM CLEANER: MODEL NO. 30

Designed c. 1937[14]
Aluminum, chromium-plated and enameled steel,
steel, vinyl, plastic, rubber
18.5 x 58.5 x 21.5 cm
Produced by Electrolux Corporation,
Old Greenwich, Connecticut
B182

Resembling a hybrid of a rocket and a sled, this revolutionary design looks as if it can propel itself around the house. The front view in an archival drawing (fig. 93) emphasizes its train-like form.[15] With its canister and runners, it challenges the traditional wheeled, upright, bag-type vacuum cleaner in American households. Its separation of motor and suction unit and use of a hose make many attachments possible for different kinds of cleaning, including the interiors of cars. And the

vacuum is light enough to perform as an upright, once its hose is removed and the wand is inserted directly into the cylinder. Furthermore, it has space-age stylishness: its aluminum parts and shiny chromium plating contrast with the textured gray leatherette covering its body. Soon after its introduction in 1937, this Electrolux, Model No. 30, sold to nearly a million households in one year.[16]

Though identified with American ingenuity and marketed door-to-door, the Electrolux canister design was invented in Sweden in 1918 and the cleaner was exported to the United States beginning in 1924. In 1931 manufacturing began in Old Greenwich, Connecticut; and in 1937 Lurelle Guild designed the casing for this, the most popular Electrolux type. Guild's gifts in designing elegant aluminum vessels for such manufacturers as Kensington Inc. (cat. 96–97) served this appliance well.

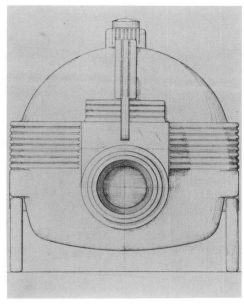

Fig. 93 Lurelle Guild, drawing of elevation of *Electrolux* vacuum, pencil on paper. Special Collections, Syracuse University Library, Syracuse, New York.

35. Harold S. Ryden
VACUUM CLEANER: MODEL C6EPB, *COMPACT ELECTRA*

Designed c. 1955[17]
Aluminum, steel, plastic
30 x 48 x 21 cm
Produced by Interstate Precision Products
Corporation, Anaheim, California
The Liliane and David M. Stewart Collection
SHLSL 2003.20

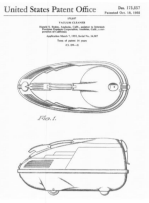

Fig. 94 Harold S. Ryden, patent drawing of "Vacuum Cleaner," detail showing plan.

The vigorous survival of streamlining into the 1950s is demonstrated in Harold Ryden's dynamic design for a vacuum cleaner. In plan (fig. 94), its form adheres to the streamlined dictum of a perfect teardrop, and the speed-line perforations at its nose and the speed banding of its body give the compact design the sense of rocket propulsion. Whereas the Guild canister-type vacuum (cat. 34) is as sleek as a train, the Ryden example is compressed into bulkier form, but one that nevertheless has the shape of velocity. Originally covered with enamel paint, this machine could have been conceived in the 1930s: only its special spherical casters give it away as a 1950s creation.

36. Peter W. Lahr
Floor Polisher: Model No. 623.1925, Craftsman

Designed c. 1948[18]
Enameled and chromium-plated steel, aluminum,
plastic, bristles
122 x 23 x 12.5 cm
Produced by S. C. Johnson & Son, Inc., Racine,
Wisconsin, for Sears, Roebuck and Company,
Chicago, Illinois
B464

Seen from the side, this floor polisher is streamlined
in the tear-shaped forms of its stepped side panels
as well as the perforated speed lines across its top,
which function for ventilation. The brush continues
the curve of the top in this sleek design. Stippled
light blue enamel covers the entire surface of
the polisher, which displays its *Craftsman* label
prominently in a rectangular plate at the top. Small
and space-saving, the appliance could easily be
stored with its body in a vertical position. Aspects
of late streamlining, its pastel enameling, somewhat
boxy body, and literal as well as visual lightness,
reveal its postwar origins.

This is one of many domestic appliances in
Sears, Roebuck's *Craftsman* line, which the giant
mail-order retailer introduced in 1927. The retailer,
which opened stores at the turn of the century,
continues to sell *Craftsman* home-improvement
machines today at popular prices. The designer
Peter Lahr assigned the patent to S. C. Johnson
& Son, Inc., the well-known manufacturer of wax
products and cleaning fluids in Racine, Wisconsin.
A similar floor polisher was advertised by S. C.
Johnson in 1930 in *Better Homes & Gardens*,[19]
indicating that S. C. Johnson probably manufactured
this floor polisher for Sears's *Craftsman* line.

According to the 1948–49 Sears catalogue, this
floor polisher sold for $29.95 and was "Amazingly
easy to use. No rubbing! No hand polishing!
No kneeling! Just put on the wax, then guide
the *Craftsman* Polisher over your floors as you
would a vacuum cleaner. Weight of polisher
provides necessary pressure to make your floors
beautiful."[20]

37. Louis Vavrik
Sander/Polisher: Model 207256L, Craftsman

Design c. 1945[21]
Steel, plastic
15 x 13 x 25 cm
Produced by The American Floor Surfacing
Machine Company, Toledo, Ohio, for Sears,
Roebuck and Company, Chicago, Illinois
B664

This design for what Vavrik called a "Surface
Treating Machine" in his patent application reveals
his unusual skills in giving aerodynamic vitality
to power tool forms. This machine is all smooth
curves, from its rounded body to its handle, whose
S-shape continues in its electrical cord. Resembling
a toy elephant head with a two-toned trunk, this
appliance promises power and control. Adhering
to the canons of streamlining, perforations like
speed lines cool the motor at the top front
and the base, while the contrast of the colors
of the plastic and the sheen of the steel animate
the total. Vavrik has used streamlining successfully
to give a noisy machine that sands, buffs, and
polishes a friendly face.

38. Albert Edwin Emmons
Electric Lawn Mower: *REM* Model

Designed c. 1946[22]
Steel, enameled aluminum, rubber
119 x 40.5 x 57.5 cm
Produced by Rumsey Products Inc.,
Seneca Falls, New York
B162

Designed immediately after World War II, this electrically driven lawn mower exemplifies the continuing taste for streamlining in its smoothly contoured aluminum cowling, which conceals the large rotary blades and motor beneath it. Around the front, a toothed skirt (seen to advantage in the patent drawing, fig. 95), prevents twigs from slipping into the machinery, and on the motor face a series of air vents extends the faintly menacing persona. If the electric cord is long enough, no tall grass is safe. Yet the original peachy-beige enamel, now restored, and the overall bell shape of the mower make it look friendly to the housewife and teenager, as well as to Father.

The need for lawn care tools ballooned after the war as the GI Bill made low-cost loans to returning servicemen who wanted to own homes. They encouraged the development of tract housing in the suburbs, which had begun in the late 1930s, and the battle for manicured lawns was joined. The genealogy of lawn mowers is Anglophone, as the appeal of park-style greensward seems to be. The first home lawn mowers was a British invention of 1830 (a cutting cylinder from the textile industry given a plow-like wheeled frame), and gas- and steam-powered mowers appeared in the 1890s.[23] Compared to models of the late 1930s with exposed parts,[24] this mower exudes a sense of power and efficiency. Its works are hidden, for safety and good looks.

Fig. 95 Albert E. Emmons, detail of a patent drawing of "Electric Driven Lawn Mower."

---

39. Designer unknown
Hedge Trimmer: Model No. 283, 25651, *Craftsman*

Designed c. 1948
Steel, aluminum, brass, rubber
17 x 30.5 x 29.5 cm
Produced for Sears, Roebuck and Company,
Chicago, Illinois
B439

"Good fences make good neighbors," goes the old saying. And if the divisions between properties are made or prettily concealed by hedges, they inevitably need clipping to indicate that man, not nature, has the upper hand. Not only does this motorized trimmer save effort relative to hand shears, but it looks more efficient, and assures dependable quality at a reasonable price. The canted handle offers a secure grip, while the speed lines on it—the emblem of streamlining—echo the horizontal grooves wrapping around the sides and back of the bullet-shaped body.

The *Craftsman* label, which appears three times on the trimmer, was a somewhat nostalgic and wishful choice of name by Sears, Roebuck. The line's growth market was in middle-class, do-it-yourself homes kept up by increasingly urbanized workers. Their yards were small enough to be covered by electrical extension cords. Their wiring, owing to provisions of the Federal Housing Act, could serve the demand of power tools.[25] And their energy costs were less to them than wage earners' physical effort. After a week at work, they wanted to trim the privet as fast and easily as possible. These homeowners continue to be the prime customer for *Craftsman* tools. According to the Sears, Roebuck and Company catalogue, this electric hedge trimmer sold for $29.50, and an extension attachment was sold separately to make it possible to "use this tool as a long-handled power grass trimmer for lawn edges, under shrubbery, or overhead trimming."[26]

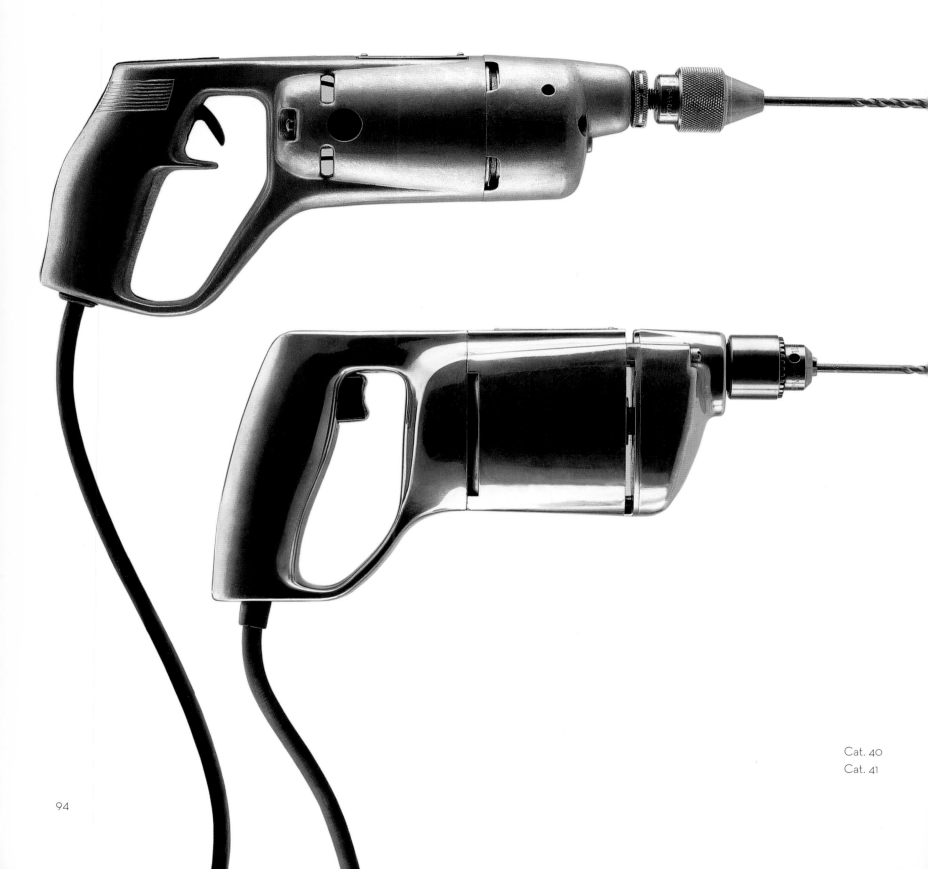

Cat. 40
Cat. 41

40. Designer unknown
ELECTRIC DRILL: MODEL NO. 626, 25751,
DUNLAP
Designed c. 1948[27]
Steel, aluminum
11 x 31 x 6.5 cm
Produced for Sears, Roebuck and Company,
Chicago, Illinois
B199

41. John R. Morgan
ELECTRIC DRILL: MODEL NO. 315, 7711,
CRAFTSMAN
Designed 1940-50
Aluminum, steel, brass
13 x 27 x 6 cm
Produced for Sears, Roebuck and Company,
Chicago, Illinois
B193

42. Designer unknown
ELECTRIC DRILL: MODEL NO. 250
Designed 1935-40
Steel, aluminum
12 x 31 x 8 cm
Produced by Skilsaw Inc., Chicago, Illinois
B204

A pistol and an electric drill have much in common. Both trigger a piece of metal to put a neat hole into a resistant body at high speed. Handymen must have liked the weapon analogy for these three drills, which all have pistol grips and typify the streamlining of power tools in the 1930s and 1940s. In all three examples, the handle, trigger, and motor housing compose a compact, continuous bullet-shaped body. The grip of each drill is curved to fit the palm and direct the torpedo-like drill head, and the smooth, shining, unornamented surface of the total means easy care. In 1945 the artist Saul Steinberg, then curator of an industrial products exhibition, commented: "You always find good design in work things."[28]

That said, subtle formal variations in these three drills nevertheless reflect their different selling points or brand identities. John Morgan's designs for *Craftsman* tools are typically chunky: the

squared-off handle and body of cat. 41 relate to his contouring of his earlier air compressor, cat. 50. The body of the Skilsaw drill is a plump tapered sphere, whereas the longer cylinder of the *Dunlap* drill suggests it offers more precision than power. Of course the drills also competed in price, number of drill bits, and so on, but their appearance was a marketing point.

All three of these drills are portable and corded. The "in-line" design, with the pistol grip lined up with the bit, increases accuracy, while the trigger allows the user to vary the speed or to turn the motor off and on. These features made the first such drill, patented c. 1915 by Duncan Black and Alonso Decker, Sr.,[29] an immediate success. Skilsaw was founded in 1924 as the Michel Electric Handsaw Company and renamed Skilsaw in 1926. Contemporary drills have not changed significantly from these streamlined versions, although lighter materials today, including plastics, have replaced the cast iron and much of the steel of the sturdier earlier models, and many of today's drills are conveniently cordless (the battery-charged, cordless drill was invented in 1961). *Dunlap* and *Craftsman* are brand names still to be found in home woodworking shops and on building sites.

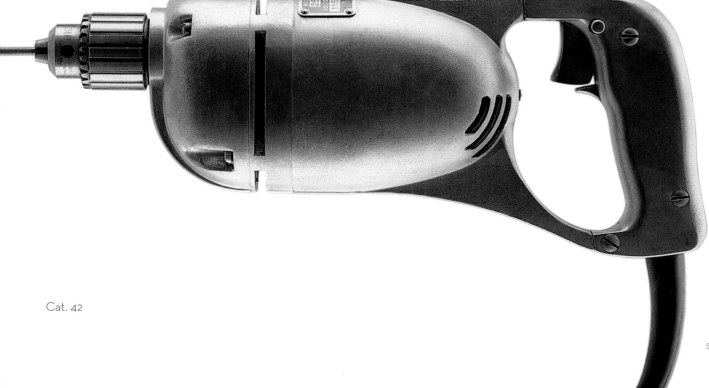

Cat. 42

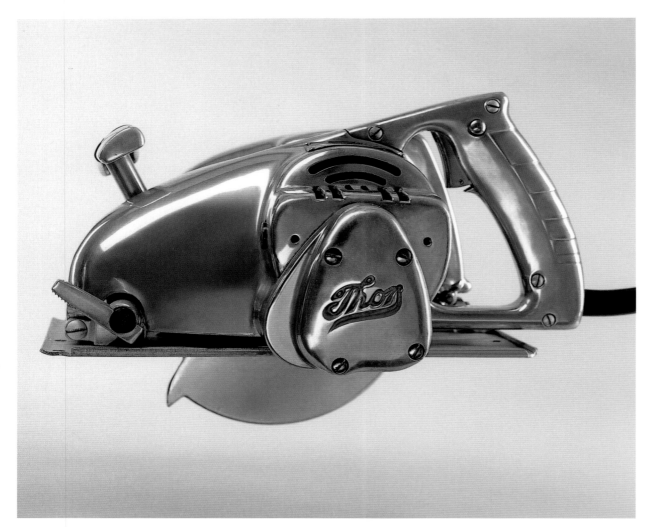

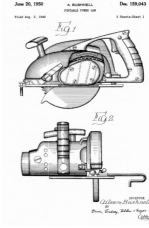

Fig. 96 Aileen Bushnell, patent drawing for "Portable Power Saw."

43. Aileen Bushnell
ELECTRIC CIRCULAR SAW:
MODEL NO. 6743, *THOR SILVER LINE*
Designed c. 1949[30]
Aluminum, steel, plastic
23.5 x 36 x 23 cm
Produced by Independent Pneumatic Tool
Company, Aurora, Illinois
B244

44. Louis Vavrik
ELECTRIC CIRCULAR SAW:
MODEL NO. 207.25602, *CRAFTSMAN*
Designed c. 1945[31]
Steel, aluminum, plastic
29.5 x 39 x 24 cm
Produced for Sears, Roebuck and Company,
Chicago, Illinois
B463

Both of these designs for circular saws are streamlined in their swelling forms, aerodynamic curves, and gleaming aluminum bodies. But aspects of their styling differ to suggest their different selling points. The *Thor Silver Line* was named after the Norse counterpart of Zeus and the god of the forge, doubtless to suggest the strength of its motor and the power it gave the user. Its patent drawing (fig. 96) illustrates the complexity of the design, with teardrop, cylindrical, and oval shapes played against angular forms, like the U of the handle, to create a highly sculptural totality. The handle, ridged for firmer gripping, recalls that of traditional hand saws.

No such old-fashioned associations cling to the *Craftsman* power tool. Here a sense of speed and precision is evoked by the sweeping teardrop form of the unified design. The handle is an S echoing the shape of the machine, a line accented in dark plastic and extended in the electrical cord. The motor is vented by an oval grille whose horizontals continue in speed lines on the side of the machine. And the user guides the saw with a circular knob, also in dark plastic, which completes the rhythmic curves of the total. These variables in the shape and placement of the grips distinguished the tools and made them more competitive. Consumers could choose the product that fit their tasks and physical abilities. Not just cosmetic, the design differences forecast the impact of wartime ergonomic studies on product appearance in the 1950s.[32]

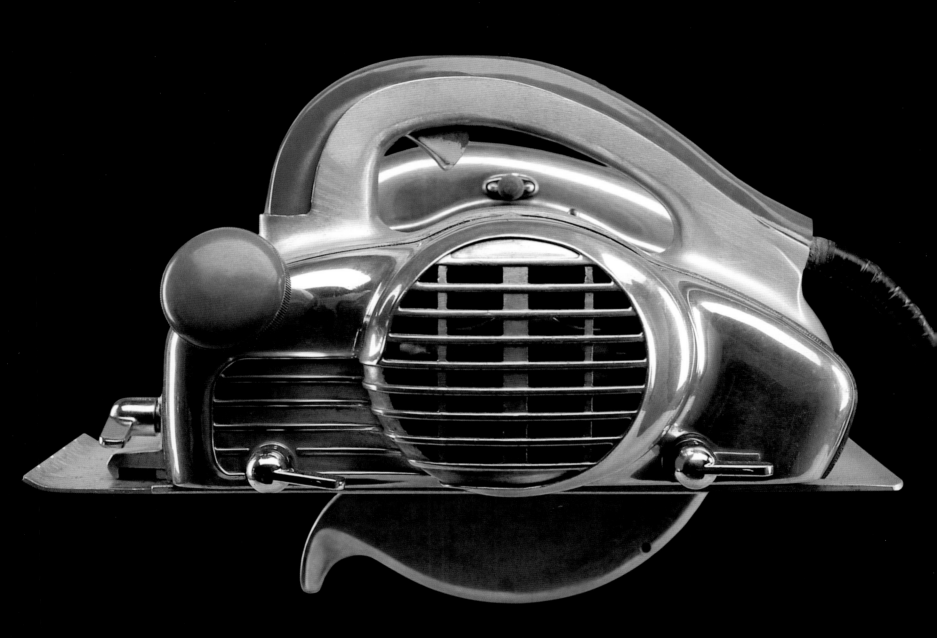

Cat. 44

45. Arthur N. Emmons
Peter Müller-Munk
ELECTRIC SANDER/POLISHER:
MODEL A3, *TAKE-ABOUT*
Designed c. 1951[33]
Steel, chromium-plated steel, plastic, felt
19 x 40 x 12.8 cm
Produced by Porter-Cable Machine Company,
Syracuse, New York
B574

46. Designer unknown
ELECTRIC SANDER/POLISHER:
MODEL NO. 110.7820, *CRAFTSMAN*
Designed c. 1955[34]
Steel, chromium-plated steel, plastic, felt
16.5 x 24.5 x 9 cm
Produced for Sears, Roebuck and Company,
Chicago, Illinois
B590

47. Stephen A. Crosby
Peter Zasadny
ELECTRIC SANDER:
MODEL NO. 1000, *SPEEDMATIC*
Designed c. 1946[35]
Steel, plastic, aluminum, rubber
18.5 x 21 x 13 cm
Produced by Porter-Cable Machine Company,
Syracuse, New York
B161

Of all the steps in carpentry or cabinetmaking, sanding may be the most tedious. Lightening and speeding this exacting labor was the achievement of the power sander, which came on the market in the early twentieth century. As handymen in the 1940s worked to upgrade their houses by finishing their basements or adding bookshelves, cabinets, or even bars to existing rooms, such machines became essential tools. To appeal to the home improvement buff, they had to be easy to use and powerful.

All three of these products convey such qualities through their streamlined designs. The bodies gleam with chromium-plated steel, the vents serve as speed lines, and the thick handles swoop up toward their motors evoking the forward thrust of the sanding.

Stephen Crosby, who designed the stapler seen in cat. 15, has shaped the motor of his sander as an elegant architectonic tower with a buttress-like handle and twin parabolas at each side of the base. With all its parts encased in a continuously contoured form topped by a canted helmet shape, this sander looks ready to move forward. Crosby's 1946 design specifications refer to his earlier 1943 patent for an "electric sanding machine or the like" (fig. 97), which illustrates the same design but with slight modifications.[36]

Just as streamlined, though horizontal in form, the *Take-About* sander resembles a locomotive and conjures up the movement and speed of one of the Streamliners. Its corners are curved and its handle and motor casing are one sculptural form with horizontal perforations for ventilation. The more rectilinear *Craftsman* machine, like the *Take-About*, has the functional advantage of being able to polish as well as sand.

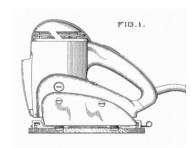

Fig. 97 Stephen A. Crosby, detail of a patent drawing for "Electric Portable Rubbing Machine or the Like."

Cat. 45

Cat. 46

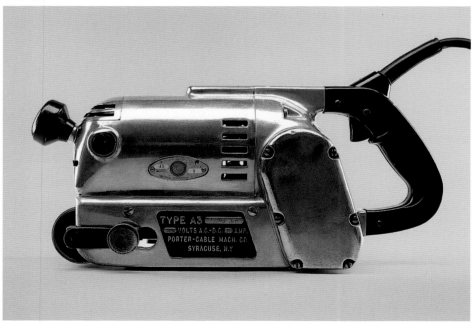

48. Roland A. Manning

AIR COMPRESSOR

Designed c. 1938[37]

Cast iron, steel, brass

28 x 37 x 21 cm

Produced by The Electric Sprayit Company,
Milwaukee, Wisconsin

B561

49. Sundberg-Ferar Company

in collaboration with

Harold R. Gamble and **Donald J. Peeps**

AIR COMPRESSOR

Designed c. 1946[38]

Enameled cast iron, brass, chromium-plated steel

28.5 x 37 x 19 cm

Produced by The DeVilbiss Company, Toledo, Ohio

B594

50. John R. Morgan

PORTABLE AIR COMPRESSOR: *CRAFTSMAN*

Designed c. 1935–40

Steel, aluminum, paint

25.5 x 32 x 17 cm

Produced for Sears, Roebuck and Company,
Chicago, Illinois

B153

To the handyman in a hurry, brushes are too slow for painting all but intricate spaces or objects, and rollers cover only big flat surfaces like walls with any efficiency. The paint sprayer, on the other hand (fig. 99), permits speedy execution and gives glistening surfaces the look of uniform mechanical perfection. Attached by a hose to an air compressor, the paint sprayer was and remains the tool of choice for the hobbyist home painter and the contractor alike. According to a testimonial in a 1955 advertisement, the spray gun "fully covers any surface with less labor. A bridge job requiring 15 brush painters, for example, can be done in the same time by a two-gun spray crew!"[39]

Like the paint sprayers they powered, these three air compressors are animated with different kinds of streamlining to catch the consumer's eye. While the sprayers are designed to suggest they can be easily and swiftly used, the air compressors convey strength and energy yet stability. Once plugged in, their heavy housings were meant to remain stationary, while their powerful motors, cooled by prominent, dramatically repeated vents, compressed all the air needed for a task. In all three of these machines, the vents wrap around the compressor bodies, and in cat. 49 and 50, they are accented with hot red enamel, which also sets off the letters of the manufacturer's name.

The body of the Sundberg-Ferar compressor is a tapered upright sphere with both vertical and horizontal vents; John Morgan's styling is more cubic, with rounded corners and a rectangular grip; while Roland Manning's machine (cat. 48), designed en suite with his spray gun (fig. 99) and having the same patent date, resembles the prow of an ocean liner. If such vessels suggest they can sail the seven seas, the owner of this compressor is encouraged to think he can sail through a mere paint job.

According to a contemporary account, the DeVilbiss air compressor was designed by the prominent Detroit firm of Sundberg-Ferar in collaboration with the engineering department of the DeVilbiss Company in order to add "sales appeal and a coherent, designed-for-the-purpose look to a carefully engineered compressor."[40] The challenge was "to integrate the air intake, the handle, the compression cylinder, and the motor into a smoothly contoured unit." Three years after its patenting, *U.S. Industrial Design* could report that "the saving in weight" of the design and "the compact, efficient, functional appearance have so appealed to consumers that increased sales have already justified the [company's] investment" in retooling.[41]

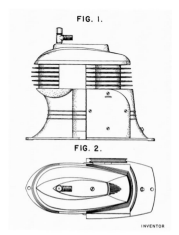

Fig. 98 Roland A. Manning, detail of a patent drawing for "Air Conpressor."

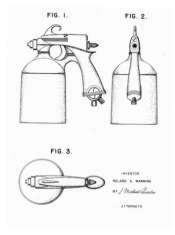

Fig. 99 Roland A. Manning, detail of a patent drawing for *Sprayit* paint sprayer.

Cat. 49

Cat. 50

51. Egmont H. Arens
Theodore C. Brookhart
MEAT SLICER: MODEL No. 195, *STREAMLINER*
Designed c. 1942[42]

Aluminum, steel, rubber

47 x 44.5 x 32.5 cm

Produced by the Hobart Manufacturing Company, Troy, Ohio

B030

The harmoniously scaled, voluptuous components of this meat slicer transform a functional object into sculpture. Streamlining is seen in the multiple elliptical curves throughout the design and the gradual, sensuous transitions from part to part. The gleaming rounded forms, which shield the blade and moving parts within and allow easier cleaning, are reminiscent of streamlined trains. The patent for the appliance shows four views of the machine, of which one is illustrated here to indicate the functional qualities of the design (fig. 100). Its continued production until 1985 attests to its efficiency and the long-lived popularity of streamlined design in twentieth-century America. Although the word "STREAMLINER" appears twice on this model of the meat slicer, it was not used on later models, reflecting changes in taste and marketing. After 1945, the term "streamlining" was in general used less frequently in advertising in architectural periodicals, suggesting that this example is probably an earlier model. A second example of the meat slicer in the Brill Collection lacks the "streamliner" stamp but instead has a model number.

This Hobart product was designed for use in delicatessens, hotels, and restaurants rather than in single-family kitchens. Hobart Manufacturing was and still is a leading producer of appliances for commercial food preparation.

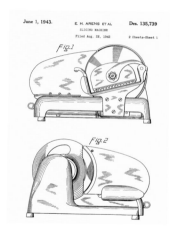

Fig. 100 Egmont H. Arens et al., patent drawing for "Slicing Machine."

52. Arthur W. Seyfried
Peter W. Lahr
DRINK MIXER: MODEL 51
Designed c. 1952[43]
Enameled and chromium-plated steel, rubber
36 x 17 x 13.5 cm
Produced by Hamilton Beach, Racine, Wisconsin
B607

An egg-shaped mixer for a milkshake or malted, this elegantly curved appliance was designed to speed the process of blending and aerating drinks. The cloverleaf blades of the "agitator" are movable, and allow the operator to plunge the shaft easily into frozen ice cream. Flick the switch and, according to the 1941 utility patent application, the machine will "mix liquid or powdered or semi-solid ingredients in liquid beverages quickly and efficiently."[44] The mixer looks as smooth and cool as the drinks it delivers. Its white enamel, set off by chromium-plated working parts, spells out how hygienic is its operation and how healthy its dairy beverages. What could be more elemental and nourishing than an egg? This spherical motor housing tops a bone-like support on a U-shaped base, into which the liquid container nestles, and the total suggests how delicious this form of calcium ingestion can be. Period photographs show the mixer widely used in diners and drugstores.

53. Albert W. Scarratt
Raymond L. Loewy
William H. Harstick
CREAM SEPARATOR
Designed c. 1939[45]
Cast iron, metal, aluminum, wood
119 x 52.5 x 54 cm
Produced by International Harvester Company, Chicago, Illinois
B362

The continuous metal sheathing typical of the streamlined style had sanitary as well as aesthetic advantages for this cream separator. Earlier designs "were hard to clean, due to their many recesses, cavities and exposed areas," the designer Raymond Loewy observed in his autobiography. "I believed impeccable cleanliness was essential in such a machine."[46] To that end, he replaced the four-legged base of the past with a circular pedestal and absorbed the traditional belt-and-wheels mechanism into the swelling body of the separator (fig. 101). All cast-iron parts of this example were enameled white and beige to complete the hygienic associations, while the vessels for the cream were ever-shining aluminum for ease of care. A sculptor's sense of proportion and form gives the goblet-shaped device a memorable presence, half-humanoid, half-mechanistic.

Although Loewy is credited with the sensuous design of this much-published machine, the patent specification lists three designers—evidence of the collaborative effort necessary in industrial design. "The industrial designer never works alone," Loewy wrote. "As a rule, he is one of a trio (backed by dozens of assistants) whose duty it is to solve the design problem. He, the engineer, and the cost analyst constitute the force whose task it is to consider every minute phase of the undertaking and to solve it with speed, thoroughness, and finality. . . ."[47] Depending on the project, this collaboration might be within Loewy's growing office, or between Loewy and his staff working with expert outside specialists, who often included the staff of the corporate client.[48]

Although the McCormick and Deering companies merged in 1902 with others to form International Harvester Company, the firm continued to use the McCormick-Deering name because of ongoing lawsuits against the merged companies. Even by 1939, when the cream separator was produced, the McCormick-Deering name was prominently displayed as a brand on the product. The patent specifications, however, list International Harvester Company alone as the manufacturer.

Fig. 101 Photograph showing before and after views of cream separator, produced by McCormick-Deering et al. From Raymond Loewy, *Industrial Design*, 1979.

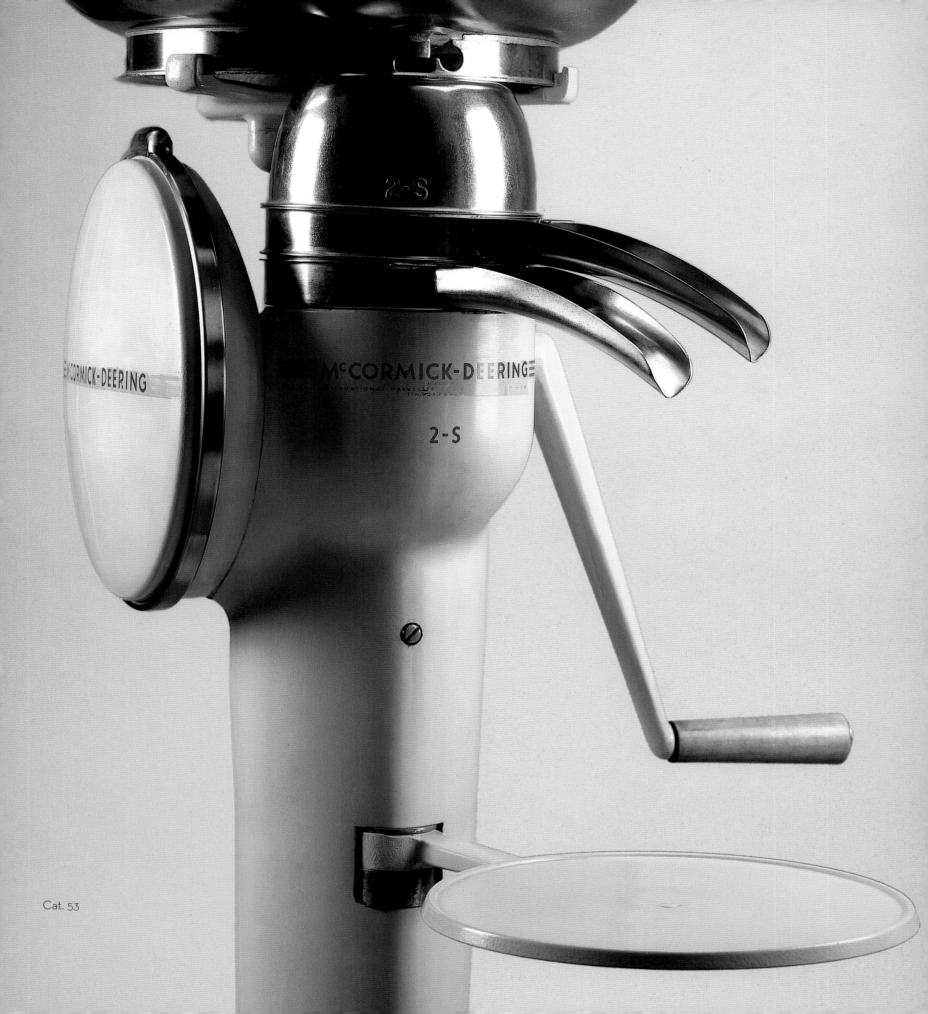

"AMAZING APPLIANCES"

Streamlining the Kitchen and Bath

3

The American kitchen and bathroom that developed in the 1930s would be familiar to us today. Styled with streamlining, these rooms provided a complementary setting for the plethora of streamlined appliances invented or improved and patented in that decade. Here modernity in technology and design was wholeheartedly embraced in the home.

These updated settings reflected the construction boom in middle-class housing following World War I and the modernization of municipal sewer systems and utilities. By 1907, 8 percent of American houses were wired for electricity, but by 1920, 35 percent of homes enjoyed electricity at any time of the day,[1] and by 1930 over 85 percent of urban homes were electrified.[2] With the New Deal, two-thirds of all housing in the nation was wired for appliances as well as electric light.[3] Here was the power for the labor-saving inventions made for the kitchen from this period on, and here was the mass market for the modern bathroom with its matching sink, toilet, built-in tub and shower, and its electrical grooming devices. Manufacturers were so successful in reaching American consumers that between 1930 and 1940 the annual use of electricity per home doubled, because of the vastly increased reliance on electrical appliances and the lower cost of power.[4]

In the 1920s and 1930s the modernized kitchen and bath became the domestic status symbols they remain to this day. In each, the housewife exercised her taste and power over household consumption, determining the look of the rooms and the choice of appliances. Credited with making 80 percent of all consumer purchases, she was encouraged by advertisers to see herself as an executive and literally a homemaker. She was "The Little Woman, G.P.A." or general purchasing agent, in the words of one advertisement. "Businesses may have their treasurers, their controllers, but homes have their wives who do the same work in 25 million independent businesses, the households of America."[5] In the kitchen and bath—symbolically powerful sources of family meals and personal hygiene—women were urged to adopt streamlined design, in both spatial layouts and the styling of equipment. The up-to-date appearance of these rooms would signal the family's financial health in the Depression's dark days, while the presence of even one brand-name appliance, such as a Dormeyer mixer or Schick electric shaver (cat. 73, 89), would allow middle-class owners to associate themselves with the wealthy who used the same goods.

The Kitchen

"A Man's Castle is a Woman's Factory!" asserted an ad for General Electric appliances in 1934. Picturing a woman in her gleaming kitchen, the copy pressed the reader to imitate her and to "modernize with the Ten Best Home Servants," including an electric refrigerator, cooking range, and dishwasher.[6] "The servant problem" was one subtext, for live-in domestics had been disappearing since the 1890s, lured by better-paying jobs in factories and later in offices; and their numbers were further diminished by restrictive immigration policies from World War I on. The housewife needed a set of labor-saving machines and a step-saving kitchen design to lighten her heavier burdens.

More efficient "kitchens of the future" had been seen in world's fairs since the 1933 *Century of Progress Exposition* in Chicago, yet that all-electric display promoted efficiency only in power, not in design. Typical kitchens of c. 1890–1920 were workspaces with separate pieces of furniture for food preparation, clean-up, and storage (fig. 102). The "rationalized" kitchen emerged in the 1920s in Europe among German architects and designers who looked to the United States. They were inspired by the time-motion studies of Frederick W. Taylor and their impact on the American factory assembly line, and also by the writings of Christine Frederick, among other American experts in domestic engineering of the 1890s–1910s. Frederick was one of the most influential American women to be concerned with "bringing the science of efficiency to the home." In her book, *Housekeeping with Efficiency*, she asked: "Do we not waste time by walking in poorly arranged kitchens?"[7] Comparisons between "bad and good" and "before and after" kitchen designs proliferated (fig. 103), making women conscious of the steps necessary in preparing meals, from bringing groceries into the house to taking food to and from the dining room.

The Germans applied Taylor's and Frederick's concepts in their new kitchens and equipped them with modular cabinets modeled on the standardized furniture pioneered by their countrymen before World War I. Promoting the work of the Bauhaus in Weimar, the model house named Haus am Horn of 1923 presented a kitchen by Marcel Breuer, which is credited as the first design with continuous countertops and cupboards above and below them (fig. 104).[8] The next steps in streamlining food handling were taken by American manufacturers. "When ranges, sink and counters were

Fig. 102 Kitchen, c. 1900. From *The Architectural Forum*, October 1937.
Fig. 103 "Before" and "After" kitchen plans, 1936. From *American Home*, 1936.

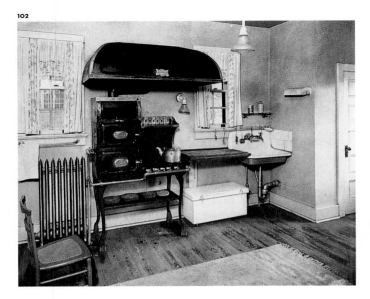

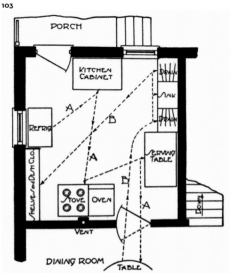

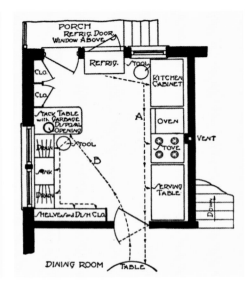

104

105

106

Fig. 104 Bauhaus Kitchen, Haus am Horn, 1923.
Fig. 105 Kitchen, c. 1936. From *The Architectural Forum*, June 1936.
Fig. 106 Advertisement for General Electric Unit Kitchen. From *Pencil Points*, January 1937.

designed to make a continuous working surface," wrote one American observer in 1936, "the streamlined electric kitchen became a reality."[9]

The "integrated kitchen" in America had ensembles of strandardized, modular cabinets and large appliances efficiently organized in a purpose-built space (fig. 105). It was "an industrially designed laboratory for food preparation," proclaimed the Cheneys in 1936.[10] Its electrification and the consequent replacement of the icebox in the pantry with a refrigerator furthered the streamlining of the kitchen design. As seen in General Electric's "Unit Kitchen" (fig. 106), the range, sink, and refrigerator were placed in a tight triangle (a step-saving arrangement favored today), while space was liberated in the kitchen for a desk (fig. 108), and in the pantry for laundry equipment (presumably served by a centralized plumbing system). In fig. 106, the housewife scrapes plates into a garbage disposal in her sink, then puts them in a top-loading dishwasher to her left, all without taking a step. The advertisement copy underlined the point of an inset illustration: the "Unit Kitchen . . . will fit any plan—one wall, L-shaped or U-shaped kitchens. It includes G-E Refrigerator, G-E Range, G-E Dishwasher-sink, G-E Garbage Disposall, cabinets, work surfaces, wall splasher, and lumiline lighting. All units are pre-fabricated and interchangeable."[11] This line of GE products allowed families the maximum of planning choices, in keeping with their budgets and space. Though not streamlined in style, the kitchen was streamlined in organization, with continuous cabinetwork and countertops and integrated appliances.

Streamlined styling was easy to apply to such a kitchen (fig. 109): rectangular corners were simply curved and horizontal pulls and/or horizontal bands were added. "Rounded cabinet corners give a streamlined effect—and are safer," claimed a contemporary writer.[12] In the kitchen in fig. 107, the linoleum is banded to accent the U-shaped work center and a long, wraparound window over the sink gives the requisite view over the lawn. In Brigsteel's *Kitchen of Tomorrow*, 1935 (fig. 108), streamlined efficiency is summed up in the cylindrical cooking island topped by a Bauhaus-style

107

108

metal lamp. And though this model kitchen evokes spacious suburbia with trees outside its ribbon window, the breakfast table is a space-saver, dropping down from built-in display shelves in the wall. This table, and the desk and phone, indicate the evolution in the late 1930s of the one-purpose, "laboratory" kitchen into a multi-purpose family space.

In the second half of the 1930s, the whole family began to move into the middle-class kitchen, whether in response to more informal lifestyles, the pressures of limited space, or both. In some apartments and homes, the dining room was eliminated entirely and transported to the kitchen as an eating area. And appliances associated with other rooms, such as the clothes washer and dryer, came into the kitchen as part of the new family center. In a December 1940 advertisement, the Crane Company, a prestigious Chicago manufacturer of kitchen and bathroom equipment, asked: "What is a kitchen, anyway? Nowadays, in addition to its kitchen functions, it is likely to be a sewing room-ironing room-dining room-study-recreation room—even a nursery!"[13]

In the imagery of the 1930s, kitchens are only intermittently pictured with refrigerators, depending on the advertiser, for the refrigerator was the one appliance that, with its upright bulk, necessarily broke the sweeping horizontality of the streamlined kitchen. Yet as the biggest and most expensive item in that room, it was the epitome of the technological, styling, and price changes that made the mid- and late 1930s a time of renewed consumerism. The old icebox, once outside the kitchen to be nearer the delivery of ice, was a cabinet-like container on legs. For its electrified descendants designers simply added a motor to the legged boxy shape, as in GE's *Monitor Top* model of 1932 (fig. 110). But a new form was invented for the new technology in 1934 when the celebrity industrial designer Henry Dreyfuss unveiled his *Flatop* for GE (fig. 111). The motor was incorporated in the base of the taller casing, a rectangular form with set-back sides; and the legs disappeared into a narrow recessed base. The same year Sears, Roebuck, which had begun selling refrigerators in its mail-order catalogue in 1931, answered with the *Coldspot* model by Dreyfuss's rival Raymond Loewy. Loewy transformed the rectilinear Dreyfuss design into his signa-

Fig. 107 Streamlined kitchen, c. 1937. From *The Architectural Forum*, August 1937.

Fig. 108 *Kitchen of Tomorrow*, Brigsteel exhibit at the National Association of Master Plumbers Convention, 1935, Briggs Manufacturing Company, Detroit, Michigan. From *The Architectural Forum*, August 1935.

Fig. 109 Streamlined kitchen in advertisement for Westinghouse Refrigerators, c. 1940.

109

WESTINGHOUSE REFRIGERATORS

For better Living in the American Way

ture streamlined idiom by rounding the appliance's corners and turning it into a unitary shape. In his 1937 model (fig. 112), he accented horizontality in his streamlining, making the earlier vertical handle into an elongated horizontal one and adding speed lines to the bottom corners of the refrigerator. The casing of enameled sheet steel now extended without interruption to the floor.

Loewy's styling adjustments of 1935–38 were more cosmetic than technical. They reflected industry's acceptance of "planned obsolescence," or "creative waste," in the words of Christine Frederick in *Selling Mrs. Consumer*, 1929. Improving the hardware—introducing rustproof aluminum shelves, for instance—and updating the design added value for style-conscious consumers. They were encouraged to want the latest model as a new purchase, or to consider upgrading even if their old refrigerator was still functioning well. Thus streamlining by the masters of the style stoked the economic engine of consumption.

Styling was only one of the factors, however, that brought refrigerators into 44 percent of American homes by 1940, up from the 17 percent that had iceboxes or power refrigeration in 1927.[14] Low-cost, federally insured loans and other incentives to home owning and modernization through electricity and power appliances were part of the New Deal. Because electrical appliances such as refrigerators and ranges were sold cooperatively through certain federal programs, the government could challenge manufacturers to compete in lowering their prices. In 1934 Westinghouse more than halved the price of its cheapest stove, while GE beat out Sears on economy refrigerators, $74.50 to $94.50.[15] Meanwhile, home building under the National Housing Act of 1934 required outlets for portable power appliances as well as electric lights. If refrigerator ownership more than doubled across the United States in the 1930s, one might assume there were even greater increases in small appliance sales where unit costs were much lower. On her sweeping countertop, Mrs. Consumer could flaunt her choices from an ever-growing smorgasbord of power cooking aids.

The pages that follow here illustrate some of those choices, and others are visible in a *House Beautiful* survey of "Current Equipment" in 1938 (fig. 113). Mixers with juicer attachments, deep fryers, warmers, rotisseries, blenders, waffle irons, and popcorn poppers are just a few of the offerings. Many of the appliances were streamlined for sales appeal, but also for ease of cleaning and efficient storage. In some cases, the designs were marketed as stylish enough to travel from the

Fig. 110. Designer unknown, *Monitor Top* refrigerator, General Electric, 1932.

Fig. 111. Henry Dreyfuss, *Flatop* refrigerator, General Electric, 1934.

Fig. 112. Raymond Loewy, *Coldspot* refrigerator, Sears, Roebuck and Company, 1937.

kitchen to the rumpus room or even the dining room. "The Best-Dressed Products Sell Best," asserted a headline in *Forbes* magazine as early as 1934.[16] The housewife could express her individuality through the selection of attractive, efficient appliances and feel up-to-date with a small purchase. These tools would help her improve and speed her cooking, leaving her more time to spend with her well-fed family.

The Bathroom

If the modern kitchen began as a laboratory and evolved into a family center, the modern bathroom began as a clinic and developed into a spa, complete with sleek personal grooming devices (cat. 83–90). Concerns about hygiene had originated with the public health movement of the late nineteenth and early twentieth centuries, when it was first understood that cleanliness was crucial to limiting the spread of communicable diseases. The fixtures of today—the sink, toilet, and bathtub with running water—developed in the second half of the nineteenth century. At the same time, showers were recommended for bathrooms, as well as for the public baths that cities began building for the working class. All classes looked down on the "great unwashed masses" and encouraged the manufacture of bathroom appliances through their purchases. The Dada artist Marcel Duchamp was only half-joking in 1917 when he claimed that "the only works of art America has given are her plumbing and her bridges," and entered a mass-produced urinal in a New York art exhibition.[17]

By the 1930s, designers saw the bath, like the kitchen, as a modern setting of machine-age efficiency and modular parts. A number of writers and exhibitions extolled the virtues of industrial design in this space and its appliances as art. In *Art and the Machine* (1936) the Cheneys wrote:

> The bathroom, too, is functionally honest, immaculately clean, joyously bright. It has claimed the attention of leading architectural and industrial designers. It is here that the inventor-artists have made their first large gains in marketing prefabricated units, comprising the whole room or a single major plumbing unit and its adjacent wall. It might be noted that in thus perfecting and standardizing the bathroom and the kitchen—not to say establishing their aesthetic—the moderns have glorified first those parts of the home that used to be considered mere utility adjuncts not of any importance in the artistic architect's work. . . .[18]

In 1937, Buckminster Fuller patented a prefabricated bathroom for existing homes and those in construction (cat. 78), with plumbing, electrical wiring, and appliances all in one unit. The sheet steel facility was intended to streamline bathroom manufacture and installation; at the same time, it is a streamlined design modeled on the space-saving "heads" in ships. Less visionary but more popular was Henry Dreyfuss's *Neuvogue* line for the Crane Company (fig. 115), which included sink, toilet, and built-in tub as elements the buyer could assemble and place at will. Here Dreyfuss gave streamlining a restrained, even classicizing form: the appliances are simplified geometric solids with bands accenting their symmetry and chromium-shiny hardware.

What a far cry from the bathroom of the turn of the century (fig. 114). American homes had indoor plumbing from the 1830s on, but as late as the 1890s bathrooms resembled other rooms in the house with furniture, draperies, carpets, and bric-a-brac. By the 1920s and 1930s, however, the bathroom paralleled the kitchen in integrating equipment, and it too began to show streamlining as sharp corners were rounded and porcelain forms were stripped of detail. The tub, for example,

Fig. 113 "Current Equipment." From *House Beautiful*, November 1938.

lost its nineteenth-century feet and its isolation in the room like a separate piece of furniture. Instead, it was built in, an evolution that began early in the century and was complete by the mid-thirties. The bathroom with a footed tub was considered "Old-fashioned—unsightly—an irritation to the family," while the built-in tub was "Beautiful—modern—clean—inviting—easy to keep spick and span."[19] While living rooms of the 1930s might have Chippendale reproductions with claw-and-ball feet, that feature was banished from the bath along with any associations with furniture.

The ideal bathroom had low-maintenance, high-gloss surfaces of tile, porcelain, glass, and enamel, in addition to a built-in tub, separate shower, and shelves with sliding glass doors (fig. 116). Curving walls, mirrors, and lighting with speed line accents united the space. While towel and soap manufacturers invited consumers to bathe not just once a day but more often,[20] such designs suggested that the process could be fast. Here the American family, if conservative in its tastes elsewhere, was most often modern. Even in the revival-style houses widespread in the 1930s, "kitchens and bathrooms are almost wholly rational and by all odds the most satisfactory rooms in the house," wrote the designer Walter Dorwin Teague. "Modern design entered the American home not through the front door," he concluded, "but by way of the kitchen, bathroom and garage."[21]

114

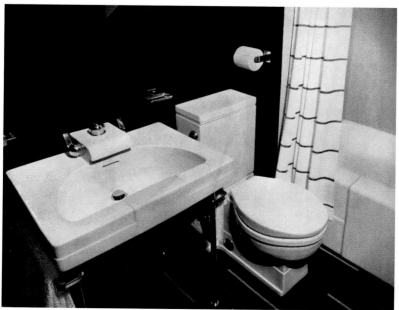

115

116

54. Designer unknown
ROASTING PAN
Designed c. 1935–40
Aluminum
18 x 48 x 28.5 cm
Manufacturer unknown
B219

55. Designer unknown
ROASTING PAN: ZEPHYR *STREAMLINER*
Designed c. 1935–40
Aluminum
18 x 44.5 x 25.5 cm
Produced by Schlenzig Manufacturing
Company, United States
B262

Aluminum, principally derived from the ore bauxite, was first discovered in the early nineteenth century, but it came into its own in the twentieth and became popular for utensils and appliances as well as the sheathing of trains and planes. It is lightweight, low-cost, malleable, corrosion-resistant, as strong as iron, and as conductive as copper. In the Depression years it was often substituted for steel to reduce prices. The variety of aluminum goods designed by the highly regarded Russel Wright and Lurelle Guild reflect the material's popularity, and the inventiveness of these designers popularized aluminum in turn.

These two roasting pans offer an insightful comparison in streamlining: the first design, evoking the form of a streamlined passenger ferry (fig. 117), conveys the sense of majestic forward movement. (In the mid-1930s ferries too began receiving aluminum skins, in their case to reduce load and therefore fuel costs.) Aspects of streamlining are

Fig. 117 Mazie Krebs, *Admiral*, streamlined passenger ferry, St. Louis, built in 1938.

Fig. 118 The Burlington *Zephyr*, designed in 1934, manufactured by the E. G. Budd Manufacturing Co. for the Burlington Northern Railway.

seen in the pan's teardrop shape and gently graduated, domed top. The removable top, with its moderately flared handle, slides smoothly into the base, which has flared grips at each end. Through three fluent forms and the use of aluminum, the unknown designer created a modern aesthetic statement enhanced by the reflected light from the polished surface.

The second roasting pan, though not dramatically streamlined, capitalized upon the selling notion of streamlining via its name. In stylized letters, "Zephyr" is stamped on the bottom of this roaster. Referring to the Greek god of the west wind, Zephyr was the name of one of America's most famous streamlined trains, the aluminum-faced Burlington *Zephyr* (fig. 118), introduced in the second year of the Chicago *Century of Progress Exposition*, 1933–34. Perhaps the pan's name also alludes to its weight, for aluminum was considerably lighter than the enameled steel and cast iron of previous and contemporary roasters, and it thus lightened the housewife's burden.

In this container, discreet streamlining is visible in the modified teardrop plan, the continuous bulging form of the lid, varied only by the wide ridge running its length, and the flared grips molded from the top and bottom sections. When the roaster is closed, the grips, which are placed off center on the pan and lid, join to form a single visual entity at each end.

56. George R. Coss

ELECTRIC ROASTER-COOKER: *EVERHOT*

Designed c. 1937[1]
Enameled and chromium-plated steel,
aluminum, Bakelite, plastic
28 x 50 x 33 cm
Produced by Swartzbaugh Manufacturing
Company, Toledo, Ohio
The Liliane and David M. Stewart Collection
SLSLH 2003.12

As women moved from the home to the workplace in the early twentieth century, new products such as the electric roaster were introduced as conveniences to fit varying family schedules. This electric roaster allowed the chef to prepare one or two dishes in advance and leave them to cook at a low heat over several hours, so that children could serve themselves even "if the mother is not present."[2] At the same time, the roaster-cooker was promoted as attractive enough to enter the dining room. In an *Everhot* brochure Mother serves dinner from the roaster to the family gathered at the dining table. According to the brochure, half-round insert pans and steamer and broiler attachments in aluminum were extras for certain models, including this one.

For larger meals, *Everhot* "electric cooking chests" were available in larger-capacity rectangular form and a variety of colors. In 1938 the manufacturer undertook an advertising campaign with *Good Housekeeping* magazine, and the chest was later awarded the *Good Housekeeping* seal of approval.[3] In the still-cost-conscious late 1930s, the chest was promoted as economical as well as swift in operation. "Oven preheats to 500 degrees in 18 minutes for complete meal cooking. . . . Brings efficient electric cooking to the average home for a small investment and low operating cost. Can pay for itself out of savings it makes in the grocery budget."

Streamlining is seen in the roaster's rows of banding at top and bottom and on both sides of its logo and temperature dial, its grooved handles, and shining domed cover. It was offered in ivory or tangerine enamel, suggesting the variety of color schemes for kitchens of the day, from the hygienic to the vivid.

57. Charles P. Strite
TOASTER: MODEL NO. 1-A-1, *TOASTMASTER*
Designed c. 1925
Chromium-plated steel, Bakelite, rubber
26 x 18.3 x 12 cm
Produced by Waters-Genter Company,
Minneapolis, Minnesota
B055

58. Designer unknown
TOASTER
Designed c. 1940
Chromium-plated steel, steel, Bakelite
19.5 x 25 x 15.3 cm
Produced by Westinghouse Electric Company,
Mansfield, Ohio
The Liliane and David M. Stewart Collection
SHLSL 2002.24

59. Donald Earl Dailey
TOASTER: MODEL NO. 1481,
PROCTOR AUTOMATIC POP-UP
Designed c. 1947[4]
Chromium-plated steel, Bakelite, aluminum, plastic
18.5 x 27.5 x 17 cm
Produced by Proctor-Silex, Philadelphia,
Pennsylvania
B386

Fig. 119 Advertisement for Toastmaster from
Ladies' Home Journal, December 1929.

The earliest of these three appliances, the
Toastmaster of c. 1925, marked a technical
breakthrough. "The World's Most Completely
Automatic Toaster," according to its advertising
(fig. 119), it was the first spring-loaded or pop-up
toaster, able to brown both sides of the bread
slices at once and eject them when done,
automatically turning off the current. "No Toast
Turning or Watching—No Burnt Toast . . . you read
your paper—*in peace*." Between 1927 and 1929,
the ad claimed, it "has supplanted all other less
modern toasters in over 465,000 homes."

Part of the modernity of the *Toastmaster* lies in
its styling, but its streamlining is restricted to details,
typifying its mid-1920s date. Rows of horizontal
perforations to vent the heat and the rounded front

Cat. 57

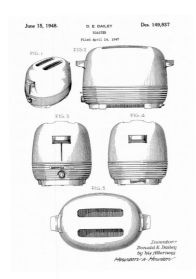

Fig. 120 Donald E. Dailey, patent drawing for "Toaster."

and base of the machine are progressive elements, but they adorn a flat-sided upright form. Though it is fully chrome-plated—with "No advance in price!"—the *Toastmaster* betrays its origin in the thin rectangular toasters with drop-down sides of pre-automatic days.

The Westinghouse toaster of c. 1940, cat. 58, also presents a rounded end on a rectangular form, but it is a unified and more horizontal design. The dark Bakelite base and top conform to the fluent lines of the wraparound chrome-bright body, which is set off by stepped and etched banding. The appliance is lower and wider than its predecessor, reflecting 1930s aesthetics. When removed and inverted, the top becomes a toast rack.

In the latest toaster shown here, the *Proctor Automatic Pop-Up* of c. 1947, cat. 59, the form is simplest. Fully rounded, the chromium skin ends in the parallel, horizontal speed grooves of 1930s streamlining, indicating that the device retained its potency well into the 1940s. No joints are visible: instead, the toaster's continuous shape recalls its source in a clay model, a step in designing that was common in the 1930s and continued in the postwar period. The toaster's dark, slightly recessed base makes its glistening body appear airborne. As seen in the four views in the patent drawing (fig. 120), the machine is almost completely symmetrical: a handle at one end matches the control lever at the other; the electrical socket rhymes with the heat dial that lets you choose "doneness." A Proctor brochure pointed out one of its conveniences: an "exclusive slide-out crumb tray."

Cat. 58

Cat. 59

Cat. 59

60. Designer unknown

POTATO BAKER: *TOP-O-STOVE*

Designed c. 1935[5]

Aluminum

10 x 18.5 x 11 cm

Produced by Na-Mac Products Corporation,

Los Angeles, California

B526

Shaped like a baby zeppelin and supported by streamlined glides, this appealing object allowed the owner to bake just one potato, skewered on an inner prong. The streamlined handle, placed horizontally, held the two halves of the cooker together. When raised, the handle opened the toylike appliance. Placed in the oven, the highly conductive aluminum enclosure provided concentrated heat, speeding up the baking process.

Its utility patent asserted that the food in the baker could be "kept free from a heated surface which might otherwise endanger scorching the article being cooked." This invention was "particularly well adapted for use of campers for baking articles in an open-fire." Aluminum foil of course does a similar job, but it lacks the space age charm of this appliance, which customizes potato baking for one.

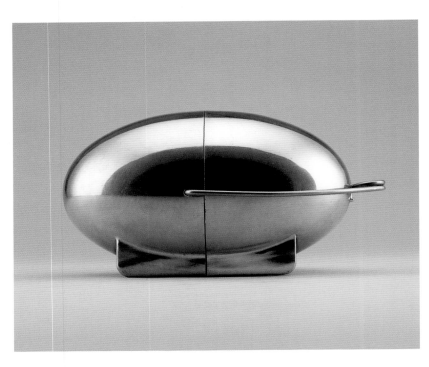

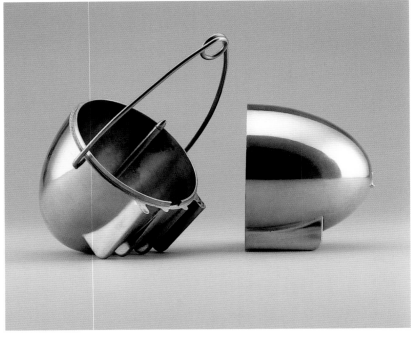

61. Designer unknown

PORTABLE ELECTRIC RANGE:

MODEL NO. D, *CLOVERLEAF*

Designed c. 1935-45

Aluminum, porcelain, rubber, plastic, steel

15.2 x 30 x 20.2 cm (closed)

Produced by Camco Products, Inc.,

New York, New York

B072

Teardrop in plan, the aerodynamic form of streamlining, this hinged "range"—or triple hot plate—will not only boil water but also heat two additional dishes. With plates swiveling out from a single fulcrum, the device gives the user the choice of heating one, two, or three vessels simultaneously—the maximum convenience in a compact form. The burners are circular ceramic plates with electrical coils winding inside molded grooves. Its simple shapes and simple forms and smooth metal surfaces mean easier cleaning. When separated, the tiered structure with its bold cylindrical supports resembles futuristic buildings like those in New York's 1939 *World of Tomorrow* exhibition (fig. 47). Sharing elemental, repeated, streamlined forms with such structures, the *Cloverleaf* hot plate is functionalist architecture for the kitchenette.

Cat. 61

62. John Gordon Rideout
for **Van Doren and Rideout**
WATER KETTLE: MODEL NO. 4133M,
MAGNALITE
Designed c. 1933
Aluminum, magnesium, and nickel alloy,
enameled wood
17.5 x 24.5 x 22 cm
Produced by Wagner Manufacturing Company,
Sidney, Ohio
B026

63. James H. Reichart
WHISTLING WATER KETTLE
Designed c. 1944[6]
Aluminum, Bakelite, brass
18 x 24 x 23 cm
Produced by Excel Manufacturing Corporation,
Muncie, Indiana
B414

64. Designer unknown
WHISTLING WATER KETTLE
Designed c. 1940
Glass, chromium-plated steel, Bakelite, aluminum
20 x 19.5 x 17.5 cm
Manufacturer unknown
B354

Is there an ideal form for a water kettle—or any vessel, for that matter? Manufacturers, dependent on new product lines for their business survival, generally evaded the issue, but designers and critics debated it from the 1920s on. Conceived by John Gordon Rideout, the *Magnalite* kettle, cat. 62, benefited from the general favor among progressives for simple solids. In his classic textbook, *Industrial Design*, the designer Harold Van Doren illustrated this as an example of the bold geometry he recommended for three-dimensional objects.[7] Although he viewed the cube and "its elastic variations" as the most useful forms, he also praised the sphere or half-sphere, as seen in this kettle. In later writing, he complimented the functionalism of the utensil's elements. "Old models had a handle that flopped over the side where it could be charred by the fire. Pouring and filling were awkward. He [the designer Rideout] placed the handle grip off center, made it rigid instead of loose, and fixed the kettle so you could fill through the spout."[8]

The forward-canted, ovoid wooden handle of this kettle is part of its streamlining, which is also seen in its domed shape and its tapering spout, which barely interrupts the body's curved contouring. The low metal form is attractive and also distributes heat evenly; it is of "Magnalite," a long-lasting magnesium-aluminum-nickel alloy that

the manufacturer patented under the trade name "Wear-Ever."[9] Such alloys were cheaper and lighter than steel, a benefit during the Depression when cost-cutting was important to maintain product sales.

Even lighter in weight and lower in profile than the *Magnalite* kettle is the aluminum water kettle, cat. 63, by James H. Reichart for Excel Manufacturing. Its spout has a perforated lid, causing it to whistle when the water boils, and its long flaring handle with Bakelite grip echoes its flying saucer-like silhouette. A brass indicator above the spout moves across the gauge as water fills the container, indicating quantities from two to eight cups. Below the handle is stamped "Sears Maid of Honor," a slogan typifying the period's taste for puns and indicating the product's distribution through Sears, Roebuck.

The glass water kettle, cat. 64, lets the user see the water level, and its rows of repeated bands at the bottom and midsection offer guidelines to amounts as they articulate the kettle's spheroid shape. Equally curvaceous are the graduated domed lid and arched Bakelite handle attached to the forward-thrusting spout. This kettle also whistles.[10]

All three of these vessels have distinct, individual merits. And indeed the production to this day of different kettles indicates that the question of how to boil water has no final answer.

Cat. 63

Cat. 64

65. Michael S. Desser

PAIR OF CONDIMENT SHAKERS

Designed c. 1936[11]

Glass, plastic

8.5 x 4 x 4 cm (each)

Produced by Owens-Illinois Company, Toledo, Ohio

B521

These petite rounded forms are streamlined with horizontal banding on their lower halves. The patent drawing shows a single design for a condiment shaker, in elevation and plan (fig. 121), but the dome-shaped, lime-green tops of the manufactured shakers have perforations that are more dynamic in placement and shape than those in the drawing. They help make the shakers look like rockets—perhaps to match the Buck Rogers fantasies that comic strips brought to the breakfast table in the 1930s.

Owens-Illinois was known for its industrial production, but in 1935 it purchased the Libbey Glass Company, which had made its name in the nineteenth century through its fine cut glass. This company continued operation as the Libbey Glass Division of Owens-Illinois. "Owens-Illinois" and the patent number are impressed on the bottom of each container, a rare feature possibly intended to publicize the parent company's move into glass products. The use of glass widens the function of these shakers, since the user can see whether they hold salt, pepper, cinnamon, or another condiment. Of pressed glass, these friendly little containers show Owens-Illinois's effort to reach middle-class consumers.

Fig. 121 Michael S. Desser, patent drawing for "Condiment Shaker."

66. Herbert C. Johnson
JUICER: MODEL NO. JK-50, *JUICE-KING*
Designed c. 1945[12]
Chromium-plated and enameled steel,
aluminum, enameled wood, rubber
19.5 x 26 x 16 cm
Produced by National Die Casting Company,
Chicago, Illinois
B215

67. Joseph M. Majewski, Jr.
JUICER: *JUICE-O-MAT*
Designed c. 1937[13]
Chromium-plated and enameled steel, steel,
aluminum, rubber
21.5 x 17 x 15 cm
Produced by Rival Manufacturing Company,
Kansas City, Missouri
The Liliane and David M. Stewart Collection,
gift of David A. Hanks in honor
of Eric and Nannette Brill
SHLSL 2002.15

When vitamin C was isolated in the ultra-health-conscious early 1940s, it sparked a national craze for drinking fresh-squeezed orange juice. The beverage became popular and designs for juicers proliferated, all using lever action to maximize the user's strength. In the *Juice-King*, curves unite the design, from its horseshoe-shaped stand to the horizontal banding accenting its cylindrical container to the latch that lifts its top, allowing the user to insert an orange half. The equally aerodynamic shape of the side handle suggests that squeezing the fruit will take little work. Inside, a removable perforated disc allows the juice to pass, but not the seeds.

The juicer designed by Majewski is streamlined, and its parts are unified in a single, sweeping, hooded form. Seen from above, as in the patent drawings (fig. 122), it has a teardrop shape, and its moving elements—the top and handle—are highlighted by their chromium plating with speed lines. The user places his or her glass on the extended stand, lifts the arm, which raises the top, inserts the orange half, and then presses the arm down: voilà, fresh juice. The contrast of mirror-bright chromium and red enamel in the *Juice-o-Mat* adds to the allure of the helmet-shaped appliance.

Its name plays on the word "automatic" (as in Automat), suggesting the ease and speed of its operation. According to an advertisement in a contemporary periodical, the "Streamline Juice King," which bore a striking resemblance to the *Juice-o-Mat*, was available at Bloomingdale's department store in Manhattan in different colors to suit the up-to-date kitchen—"ivory with red, blue, green or chrome, and red and chrome." The price was $2.95.[14]

Cat. 67

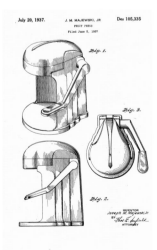

Fig. 122 Joseph M. Majewski, Jr, patent drawing for "Fruit Press."

Cat. 66

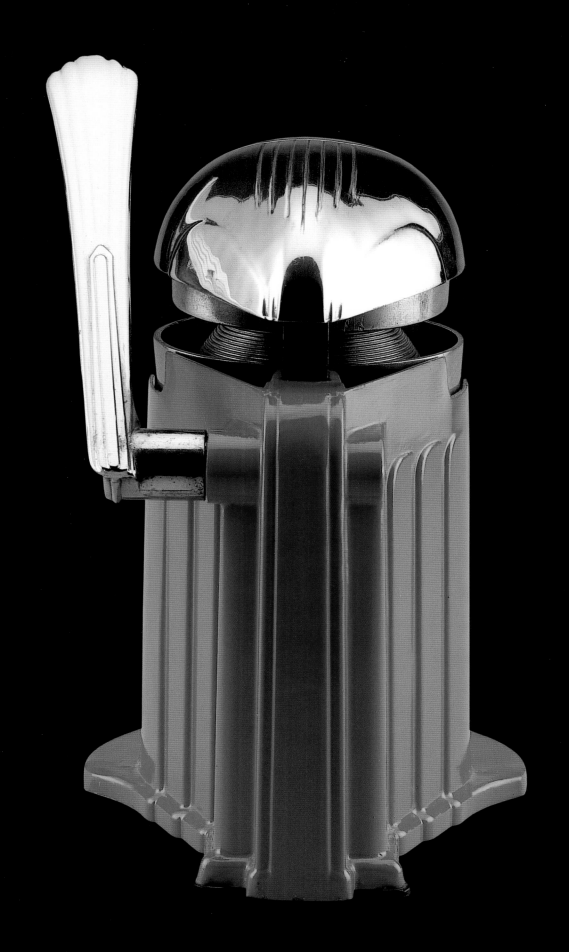

68. Joseph Palin Thorley

REFRIGERATOR PITCHER: *PEASANT WARE*

Designed c. 1940
Glazed earthenware
19.4 x 23.5 x 9 cm
Produced by The Hall China Company,
East Liverpool, Ohio
The Montreal Museum of Fine Arts,
The Liliane and David M. Stewart Collection,
gift of Geoffrey N. Bradfield
D86.127.1 ab

69. Ralph E. Kruck

REFRIGERATOR PITCHER: *GENERAL*

Designed c. 1939[15]
Glazed earthenware
21.2 x 19.5 x 12 cm
Produced by The Hall China Company,
East Liverpool, Ohio
B430

Fig. 123 Advertisement for Westinghouse refrigerators, c. 1935-40.

70. Attributed to Ralph E. Kruck

REFRIGERATOR LEFTOVER DISHES: *GENERAL*

Designed c. 1939
Glazed earthenware
10 x 17 x 10 cm (each)
Produced by The Hall China Company,
East Liverpool, Ohio
The Liliane and David M. Stewart Collection,
gift of David A. Hanks in memory
of Claude Beaulieu
SHLSL 2002.22 and B540

Responding to the growing use of refrigerators in the United States in the 1930s, Hall China produced space-saving earthenware containers in a variety of bright colors, such as yellow, green, and red, for storing and chilling leftover foods and liquids. The cobalt blue pitcher by Thorley has a continuous, unitary, streamlined form, with a handle carved out of the lean body of the vessel and a spout that barely extends from the opposite side. Three grooves ringing the base form speed lines, one of the signatures of streamlining since the 1930s.[16]

Hall designed and produced special lines of containers for Westinghouse and other refrigerator manufacturers, which used the attractive products to catch consumers' eyes and lead their attention to their appliances. If they bought one, the containers came with it. Hall sold the *General* design in 1939 as an accessory specific to Westinghouse refrigerators.

Sets included pitchers (cat. 69), as well as containers for leftovers, and butter dishes.[17] Thanks to their recessed handles, the containers and butter dishes could be stacked. A 1941 Westinghouse brochure shows a refrigerator neatly stocked with this pitcher and three other covered containers in the *General* line (fig. 123). The refrigerator ware has the same horizontal bands as the appliance's drawers and decorative exterior base. In the brochure illustration, an S-shaped motif unites the depiction of the refrigerator and its model logo, a cameo of Martha Washington. The appliance is "styled for today, yet reminiscent of Mount Vernon," according to the advertisement, which suggests that even the American flag is streamlined.

From the 1920s through the 1960s Hall China pioneered in hiring modern designers to create its moderately priced mass-produced wares working on commission. Eva Zeisel[18] was the company's most celebrated designer, while J. Palin Thorley and Ralph E. Kruck, responsible for these vessels, were among its most productive staff. Hall adroitly marketed their designs, alongside more conservative ones, and succeeded in winning both critical and popular success for them. Not every consumer was adventurous enough to buy radically simplified dinnerware, but progressive design in kitchen ware was widely acceptable, in keeping with the demand for technically progressive appliances.

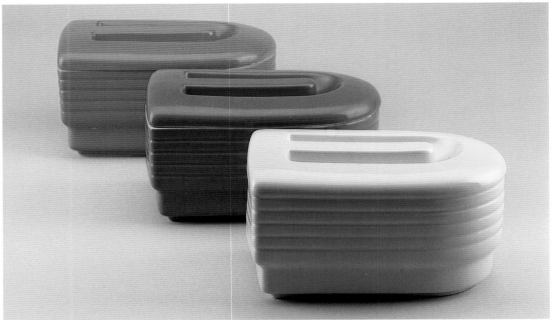

Cat. 68   Cat. 70

Cat. 69

71. Viktor Schreckengost

PITCHER: *JIFFY WARE*

Designed 1942
Glazed earthenware
17 x 18 x 9 cm
Produced by American Limoges China Company, Sebring, Ohio
The Liliane and David M. Stewart Collection
SHLSL 2003.19

Refrigerators are never big enough, in peacetime or in war. Thus the space-saving design and versatility of *Jiffy Ware* were its selling points: the straight sides of this compact pitcher (and all the vessels in the line) let it abut the other containers as well as the freezer compartment in the fridge, for faster cooling and no loss of room. The containers could nest when empty; their grips are recessed to allow the wares to be stacked.[19]

This shipshape pitcher is the most streamlined of the earthenware line. Its spout, lid, and handle form a continuous long contour in lipstick red, contrasting with the neutral hue of the body. The lid is a teardrop shape, suggesting the fluid within the vessel. And horizontal speed lines accent the pitcher's bottom and top, suggesting this ware will slake your thirst in no time.

Like *Fiestaware* (cat. 95) and the other brightly colored earthenware it followed on the market, *Jiffy Ware* responded to the less formal lifestyles that began in the 1930s and continue today. It was attractive enough to move from the kitchen to the dining room, and as an ovenproof line, it could move easily between the stove and the table.

72. Clarence M. Burroughs

ICE WATER PITCHER

Designed c. 1948[20]
Plastic
21 x 19.8 x 9 cm
Produced by The Burroughs Company, Los Angeles, California
B512

The form of this pitcher had already been achieved in ceramic, as seen in *Fiestaware* pitchers of 1936 (cat. 95), but the plastic utilized here provided an opportunity for similar streamlining in a material that allowed for a lighter, less expensive, and relatively unbreakable product. The turquoise-colored body and handle of cat. 72 form a complete circle, accented by molded bands generated from its center. Identical U-shaped bands compose the hinge of the teardrop-shaped lid, while the throat of the spout curves into the body and out again at the foot of the pitcher in an unbroken line. This suave simplification was one epitome of modernity. At the same time, the styling was functional: the narrow flat-sided pitcher fit neatly against the freezer unit in the refrigerator, keeping its contents ice-cold, and its minimal ornament assured it was easy to keep clean.

The repeated banding can be seen in the patent drawing of the pitcher showing the plan and three elevations (fig. 124). The patent specifications claimed the design to be specifically for an ice water pitcher and referred to four previously patented pitcher designs. All four were for glass and ceramic forms, including the streamlined pitcher patented by Paul Huntington Genter in 1940 for the Red Wing Potteries (fig. 125).

The four earlier designs cited in its patent application all play similar variations on the circle theme. One of Genter's ceramic pitchers of 1939 is closer to the painted biomorphs of Miró than the ideals of Plato as an exploration of nested ovals. His squat model of the same year is ridged on every surface, including the handle, in part to conceal the imperfections in cheap molded glass. Although all these pitchers had to be developed three-dimensionally, the Genter pitchers appear to have been designed in clay, the Burroughs vessel apparently with a compass on graph paper.

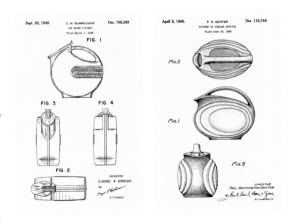

Fig. 124 Clarence M. Burroughs, patent drawing for "Ice Water Pitcher."

Fig. 125 Paul Huntington Genter, patent drawing for "Pitcher or Similar Article."

Cat. 72

Cat. 73

73. Chauncey E. Waltman

ELECTRIC STAND MIXER: MODEL NO. 3200

Designed c. 1939[21]

Enameled and chromium-plated steel, plastic

31.5 x 31.5 x 18 cm

Produced by A. F. Dormeyer Corporation,
Chicago, Illinois

B562

74. Designer unknown

PORTABLE ELECTRIC MIXER:
MODEL NO. 12 P, *MIXALL JR.*

Designed 1935–40

Chromium-plated steel, plastic

17 x 25 x 7.5 cm

Produced by The Iona Manufacturing Company,
East Hartford, Connecticut

B618

75. Attributed to Alfonso Iannelli

PORTABLE ELECTRIC MIXER:
MIXMASTER JUNIOR

Designed c. 1945

Enameled and chromium-plated steel,
Bakelite, plastic

15.5 x 18.5 x 7 cm

Produced by Sunbeam Corporation,
Chicago, Illinois

B469

76. Alfonso Iannelli

PORTABLE ELECTRIC MIXER:
MODEL NO. 400, *OSTERETT*

Designed c. 1950[23]

Plastic, stainless steel

16 x 16 x 7 cm

Produced by the John Oster Manufacturing
Company, Milwaukee, Wisconsin

B217

Electric mixers were marketed as early as the 1910s. By the 1920s, a number of them had appeared on the market with electric motors integrated into their bodies. Canny manufacturers styled them to appeal to the tastes of each decade. In the 1930s the motors became small and reliable enough to make the mixer a more popular object and streamlining was widely applied to the metal casing.[22]

This Dormeyer product of the early 1940s is a stationary tabletop model, but its teardrop-shaped base and torpedo-like motor unit suggest meal preparation will be speedy and efficient. These mixers were proud possessions and often one of the few appliances left out on the counter, as seen in period photographs of immaculate all-white kitchens.

The styling of these three portable mixers is a far cry from that of earlier standing models (see cat. 73), and it underlines their new convenience. All three allowed the housewife to beat ingredients anywhere—on the stove or the breakfast table, not to mention the kitchen counter. Each answered its company's need to sell more products by diversifying its lines. While using the same motors, hand-held mixers supplemented stationary mixers in the fully equipped kitchen or they substituted for them, saving space and money, in the modest household. The Oster Company marketed its *Osterett* as an affordable extra, its brochure trumpeting, "Oster quality products for better living . . . perfect giving."[24] Each of these three designs promotes a different virtue of the machine.

The *Mixall Jr.* (cat. 74) radiates strength through its stout, shining body and the long conforming handle notched seamlessly out of it, all in

Cat. 74

chromium-plated steel. Three stepped indentations adorn each side of the tapered tail; and the last of them is perforated to vent the motor. The blunt line of the nose is echoed in the straight, flat termination of the base. This mixer resembles a cross between an iron and an electric sander: it looks like a woodworker's power tool.

The *Mixmaster Junior* (cat. 75), on the other hand, has a dramatically tapered handle, a black Bakelite arc that contrasts with its small white-enameled body. The curve of the handle continues in the body and ends in a projection on which the total can rest. This appliance looks easy to grip and speedy to use.

The *Osterett* (cat. 76) climaxes the apparent trend to simplification and spells out lightness through its design. Shorter than the other hand-held mixers, weighing under two pounds thanks partly to its greater reliance on plastic, it is "not tiring to use," according to its brochure. It has no handle. Its bullet-shaped body echoes the simplest form of a high-speed train engine, emphasized by the raised horizontal band around the middle and the vertical perforated lines at the end. In place of a train searchlight, a Phillips head screw secures the two halves, and the script lettering "Osterett" is placed where a train name would be. In its multiple views of the mixer, the patent drawing (fig. 126) illustrates these train-like qualities. Slight variations can be seen between the patent drawing and the manufactured item, including the use of vertical slits in the drawing and horizontal ones in the actual object. The views highlight the sweeping horizontal of the mixer's body.

Alfonso Iannelli, designer of both the *Osterett* and the *Mixmaster Junior*, was famous in architectural circles for his cubistic sculptures for Frank Lloyd Wright's Midway Gardens, 1913–14. Beginning in the 1920s he also undertook industrial design work and conceived a variety of home appliances, notably for Sunbeam. Simultaneously he pursued his successful career as a sculptor in an abstracted figural style, taking commissions for public sculpture, including reliefs for pavilions at the Chicago World's Fair of 1933. The changes in his idiom for both fine and applied arts from the teens through c. 1950 reflect one tendency in modern abstraction, toward the elemental.

Cat. 75

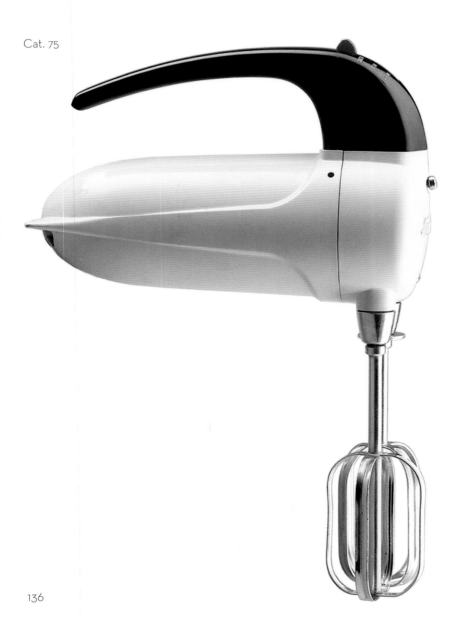

Cat. 76

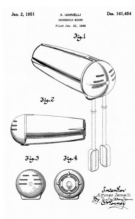

Fig. 126 Alfonso Iannelli, patent drawing for "Household Mixer."

Osterett ®

77. Donald E. Grove and Jackson D. Comstock
BLENDER: MODEL NO. 48,
HOLLYWOOD LIQUEFIER
Designed c. 1941[25]
Bakelite, plastic, steel, rubber
36 x 22 x 13.8 cm
Produced by Machine Craft Manufacturing Co.,
Los Angeles, California
B609

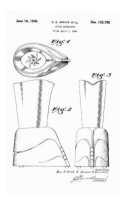

Fig. 127 Donald E. Grove et al.,
patent drawing for "Juice Extractor."

Frozen daiquiris and vegetable juice tonics, foaming milkshakes and pureed soups: the *Hollywood Liquefier* looks capable of making these and more foodstuffs in record time. The metaphor of its styling is nautical. The base housing the motor is shaped like an ocean liner's prow, with molded S-curves at the bottom resembling twin breaking waves, seen in the patent drawing (fig. 127). The jaunty cap on the liquid container has a streamlined vertical flange for easy gripping, and the glass container is oval in section and flaring like a ship's funnel. Such machines are more versatile than the malted mixer with its simple rotating rod (cat. 52), since they chop substances finely enough to turn them into liquids at the same time that they aerate them. Better known today as "blenders," they were popular for home and commercial use from the 1930s on; and in conventional tapered, cylindrical forms, they make the fruit "smoothies" of the twenty-first century.

78. Richard Buckminster Fuller
BATHROOM: *DYMAXION*
Designed c. 1930[26]
Tin-antimony alloy-plated copper
96.5 x 162.6 x 162.6 cm
Produced by Phelps Dodge Corporation,
New York, New York
The Montreal Museum of Fine Arts,
The Liliane and David M. Stewart Collection,
gift of Samuel L. Rosenfeld in memory
of June S. Rosenfeld, through the American
Friends of Canada
D1996.102.1

Buckminster Fuller's years at the Naval Academy and in the U.S. Navy are reflected in the pocket sizing and streamlining of his prefabricated *Dymaxion* bathroom, (cat. 78, fig. 129) which he developed in its first prototype in 1930 and patented in 1940. The tub (which has shower hardware) forms one component, the toilet and washbasin another, and the two rectangular units—each die-stamped in one piece—come from the factory ready to be joined together and installed in a building under

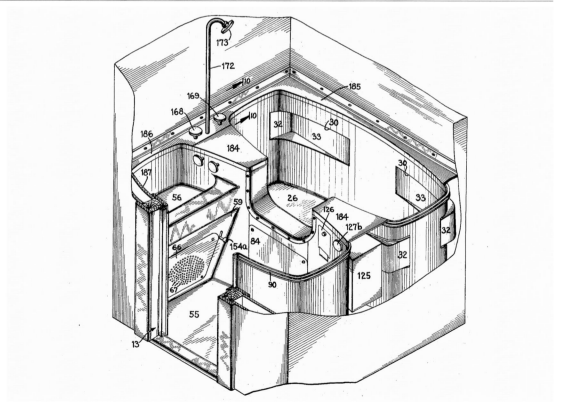

Fig. 128 R. Buckminster Fuller, detail of a utility patent drawing for "Prefabricated Bathroom."

construction or one already built. Streamlining is seen in the continuous sculptural forms of all elements of the bathroom, in contrast to contemporary bathroom designs with their separate rectilinear components. Two of these baths, including this example, went into a

remodeled Manhattan townhouse, where, as *The Architectural Forum* reported in September 1938, they "occupy only slightly more space than normally required by one" (fig. 129). The townhouse owner, Jasper Morgan, a friend of Fuller's, was a naval architect. A cutaway perspective view of the bathroom is seen in the patent drawing (fig. 128).

Space-saving was not Fuller's primary goal. The prefabrication was intended to cut the installation costs that help make bathrooms (and kitchens) the most expensive rooms to construct in any house. The *Dymaxion* bath sections could be transported easily to their spaces and easily installed thanks to their integrated fixtures. Designed to be made of lightweight fiberglass-reinforced plastic, the bath would also have been cheaper in materials and shipping than any existing types. Unfortunately, however, technology then was not advanced enough to fabricate the bath as one unit, and so this compact conception saw light only in twelve prototypes in 1936–38, made of copper plated with a tin and antimony alloy. In the 1970s, after Fuller's patent had run out, the design was realized exactly to his specifications by a German firm. The molded sink-and-toilet bathrooms in today's planes and trains are indebted to it.[27]

"Dymaxion" is Fuller's neologism based on "dynamic," "maximum," and "tension," key words in his design philosophy and futuristic work. He

applied it most famously to his *Dymaxion* house, 1927–46 (fig. 130), which was intended to have this bathroom and embodies all its elements. The house is prefabricated, compact (a round, 1,075-square-foot structure with two bedrooms), lightweight, and portable. At three tons, of aluminum and Plexiglas, it weighed about one fiftieth of a conventionally built house and could be packed and shipped by air. Like the *Dymaxion* bath, the house was designed to serve mass needs for comfort at low cost while conserving natural resources. Hung from a central utility "mast," it was a structure in dynamic tension, and it derived maximum benefit from the minimum of new industrial materials.

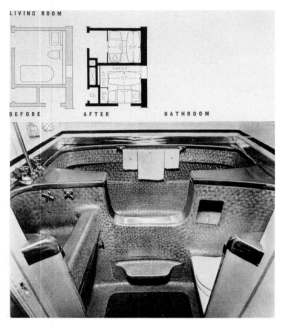

Fig. 129 Before and after remodeling, plans of bathroom in Jasper Morgan townhouse, New York, New York. *The Architectural Forum*, September 1938.

Fig. 130 R. Buckminster Fuller, *Dymaxion* House, 1927-46.

---

79. Henry Dreyfuss
BATH SPOUT AND VALVE CONTROLS:
NEUVOGUE
Designed c. 1936[28]
Chromium-plated steel, iron, copper, brass, partially enameled
26 x 23.5 x 27.5 cm
Produced by Crane Company, Chicago, Illinois
B148

80. Henry Dreyfuss
Roy H. Zinkil
SINK: *NEUVOGUE*
Designed c. 1936[29]
Porcelain, chromium-plated steel
92.5 x 68 x 56.5 cm
Produced by Crane Company, Chicago, Illinois
B613

One of the most famous of the bathroom lines of the 1930s was Henry Dreyfuss's *Neuvogue* for Crane, the prestigious bath appliance and fixture manufacturer of Chicago. The line, which included bathtubs, sink basins with stands, toilets, and chromium-plated faucets and handles, remained in production through the mid-1940s.[30] The sink design of 1936 is simpler, uniting these controls on one

hooded porcelain form. Its streamlining appears in its rounded corners and horizontal banding.

Faucets and water control knobs are the jewelry of bathroom sinks and tubs. Like the painted or molded decoration of nineteenth-century pitchers and washbasins, they announce their owners' tastes and incomes. The difference, of course, is that they must function to allow regulation of water, but after satisfying that requirement, their forms can be designed to embody virtually any aesthetic. Dreyfuss's *Neuvogue* bath spout and dual valve control unit make mechanical efficiency look glamorous. His metaphor is Bauhaus geometry,[31] which the 1932 Museum of Modern Art exhibition of modern architecture had done so much to promote. The half-spheres of Dreyfuss's knobs openly display the screws attaching their long rectangular handles; and the horizontal banding of the knobs, is an element of streamlining. The spigot, rectangular in section, extends bluntly from a rectangular plaque.

These Platonic shapes are chromium-plated to be richly reflective, and they sport grooves at their terminations as a reticent kind of styling, like tailored cuffs. In Dreyfuss's built-in tub and shower for Crane (fig. 131), this hardware looks bold and masculine, accompanied by recessed soap dishes and a vertical support bar in the same chromium-plated finish. The tub is also streamlined with its curved corners and a horizontal groove bisecting its body.

Dreyfuss's sink for Crane harmonizes with the tub in its play of geometries. Like the tub, it is a porcelain rectangle, horizontally grooved on its exterior, and its symmetry is accented by a broad vertical band that extends over its thick rim at its front. In the sink, the band continues visually in the porcelain housing for the water controls, a curved raised rectangle with the drain control on top and the hot and cold valves on each side. These controls, like the tub's, are simple hemispheres with handles set at right angles. Their mirror-bright chromium plating continues in the sink's legs, two U-shapes with towel bars. More traditional homeowners could choose a porcelain pedestal for this sink, but the bent steel connotes modernity. Though some nineteenth-century sinks had metal supports, chromium-plating had only become commercially available in 1925, and bent steel structures recalled the Bauhaus, where Marcel Breuer is thought to have designed the first chair with it that year. Dreyfuss's designs, according to Crane's advertisement, composed "The Bath of Tomorrow." The name "Neuvogue" for the line implies that this bathroom has both Germanic hygiene and Gallic high style.

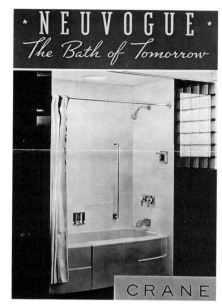

Fig. 131 Cover of *Neuvogue* brochure, Crane Company, Chicago, Illinois.

Cat. 80

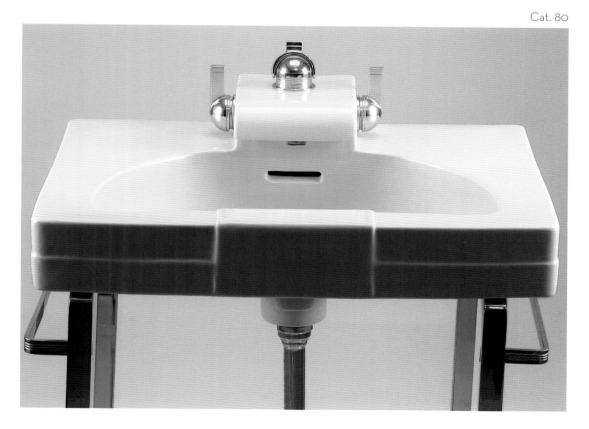

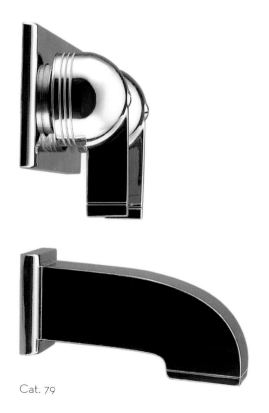

Cat. 79

81. Russell E. Vanderhoff

SCALE: *HEALTH-O-METER*

Enameled steel, steel, glass, linoleum

Designed c. 1933[32]

16.5 x 39.5 x 27.3 cm

Produced by Health-O-Meter Scale,

Chicago, Illinois

B422

82. Henry de Segur Lauve

SCALE AND VALET STAND: MODEL NO. 6341

Designed c. 1960[33]

Enameled and chromium-plated steel,

aluminum, rubber

115 x 53 x 57 cm

Produced by Fairbanks, Morse and Co.,

Chicago, Illinois

B088

The health consciousness of the 1920s and 1930s, and America's love of self-improvement, gave birth to home-use scales as accoutrements of upscale baths. Catering to the public's concern for attractive appearance and good health, manufacturers of scales simplified their doctor's office models for home use in the 1930s. "Streamlined beauty comes to the bathroom in this attractive bathroom scale," claimed a contemporary writer describing the cat. 81 scale. "Even the dial is of a new, easy to read aeroplane-type. Available in a large variety of colors."[34] Parts were concealed within the base, while the dial marking the crucial data was accented. Elements of the streamlined style convey the product's modernity: all corners are rounded, and the circular dial is held within a teardrop form. Linoleum patterned to simulate marble, increasingly popular in the 1930s, covers the scale's surface. It could measure owners weighing up to 300 pounds. A circular steel knob adjusts the weight measure.

Tall types such as the Fairbanks, Morse example, cat. 82, probably migrated to homes from doctors' offices, or they might have been marketed for both family and medical use. With this svelte model in ochre enamel, the manufacturer intended to appeal to the widest possible audience. His scale is a sculpture, in which the tall tapering shaft plays against the horizontals of the weight-measuring devices, as well as the decorative horizontal bandings accenting them and the off-center logo of Fairbanks, Morse. The clean lines of the scale seem to bear witness to the trustworthiness of its weight measurements. Its *moderne* styling assures users that their physical absorption is chic and contemporary. Lest their weights be increased by clothing and pocket change, the scale has a shaped valet hanger at the back and a dished shelf in the front for keys and coins. These features, which can be seen in the detail of the patent drawing (fig. 132), give the scale multi-purpose function. Surprisingly, the scale was designed in 1960, not 1930, yet the only characteristic of the later streamlined style is the flattened form seen in both the base and shaft of the scale. Otherwise, the scale looks like a 1930s product.

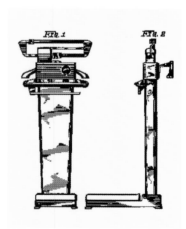

Fig. 132 Henry de S. Lauve, detail of a patent drawing for "Combination Scale and Valet Stand."

Cat. 81

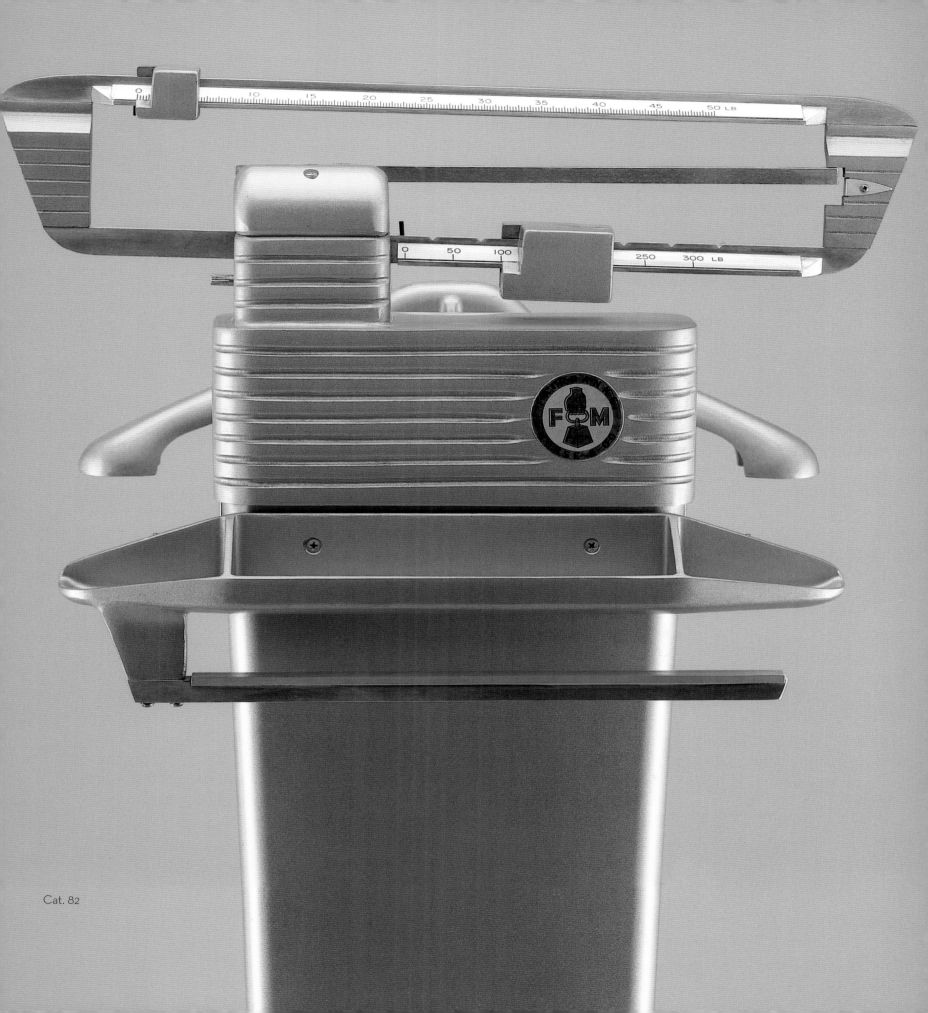

Cat. 82

OFF

Cat. 83

83. Harry S. Preble Jr.

HAIR DRYER

Designed c. 1944[35]

Bakelite, chromium-plated
and enameled steel, paint

14.5 x 10.8 x 6.5 cm

Produced by The A. C. Gilbert Company,
New Haven, Connecticut

B185

84. David Chapman

HAIR DRYER WITH STAND

Designed c. 1937[36]

Chromium-plated steel, plastic, brass

23.5 x 9.5 x 11.5 cm

Produced by Knapp-Monarch Company,
St. Louis, Missouri

B470

85. Designer unknown

HAIR DRYER: MODEL NO. 787, *ESKIMO*

Designed 1935–40

Chromium-plated steel, painted wood, Bakelite

26 x 21.3 x 15 cm

Produced by Bersted Manufacturing Company,
Boonville, Missouri

B610

Who has time to go to the hairdresser? Cat. 83, a small, compact, and effective appliance made by The A. C. Gilbert Company, is designed for quick, manual, home use by either sex, unlike the helmet-shaped, stationary dryers of beauty salons. The bullet-shaped handle of the dryer and its curved motor housing are grooved, and these horizontals are accented by the chromium-plated perforations through which the hot air is blown. Additional small perforations on the dryer's top vent the motor.

The user activates the off-on mechanism by simply twisting the handle end. A circular wall mount lets the user place the dryer at arm's reach. In this personal appliance, function, form, and decoration are one.

The brightly polished Knapp-Monarch hair dryer (cat. 84) has a teardrop shape, with a stepped domed casing for its motor and venting perforations in a flowerlike pattern. Even the small button to adjust the heat is streamlined with speed lines. The shaped handle swivels and the nozzle tilts for the user's convenience.

The *Eskimo* hair dryer (cat. 85) has the teardrop shape of the Knapp-Monarch model but with horizontal perforations to vent the motor rather than a flower formation. Its stand allows it to function standing upright, freeing the hands of the user, and the painted wood support—also an elongated teardrop shape—contrasts with the glistening chromium plating of the grooming device.

Cat. 84

Cat. 85

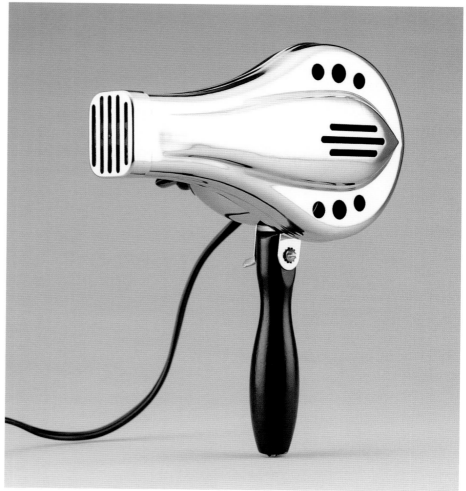

Cat. 86

86. Designer unknown
MASSAGER: *ROLL-A-RAY*
Designed c. 1935–40
Bakelite, rubber
18 x 20.5 x 12 cm
Produced by The O. A. Sutton Corporation,
Wichita, Kansas
B270

87. Casper J. Miller
MASSAGER: MODEL NO. 700, *RELAX-IT*
Designed c. 1951[37]
Chromium-plated steel, rubber
16 x 19.5 x 9.8 cm
Produced by The Relax-it Massage Company,
Hollywood, California
B501

Combining heating coils for warmth and a motor for vibration, the hand-held massager was a health-oriented appliance created in the 1910s from existing electrical devices. The *Roll-a-Ray* looks like a cross between an iron and a vacuum cleaner, and in profile it resembles a locomotive with its handle as the smoke. The severity of the uniform brown Bakelite housing is relieved by *Roll-a-Ray* stamped in playful script on the front, where a locomotive's logo might be. Visible below are the rolling discs that give the device its name. The wavy pattern on its packaging suggests both modern speed lines and the waves of heat radiating from the machine. Its advertising claims it offers "penetrating heat massage for home reducing and an aid in the relief of discomforts arising from rheumatism, lumbago, muscular aches, physical aches." Its name "Roll-a-Ray" implies it can roll away pounds with its heat rays.

The *Relax-it* massager (cat. 87), on the other hand, looks anything but relaxed. An elongated, chromium-plated steel sphere, with speed line perforations on its front, a long conforming steel handle, and four broad rubber wheels, it combines traits of a zeppelin, racing car, food mixer, and roller skate.

Cat. 87

88. Designer unknown

MASSAGER: *VITALATOR*

Bakelite, chromium-plated steel, rubber
Designed c. 1950[38]
7 x 11.7 x 7 cm
Produced by The A. C. Gilbert Company,
New Haven, Connecticut
B350

Do-it-yourself therapy for sensations of health and well-being, available at home without work or expertise: how many products can deliver such pleasures as the hand-held massager? The brochure packed with the *Vitalator* massager explains: "Three elements are necessary in massage: pressure, motion and skill. In Vitalator massage, only *pressure* is left up to you. The *motion* and the *skill* are neatly packaged in this marvelous little machine." For anyone who is tired, "for muscle and foot fatigue," the *Vitalator* is "that magic machine that brings to you—at home—all the eagerly sought advantages of 'Swedish' massage." The user slips the straps over his or her hand, turns on the machine, and applies pressure through the fingers, which convey its vibrations. The device is chunky, small, and toy-like; it looks like a child's train engine with venting grid in front. "Take *Vitalator* with you when you travel. Have its unusual benefits always at hand." Both men and women are potential customers, as the brochure photographs show, for "all the invigorating tingle, all the soothing relaxation that comes with pulsating massage."

The utility patent application was for the invention of "a device especially designed for the application of vibratory massage, such as frequently used by barbers in giving face massages, or by physicians. . . ." Although the sexual uses of this vibrator are not mentioned in the patent specifications, it was intended for them and quietly promoted by word of mouth to stimulate marital relationships.[39] Although the designer of this *Vitalator* is unknown, it could be by Robert Heller, based on his other industrial designs for the Gilbert Company, including the *Airflow* fan (cat. 114) and the interior of the firm's New York showroom (fig. 152). The Gilbert firm was best known for its toys, in particular trains and *Erector* sets for boys.

89. Designer unknown

SHAVER: MODEL NO. S

Designed c. 1935–40

Plastic, steel

3.2 x 10.5 x 4.5 cm

Produced by Schick Dry Shaver, Inc.,
Stamford, Connecticut

B052

90. Raymond Loewy

SHAVER: *COLONEL*

Designed c. 1942[40]

Bakelite, steel, enameled aluminum, rubber

3.8 x 12 x 4.8 cm

Produced by Schick Dry Shaver, Inc.,
Stamford, Connecticut

B578

Cat. 89   Cat. 90

Known to this day for its business built exclusively on electric shavers, Schick was one of the pioneering manufacturers that turned the straightedge razor, razor strop, and lathered shaving brush into relics of the past. Cat. 89, a dark, compact, palm-sized shaver, came with a detachable electrical cord and a twenty-six-page booklet of instructions. "You are the owner of the most modern and efficient shaving instrument yet devised," it announced. ". . . Because the Shaver has no blade it cannot cut or nick your skin. Handle it with perfect confidence!" The tilted globe logo on the top evoked flight. Service for it, according to the booklet, was available from Bangkok to Zurich; adapters and resisters for various voltages and plug types were available; and it could be used in "Pullman Trains . . . Leading hotels throughout America . . . Most commercial boats [and] Automobiles." A "Travelers' Combination Set," with one 110-volt and one 32-volt shaver and one shearing head, cost $25; a single deluxe shaver in a "handsome, durable box" cost $16.50.

When Raymond Loewy redesigned the shaver in 1942, Schick introduced both improved shaving and more attractive styling. The celebrity designer incorporated the new "double header"—or pair of shaving heads—into a brighter, two-toned casing with bands on the front and a redesigned logo spelling "Schick" in elongated letters. Simpler and more continuous in form than its predecessor, Loewy's shaver is a modified teardrop shape rather than a flat-sided oval. The colors separate the head from the body without interrupting its curve. This design seems to guarantee a safe, fast shave. It came in a snap-hinged box, which could be used for travel.

"FLASH-AND-GLEAM BEAUTY"

Streamlining the Living Space

4

If streamlining entered American households first through the kitchen and bathroom, it came only gradually to the other portions of the house—the living, dining, and bedrooms. Thus, in the 1930s average Americans might have used a modern all-white kitchen, but the canapés they prepared there for cocktails would be presented in a traditionally furnished living room and meals would be served in a revival-style dining room. This stylistic schizophrenia was widespread in the United States and was understandable in a decade that sought both reassurance in America's cultural history and solutions in its technological progress. Kitchens and baths were up-to-date, on the models of laboratories and hospitals, but the living and dining rooms, the heart of the house, were the expression of the family's primary aesthetic values, and those values were most often culturally conservative. As the century progressed, the dining room lost its primary importance, replaced by the live-in kitchen and recreation room, but it survived as a status symbol in many households even though it was less frequently used. Status was invested in historic styles, such as American Colonial, Georgian, or French Provincial furnishings, and their current imitations. The equivalent in American painting of the period lay in the opposing movements of Regionalism, which depicted scenes of frontier heroism and heartland farms, and the American Abstract Artists, who pursued the ideals of Mondrian and de Stijl. Nativism and internationalism: the twin concerns could be seen in the culture at large and the individual home.

Architects and interior designers in the 1930s who worked in the modern style sometimes provided streamlined furniture for domestic interiors or designed entire streamlined rooms. In architectural periodicals, critics discussed the advantages of modern versus traditional: "If you like a room as streamlined as a plane, efficient as an office, neat as a filing cabinet, Modern's the answer."[1] But another critic claimed: "Despite the wide publicity that has been given Modernist architecture, the average American is reluctant to adapt it when he is making an investment in a home. . . ."[2] Nevertheless, streamlined rooms were celebrated over those in the Cubo-Futurist style. In the late thirties, a critic for *Creative Design* favorably compared a room of 1934 with one of 1929, both exhibited at The Metropolitan Museum of Art: "In only five years all the awkward points (can you find 168?) had been swept out . . . in favor of the circular smooth flowing curves and contrasting textures which we have come to know as 'modern' or 'contemporary' design."[3]

Streamlined modern interiors by leading American industrial designers included Raymond Loewy's own penthouse of 1937 in a New York apartment building (fig. 133). Here the designer

133

Fig. 133 Raymond Loewy, living room in Loewy penthouse, 580 Fifth Avenue, New York City, 1937.
Fig. 134 Donald Deskey, rendering of the living room for the Eleanor Hutton Rand apartment, New York City, c. 1934. Pen and black ink, brown, blue-green opaque watercolor over graphite on board. New York, Cooper-Hewitt National Design Museum, Smithsonian Institution, Gift of Donald Deskey.
Fig. 135 Donald Deskey, living room, Eleanor Hutton Rand apartment, New York, c. 1934.

transformed a conventional box-shaped room through streamlining. Loewy replaced the centered fireplace mantel, typical of the traditional living room, with a low, sweeping, off-center form. This dramatic feature was rectangular on the left and balanced by a curvilinear side on the right. Its horizontal orientation was emphasized by a horizontal recess for books to the left of the fireplace opening; the streamlined curves were echoed in the vase-shaped sconce, which provided indirect lighting, and in the unframed circular mirror, which replaced the rectangular, picture-like mirror of the traditional interior.

The overall horizontality of Loewy's living room, another characteristic of streamlined interiors, was achieved by maintaining all furniture at a single low line, following the lines established by the mantel. In the seating, the sharp zigzag edges of the modern furniture of the 1920s have given way to the curvilinear forms of the 1930s. The cabinet is a strong streamlined form as well, with curved corners and continuous horizontal pulls. The overall effect is harmonious, with the sense of ease and relaxation that curved elements convey, evoking an elegant yet informal lifestyle in a modern apartment.

Loewy's contemporary, Donald Deskey, was also known for his chic domestic interiors of the late 1920s and early 1930s. One of a small group of private commissions that Deskey accepted was a living room for Eleanor Hutton Rand, c. 1934, located in Washington Mews, New York City. The room, an exquisite streamlined remodeling, is seen to advantage in Deskey's rendering (fig. 134). The design as executed (fig. 135) followed Deskey's vision closely but with minor compromises.[4] Nevertheless, the Rand living room illustrates Deskey's fascination with streamlined shapes as well as new materials. The linoleum flooring, with double lines conforming to the furniture plan and

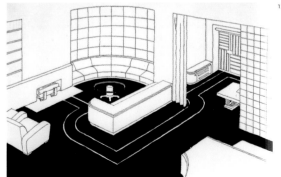

134

135

echoing the furniture forms, helped provide continuity from one room to another as well as streamlining on yet another plane.

Deskey also conceived a sophisticated dining room for the Richard Mandel residence (see fig. 57), in which the understated furnishings allow the room's curving window end to "star." By day the white-walled room is bathed in light: at night the glass-topped table and buffet shine with reflected and hidden sources of artificial illumination, and the windows are outlined with lights concealed in grooves around their perimeters.[5] The air of serene and spacious luxury culminates in the view down over the countryside, a locale that makes such space possible, in addition to the Mandel wealth.

At the same time that Deskey designed deluxe dining rooms beyond the confines of the city apartment, a new domestic interior arrangement was emerging for many middle-class Americans. This transition represented a change in space utilization from the formal dining room to the informal eat-in kitchen and recreation room, reflecting an evolving lifestyle for many families in the United States. A contemporary article describes these changes: "The dining room as a separate unit is gradually being eliminated by the modern home planner who reasons, rightly, that few people can afford the luxury of a room used only three times a day. . . ."[6] The changed domestic interior reflected a new consolidation and simplicity in planning: "Many families are ready, for the sake of really expansive, spacious interiors, to let their houses be resolved into just two major divisions: the place for living and recreation (with a kitchen and garage attached) and the place for rest and sleep (serviced, of course, by bathrooms)."[7] Although the dining room survived the rigors of the Depression, its status was diminished.

How can the domestic interior be associated with the aesthetics of speed and streamlining? This was explained by the Austrian-born designer Paul T. Frankl, an émigré to America in 1914. Known for his Art Deco interiors of the 1920s fitted with his signature "skyscraper" furniture, Frankl successfully made the transition to the streamlined modern style in his furniture and interiors of the 1930s.[8] He wrote that the new aesthetic was based on streamlining and speed, "which widened one's horizon and gave a fourth dimension." This style, he continued, "today is not restricted to rapid transit, but has been introduced in fashions, in decoration and in architecture . . . [It is] expressed by new shapes and forms typical of our age and born in the wind tunnel of the aeronautic laboratory. . . ." The new furnishings, like the new automobile, would be low, a characteristic of a more informal age. They would make use of new materials and rest on low pedestal bases, preventing the dust collection occurring under conventional furniture legs. Printed upholstery fabrics were banished, and monochrome textiles or leathers were substituted, leaving the emphasis on the continuous lines of the room.

A contemporary critic remarked on these changes in describing the apartment Frankl designed for his own use (fig. 136): "Much of the furniture is now built in and new materials are employed. A broad band of cork as an extended fireplace mantel gives the studio a horizontal character. . . ."[9] Built-in recesses for books were space savers, and also contributed to the overall horizontality. Cork—a new material to surface furnishings—adds its warm brown to the harmonious color scheme.

Frankl, Deskey, and Loewy all created fashionably modern living rooms of different characters, demonstrating the variety possible within the dictums of the streamlined style in interior architecture.

Fig. 136 Paul T. Frankl, living room, Frankl apartment, New York City, c. 1934. From *House & Garden*, July 1934.

137

138

Bedrooms could also be streamlined, though they were less frequently illustrated in period-icals than the home's principal rooms. In an apartment for Roger Wolfe Kahn, a wealthy impresario of jazz, Frankl designed a strikingly streamlined bedroom dominated by curves (fig. 137). The huge mirror, a segment of a circle, rhymes with the round features of the room, in particular the circular bed and conforming headboard. The mirror rises from a low, streamlined vanity shelf unit, with pre-dominantly rounded accessories. Even the calla lilies were chosen for their graceful lines. The room "gains its restfulness by the dominant whites and its charm by the curves,"[10] cooed Frankl in a July 1934 article in *House & Garden*. The design was applauded for its refusal of the jagged *moderne* style. "Among the newer tenets of the modernist is the abandonment of grotesque angles and the substitution of the curve. The former lacked charm; the curve is beginning to bring an air of grace into our contemporary rooms."[11]

Streamlining could also be achieved in a domestic interior solely through individual furniture pieces. Tubular steel furniture designed by Marcel Breuer, Charlotte Perriand, and Ludwig Mies van der Rohe had originated in the mid-1920s and its curves provided relief to the strict hard-edged geometry of International Style interiors. Tubular steel lent itself to streamlining and in many 1930s interiors such furniture represented modern glamour. This work could be used in both com-mercial and residential interiors, where it harmonized with curvaceous upholstered furniture of simplified form.

In American domestic interiors, there was a delicate relationship between streamlining and the International Style. This was seen in the curved dining room and the theatrical barroom below it in the otherwise geometric Mandel house (see figs. 57 and 58). It was also evident in the living room that William Lescaze designed for the Raymond C. Kramer townhouse of 1934–35, in New York City (fig. 138). Lescaze distinguished the entry area from the living space with a large streamlined bookcase, which dominates an otherwise straightforward, rectilinear International Style interior. The low form with its three continuous shelves and curved corners offered a strong counterpoint

Fig. 137 Paul T. Frankl, bedroom, Roger Wolfe Kahn apartment, New York City, c. 1934. From *House & Garden*, July 1934.

Fig. 138 William Lescaze, living room, Raymond C. Kramer house, New York City, c. 1934–35.

154

to the strict geometry of the room. The large bouquet of flowering branches also helped relieve the hard lines of the architecture. These variations seen in International Style American interiors were perceived by a sensitive critic writing for a London publication, who described the variety possible within modernism: "The modern style, international though it is because it has grown up in many countries and has certain fundamental unities, is nevertheless varied. Different social and individual needs must be met, different methods of manufacture taken into account and regional tastes provided for. In the United States, where the contemporary fashion developed much later than in Europe, these variations are most evident."[12]

While most streamlined modern domestic interiors are associated with apartments in the largest of the American cities,[13] the Walter Edwin Bixby residence designed by Kansas City architect Edward W. Tanner, with interiors by Kem Weber, between 1936 and 1937, is a splendid example in a vibrant, smaller city in the Midwest. Fig. 139 shows the entrance hall and the wide curve of the stairs of this grand residence, which was identified at that time with the International Style. A contemporary periodical noted "the manner in which the inlaid linoleum accentuates the circular theme," as well as the color scheme: "The floor is shades of gray with accents of black and coral. The stairs are carpeted in warm gray, and the stair rail is satin silver finish with a black marble base."[14] The curves and counter-curves contribute to a symphony of streamlined forms.

Objects destined for the domestic interior of the 1930s were primarily updated, streamlined versions of products invented in previous decades. Thus, clocks, fans, and smoking and cocktail equipment incorporated improved mechanical inventions and were encased in new, aesthetically pleasing forms, while vases, bowls, and the like were similarly simplified.

Social customs popular in the 1920s, such as smoking and cocktail drinking for both sexes, continued to be fashionable in the 1930s. Numerous advertisements with prominent stars and socialites demonstrated that the pleasures of a stylish and sophisticated life included smoking and drinking. Accoutrements for cigarettes and pipes were prominent in the domestic interior through the streamlined era and beyond. Before and after Prohibition ended in 1933, the decorative utensils developed for cocktails were often seen in domestic interiors; for the well-to-do, special rooms were designed as bars, as seen in the Mandel house (see fig. 58); while in the average household, a streamlined bar trolley traveled from the kitchen to the living room.

Although streamlining primarily affected the surface appearance of the domestic interior, another development affected the occupants' comfort: air conditioning for the home. This convenience allowed interior designers greater freedom. Paul Frankl was able to design a living room in shades of white, with accents of a pale blue, because modern air-conditioning, "which does not require the opening of windows, makes it possible to use white even in cities with dust-laden air."[15] Individual air conditioning units might also be streamlined machines in their own right. These technical achievements were widely promoted in articles and advertisements in periodicals of the day. For homeowners, room air conditioning units competed with central air conditioning for business.[16]

Streamlining in the domestic interior was also expressed in built-in furnishings and versatile designs developed as space savers. For example, upholstered chairs were low enough to slide under tables or desks and sturdy enough to allow one to perch on their arms. The design of smaller houses required an effort to use all space efficiently: according to a contemporary account, "The development of wall areas for use and storage is simply an adaptation of those planning principles which have in recent years given us better and more convenient kitchens in small spaces."[17]

Fig. 139 Kem Weber, entrance and stair, Walter Edwin Bixby house, Kansas City, Missouri. From *House & Garden*, June 1938.

A pinnacle of thrifty space-planning was reached in the petite studio that John Vassos designed for the photographer Margaret Bourke-White in New York's Chrysler Building (fig. 140). "The built-in fitments," wrote a contemporary critic in 1933, "are as conveniently and economically planned as those in a ship's cabin."[18] Aluminum and frosted-glass lighting fixtures were built in, as were the bookcase and desk, whose heavy plate glass added gleaming transparency to the compact interior. The Venetian blinds were of corrugated aluminum, and there was even space for an aquarium for tropical fish and a cage for the pet alligator she acquired in 1932.[19]

Ambient lighting, theatrical or subtle, was an important part of the streamlined interior, and much was achieved with new inventions in this field, such as fluorescent lighting, which migrated from factories and offices into homes. "Watch fluorescent illumination," a contemporary critic of the New York World's Fair prophesied, "it is the nearest thing to daylight!"[20] Introduced in 1938, fluorescent lighting provided a new source of low-cost illumination—and was used initially in utility areas of the house.[21] Fluorescent tubes accented streamlining with their rounded forms and extended lines. Indirect lighting was also part of the streamlined aesthetic, as seen in Deskey's work, and it could be employed to create illusions of space. In his own penthouse living room (fig. 133), Loewy exploited it in his vase-shaped sconce. Such built-in lighting eliminated some of the lamps that cluttered conventional interiors, part of the paring-down of bric-a-brac that contributed to the stylish simplification of streamlined interiors. Recessed lighting in dropped ceilings and lighting in troughs or cove moldings at or near ceiling lines were other devices used to bypass the lamp.

As distinctive as such lighting were a number of color schemes. Compared to the palettes of the 1920s, colors became lighter and brighter in tonality, though a wide range was utilized for the domestic interior. With the prevalence of aluminum and chrome-plated objects, the effect was cool, silvery, and shining. Loewy's penthouse was visually enlarged by the dark-to-light progression from the broadloom carpet in mulberry to the mulberry and gray upholstery and the gray-green walls. The furniture was lacquered gray and given chromium pulls, and a metal table had gunmetal trim.[22] For the new trains of the New York, New Haven & Hartford Railroad, The Sherwin-Williams Company announced a new color scheme that a contemporary critic termed "streamlined." Far from the drab interiors associated with railroad cars, the car's ceilings and sloping cornices were painted white to reflect as much light as possible downward over the seats. A "very soft pastel shade of the color selected for the car is then carried from the cornice to the window heads. . . ." Windows were brought together by a color band of a deeper, restful, and lower-reflecting shade of the theme color.[23] Obviously the traveler's comfort was being defined in increasingly subtle ways.[24]

Space-enhancing color schemes of lighter hues, indirect and ambient lighting, built-in furnishings and examples in tubular steel, and air conditioning were amenities associated with modernity that entered the homes of the 1930s. And so did the streamlined objects in this section. All these elements could be integrated into both traditional and modern interiors. Re-creations of familiar eighteenth-century styles for the domestic interior—beginning with the Centennial celebration of 1876—were in vogue in America from the late nineteenth century through the late twentieth century and beyond. A few urban sophisticates wanted streamlined living areas, but most consumers were pleased with streamlined objects alone to give a contemporary note to their traditional décor.

Fig. 140 John Vassos, studio for Margaret Bourke-White, Chrysler Building, New York City, 1933.

91. Kem (Karl Emanuel Martin) Weber

ARMCHAIR: AIRLINE

Designed c. 1934–35
Birch, ash, wool upholstery, cotton batting
80.7 x 93.5 x 64.1 cm
Produced by Airline Chair Company,
Los Angeles, California.
The Montreal Museum of Fine Arts,
The Liliane and David M. Stewart Collection,
gift of Geoffrey N. Bradfield
D85.172.1

The name *Airline* given to this chair is an amusing pun that associates it with speed and flight. Its lines are windswept and rounded; it looks intended for an airliner's lounge, if not an airliner itself. In fact, Kem Weber designed the armchair for use in modern interiors (fig. 141). He was driven, he wrote, by "the desire to make a comfortable, hygienic and beautiful chair inexpensively," using mass production tooling of bent and laminated wood. That he shared the goals of celebrated modernist architects such as Gerrit Rietveld, Ludwig Mies van der Rohe, Marcel Breuer, and Alvar Aalto was noted in a contemporary article that compared *Airline* to a bentwood chair by the Finnish master. Yet Weber was as inventive as his European predecessors: his knock-down design, which could be packed in a flat, square box, was inexpensive to store and ship, and easy to assemble (fig. 142). Still, as a contemporary critic remarked, the chair had "strength far out of proportion to the lightness of the individual parts."[1] The same article illustrated Alvar Aalto's plywood armchair of 1932 opposite. Another critic of the time observed that "The construction is based on the principle of the laminated bows used by the Egyptians and since forgotten. It is the most powerful method for combining strength and resiliency, according to Mr. Weber. Every part is a structural necessity. The chair is light and free from corners. Dust-catching box upholstery is eliminated."[2] A recent admirer of Weber's design praised the interlocking frame as allowing "the designer to dispense with rear legs, thereby offering the sitter a comfortable, resilient seat, one that symbolically reminded the sitter of the structural triumph of the designer over the natural laws of gravity."[3] *Airline* is thus streamlined in both senses of the word: its low sweeping lines look aerodynamic and its unornamented design is elegantly minimalist; there are no superfluous parts.

Fig. 141 Harwell Hamilton Harris, library of Cecil J. Birtcher residence, Los Angeles, California, 1941-42.

Fig. 142 *Airline* armchair in package and during assembly.

92. Kem Weber
LOUNGE CHAIR

Designed 1934
Chromium-plated steel, leather, wood
80 x 99.5 x 75 cm
Produced by Lloyd Manufacturing Company,
Menominee, Michigan
The Liliane and David M. Stewart Collection
SHLSL 2003.17

The dazzle of this tubular steel lounge chair derives in part from its daring simplicity. Its profile could have been drawn with three strokes, like an Eric Mendelsohn sketch: the tilted right angle of its seat, the elongated teardrop of its support. In three dimensions, the dark thick rectangles of the capacious leather-covered cushions contrast with the chromium-bright teardrops of steel, which unite arms and legs in their continuous forms. Weber's conception of a unified chair support distantly recalls that of Michael Thonet's bentwood rocker of the 1880s, beloved by both Art Nouveau designers for its arabesques and by modernists for its structural exploitation of the tensile strength of bentwood in a beautiful and functional mass-produced object. But Weber also knew the current vogue for furniture in tubular steel: he had been in Europe in 1925 when Marcel Breuer is thought to have designed the first chair out of it, and as the principal of his own firm (established in 1927) and an art teacher (1931–41) he was doubtless familiar with the tubular steel seating by Le Corbusier, Mies van der Rohe, and others that Americans began adapting in the late 1920s. In addition, Weber knew metalworking: he had designed small objects in silver in 1928–29[4] (cat. 94). Thus this chair benefits by the possibilities of welding. The joining of each steel loop is virtually invisible, and there are three loops for each support, welded side by side and forming the structural equivalent of speed lines. Cross pieces are welded to the supports at front and back to hold the cushions, but they are hidden in most views by the cushions, allowing the seat to seem suspended. As a whole, the low-slung chair looks both luxuriously comfortable and dynamic, attributes that assured Weber's success as an industrial designer in Southern California.

Weber's chair was part of a line of modern tubular steel furniture that he designed for Lloyd Manufacturing Company. Other examples of the lounging line are seen in a series of Weber's watercolor renderings.[5]

93. Gilbert Rohde

ARMCHAIR: *Semi*

Designed c. 1935
Chromium-plated tubular steel, vinyl upholstery
81 x 53.5 x 58.5 cm
Produced by The Troy Sunshade Company,
Troy, Ohio
The Liliane and David M. Stewart Collection,
gift of Dr. Michael Sze
SHLSL 2002. 11

This chair by Gilbert Rohde belonged to one of the more successful and attractive lines of American tubular steel furniture, introduced in 1933.[6] By the early 1930s tubular steel furniture had become chic and pervasive, as seen in the range of designs in contemporary periodicals. The Troy Sunshade Company promoted such furniture as stylishly modern and multi-purpose. According to its fall 1935 "Streamline Metal" catalogue, "In this day of Streamline trains, motor cars and modern buildings it is very natural that furniture designs also be in keeping with this Modern Age. . . . Not only is Troy Streamline Metal smart and alluring, but the steel furniture is unbreakable, light and graceful . . . suitable for use in the Home, Office, Club, Hotel,

Fig. 143 Oasis Lounge of the Chittenden Hotel, Columbus, Ohio. From the catalogue *Troy Streamlined Metal*, The Troy Sunshade Company, Troy, Ohio, 1935.

Restaurant, Cocktail Lounge, Bar or Store."[7] This chair, described as a "semi-arm chair" and available in a choice of polished chromium or lacquered steel, was used in the Oasis Lounge of the Chittenden Hotel, Columbus, Ohio (fig. 143), lending its openwork curves to the semicircular banquette arrangements.[8] At the back of the room can be glimpsed a version of the seating that helped launch tubular steel furniture, Marcel Breuer's side chair of c. 1925 in which back and legs are formed of one continuous bent tube. The Rohde chair is far more complex in structure, however, with its single steel tube supporting the seat at front and sides and describing arms and legs as jazzy Z-shapes. These are the shapes we recognize today as emblems of the American streamlined style.

94. Kem Weber
COVERED VEGETABLE DISH: *SILVER STYLE*[9]
Designed c. 1928–29
Silver-plated nickel steel, rosewood
9 x 25 x 25 cm
Produced by Friedman Silver, New York, New York
The Liliane and David M. Stewart Collection
SHLSL 2003.3

This covered container has the Platonic perfection of shape that is one of the attributes of streamlining in its functionalist vein. The beauty of the circular lid and dish—near-replicas of one another—derives from their sheer silvered surfaces, the graduated tiers of the low form, and the contrast of shape and material offered by the rosewood handles held by semicircular flanges. These costly materials play off the industrial associations of the form, which Kem Weber valued as an expression of its manufacture. "That a surface is plain or without ornamentation does not necessarily mean that the object is modern in the true machine-age sense. It is only when the effect grows out of the designer's consideration for the machine tooling that one can logically claim a place for the product in the machine-age complex."[10] This definition of modernity recalls that of Bruno Paul, the early twentieth-century German designer with whom Weber studied in Berlin in 1908–12. (See Introduction on the links between early modern European design and American streamlining.)

Weber's presence as artist is felt in the flourish of his stamped signature with logo on the bottom of the dish, which attests to the reputation he had gained after opening his own design studio in Hollywood after becoming a U.S. citizen in 1924. The signature also reflects the emerging prominence of the industrial designer in American manufacturing and marketing. A drawing for the dish showing the elevation and the perfect circles of the plan is in the Weber Archives at the University of California at Santa Barbara (fig. 144). The work's architectonic quality was caught by a recent observer, who compared it to the terraced, flat-roofed Mandel house and other streamlined buildings (figs. 48 and 50).[11]

The occasion of the Friedman Silver commission to the West Coast designer was Weber's participation in the New York exhibition *International Exposition of Art in Industry*, organized in 1928 by the giant department store R. H. Macy and Company. Weber was one of only three Americans included,[12] suggesting how prescient was his styling in the late 1920s. By the 1930s Americans would dominate the design and consumption of streamlined products.

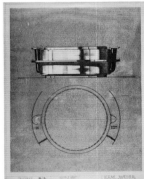

Fig. 144 Kem Weber, drawing of elevation and plan of covered vegetable dish, pencil on paper. Kem Weber Collection, Architecture & Design Collection, University Art Museum, University of California, Santa Barbara.

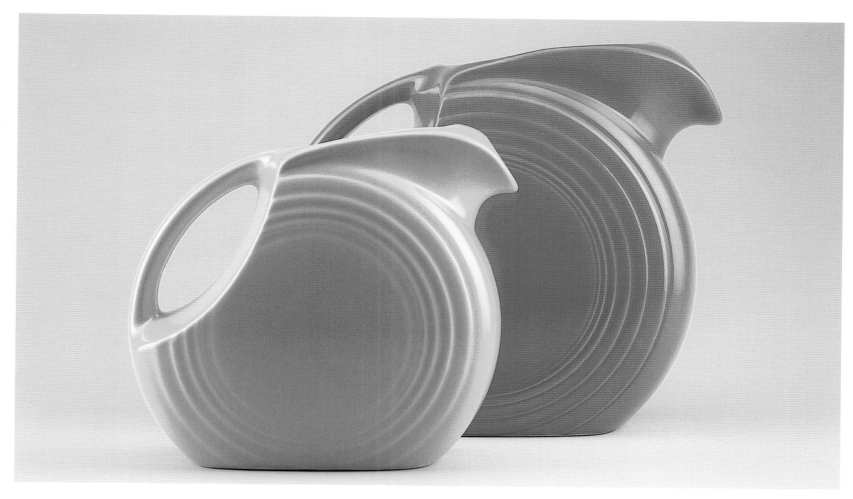

95. Frederick Hurten Rhead

Two Pitchers: *Fiesta*

Designed c. 1936

Glazed earthenware

2003.4: 18.5 x 20 x 11.5 cm

2003.5: 15 x 16.5 x 9 cm

Produced by the Homer Laughlin China Company, Newell, West Virginia

The Liliane and David M. Stewart Collection

SHLSL 2003. 4-5

Fig. 145 Designer unknown, "Homemaker's Recipe File," depicting a *Fiesta* platter and salt and pepper shakers, c. 1940, marked "Prepared by The Home Service Department of The Gas Company," referring to the Ohio Gas Company.

Introduced in 1936, *Fiestaware* appealed to many consumers with its bright colors, modern design, and affordable pricing. Promotions of the 1930s and 1940s (fig. 145) ballyhooed the complete lines, with services for the dining table as well as the kitchen, and encouraged homeowners to customize their collections by mixing and matching hues. A contemporary advertisement proclaimed *Fiestaware* as "a California fashion that has captivated the nation. . . . It is superbly shaped . . . with its rainbow colors," which included red, cobalt blue, ivory, yellow, turquoise, and light green.[13]

Fiestaware's designer Frederick H. Rhead, who came from a family of potters dating to the nineteenth century in Staffordshire, England, and who had worked in very different Arts and Crafts styles in the 1910s–1920s, described the design process in 1937: "It was decided that the *Fiestaware* pitcher would have a streamlined shape, but one not so obvious as to detract from the smooth surface and various colors of the ware. It was

to be a pleasantly curving form and convex rather than angular. A concentric series of rings was added, graduating in width, with those nearer the edges being more widely spaced. Color was to be the chief decorative note."[14]

These two pitchers demonstrate streamlining in their dramatic, forward-slanting spouts and their play with the elemental form of the circle. The curves of the body are emphasized by the concentric rings molded on the sides and the conforming handles, which complete the circle. The small-mouthed spouts prevent pieces of fruit or ice cubes from falling into the matching tumblers during pouring.

Cat. 96

Cat. 97

96. Lurelle Guild
BOWL: *SHERWOOD*
Designed c. 1937[15]
Aluminum
6.7 x 26 x 26 cm
Produced by Aluminum Company
of America (Alcoa), Kensington Inc. Division,
New Kensington, Pennsylvania
B062

97. Lurelle Guild
VASE: *SHERWOOD*
Designed c. 1934[16]
Aluminum
24.5 x 11.5 x 11.5 cm
Produced by Aluminum Company
of America (Alcoa), Kensington Inc. Division,
New Kensington, Pennsylvania
B012

Beginning in 1932 Lurelle Guild designed numerous wares in aluminum for Alcoa, and none so elegant as his lines for Kensington Inc., launched in 1934 by the Alcoa subsidiary. Alcoa was determined to take aluminum out of the kitchen and expand its market, and so it commissioned Guild to match the success of Russel Wright's "designer" aluminum goods in the early 1930s. Kensington ware was sold in gift and silver departments, not as utensils in houseware divisions. Thanks to massive promotions and displays, it became popular as presents, even for weddings.[17] The beauty of Guild's vase and bowl helps to explain why.

In their exquisite proportions, both vessels exude an air of restrained, modern good taste. The low, elemental, circular form of the bowl and the banding of its base are tenets of streamlining, and these traits typify the simple, tall cylindrical vase as well. These forms reflect the spinning process used to shape the aluminum, while their plain surfaces display the attractive qualities of the material. A Kensington advertisement of 1934 praised aluminum for its lightness, luster, low price, and easy care: "A new metal has come to grace your home. . . . Light, lovely, gracious, it glows with the soft luster of old

silver. Yet it is hard, to stand scuffing, and it knows no tarnishing, accepts no stains. . . . And Kensington ingenuity in manufacturing has made possible price tags that are far lower than such fine craftsmanship usually commands. . . ."[18] Both the vase and bowl were part of Kensington's *Sherwood* line,[19] a place name with poetically sylvan associations. The vase sold for $4.75 and was described as "intended for medium to long-stemmed flowers. Unadorned, the soft luster of Kensington metal is sufficient unto itself. . . ."[20] The *Sherwood* bowl was meant to hold flowers, fruit, or candy and to accompany matching candlesticks. It sold for $6.00.[21] Easy to use and to keep clean for casual entertainment, aluminum wares such as these were ideally suited to the new domestic interior reflecting the changed role of women—one in which they were hostesses without servants or time to polish serving pieces.

In 1934, when Lurelle Guild's designs for Kensington Gift Ware were introduced, he was named as one of America's ten foremost industrial designers by *Fortune* magazine.[22] His gifts evidently lay in making modern styling acceptable, even desirable, and in making modern materials look luxurious in small consumer products.

98. Peter Müller-Munk
Pitcher: *Normandie*
Designed 1935
Chromium-plated brass
30.4 x 24.4 x 7.7 cm
Produced by Revere Copper
and Brass Company, Rome, New York
The Montreal Museum of Fine Arts,
The Liliane and David M. Stewart Collection,
gift of Geoffrey N. Bradfield
D83.131.1

Peter Müller-Munk, a Berlin émigré like Kem Weber, was first known for his artistic work as a silversmith before he moved on to become an industrial designer in the 1930s. The *Normandie* pitcher reveals his delight in the reflectivity and tensile strength of chromium-plated sheet metal. Both its form and its name are derived from the celebrated French steamship whose maiden transatlantic voyage occurred the same year that Revere introduced this pitcher. According to the company catalogue of 1936, the pitcher was "inspired by the leaning streamlined stacks of the famous French liner."[23] Made of a single sheet of brass, the canted body is closed at the front with a thin metal strip that is also used around the base and rim. In its teardrop plan, smooth windswept curves, and conforming handle, it embodies aerodynamic streamlining at its minimalist best. Unornamented form and function are one.

Christopher Wilk points out that Russel Wright led the way in designing modern metal accessories for the table in 1929.[24] Companies that manufactured copper, brass, and aluminum for industrial uses, such as Revere and the Chase Brass and Copper Company, saw the benefits of diversifying and entering the housewares market. Housewives who could no longer afford the cost of silver serving pieces, or the time to polish them, were happy consumers. They and Müller-Munk made the transition to easier-care metalwork, and fostered a taste that most American households still maintain.

99. David Chapman
SIPHON BOTTLE
Designed c. 1940[25]
Chromium-plated and enameled steel
20.5 x 12 x 12 cm
Produced by Sparklet Devices, Inc.,
Division of Knapp-Monarch Company,
St. Louis, Missouri
B576

100. Worthen Paxton
Norman Bel Geddes
SIPHON BOTTLE: *SODA KING*
Designed c. 1938[26]
Chromium-plated and enameled metal,
brass, paint, rubber
25.4. x 10.1 x 10.2 cm
Produced by Walter Kidde Sales Company,
Bloomfield, New Jersey
The Montreal Museum of Fine Arts,
The Liliane and David M. Stewart Collection,
gift of Fifty/50
D88.134.1

101. Rolph Scarlett
DESIGN FOR SIPHON BOTTLE AND GLASSES
Designed 1935–1940
Graphite, crayon, and gouache on paper
39.1 x 32.4 cm
The Montreal Museum of Fine Arts,
The Liliane and David M. Stewart Collection,
gift of Mr. and Mrs. Samuel Esses through
the American Friends of Canada
D91.395.91

With Prohibition, more Americans began to drink at home, giving rise to the cocktail party. New forms in furniture and accessories were created for this kind of entertainment. Mixed drinks grew in popularity thanks to the uneven quality of bootleg liquor, and cocktail shakers and glasses appeared in a variety of forms. Even the soda water bottle acquired a new shape, as seen in these smooth, streamlined, rocket-like siphons and the design for one with matching glasses. "An object is *streamlined*," wrote Norman Bel Geddes, "when its exterior surface is so designed that upon passing through a fluid such as water or air the object creates the least disturbance in the fluid in the form of eddies or partial vacua tending to produce resistance."[27]

All these siphons play variants on the round tapering form of a torpedo. The Chapman bottle for Sparklet offers the cheerful contrast of red top and chromium-shiny body, and indented bands around both make gripping them easier. The Scarlett drawing shows an elongated nozzle and the siphon resting its banded bottom on semicircular extrusions, like a launching pad. Most elemental is the *Soda King* by Paxton and Bel Geddes: its spout and operating button scarcely inflect its continuous contour. Its modernity derives from its stylish silhouette and the contrast of color and gleam. Streamlining bolstered the sales appeal of each of these devices and their differences gave consumers options in self-expression. Marketing underlined these differences. The *Soda King* is clearly stamped "Norman Bel Geddes" on the bottom as the designer. The design patent, on the other hand, is ascribed to Worthen Paxton, an employee in the Bel Geddes office. The nature of their collaboration on this siphon is unknown, but clearly the *Thin Man* crowd of sophisticated drinkers was expected to appreciate the Bel Geddes name at their home bars.

Sparklet, on the other hand, wished to promote its siphon's uses beyond the cocktail hour. It marketed the Chapman siphon as providing drinks "for the youngsters when the gang gathers at *your* house!"[28] Chocolate sodas and milk shakes, "fruit sparkle" drinks of fruit syrups you could carbonate, and ice cream made without a churn were some of the treats the manufacturer assured. All this was economical too: the siphon let you "make your own Sparkling Club Soda out of ordinary tap-water in seconds" and "Champagne from inexpensive Sauterne, Sparkling Burgundy from ordinary still wine."

Cat. 100

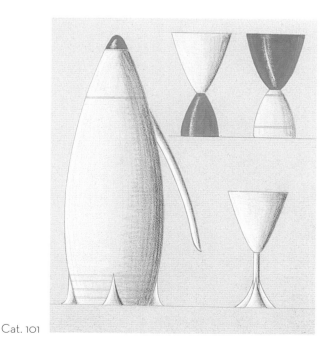

Cat. 101

102. Rolph Scarlett
DESIGN FOR COFFEE SERVICE
Designed 1935–40
Graphite, crayon, and gouache on paper
39.1 x 32.4 cm
The Montreal Museum of Fine Arts,
The Liliane and David M. Stewart Collection,
gift of Mr. and Mrs. Samuel Esses through
the American Friends of Canada
D91.395.127

Scarlett's taste for decorative linearity blossoms in this fanciful design for a coffee service. The circular forms of the vessels are energized by repeated diagonal bandings covering their surfaces, and their handles arch over them, stressing the circle motif and the windswept look of the total. In the coffee pot and creamer, the handle also serves as a spout, observing the simplification typical of modern

design. This may have prevented the manufacture of this design, however: the molding of the complex form would have been costly, and the lids beneath the extruded handles would have been difficult to remove.

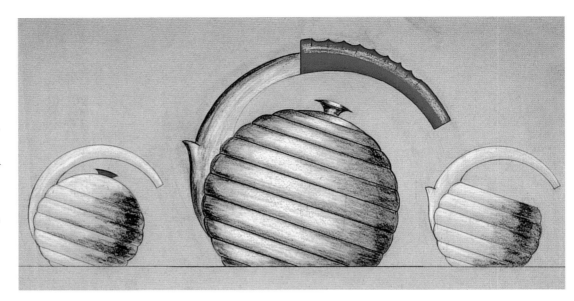

103. Harry (Arieto) Bertoia
COFFEEPOT AND CREAMER
Designed c. 1937–43
Pewter and stained wood
17.8 x 19 x 14.3 cm (coffeepot)
Executed by Harry Bertoia
The Montreal Museum of Fine Arts,
The Liliane and David M. Stewart Collection
D89.192.1 and 2

104. Harry Bertoia
DRAWING FOR COFFEE SERVICE
Designed c. 1937–43
Pencil and charcoal on paper
68.3 x 122.5 cm
The Montreal Museum of Fine Arts,
The Liliane and David M. Stewart Collection
D89.199.1

A comparison of Harry Bertoia's coffeepot and creamer to their preliminary drawing suggests the impact of U. S. streamlining in the late 1930s. The industrial designer and sculptor was teaching at the Cranbrook Academy of Art in Bloomfield Hills, Michigan, beginning in 1938, and channeling aspects of modernist art and French design of the 1920s and early 1930s. Bertoia's drawing recalls the overlapping circles of Robert Delaunay's Orphist paintings begun in the 1910s; and its compass-drawn circles, segments of circles, and repeated curves dominate the finished coffee service. The inside of the coffeepot handle completes the perfect circle of its form. In the

service as realized, concentric circles even appear on each vessel's body, the result of the spinning process of pewter manufacture.[29] But Bertoia did not let the circle rest. In the finished service, the bodies of the vessels are not in fact ball shapes but sharp-pointed ellipses. Their bases are also pointed and made, like the bodies, of bent pewter sheets welded at their edges. The tilted mouth of the creamer and its lack of handles stress the forward action implicit in all these forms. These design choices give the service the dynamism associated with streamlining. Though it nods to French art, it also asserts the American style.

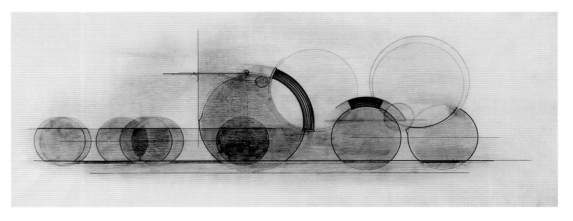

105. Walter Dorwin Teague
DIGITAL CLOCK: MODEL NO. 8B04
Designed c. 1937[30]
Bakelite, aluminum, enameled and stainless steel
9 x 19 x 9.7 cm
Produced by General Electric Company,
Cleveland, Ohio
B040

106. Kem Weber
DIGITAL CLOCK: MODEL NO. P40, *ZEPHYR*
Designed 1934[31]
Brass with partial bronze plating, plastic, enamel
9.1 x 20.3 x 8.3 cm
Produced by Lawson Time, Inc.,
Alhambra, California
The Montreal Museum of Fine Arts, gift
of David A. Hanks in memory of David M. Stewart
D88.136.1

107. Walter Dorwin Teague
DIGITAL CLOCK: MODEL NO. 8B11
Designed c. 1937[32]
Bakelite, enameled and stainless steel
9.5 x 20.3 x 10.2 cm
Produced by Warren Telechron Company,
Ashland, Massachusetts
B024

Weber's sweeping design of 1934 for a digital clock and Teague's two clocks of 1937 for different companies reveal the differences between these two masters of the streamlined style. Primarily in black Bakelite, Teague's designs are both low rectangles of nearly the same dimensions set on plinths like classical architecture, with their digital windows placed in the middle of their long sides. The model for General Electric (cat. 105) is the more symmetrical, having a raised and projecting central portion. Its streamlining is reticent, seen in the case's only slightly rounded corners and the pale, fluted, inset base, like an austere underskirt. Teague's model for Warren Telechron (cat. 107), on the other hand, has a curved top, with a raised fluted band wrapped over it, and a grooved band containing the digital window on its front. These cases are conservative in their modernity and refined in their proportions and detailing. They recall that Teague carefully studied eighteenth-century arts and distinguished himself at the Calkins & Holden advertising agency in 1908–12 for his elegant illustrations.

Weber's arresting S-curve design, by contrast, combines the brio of an Eric Mendelsohn sketch[33] with a metal sculptor's awareness of materials. Though rectangular in plan like Teague's products, Weber's brass clock is curved at its top left and rounded at its right side, forming a continuous, horizontal, marquee-like shape. This is dramatized by an ornamental brass strip drawn from the side over the top and a swooping brass-plated band that integrates the white digital window on the face. The total rests on bronze-plated pad feet (some models

have ball feet), which lighten the effect. Like his chromium-plated steel and leather lounge chair and his silver-plated covered dish (cat. 92 and 94), this clock is opulent in the colors and sheen of its metals and immediate in the impact of its simplified form.

Time and speed are embodied in Weber's clock, which is named *Zephyr* (Greek god of the winds) perhaps after the streamlined train introduced in 1934 by the Burlington Northern Railroad (fig. 118). A digital clock, it appeared only a year later than the first digital model launched by Warren Telechron, the manufacturer of Teague's clock. *Tide*, the advertising industry magazine, heralded the 1933 introduction, noting that "clocks without hands and without anything resembling a clock face" were first imported to the United States by a French clockmaker in the 1890s, and observing that in digital clocks, numbers rotate into a window like figures in a cash register.[34] At a money-obsessed moment in American history, the association was positive.

The stylistic distance between Warren Telechron's anonymous clock of 1933, its successor of 1934, the *Minitman* (fig. 146, top),[35] and Teague's and Weber's designs of 1934–37 illustrate the way that streamlining transformed product design. The first two clocks are upright boxes, but the later of the two is unornamented and has architectonic setback sides. Its raised top remains in Teague's clock, cat. 105, but both of his timepieces are horizontal forms, and his later model features rounded corners and speed lines. Weber's design is all long, low, rounded corners and speed lines. For these designers, the locomotive had toppled the skyscraper as the master metaphor of the era.

Fig. 146 Advertisement for Warren Telechron clocks, from *House & Garden*, April 1934.

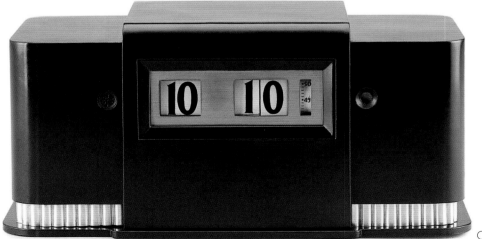

Cat. 105

Cat. 107

108. Raymond Loewy
TALL CLOCK AND RADIO: *COLUMNAIR*

Designed c. 1930[36]
Mahogany and oak veneer, enameled steel,
Masonite, fabric
152.8 x 34.5 x 27.5 cm
Produced by Westinghouse Electric
and Manufacturing Corporation, Meadville,
Pennsylvania
B358

Loewy's tall clock and radio of 1930 is a hybrid of old and new in its style, allusions, and technology; it marks a transition in the form language of streamlining. It alludes to eighteenth-century "grandfather" or tall clocks in its proportions and housing of mahogany and oak veneer, and it also references Paul T. Frankl's "Skyscraper" furniture of the 1920s with their stepped-back silhouettes. But its "exposition style" or Art Deco aspects are overshadowed by Loewy's early use of streamlining. All of the clock-radio's edges are curved, even the corners of the rectangular clock face, and horizontal speed-line banding marks the base and the division between the top and body. At the same time, the clock's height is emphasized in line and color by the panel of oak veneer that runs from the face to the floor, veneer also used on the stepped sides. The radio controls are inset into the right side.

Loewy's columnar design of the *Columnair* as modern wooden cabinetwork is an early solution

to the aesthetic challenge posed by radios. By the late 1920s they were display pieces in as many homes as telephones, and they adorned living rooms in cabinets styled to accord with widespread conservative tastes in décor. But revival-style containers for the new and exciting technology increasingly dissatisfied consumers. In 1930 Westinghouse held an international contest for "the best ideas on beautifying radio cabinets."[37] From the 75,000 entries from fifty-eight countries, the manufacturer learned that present-day designs were objectionable—at least to the contestants— and that buyers wanted cabinets requiring less floor

space, as well as units combining an electric clock with the radio.

With this data, Westinghouse commissioned Loewy, who had opened his design office the year before, to design the *Columnair* clock-radio. The *Columnair* was extravagantly promoted, primarily through two unusual photo shoots: one 307 feet underground at the Bridal Altar in Mammoth Cave in Kentucky, and the other in a zeppelin floating over Manhattan.[38] The P. T. Barnum flair of these stunts illustrates the extremes that 1930s advertising reached in marketing products to Americans.

Fig. 147 Raymond Loewy, detail of a patent drawing for "Radiocabinet."

109. Isamu Noguchi

SHORTWAVE RADIO TRANSMITTER:
RADIO NURSE

Designed c. 1937[39]

Bakelite

21 x 16.5 x 16.5 cm

Produced by Zenith Radio Corporation, Chicago, Illinois

B573

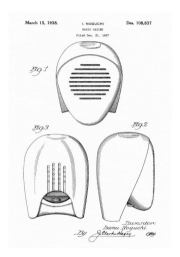

Fig. 148 Isamu Noguchi, patent drawing for "Radio Casing."

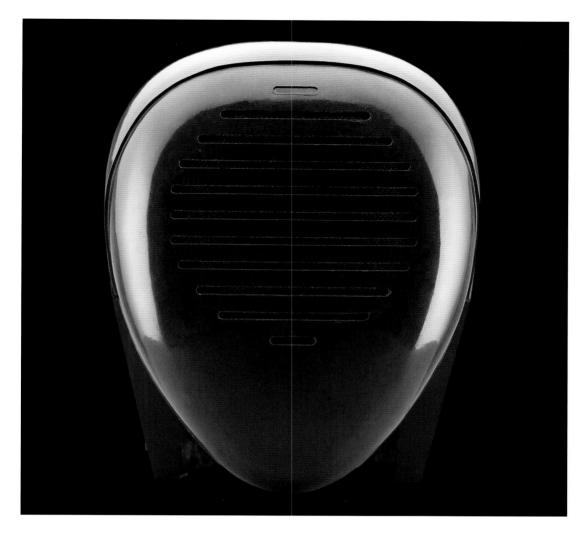

The idea for *Radio Nurse*, a wireless intercom system for home use, came from the president of the Zenith Radio Corporation, whose first child was born in 1937. Fearful she could be kidnapped, like the aviator Charles Lindbergh's child in 1932, he rigged a microphone over her crib, attached it to an amplification system, and set receivers around the home to let him listen for any sounds. His satisfaction with the results led him to put the device into production, commissioning the sculptor Isamu Noguchi to realize his idea for a receiver shaped like a head in a nurse's cap. Both the receiver and transmitter used the home's electrical wiring for "broadcasting." Sold to families to let them monitor invalids and the elderly as well as infants, Noguchi's design in Bakelite won first prize in the household category from the magazine *Modern Plastic* in 1938 and was exhibited at the Whitney Museum of American Art in 1939.[40]

In a 1941 *House & Garden* survey of sixteen home safety devices, it was cited as costing $24.95, a luxury price, between the chain ladder for $20 and up, and the tear gas machine gun for $37.50.[41]

Noguchi's conception of *Radio Nurse* suggests the affinity between streamlining and organic forms in progressive art of the 1930s. Its stylized teardrop-shaped head is crossed by the horizontal sound perforations resembling speed lines found in radio grille work; it rests on its "chin" and the curve of its "cap" with compact self-sufficiency (fig. 148). In the spherical forms of its dark Bakelite, it suggests the mask-like portrait heads that Noguchi made to support himself through the Depression. It was removed from production in 1942 for technical, not aesthetic, reasons: many neighbors could overhear the conversations of those who used the device. *Radio Nurse* is the ancestor of today's "baby monitor."

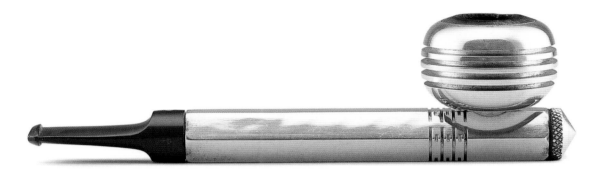

Cat. 110

110. Designer unknown

SMOKING PIPES
Designed c. 1930-40
Aluminum, wood, Bakelite
Streamliner[42]: 4.2 x 13.6 x 3.8 cm
4.2 x 14.7 x 3.5 cm
4.2 x 14.7 x 3.8 cm
Manufacturer unknown
B167

111. Wayne Leser

SMOKING PIPE:
AIR COOLED STREAMLINER
Designed c. 1941[43]
Burl walnut, Bakelite
4 x 15.2 x 3.6 cm
Manufacturer unknown
B506

Bing Crosby was rarely without a pipe. Advertisers encouraged smoking as one of the personal compensations one could enjoy (and afford) even during the Depression. The accoutrements of the stimulant, like those for cocktail drinking in the 1930s, were updated with streamlining to appeal to urban sophisticates.

The source of the trio of aluminum pipes (cat. 110) is unknown, but their nearly identical bowl and stem shapes and comparable dimensions suggest they had the same manufacturer. The pipe with four incised speed lines on its pointed stem is stamped "Streamliner"; the one with three deep grooves (rather than four) in its bowl is stamped "Bryson Pat. Pending," indicating the designer or maker, who are as yet unidentified. The third pipe has no marks.

In the language of flight through water or sky, the burl walnut pipe (cat. 111) is described as "air finned" in its patent application (fig. 149). The application identifies Wayne Leser as the designer.

Though Leser chose a hard wood traditional for pipes rather than aluminum, that quintessentially modern material, the designers of all four of these items were inventive in using streamlining to improve looks and performance. The deep parallel grooves of each bowl allow air cooling and therefore longer burning of the tobacco and a more comfortable grip. The teardrop shape of the bowl in Leser's design is attractive to the hand and eye.

Unlike conventional pipes, which were generally curved in profile, these are all functionalist designs that set stem and bowl at right angles. With such bold geometries and streamlined grooves, these smoking tools conveyed modernity.

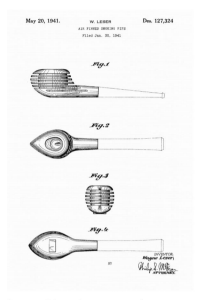

Fig. 149 Wayne Leser, patent drawing for "Air Finned Smoking Pipe."

Cat. 111

112. Designer unknown

RING

Designed c. 1945
Silver, rhinestones
2.5 x 2 x 2 cm
Produced by Kramer Jewelry Creations,
New York, New York
The Liliane and David M. Stewart Collection
SHLSL 2003.21

Even jewelry was streamlined in the 1930s, and the continued popularity of the style is demonstrated by this rhinestone and silver ring, designed c. 1945 by Kramer Jewelry Creations. Teardrop-shaped layers of silver form the sides of the ring, and they are graduated toward the centrally placed crystal flanked by smaller crystals. Heavy, symmetrical, and streamlined in its teardrops and cool sheen and sparkle, the costume piece was probably inspired by diamond and platinum jewelry of the 1930s, when it would have been a chic finishing touch to one of the streamlined fashions of the day. Perhaps it was worn with a bias-cut ivory satin evening gown by Madeleine Vionnet that swept from bust to heel in a single sinuous line. Or it might have "accessorized" one of the white crepe lounging ensembles designed by Adrian for Jean Harlow in one of her movie roles as a platinum-blonde vamp. Certainly, the styling of this costume ring was no fluke, for fashion interested the streamlined designers.

In 1939 *Vogue* magazine asked nine of them—including Teague, Loewy, Dreyfuss, Deskey, and Arens—to design a dress for the "Woman of the Future," and they did (fig. 150). Several predicted that tomorrow's woman "will be tall and slim," and Deskey added that she would be fit, able to wear his design of a translucent, neo-Grec gown.[44] Already Loewy had outlined the progression of female dress toward pared-down simplicity in one of his "Evolution Charts." He and his fellow designers believed in the logic and functionalism of streamlining, as well as its sales appeal and near-

universal applications. That it could and should affect fashion—including jewelry—was inevitable.

The c. 1945 dating of this ring is suggested by its mark. Kramer Jewelry was founded in 1943 and continued in business in New York until 1980.[45] Its production of Christian Dior jewelry in the United States during the Parisian couturier's heyday in the 1950s indicates the sophistication of its target audience, an audience implied by the ring.

Fig. 150 Wedding gown designed by Egmont Arens. From *Vogue*, February 1939.

113. Designer unknown

BED SPOT LAMP

Designed c. 1945
Bakelite, plastic, brass, enameled steel, felt
19 x 18.3 x 10.5 cm
Produced by Eagle Lighting, United States
B584

"Reading in bed is not injurious to the eyes," warned a contemporary writer, "*if* there is adequate, glareless light on the reading page. So-called bedlamps—the kind that hang on the back of the bed—are invariably designed for their decorative value only and are not good to see by."[46] *This* brown Bakelite lamp, however, would have been

approved. It takes a larger-than-usual bulb for more illumination, and a ball joint allows the head to rotate, directing the light. A chain pull turns the lamp on and off.

In form, the Eagle lamp imitates the spotlights on the hoods of such luxury cars as the 1929 Cadillac *LaSalle*. Graduated bands animate its football shape, and three raised speed lines embellish the front of the bracket that attaches it to the bedstead. Such streamlining was not required by the need to house the bulb and its wiring. Nor was its metaphoric association apropos. Streamlining for both this bed lamp and the casket advertised in 1937 (fig. 10) reflected fashion, not function: the users of both items were at rest.

114. Robert Heller

FAN: *AIRFLOW*

Designed c. 1937[47]

Enameled and chromium-plated steel,
aluminum, enameled cast iron

23 x 32.5 x 39.5 cm

Produced by The A. C. Gilbert Company,
New Haven, Connecticut

B029

115. Robert Davol Budlong

FAN: MODEL NO. D22-TL, *ZEPHYR*

Designed c. 1936[48]

Aluminum, painted cast iron, steel

72 x 83.5 x 36.5 cm

Produced by Edgar T. Ward Co., Inc.,
Chicago, Illinois

B646

116. Richard Ten Eyck

FAN: MODEL NO. 12P1, *VORNADO*

Designed c. 1945[49]

Enameled and chromium-plated steel,
aluminum

61.5 x 51.5 x 50.5 cm

Produced by the O. A. Sutton
Corporation,
Wichita, Kansas

B570

Early electric fans had pedestal bases and
cylindrical motor housings; their air-circulating
powers were only minimally suggested, for example,
in the wavy wires of their safety cages (fig. 151). But
from the mid-1930s on, designers of these home
appliances found new airplanes irresistible as a
styling source. When the *Zephyr* and *Airflow* fans
appeared in 1936 and 1937, streamlined planes had
been carrying mail for over four years, and the
Douglas DC-3 plane had just been introduced,
making coast-to-coast passenger flight possible. The
propellers of planes and the blades of fans function
identically: designers such as Budlong and Heller
must have considered it logical as well as attractive
to style the bodies of their home appliances like
aircraft motor cowlings.[50]

In his *Zephyr* (cat. 115), a floor model on a cast-
iron base, Budlong used aeronautical forms in its
steel teardrop foot, curved shaft, and hemispherical

Cat. 114

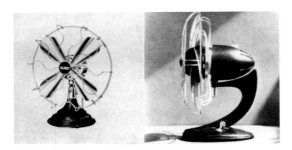

Fig. 151 Before and after views of A. C. Gilbert fan, from *The Architectural Forum*, October 1940.

motor housing. The housing's three fins made it easier to grasp and move the heavy machine, but their primary purpose was aesthetic. On the front of the wire safety cage four wires have the expected rippling forms.

Even more streamlined is Heller's *Airflow* table fan (cat. 114). Rising from a teardrop base, its shaft sweeps backward and then forward to support its spheroid motor housing. This shaft design enables the fan to be "raised or lowered to direct the flow of air to any desired angle," according to an article in the March 1937 *Architectural Forum*. The text goes on: "Instead of the usual driving arm, the fan employs an actuating pin operated by gears, which works in a groove in the base running parallel to the

motor housing. The redesign of this mechanism has contributed to the beauty and simplicity of the streamlined form of the fan.... The 10 in. blade size, finished in telephone black with metal parts chromium plated, will retail for $9.95."[51] The allusion associates the fan with the increasingly essential telephone. A desk or table carrying both conveniences would have been ultra-modern.

In addition to such fans, Heller also designed the New York showroom for The A. C. Gilbert Company, a firm known for the high-quality design of toys as well as electrical appliances. As illustrated in the June 1937 issue of *The Architectural Forum* (fig. 152), the showroom was complete with tubular steel furniture and ashtray stands.[52] On the sleek continuous shelves several versions of the *Airflow* are displayed, along with Gilbert's blenders, juicers, and the like. The total showcases the company's masterly use of streamlining for a unified brand identity. Its modish style was a selling point: the display is headlined "The World's Smartest Lines of Electric Fans and Appliances."

Designed at the end of World War II, the *Vornado* fan (cat. 116) represents the sober geometric simplification of the later streamlined style. As suggested by its name, which combines parts of the words "*vortex*" and "*tornado*," the

Vornado works on different principles from the *Airflow* and *Zephyr*. It was developed by the O. A. Sutton Corporation from its experience as a manufacturer of structural frames for the aircraft industry. The air movement is centrifugal and depends on two nested cones spun from strip aluminum. It is also quieter than conventional fans. According to the designer, Richard Ten Eyck, most electric fans "jostle" the air; the *Vornado* provides a directed column of it.[53]

Ten Eyck's design is streamlined from its script logo, *Vornadofan*, on the grille, to its stepped shield-like base. The fan's truncated, bullet-shaped form resembles an airplane's propeller shaft. This form also protects the cones and blades inside, preventing damage during shipping and use and assuring safety. Ten Eyck's streamlining is both practical and attractive.

The *Vornado* is an example of a company's swift and successful retooling from wartime to peacetime production. Ten Eyck recalls "the long lines of workers being terminated" after the Armistice. "Were they going to be part of another Depression? . . . My job was going to be creating things to create new jobs."[54] The imagery of airplanes, as seen in the fan, has also changed, from pizzazz to blunt power, perhaps in response to the war.

Fig. 152 Showroom for The A. C. Gilbert Co., New York City, designed by Robert Heller, from *The Architectural Forum*, June 1937.

Cat. 116

Cat. 116

117. Wayne A. Gustafson
HEATER: MODEL NO. 3000-B, *SOLAIRE*
Designed c. 1946[55]
Enameled and chromium-plated steel,
anodized aluminum, Bakelite
28.5 x 19 x 30 cm
Produced by M. S. Aviation Co.,
Minneapolis, Minnesota
B453

118. David Chapman
FAN HEATER: *HEAT KING*
Designed c. 1948[56]
Enameled and chromium-plated steel, aluminum
56.5 x 25 x 21 cm
Produced by the National Die
Casting Company, Chicago, Illinois
B451

Electric heaters and fans direct air with the same
kinds of motors, but to heat the air requires a
conductor, and to protect the user and conserve
the warmth requires a thick casing. Called a "space
heater" in its patent application, the *Solaire* heater
has a sunburst and "MS" monogram as its logo,
promising radiant "natural" heat. It is streamlined in
its stepped teardrop-shaped base and its missile-
like body, which closely resembles an airplane
motor. Heat radiates out of concentric rings of
aluminum enameled bright red on both sides, which
contrast with the green stippled surface of the
body, the Bakelite handle accenting the streamlined
silhouette, and the chromium-plated band
concealing the joint between the body parts.
This space heater looks ready to be launched.
Indeed, the manufacturer M. S. Aviation Co.
of Minneapolis, a partnership of John E. Magner
and Warren J. Schneider, also made engines for
small aircraft. No wonder *Solaire* looks
aerodynamic.

Airplane imagery is also incorporated in the
Heat King standing heater. Resting on a stepped
teardrop-shaped base, its machinery is protected
by a truncated hemisphere evoking an airplane
motor. The concentric rings on its back are
signatures of streamlining, and it too incorporates
a stippled surface, in brown, which contrasts
with its brilliant chromium plating.

Cat. 118

119. Dr. Peter Schlumbohm

GARBAGE PAIL: *CINDERELLA*

Designed 1930–40
Aluminum, maple, cork
29 x 29 x 29 cm
Produced by Dr. Peter Schlumbohm,
New York, New York
B025

In *Cinderella*, Schlumbohm has transformed the lowly cylindrical garbage pail of tradition into a dynamic streamlined object whose conical form and undecorated surfaces suggest a futuristic age. Its graduated horizontal banding extends from a circular maple foot resting on a cork base to the flattened circular finial of its shiny aluminum lid. The cork used below the maple base was, like aluminum, a material favored in the 1930s. The overall look is one of scientific hygiene and Machine Age perfection. According to its marks, Schlumbohm, a German-born chemist, was the manufacturer as well as the designer of the container, which was part of his *Fahrenheitor* product line.

Intended for apartment living, Schlumbohm's small-scale receptacle was handsome enough to be used in any room, "in the kitchen, living room, den, bathroom," according to its literature.[57] "Folded-in wax paper linings" would make disposal of wet garbage easy. This was inventive in the era before plastic bags and containers, when electrical garbage disposals were rare. *Cinderella* was also apparently a dress rehearsal for Schlumbohm's most famous invention, the *Chemex* coffeemaker, marketed from 1941 to the present (fig. 153).[58] Its folded paper inserts filter the coffee as well as easing the removal of the grounds; it is an hourglass shape of glass, a doubling of *Cinderella's* cone shape.

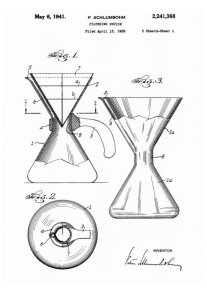

Fig. 153 Peter Schlumbohm, patent drawing for "Filtering Device."

Cat. 119

"WON'T YOU HAVE FUN"

Streamlining Recreation

5

Entertainment boomed in the Depression as a distraction from economic woes and political worries. Dance crazes and marathons, roller derbies and figure skating competitions, along with golf, tennis, bowling, and cycling were among the activities drawing avid participants, who invested in the latest streamlined equipment. Meanwhile spectator sports from baseball to horse and automobile racing were broadcast to throngs of fans, and the radio displaced the dining table as the family's communal center. A hit parade of songs came over the airwaves, and aficionados of swing, Broadway show tunes, and classical music could buy 78 rpm records to spin on new portable phonographs and dance or listen to them in a new part of the house called the rumpus room.[1] All of this could be photographed, and it was: slide shows and home movies recorded family events and vacations, which were promoted as yet another means of stimulating the economy. Miniature cars, trains, and planes let children dream about the fast travel increasingly available to their parents, and new model toys from scooters to sleds were streamlined to suggest their speed. Those fortunate Americans "in the money" had a rainbow of new ways to spend it.

For the three out of four Americans who kept their jobs during the Depression, leisure time became increasingly abundant. To widen employment opportunities, a forty-hour working week was introduced in 1935, down from the average sixty-hour week at the beginning of the twentieth century. Saturdays as well as Sundays were days off for more Americans. Of the increased number of objects created to accompany play, many were subject to the new sleek machine aesthetic. Entire rooms devoted exclusively to amusement multiplied in American homes, in many cases replacing the traditional dining and living rooms as the family center and entertainment site and reflecting more informal and family-oriented lifestyles. A contemporary critic claimed: "Instead of the formal parlor of the 1890s, today's house frequently has a *recreation* or game room, usually located in the basement. . . ."[2] Another period article specified: "Such a room may be devoted to entertainment which requires exertion of some sort (i.e. billiards, ping pong, fencing, etc.) or to more sedentary indoor sports (bridge, games, drinking, etc.)."[3] A deck of *Streamline* playing cards would fit such a space (fig. 157).

For the wealthier homeowner, a special room for entertainment might be included in plans for a new house. The Kansas City insurance executive Walter Edwin Bixby, for example, employed the architect Edward W. Tanner to design his modern house; it had a flat roof with white stucco walls and long, horizontal expanses of glass. Tanner's blade-shaped plan centered on an open two-story stair hall (discussed on p. 155) with a basement rumpus room directly beneath. Between 1936 and 1937, Kem Weber executed the interiors (figs. 154 and 155)[4] The swooping lines of the serpentine banquette and ceiling lighting that curl through the room, as well as the semicircular bar and low-slung, curvaceous furniture, give the open space the look of a streamlined lounge in an ocean liner.

"Club" rooms were furnished with a variety of new equipment for adults' and children's indoor activities and closets and shelves for storing items from roulette wheels and Monopoly boards to miniature golf putting greens. "Almost everything in the room is burn-proof, alcohol-proof, servant-proof. . . . Here everything is on the side of informality, gaiety, lightness." Modern interior styling, including streamlining, was welcome: "This is the place where the house lets go, no matter how Georgian the rest of it may be."[5]

For modest households the game room might be carved out of an existing interior space, in particular the basement, seen for example in the Albert W. Haddock residence in Wilmington, Delaware (fig. 156). Although this basement area is not streamlined itself, the redesigned and finished space (with club chairs and a ping-pong table) capitalizes, according to the Cheneys, on "the cleanliness and beauty of modern heating equipment, here a streamlined General Electric oil-burning furnace."[6] For these champions of industrial design, the gleaming cylindrical furnace made the room more beautiful, while it fulfilled the humdrum practical requirement of heating the house.

The end of Prohibition in 1933 did not end the custom of drinking cocktails at home, or of entertaining with cocktail parties and gatherings with music and dancing. In response to the growing ritual of the cocktail hour, a bar was often included in the game room for hospitality in the evening hours. According to a contemporary writer, "there is no limit to the actual size of the bar. The smallest bar installed by one manufacturer takes up to four feet of space, and the largest is 140 feet long. In fact, an ordinary-sized closet can be converted into a satisfactory bar."[7] For those

155

156

Below, left, **Fig. 154** Kem Weber, rendering of rumpus room for Walter Edwin Bixby house, Kansas City, Missouri, 1936–37. Watercolor and graphite on board. Architecture and Design Collection, University Art Museum, University of California, Santa Barbara. Gift of Erika Weber.

Top, **Fig. 155** Kem Weber, rumpus room for Walter Edwin Bixby house, Kansas City, Missouri, 1936–37.

Above, **Fig. 156** Albert W. Haddock residence, Wilmington, Delaware, with General Electric oil-burning furnace. From Cheney and Cheney, *Art and the Machine*, 1925.

Below, **Fig. 157** *Streamline* playing cards, c. 1935–40, Eric Brill Collection.

154

157

Fig. 158 John Vassos, "Musicorner," from the "Americans at Home" exhibition, New York World's Fair, 1939.
Fig. 159 Mark D. Kalischer, architect, Adelphi Theatre, Chicago, c. 1935. From *Architectural Forum*, August 1937.

who could afford it, a separate room exclusively for a bar might also be designed, as seen in the Mandel house of 1933–35 (see figs. 58–59). The curve of its streamlined bar encouraged sociability. Here was a house that also provided many additional amenities for active amusement such as a swimming pool, squash court, and tennis court.

For passive pleasure, console radios and phonographs became an essential part of the comfortable upper-class and middle-class home, and built-in versions can be seen in the "Musicorner" designed by John Vassos for the "Americans at Home" exhibition at the New York World's Fair of 1939 (fig. 158). The soon-to-be ubiquitous television shown here was first introduced to the American public at that *World of Tomorrow* fair, and the invention would quickly lead to renaming this space the TV room. In the Vassos room, curved horizontal elements contributing to its streamlined modernity include the built-in bookcases and the curved flower planter beneath the wraparound window. Streamlined, built-in, upholstered seating welcomes the guests, and the accoutrements for serving cocktails are on the coffee table. This compact multipurpose room was designed for snug and effortless sociability: the conversation pit of the 1960s and the couch potatoes of the 1980s were not far away.

Among the products enhancing leisure, none was as revolutionary as radio. Broadcasting entertainment as well as information, radio intensified consumerism and the sense of national identity in the 1930s. President Roosevelt's "fireside chats," Jack Benny's comedy, Metropolitan Opera performances, Orson Welles's *War of the Worlds* drama, and such serials as *The Green Hornet* and *Little Orphan Annie* suggest radio's range: abundant, diversified programming, which had become continuous in 1926, reached virtually every taste, and the runaway popularity of the medium led to increased manufacturing of various radio types, lower product costs, and equipment miniaturization—in the evolutionary pattern evident later in personal computers and iPod music players. By 1929, Americans had bought 4.4 million radios, doubling the cost of home energy use; four years later, they owned 24.4 million models, many in the streamlined forms described here (see cat. 125–130).[8] According to a contemporary article, radios outnumbered telephones by 8 million sets in 1934, and there were some 2 million more radios installed in cars.[9]

Hollywood came close to rivaling the mass appeal of radio in the 1930s. Benefiting from the emigration of talent from Nazi Germany, American films included screwball comedies, Marx Brothers slapstick, hard-boiled detective stories, costume epics like *Gone With the Wind* (1939), and Busby Berkeley song-and-dance extravaganzas. Streamlined sets for such musicals and interiors for such dramas as *Grand Hotel* (1932) reinforced the identification of aeronautical style with sophistication and modernity.[10] By 1938, more than 80 million movie tickets were sold each week, to 65 percent of the U.S. population.[11] The movie theater, adapted from the vaudeville stage, became a picture palace in the 1920s to match the fantasies of this mass audience.

Although movie theater architecture drew on many revival styles, the streamlined modern was a popular option, as seen in the Adelphi Theatre in Chicago (fig. 159), designed by Mark D. Kalischer, c. 1935. Streamlining is notable in the multiple curves of the marquee and its horizontal banding, and in the façade, which curves in toward the ticket booth and entry doors, all aglow with neon and chromium plate. This formula appeared with variations throughout the United States, from large cities to small towns. Noteworthy graphics were often part of the drama of the showy architecture. A contemporary critic reported that most theaters then employed a type of sign in which "opaque letters are silhouetted against a background of frosted glass illuminated from behind. This arrangement is not only more attractive . . . but it is also more readable, and simplifies the construction of the letters themselves."[12] Here the graphics accord with the streamlining: the horizontally elongated letters in "Adelphi" appear on two prominent horizontal lines that span the front edge of the marquee.

Streamlining took Hollywood glamour to urbane restaurants and especially to their bars. A good example can be seen in one of the Longchamps restaurants in New York (fig. 160) designed collaboratively by the architect Louis Allen Abramson and the painter/designer Winold Reiss in c. 1936. Each establishment in the famous and chic New York chain was decorated around a different theme, and this Longchamps provided the epitome of streamlining. The emphatic horizontal banding of the curved bar was echoed in the ceiling and in the tubular steel stools. According to a contemporary account, the bar was "topped with teak, has a tufted facing of alternate vermilion and white fabricoid stripes which is indirectly lighted." The back bar was of bronze and glass, with red and black terrazzo flooring. Draperies were of red Cellophane.[13] On the exterior of another restaurant in the chain (fig. 161) the words "Longchamps" and "Restaurant," "Café," and "Bar" glistened in thin silvery letters on a black ground, while a curved marquee and rounded railings led the customer to the revolving entrance door.

Another aspect of amusement in the 1930s implicitly involved traditional American concerns for self-improvement and public health. "One of the outstanding phenomena of the past decade," read an article of 1937, "has been the tremendous increase in the amount of leisure, much of it enforced. . . . [A question] facing America today is how this free time may be so utilized as to contribute to the enrichment of our people, rather than becoming a liability or even a menace."[14] Public recreation projects were designed to respond positively to the numbers of idle Americans and also to generate building jobs in the process. Foreclosures had put more land in municipal hands, while expanded highways allowed vacationers access to more distant parks and beaches. Both relief funds and low-cost labor enabled city governments from New York to Los Angeles to carry out ambitious plans for public benefit.

Most far-reaching as a master builder with public funds was New York's Robert Moses, the powerful Parks Commissioner of New York City (1934–1960) and head of the Triborough Bridge and

Fig. 160 Louis Allen Abramson, architect, and Winold Reiss Studios, interior decoration, Bar, Longchamps Restaurant, New York City, c. 1936. From *American Architect and Architecture*, December 1936.
Fig. 161 Abramson and Reiss Studios, exterior, Longchamps Restaurant, New York City.

160

161

Fig. 162 Photo-collage, Astoria Swimming Pool, New York City Department of Parks, c. 1936. From *American Architect and Architecture*, November 1936.
Fig. 163 William Mooser, Aquatic Park, San Francisco, 1939.
Fig. 164 Antoine Courtens, Recreation Center, Domaine d'Esterel, near Montreal, 1938. From *Architectural Record*, December 1938.

Tunnel Authority (1946–1968). As early as 1936, he counted among his accomplishments the creation of "169 new parks totaling 3,357 acres, 150 new playgrounds, 3 zoos, 8 golf courses, 1 stadium, 10 swimming pools . . . [and] numerous recreational facilities along the many new parkways. . . ."[15] For many of these park buildings, the streamlined modern style was chosen as healthful and easy to keep clean.

The Parks Department, according to Moses, should provide sanitary and attractive public bathing facilities. In the fall of 1934 work commenced on the construction of eight swimming pools and bathhouse units, and three more pools were added the following year. A photo-collage of 1936 (fig. 162) of these clean, modern facilities reveals the bold canted shapes of diving boards with tubular steel railings and the repeated curves of pools and surrounding steps. The style implies Olympic-quality sport.[16]

Moses was also responsible for commissioning additional recreational facilities along the new parkways. And other cities, including Chicago and Los Angeles, had similar public projects made possible by public relief funds. New York's handsomely landscaped routes included stopping places for automobiles with picnicking facilities, cafeterias, walks, and benches. The routes themselves— of limited access, quickly connecting the city to beaches and scenic destinations—acknowledged the growing leisure use of the car and its higher speeds. Such parkway design could be said to streamline travel by car.[17]

Streamlined architecture at San Francisco's Aquatic Park suited its waterside setting. A Works Progress Administration project, designed by William Mooser in 1939 (fig. 163), the concrete, glass, and steel building provided facilities for entertaining, dancing, and eating as well as lockers and showers for its use as a bathhouse.[18] The stories step back to create observation decks, and the wraparound windows and sleek white walls complete the building's resemblance to an ocean liner.

In Canada near Montreal, the Domaine d'Esterel, a sportsman's resort developed by Baron Louis Empain in 1938, was streamlined in several of its buildings, both exteriors and interiors. The complex was designed by the Belgian-born architect Antoine Courtens,[19] a disciple of Frank Lloyd Wright who lived in the United States in 1915–19. Courtens's use of tubular steel furniture and his stylish streamlining of the recreation building (fig. 164) are a few examples of the popularity of the idiom outside the United States in the 1930s.

The amenities of these holiday destinations provided photo opportunities, and American manufacturers responded in the 1930s with a broader variety of picture-making devices. Simple, inexpensive cameras were developed for average tourists and their children to record their weekends and holidays. Flashbulbs, exposure meters, and color film became available, and streamlined design and simple directions made everyone a photographer. Even amateur filmmaking was becoming more popular: this decade saw the invention of the first motion picture camera with synchronized sound recording. The growing use of cameras by Americans was paralleled by the growing recognition of photography and film as arts.

In sum, despite the privations of the Depression, amusements multiplied for the majority of the population. Americans learned to expect affordable entertainment from national media (underwritten by advertising) as well as free activities and new or improved facilities from their towns and cities. Whether the fun came from an old sport like skating or a new medium like radio, the associated products gained "eye appeal" through streamlining. With its styling, the latest thing *looked* like the latest thing.

120. Designer unknown

COIN-OPERATED PHONOGRAPH:
PENNY PHONO
Designed c. 1939
Lacquered plywood, plastic, stainless steel, glass
108 x 55.9 x 45.7 cm
Produced by Cinematone Corporation,
Hollywood, California
The Montreal Museum of Fine Arts,
The Liliane and David M. Stewart Collection
D88.188.1

The automatic coin-operated phonograph or "jukebox" was born in the early twentieth century when a coin mechanism was added to a phonograph. Soon a machine was devised to allow a choice of multiple records to be played. By 1927, the Automatic Music Instrument Company created the world's first electrically amplified, multi-selection, coin-operated phonograph. With amplification, the jukebox could compete with a large orchestra.[1] For a nickel—or, in the case of this machine, for a penny—one could dance or simply listen to swing, ballads, jazz, or classical music, whatever was recorded on the period's 78 rpm records. In the 1930s jukeboxes brought music to increasing numbers of bars, restaurants, and diners, turning them into poor man's night clubs.

"Jook" is an African-American word meaning to dance, sometimes used with sexual connotations. The jook joint was a place for dancing and drinking, and the jukebox provided the music. Early jukeboxes were made of wood like early radios and phonographs and they looked like heavy furniture. But flashy cabinets were soon seen as selling points and design patents were filed for them from 1934 on. In 1937, Paul Fuller was first to introduce colored, illuminated plastic panels and brightly glowing tubes in his new, streamlined jukebox, the Wurlitzer model no. 24.[2] Even more streamlined was the jukebox by the John Gabel Manufacturing Company, Chicago, Illinois, called the *Gabel Kuro*, of 1940 (fig. 165), designed by the Milwaukee industrial designer Clifford Brooks Stevens.

Compared to its gaudy competitors of the late 1930s and beyond, the *Penny Phono* jukebox is a compact assertion of simplicity, symmetry, and streamlining. The three prominent horizontal fins rounding its front are echoed by the openings for speakers on top and the three stainless steel bands setting them off. At the same time the jukebox resembles a refrigerator such as Henry Dreyfuss's *Flatop* (fig. 111) in its flat top, curved corners, and clearly divided parts. With its strong horizontal banding and contrasting colors, it also looks architectural, and strikingly similar to the enameled steel entrance of Raymond Hood and J. André Fouilhoux's McGraw-Hill Building (fig. 166).[3] Yet its design is more sculptural, thanks to the pliability of plywood and fluidity of plastic. A plywood sheet was molded into a U-shape for the body, while plastic was molded for the pierced sides for the speakers above. This form would have been more difficult and expensive to achieve in sheet metal; it gives the *Penny Phono* plasticity and an apparent scale beyond its literal size.

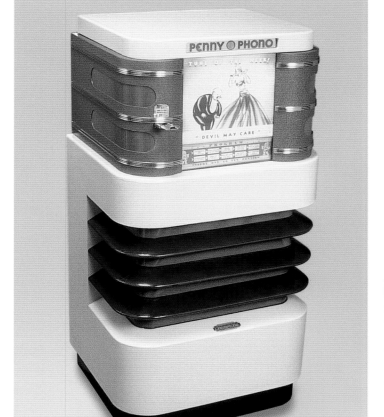

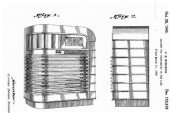

Fig. 165 Clifford Brooks Stevens, patent drawing for "Cabinet for Phonographs or the Like," detail.

Fig. 166 Raymond Hood and J. André Fouilhoux, entrance to McGraw-Hill Building, New York, 1931.

121. Designer unknown
PORTABLE RECORD PLAYER:
MODEL NO. CJM3
Designed c. 1935–45
Bakelite, steel, rubber
11.5 x 37.5 x 27.3 cm
Produced by Canadian General Electric
Company, Ltd., Toronto, Canada
B308

122. John B. Suomala
PORTABLE RECORD PLAYER
Designed c. 1939[4]
Bakelite, steel, rubber
12.5 x 32 x 21 cm
Produced by Radio Corporation
of America (RCA), Camden, New Jersey
B043

123. Designer unknown
PORTABLE RADIO/RECORD PLAYER
Designed c. 1935–45
Mahogany and oak veneer, Masonite,
aluminum, plastic, enameled steel, felt
31 x 43 x 40 cm
Produced by Stromberg-Carlson,
Rochester, New York
B383

To underline the modernity of these three portable record players, their manufacturers turned to streamlining. The playing arm, turntable, and case for the mechanism are united in a single teardrop shape in cat. 121 and 122, a shape made possible by the malleability of the plastic Bakelite. Both players are adorned with speed lines: they encircle the base of cat. 121 and emphasize the length of the arm in cat. 122.

In the combination radio and record player by Stromberg-Carlson (cat. 123), streamlining is achieved by the application of perforated aluminum banding for the speaker and station numbers. This banding wraps around the curved corner of the set at the left and ends on the front with a curve framing the radio dial. Also streamlined is the curved recessed lid with graduated banding which opens to reveal the turntable. Contrasting light and dark exterior veneers add to the dramatic impact of this model.

Cat. 121

Cat. 122

124. Designer unknown

RECORD RACK

Designed 1940–45

Bakelite, gold paint

17 x 33.5 x 27 cm

Produced by Radio Corporation of America (RCA), Camden, New Jersey

B624

Music mavens are usually torn between two impulses—to protect their discs or to have them right at hand, for easy selection and immediate acoustic gratification. Protection had its difficulties in the 1930s, when records could melt, bend out of shape, or break easily, as well as attract dust. Even kept in the boxes they were sold in, they were supposed to stand upright. The design of this rack sacrifices dust-proofing to style and convenience. Shaped like a dirigible hangar, the rack holds forty discs, ready to be plucked by the owner from

a gold-numbered slot. The records' glistening black circles would contrast with the brown Bakelite of the stand and the gold logo of the manufacturer, RCA Victor (also well known for its record and radio manufacture). The boldly simple design is streamlined with bands at its bottom and graduated supports, and the repeated slots for the records create a banded texture that conveys mechanical efficiency. Then as now, music lovers wanted to signal their cool by the look of their equipment, as well as its sound.

Whether the designer was inspired by a dirigible hanger is unknown, but dirigibles (or zeppelins) caught the popular imagination in the late 1920s and 1930s when they were considered viable means of passenger flight. The mast atop the Empire State Building was intended for mooring dirigibles, and one of Margaret Bourke-White's better-known photographs shows a dirigible emerging from its hangar (p. 14, right).

---

125. Clarence Karstadt

TABLE RADIO: MODEL NO. 6110, *SILVERTONE ROCKET*

Designed c. 1938[5]

Bakelite, plastic, fabric, rubber

16.5 x 30.7 x 16.5 cm

Produced by Chicago Molded Products Corporation for Sears, Roebuck and Company, Chicago, Illinois

B002

126. John R. Morgan

TABLE RADIO: MODEL NO. 132.807-2, *SILVERTONE AUTOMATIC STREAMLINER*

Designed c. 1940[6]

Bakelite, plastic, fabric

15.5 x 26.5 x 14.8 cm

Produced for Sears, Roebuck and Company, Chicago, Illinois

B619

127. Attributed to Raymond Loewy

TABLE RADIO: MODEL NO. 744

Designed c. 1954[7]

Bakelite, plastic, steel

18 x 28.5 x 20.3 cm

Produced by Emerson Electric Company, St. Louis, Missouri

B081

128. Designer unknown

TABLE RADIO: MODEL 67X

Designed c. 1935–40

Bakelite, plastic

20 x 34 x 20.5 cm

Produced by Motorola Inc., Chicago, Illinois

B621

129. Barton T. Setchell

TABLE RADIO: MODEL NO. 416

Designed c. 1946[8]

Bakelite, plastic

17.5 x 25.5 x 17 cm

Produced by Setchell-Carlson Inc., St. Paul, Minnesota

B588

130. Designer unknown

TABLE RADIO: MODEL NO. 62455

Designed c. 1937

Bakelite, plastic, fabric

18 x 29 x 17.3 cm

Produced by Airline Radio for Montgomery Ward, Chicago, Illinois

B659

These six table radios present lively, different, modern responses to the challenges of housing the mechanical parts of the wildly popular medium. Such designs were new in the mid-1930s and afterward. In the early 1920s radio was novel in middle-class homes and designs reflected the styles of the living rooms where they were played. Radios in *ersatz* Sheraton cabinets, neo-Gothic shrines, and so forth echoed the conservative tastes of most Americans and the relatively high cost of the equipment. But by 1930 manufacturing competition and technological innovation led to the introduction of table models at half the price of consoles. In 1933 the average radio cost $35, down from an average of $133 in 1929. This was the year that Harold Van Doren and John Gordon Rideout introduced the first plastic cabinet.[9] The Bakelite used for all six of these radios allowed their competitive pricing

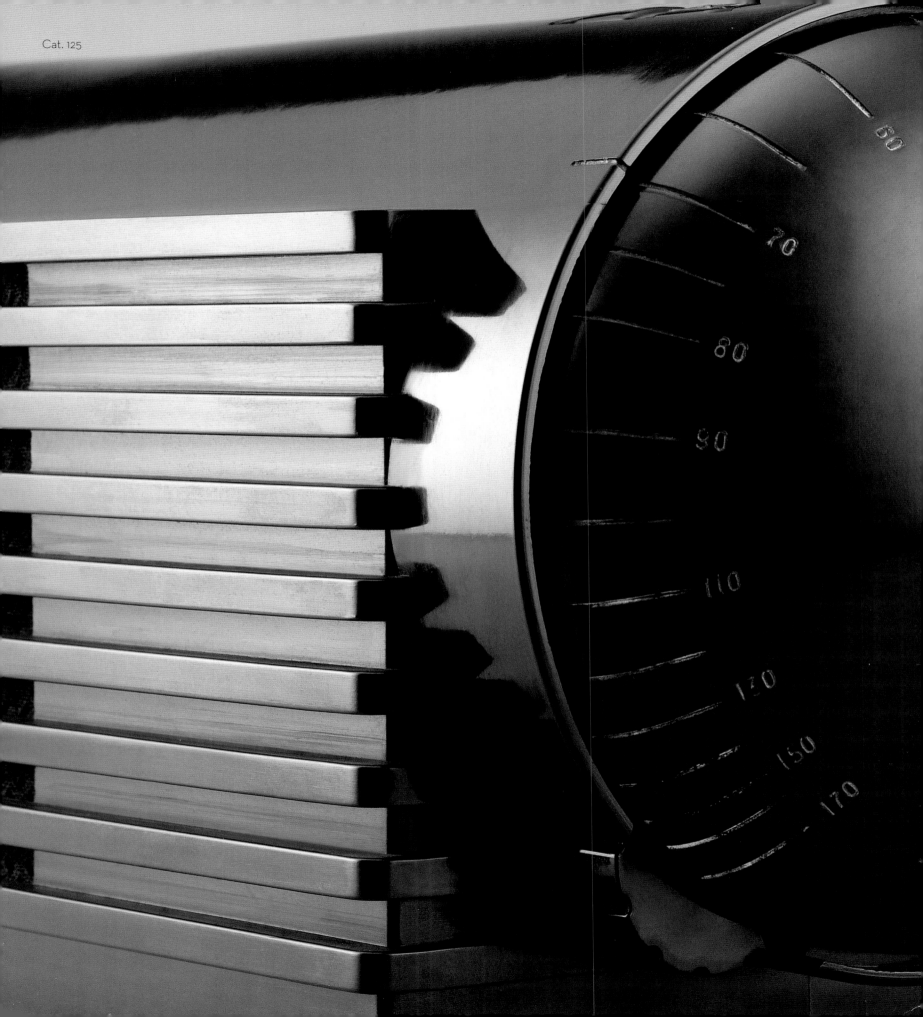

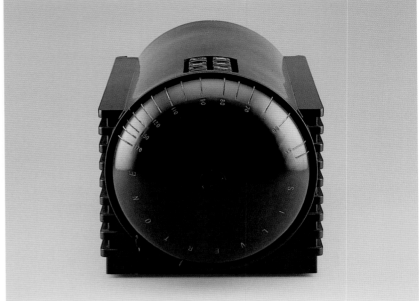

Cat. 125   Cat. 125

and fluid, even fanciful styling. Each answered the design question, was the ideal radio shape a box with streamlined fillips or another, more exciting form altogether?

The well-named *Silvertone Rocket* resembles a streamlined train engine, or a rocket in its carrier (cat. 125). Its rounded nose is the station dial, which covers one end of the radio, and the six push buttons on the top to set for special stations are flush with the surface. The speed of streamlining is also expressed in strong horizontal banding surrounding the cylindrical form. According to the 1939 Sears, Roebuck catalogue advertisement for the *Rocket* (fig. 167), this was the top of the *Silvertone* line. Available in black, ivory, or mottled walnut, it sold for $12.95. The *Rocket*, the ad claimed, was ideal for the bedroom, den, or small room and it was "as new as tomorrow . . . reflecting the architectural splendor of 1939's great World's Fair!"[10]

If the *Rocket* evokes broadcasts starring Buck Rogers and Captain Marvel, Raymond Loewy's radio for Emerson (cat. 127), resembles both a theater's proscenium arch and a rising sun. Behind this theatrical shape, the body of the radio has serrated control knobs on top, the one on the left for on/off and volume, the one on the right to dial the spectrum of stations. The sundial-like hand moves to the station selected. The body is black,

the face and dials are a rich green, and the sans-serif numbers and the letters spelling out "Emerson" offer brassy graphic contrasts.

The other table radios illustrated here are more conservative designs, but their boxiness is relieved by the rounded corners that Bakelite molding permitted and in fact encouraged. The plastic flowed more evenly into curved molds without sharp edges, and rounded forms were better able to survive shipping and use without chipping or cracking. These features of the coal-tar resin compound made it an ideal material for streamlining. The bulbous, big-shouldered shape of cat. 128 with its speedline-style speaker vents could not have been achieved cheaply in another material. The twin controls and station dial window raised from the top of cat. 129 could only have been made in a plastic.

Cat. 126 and 130, on the other hand, are replicas in Bakelite of more expensive radios made in veneered wood. Nonetheless, streamlining is evident in the parallel perforations of their speaker grilles, which fold down from the top over the front and contrast with the station dials. In cat. 126, the station numbers and dial form an extended C-shape that sweeps across the bottom with the model name, *Silvertone*, while the dial in cat. 130 resembles a telephone dial of the era, but with push buttons for the stations.

These six radios—all different in casings if not in technology—are but a sample of the design variety sparked by rival manufacturers seeking to diversify their markets. The *Silvertone Streamliner* (seen in the ad in fig. 167) cost $7.95 and, according to its 1938-39 advertising, "Approved by more than 200,000 purchasers!" By the end of the 1920s, 10 million American homes were said to have had radios.[11] By the end of the 1930s, most homes doubtless had more than one.

Fig. 167. *Silvertone* radios, from Sears, Roebuck and Co. catalogue, Fall/Winter 1938-39, p. 856.

Cat. 126

Cat. 127

55·60·70·80·100·120·140·160

Cat. 128

Cat. 129

Cat. 130

Cat. 131

131. Joseph Johnson
William Zaiser
ACCORDION
Designed c. 1938[12]
Plastic, chromium-plated steel, steel mesh,
aluminum, leatherette, rubber, fabric
20.5 x 47 x 35.5 cm (closed)
Produced by the Rudolph Wurlitzer Company,
Cincinnati, Ohio
B152

Live music was everywhere in the early 1930s, and
in many families at least one member played an
instrument. The accordion, an organ-like, hand-held
device, entertained at both public and private
gatherings. To today's eyes (and ears), it may
conjure up rural festivities in nineteenth-century
Europe. But in the late 1930s, it defended its wide
American popularity against radios and record
players with a face lift: it went streamlined, lost
weight, and cut its price.[13]

The earliest accordions (accordo is the Italian
word for chord) date from the first quarter of the
nineteenth century, and manufacturers flourished,
especially in Germany. Among them was Rudolph
Wurlitzer, whose family had made and sold musical
instruments since the seventeenth century. In 1853,
he immigrated to the United States, and three years
later, he founded the Rudolph Wurlitzer Company.[14]
Initially importing musical instruments from his
family in Germany, Wurlitzer began to produce
pianos in 1880, which led to his first coin-operated
electric piano in 1896, and then to organs for
theaters and movie houses in the days before
talking pictures.

This accordion was produced at the height
of the Wurlitzer empire in American music. Its
streamlined form was illustrated alongside an
old-fashioned type in an article of 1940 reviewing
design progress (fig. 168).[15] The simple captions
"Before" and "After" imply that the reader can easily
identify the best design. The earlier rectilinear

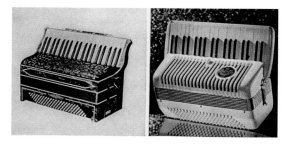

Fig. 168 Before and after views of accordion design,
from *The Architectural Forum*, October 1940.

model—literally a squeeze box—has given way
to the sensuous curves of streamlining. Horizontal
banding wraps around all sides, and additional
grooving unfurls across the top. Circular
perforations on the bottom allow air to be taken
in and expelled as the instrument is manipulated.
Ivory-colored plastic imitates the ivory of traditional
accordions. As a cosmetic touch of modernity,
the Wurlitzer monogram is placed off-center
in a disk recessed in the grooving.

132. John Vassos
HARMONICA: *ECHO ELITE*
Designed c. 1939[16]
Chromium-plated and enameled steel,
painted wood, fabric
2.7 x 19.5 x 6 cm
Produced by Hohner, New York, New York,
and Trossingen, Germany
B165

In this instance streamlining turns the harmonica—
that down-home mouth organ and children's toy—
into an elegant instrument. Rounded edges and
prominent ribbed banding circling the length of the
object give it the panache of a costly cigar case.
Additional banding accents the twenty-four blow
holes that produce music. Contrasting bright red
enamel and chromium add zest to this delightful
musical instrument, which has C and G impressed
on each side to indicate keys. The block capitals
spelling "Hohner" are cut out of the center of the
broad ribbed banding, like "Electrolux" on the
celebrated vacuum cleaner (cat. 34). Stamped out
of metal with the same die cut, the letters are
generated economically in both cases, and they remain
flush with the smooth surface of the instruments.

Although designed by an American, the
versatile John Vassos, the harmonica was made
in Germany, as the markings clearly indicate.[17]
This witnesses the prestige of Hohner, the world
leader in harmonica production until imports to the
United States were halted during World War II.[18]
Harmonica fans consider the 1920s and the 1930s
their golden age, when harmonica marching bands
were a fad, and blues, country, jug band, and jazz
recordings all included harmonica playing.[19] The
styling of the *Echo Elite* suggests it can go on
parade, or make an amateur musician look like
a professional.

133. Harold L. Van Doren
John Gordon Rideout
SCOOTER: *SKIPPY-RACER*

Designed c. 1933[20]
Painted steel, painted wood, rubber
82 x 108.5 x 26.8 cm
Produced by The American National Company,
Toledo, Ohio
B363

In the 1930s The American National Company was the largest manufacturer of children's vehicles in the world. No wonder: as their design chief, Harold Van Doren, remarked, "Children like anything that enables them to imitate their elders."[21] And what the company's toys successfully imitated were the streamlined planes, trains, and automobiles of modish America. Like father, like son, each consumer loved the contemporary look of teardrop-shaped mud-guards shielding their wheels,

continuous windblown lines (as in this scooter's front profile), and bright colors. The *Skippy-Racer* has a fire-engine-red body with white outlines, and white wheels with red outlines. In the event it needed parking, a shaped kickstand would hold it stationary without marring its aerodynamic silhouette. This snazzy scooter was highlighted in an article of 1940[22] that favorably contrasted current streamlined designs with their awkward predecessors of the early 1930s. The article itself demonstrated the strong sense of optimism and progress that the style summed up at the end of the decade.

A similarly streamlined tricycle by Van Doren and Rideout won praise from a contemporary "because the younger generation expects the latest expression of modernity in its playthings."[23] The writer noted that the design also reduced the number of stampings to a minimum, hence permitting a lower cost.

During their four-year partnership, from 1931 to 1935, Van Doren and Rideout also designed a sled and a coaster wagon for The American National Company,[24] both of which exemplify the appeal of aerodynamic styling for speed demons, no matter how small.

134. Harold L. Van Doren
John G. Rideout
SLED: *SKIPPY SNO-PLANE*

Designed c. 1933[25]
Plywood, enameled and chromium-plated steel, plastic
18.5 x 134 x 64 cm
Produced by The American National Company, Toledo, Ohio
B524

The most famous child's sled may have been "Rosebud," but Citizen Kane's amusement was Victorian compared to American National's. "Children Love Streamlining," the sled's designer Harold Van Doren announced with his illustration of the *Skippy Sno-Plane* in his 1940 text *Industrial Design*.[26]

A U-shaped tubular steel frame surrounds the sled's elongated teardrop body, flanked on each side by two elongated members, which serve as speed lines while they lighten the body weight. The curved fins for steering and the graceful runners echo the streamlined form—in this case for actual as well as symbolic speed. Stenciled in red on top is the sled's name, together with seven arrows that resemble airport landing strip guidelines. The *Sno-Plane* was ready for takeoff!

Van Doren and Rideout's design offered more than style. The utility patent application cited the sled's efficient steering mechanism and its structural innovations: it was "composed of a relatively few simple parts so designed and connected together as to provide a light, inexpensive and durable sled construction."[27]

Cat. 133

135. John R. Morgan and John S. Coldwell
ROLLER SKATES: *FLYAWAY STREAMLINED*
Designed c. 1935[28]
Chromium-plated and enameled steel, steel
9 x 27.5 x 8.5 cm (each)
Produced by Advance Manufacturing Company,
Milwaukee, Wisconsin
B174

The name of these roller skates—*Flyaway
Streamlined*—is somewhat wishful for a pair of
skates with four wheels placed wagon-style, in pairs
front and back. They are neither as fast nor as
maneuverable as ice skates, and this pair predates
by more than half a century the in-line skates of the
1990s. But the wheeled toys, which strapped onto

shoes, had satisfied skaters since the eighteenth
century who wanted the fun of ice-skating in warm
weather. The documented inventor of roller skates
was John Joseph Merlin, a Belgian who was a well-
known maker of musical instruments and
mechanical inventions.[29] In the 1930s his roller-
skating was a craze, especially for teenagers at
roller rinks and youths in roller derbies. The shiny,
heavy, clanking metal skates were inexpensive to
buy and cheap to rent; everyone could learn to
roller-skate.

The *Flyaway* model is streamlined to symbolize
the speed it assured the skater. The striking graphic
design of the accompanying cardboard box (fig. 170)
illustrates this with the name *Flyaway* in stylized
script within the outline of an airplane with speed

lines and a propeller. The patent drawing (fig. 169)
shows the skates in plan and elevation. In profile,
the skates resemble a racing car, but they also
evoke flight. A trio of arrows suggesting guidelines
for takeoff is stamped on the footrest. The fin at the
back of the heel rest also looks aeronautical, though
its purpose is not speed but to anchor the leather
strap. The teardrop shapes that grip the skater's
shoes and the chromium plating further the
associations with fast vehicles.

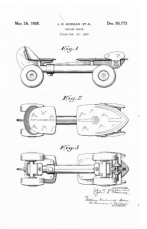

Fig. 169 John R. Morgan
and John S. Coldwell, patent
drawing for "Roller Skate."

Fig. 170 Box for *Flyaway Streamlined* roller skates.

136. Designer unknown

TOY TRAIN ENGINE: *MERCURY FLYER*

Designed c. 1938

Painted steel

21.5 x 61.5 x 16.7 cm

Manufacturer unknown

B195

Although this streamlined pull-toy train engine has "Mercury" painted on its side, a famous streamliner designed by Henry Dreyfuss in 1935, the toy form is closer to what was then the world's largest steam locomotive, Raymond Loewy's celebrated S-1 design

of 1937 for the Pennsylvania Railroad (fig. 25). Both works are streamlined in the sleek bullet-like form of the engine and the horizontal banding below. Loewy's engine had to be streamlined: the Railroad wanted to run a 1,200-ton train at 100 miles per hour and keep to that speed on level track.[30] The designer described his efforts to assure aerodynamic efficiency and control the steam: "In New York we started a scale clay model of a new steam locomotive. I had a hunch that a flat plane placed forward atop the locomotive immediately behind the smokestack and flush with it, might help. By giving this plane a slightly streamlined

configuration, like an airplane wing, it would create at high speed a depression over the engine and lift the smoke over the cab, improving forward vision on the track."[31]

The torpedo-like engine powered the S-1, and this luxurious design became synonymous with sophisticated travel. The engine itself was a star attraction at the 1939 New York World's Fair, speeding nowhere on a treadmill. As for the toy, its designer ceded to a youngster's desire to carry things in the train: the cab area is open, whereas Loewy's design presents uninterrupted air-smoothed cowling.

Toy trains and model railroads were marketed in the 1930s as educational tools, teaching Junior how to get ahead. An advertisement for Lionel Trains asked in 1932: "Do you want your son to be keen-witted, quick-thinking, resourceful. . . ? Your boy will not only have the fun of building his railroad and operating it; he will have the opportunity to tackle actual problems of railroad operation that give him training in both electricity and mechanics."[32] This train, therefore, was not a mere plaything, but a step toward an electrified model and thence to a miniature railroad set. Touted as "true-to-life to the last detail," such trains were necessarily almost as streamlined as real locomotives.

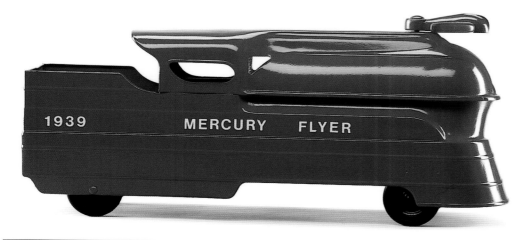

137. Designer unknown

TOY TROLLEY CAR: *STREAMLINE RAILWAY*

Designed 1935–40

Painted tin, rubber

11 x 44.8 x 10 cm

Produced by Wolverine Supply & Mfg. Co., Pittsburgh, Pennsylvania

The Liliane and David M. Stewart Collection

SHLSL 2004.5

American streetcars or trolleys were also streamlined in the 1930s, as reflected in this toy "Streamline Railway" car painted with "No. 129" on the front and "STOP" on the rear. A bell sounds when it is moved forward by hand.[33]

The form, with a strongly flared front and rear, follows that of streamlined train engines. Three bold horizontal speed lines are painted on the sides at the bottom, with accents in red and black at the top. Through the painted windows passengers are depicted enjoying the view, reading, or chatting.

The toy reminds us that most American cities had effective and widely used rail transit systems in the 1930s. The streetcar's nostalgic charm is heightened by hindsight, for the war ended the use of tin in toys as well as the vitality of public transport by trolley car.

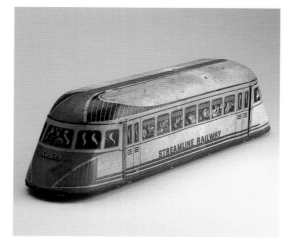

138. Designer unknown

TOY CAR: *SCARAB*

Designed c. 1935
Chromium-plated and enameled steel, rubber
9.5 x 25.7 x 12 cm
Produced by the Buddy L Toy Company,
East Moline, Illinois[34]
B273

That streamlined cars could be more efficient and faster as well as stylish was grasped by inventive designers such as Norman Bel Geddes, Buckminster Fuller, and William B. Stout. This toy pays homage to Stout's *Scarab*, designed in 1935 (fig. 171), a car ahead of its time. That rear-drive experiment had a snub nose allowing the driver maximum visibility, forecasting the Volkswagen *Beetle*, and an aluminum body of unitary construction. Because it lacked running boards, unlike other 1930s automobiles, as well as a prop shaft, its interior had unprecedented space. In this and its movable seats (only the driver's was fixed), it foretold the minivans of the 1980s. The *Scarab* never saw mass production, but it is estimated that nine were made.

Nevertheless, its mark on the public is evidenced in this toy car. On its side is its name, the manufacturer's logo, and a scarab logo, a tribute from the toymakers to William Stout. Like the full-size *Scarab*, the toy has ten windows and a unitary body of sheet metal. Wind the key on its side and it would zip away, its low body meeting little wind resistance.

Fig. 171 William B. Stout, *Scarab* automobile, 1935. From Cheney and Cheney, *Art and the Machine*, 1936.

139. Glenn W. Periman

Toy Racing Car: Gad-Jet CO_2

Designed c. 1948[35]

Enameled aluminum, aluminum, rubber

4 x 19 x 7 cm

Produced by Penco Products,
Los Angeles, California

B200

The bottom of this visionary toy racing car was originally enameled blue and the top green, perhaps associating it with the sky and open fields. It has no motor and was propelled by a CO_2 cartridge, and, like the *Scarab* car (cat. 138), it embodied a streamlined dream of the future. Although it resembled the Batmobile of the comic strip, it was probably inspired by an actual racing car, such as John R. Cobb's sleek design of 1939, reproduced in Walter Dorwin Teague's *Design This*

Day. Reaching 368 miles per hour, Cobb's car was the fastest in the world at that date. A similar racer is seen in fig. 172. As the age of jet travel was dawning in the late 1940s, the fantasy of speed and power—on land and in the air—continued to appeal to both children and adults. What would the fastest vehicles look like? In this toy and Cobb's design, the wheels are the highest element of the ground-hugging body, apart from the tail fin. The invisible driver is presumably one with the engine, as in a Futurist poem.

Fig. 172 "A Giant Racer Making A World's Record," Bonneville Salt Flats, near Great Salt Lake, Utah, postcard, c. 1940. Washington, D.C., Library of Congress, Elizabeth Dixon Hanks Collection.

Cat. 140

140. Designer unknown
Airplane Kit: Model No. GPL-5024, *Tether Streamliner*
Designed c. 1947[36]
Balsam wood, steel, plastic, paper, cardboard
Box: 4 x 62 x 16.5 cm
Airplane: 23.5 x 66.5 x 64 cm
Produced by Cleveland Model & Supply Company,
Cleveland, Ohio
B275

Since airplanes and their toy imitations require streamlining in order to fly, one wonders if the popularity of building airplane models—which began in the 1920s—helped spread the appetite for aeronautical design in the following decades. In any case, in the 1940s model planes capitalized on the thrill of flying, when it was becoming possible for middle-class travelers; on headline-making advances in jet technology, which built on wartime achievements; and on the U.S. government's encouragement of the use of model planes for aircraft spotting and identification during World War II.

This streamlined toy appears to be loosely modeled on the Lockheed P-38J *Lightning* (fig. 174), a fighter plane famous for having been used to shoot down the Japanese Commander-in-Chief, Admiral Yamamoto, in 1943. The twin-boom fuselage of the turbocharged plane is simplified to a pair of rods, but the model retains the fighter's tricycle-style undercarriage, and the plane's overall contours are more streamlined that those of the original. The kit for the model included wing de-icers and a gas-powered motor; it is shown unassembled in fig. 173 and without the motor; and also assembled for exhibition, following the original directions. The *Tether Streamliner*'s box announced that it is "Flight-Engineered" and part of an "Industrial Aviation Training Kit." All this assures the consumer of the professional education that building the model will impart. The rows of stars on the box summon up America's pride in its ace pilots and aviation records: the "Streamliner," originally a term for the trains of the early 1930s, had obviously bridged the decades with its looks and nationalist associations.

Fig. 173 *Tether Streamliner* airplane kit, unassembled.

Cat. 140

Fig. 174 Lockheed P-38J *Lightning* fighter plane. c. 1940.

141. Walter Dorwin Teague
Camera: *Bantam*
Designed c. 1933[37]
Bakelite, enameled steel, glass
7 x 12 x 3.3 cm
Produced by Eastman Kodak Company,
Rochester, New York
B074

142. Walter Dorwin Teague
Camera: *Bullet*
Designed c. 1937[38]
Bakelite, enameled steel, glass
7 x 12 x 5 cm
Produced by Eastman Kodak Company,
Rochester, New York
B116

143. Lew W. Lessler
Camera: *Flash Champion*
Designed 1939[39]
Aluminum, plastic, glass, leather
9.8 x 13.5 x 5.5 cm
Produced by Ansco, Binghamton, New York
B236

From the *Box Brownie* of 1900, sold for a dollar, to the *Instamatic* of the 1960s and the disposable cameras of today, Eastman Kodak revolutionized photography by inventing and selling economical cameras. These three products are not in that class. They witness the interest of manufacturers in reaching luxury markets as the recovery progressed from the middle of the 1930s. Such companies as Kodak and Ansco grasped that some camera buffs would pay more for the latest technology and style.

The *Bantam* cost four times more than the average amateur camera of the 1930s. It targeted the ambitious affluent hobbyist with its technological features and casing, the latter by the celebrity designer Walter Dorwin Teague, who was hired by Kodak in 1927 and retained for thirty years. As a range finder camera, the *Bantam* let one focus more easily than with a single-lens reflex model and see through the viewfinder exactly what would appear in the photograph. Its f/8 lens and ultra-rapid, machine-tooled shutter assured performance under a wide range of conditions; and while it had the convenience of roll film, its film was wider than usual, at 40 mm. All this came in a compact, die-cast aluminum body set off by a black enamel finish.

Yet the camera was small enough to be termed a "miniature"—it could be comfortably carried in a field case with a strap over the shoulder.[40]

Teague's elegant design and jewel-like detailing left no doubt that this was a deluxe precision tool. The parallel lines ringing the body evoke Saville Row pinstripes as well as speed lines, and the rounded edges of all the parts and the glistening surfaces attract both the hand and eye. This machine was for camera snobs.

Of simpler but still stylish form, Teague's *Bullet* is also sheathed in horizontal bands—a far cry from the ornament of earlier, more cubic cameras. These designs evidence Kodak's awareness of the importance of packaging. The company did not market new styling alone as justification for high prices, but used it to symbolize the improved technology of these cameras. This version of the *Bullet* camera was produced from 1937 to 1942.

The *Flash Champion* manufactured by Ansco marks another innovation in camera technology of the thirties—the flash bulb. Though soon notorious as a tabloid paparazzo's aide, it made indoor photography with existing light possible for amateurs (fig. 175). Set in this small and svelte camera, the attachment also looked ultra-modern. According to the utility patent specifications, the Ansco camera was "an improved camera, having folding or telescoping parts wherein the probability of light leakage is reduced to a minimum." Its curved streamlined body is echoed by a conforming curved section in front, and both are grooved with horizontal lines. This texture makes the camera easier to grip and attractive as well, set off by the silvery aluminum edgings that mark its working parts.

Cat. 141

Cat. 142

Cat. 143

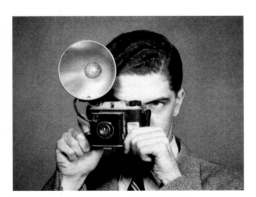

Fig. 175 Ansco *Flash Champion* in use, from manufacturer's User Guide.

144. Designer unknown

BULK FILM WINDER: *DAYLIGHT*

Designed c. 1950

Bakelite, steel

6 x 13 x 10.5 cm

Produced by Lloyd's Manufacturing Company, Houtzdale, Pennsylvania

B327

In the days before Japanese companies began price wars on film and cameras with powerful Eastman Kodak, photographers had few ways to save money on supplies. This bulk film winder was one. It allowed the user to buy 35mm film in 100-foot rolls and store it, thus saving on cost. The instruction brochure vowed you would be able to "shoot three times as much film in your 35mm camera as you are now, but at the same price." There was nothing at all complicated about reloading your own cassettes and cutting off the wanted amount of film, according to the instructions: "The very first 100 foot roll you use will more than pay for the equipment."[41] A cut-away view in the User Guide (fig. 176) shows how the cassette, loader, and door fit together.

The winder is a unified streamlined design with a stepped circular reel holding the film roll within, rounded corners, and a winding knob of circular shape. In contrasting terra cotta and brown Bakelite, with bright steel detail, this compact form fulfills its advertising: it looks efficient, economical, and easy to use. There is nothing extraneous here, illustrating how functional streamlining could become Good Design in the 1950s.

Fig. 176 Cut-away view showing interior of film winder, from manufacturer's User Guide.

145. Philmore F. Sperry

FILM PROJECTOR MODEL No. 48

Designed c. 1939[42]
Painted steel, aluminum, plastic
Projector with reels: 49 x 28 x 23.5 cm
Produced by Revere Camera Company,
Chicago, Illinois
B489

146. Designer unknown

FILM PROJECTOR:
MODEL No. P63, *APOLLO*

Designed c. 1935–45
Aluminum, steel, rubber
39 x 33.5 x 12.5 cm.
Produced by Excel Movie Products Inc.,
Chicago, Illinois
The Liliane and David M. Stewart Collection
SHLSL 2003.18

These 16mm film projectors reflect the growing appetite for home movies and motion-picture presentations in schools and sales meetings at the end of the 1930s. Hollywood was one of the few industries to boom during the Depression, and it fed the hunger for moving images, which both camera and film producers capitalized on. They needed to shield their complex projection machinery in smooth, safe cowlings and allow transport of their projectors in easy-to-carry cases. The simplicity of these containers implied that the temperamental equipment was simple to use, while their streamlined designs conjured up the ideal of movies as the communications medium of tomorrow.

On the *Apollo* projector, the arms for the film reels are united in a bold crescent that hangs from an arc extended from the tower-like body of the machine. The body's rounded top is animated with a trio of arching vents, while a circle of repeated perforated arrows vents the motor at the extended base. The glistening aluminum of the whole curvilinear composition completes the associations of the projector's name, for Apollo was the ancients' sun god and the leader of the Muses. (They may be celebrated through cinema, this model encourages us to imagine.)

By contrast, Philmore Sperry's projector is more rectilinear, but it is streamlined in the speed lines that decorate all of its parts, including its S-curved support, dark plastic base, and even its carrying case. Its arms resemble propeller or fan blades, suggesting the speed and rotary mechanics of cinema projection. Film reels can be stored in a compartment in the base, making the equipment a compact, portable entertainment center. The first sheet of its patent drawing (fig. 177) shows the projector in its two profiles.

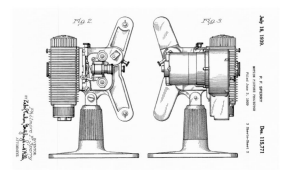

Fig. 177 Philmore F. Sperry, patent drawing for "Motion Picture Projector."

Cat. 145

Cat. 147

Cat. 148

147. Designer unknown
SLIDE PROJECTOR
Designed c. 1935–40
Aluminum, enameled
and chromium-plated steel, glass, rubber
17 x 35.5 x 28.5 cm
Produced by Emde Products,
Los Angeles, California
B517

148. Theodore G. Clement
SLIDE PROJECTOR:
MODEL NO. 1A, *KODASLIDE*
Designed c. 1947[43]
Plastic, tin, aluminum, glass, rubber
13.5 x 29 x 17.5 cm
Produced by Eastman Kodak Company,
Rochester, New York
B502

149. Theodore G. Clement[44]
TABLE VIEWER: *KODASLIDE*
Designed c. 1950
Bakelite, plastic, steel, brass, paint, rubber
31.5 x 17 x 17.5 cm
Produced by Eastman Kodak Company,
Rochester, New York
B482

In promoting its *Kodachrome* color film, Eastman
Kodak produced a variety of devices for viewing
the slides it developed. This inexpensive "daylight"
viewer was intended for use in homes, stores, and
offices. It was designed by Theodore G. Clement,
an Eastman employee, in collaboration with
the Kodak Styling Division and Camera Works
engineering department. The viewing screen, on
which *Kodachrome* slides are magnified four times,
"is slightly hooded with a simple frame to minimize
interference with the projected image," according to
a 1951 book touting recent industrial designs.[45] The
tapering form of Bakelite is streamlined through its
multiple curved parts, and five horizontal "gold-
filled" grooves beneath the screen extend around
the sides in the speed lines typical of the style.

Slide projectors have given popular entertainment
and instruction to Americans from the late
nineteenth century on: they made "magic lantern
shows" possible and used painted glass and, later,
photographic glass plates, a light source, and a lens
to magnify the projected image. These projectors
are simply smaller, streamlined versions of the big,
boxy apparatus of yesteryear. They project the
35mm color slides that Eastman Kodak developed
and has been marketing heavily to amateur
photographers since the 1930s. Though fed with
one slide at a time, such projectors allowed the
slide presentation to enter living rooms, classrooms,
and boardrooms, with a ubiquity that has only
recently been threatened by digital photography
and PowerPoint projection technology.

The forward cant of the handle on the Emde
projector and its continuation of the body's curve
announce this is a streamlined portable device.

The cylindrical form with thrusting lens resembles
a train engine with a large headlight: all this conveys
brilliance and modernity, a transformation of the
modest 35mm slide.

The Kodak projector reflects directions in
postwar technology and design. It is smaller overall
than the Emde item and boxier, although its
contours are curved and the speed lines on each
side imply it can be operated quickly and easily.
In these elements it reveals the continuing hold
of streamlining on popular imagination.

150. John R. Morgan

OUTBOARD MOTOR:
MODEL NO. MB, *WATERWITCH*

Designed c. 1937[46]
Aluminum, steel, brass, rubber
93.5 x 40.5 x 55.5 cm
Produced for Sears, Roebuck and Company,
Chicago, Illinois
B035

151. Designer unknown

OUTBOARD MOTOR:
MODEL NO. WD-4S, *WIZARD*

Designed c. 1940–45
Steel, aluminum, rubber, cast iron, paint
102.5 x 47 x 29 cm
Produced by the Kiekhaefer Corporation
for Western Auto Supply Company,
Cedarburg, Wisconsin
B017

An outboard motor does not have to be streamlined to move a boat—the horsepower beneath the cowling does that. But streamlining, as with so many products, helps sales. John Morgan's *Waterwitch* for Sears, Roebuck is a lightweight, silvery, three-quarter horsepower machine with paired teardrop fuel tanks flanking its rounded body, a structure particularly evident in the patent drawing (fig. 178). The motor's design resembles a cross between a bird and a hydroplane: it says flight. According to its first listing in the Sears, Roebuck and Company catalogue, the *Waterwitch* sold for $39.95 and was a "brand new streamlined design [which] reduces wind and water resistance."[47]

The *Wizard* WD-4S, on the other hand, suggests power as well as speed through its heavy yet sweeping motor casing. This postwar outboard offers many times the horsepower of its elegant older rival, and thus it can pull heavier, more comfortable boats or, with light vessels, get to the fish faster. Technical advances in outboard motors, according to an *Industrial Design* article of 1957, "take a good share of the credit for the boating boom. As the noisy put-put, the stifling exhaust and the stubborn rope starter became memories, the less mechanically inclined sailors—or any member of the family—can take to the water with more confidence and less expectation of fatigue."[48]

Yet styling mattered. "Though motors are being made to look like everything from juke-boxes to space helmets, design is making them the consumer's, not the mechanic's, instrument and is giving them distinct brand identity for the first time." The pair of wings like those on the sandals of Mercury, speedy messenger of the Greek gods, painted on the *Wizard*'s side reflect the company's attempt to offset the relatively leaden design of its lower cowling.

Cat. 150

Cat. 151

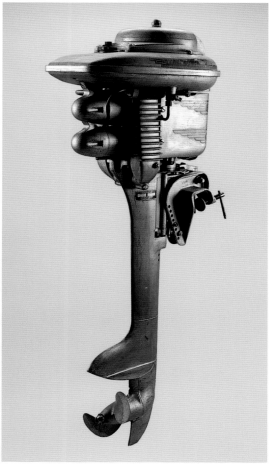

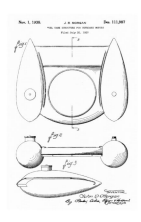

Fig. 178 John R. Morgan, patent drawing for "Fuel Tank Structure for Outboard Motors."

Cat. 150

152. Henry Dreyfuss
TRAIN LIGHT FIXTURE
Designed c. 1938
Aluminum, brass, glass
24.8 x 12.7 x 7.5 cm
Produced by Luminator, Inc., Chicago, Illinois
The Liliane and David M. Stewart Collection
SLSLH 2002.28

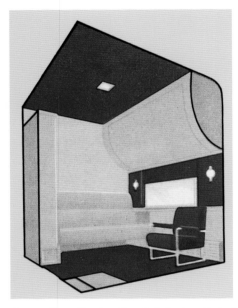

Fig. 179 Henry Dreyfuss, *Twentieth Century Limited* bedroom compartment showing train light fixtures flanking the window, from Luminator, Inc. brochure, c. 1938. Henry Dreyfuss Collection, Cooper-Hewitt, National Design Museum, Smithsonian Institution, New York.

This lamp was designed by Dreyfuss for his *Twentieth Century Limited* train, perhaps the most famous of all the streamliners of the 1930s (see fig. 26). The train ride—sixteen hours between New York and Chicago—was characterized as a "meteoric flight down shining steel rails into sunlit and starlit space realizing to the full that magical sensation of skimming the earth with no fear. . . ."[49] Dreyfuss designed not only the engine but all interiors, including details down to menus, dinner services, and glassware. He supervised the design of the lighting throughout on behalf of the New York Central Railroad, in consultation with the lighting manufacturer, Luminator, Inc., and the Design Division of the Pullman Company. According to a Luminator brochure on the design process, full-scale models were made for all lighting. Cylinder-shaped geometric forms were designed for many purposes where both general and glare-free focused lighting were used. Here the cylinder passes through a half-sphere with a formed lens for directed lighting. The design was used in the bedroom compartment, flanking the window (fig. 179). The fixture's geometric simplicity, smooth surfaces—embellished only with symmetrically placed fluted bands of speed lines—and contrasts of metallic finish embody Dreyfuss's brand of stylish functionalism. New York Central's promotions called the train design "the ultimate in conservative modernism."[50] This artful phrase suggests the range

of styling possible within streamlining. In public, heavily used spaces such as railroad cars, the style was applied reticently to the unified setting, with allusions like the banding that could seem both classicizing and modern. Objects for private self-expression and enjoyment, on the other hand, such as toys and radios, were exuberantly shaped, since manufacturers could dare to experiment given the low unit prices and need for rapid styling changes.

153. Designer unknown
KNIFE AND FORK FROM
AMERICAN AIRLINES DC-3 FLAGSHIP
Designed c. 1936
Silver plate
Length of knife: 20.5 cm; length of fork: 17 cm
Produced by International Silver Company, Meriden, Connecticut
The Liliane and David M. Stewart Collection
SHLSL 2004.7

The profile of the American Airlines Flagship DC-3 is impressed on both the top and bottom sides of this knife and fork—two of the utensils from a place setting used on one of the most famous of the DC-3 planes. The streamlined outline of the aircraft body fits into the overall design for the handle. Apart

from the sleek lines of the plane's outline, the knife and fork follow a traditional flatware silver form.

Custom-designed cutlery and dinner services were often commissioned for streamlined airplanes, trains, and ships, as signs of their luxury. For

example, Henry Dreyfuss designed dinnerware, glasses, and flatware for the *Twentieth Century Limited*. The American Airlines DC-3 presumably used this flatware beginning with its introduction of its nonstop New York-to-Chicago service in 1936.

154. Designer unknown
AUTOMOBILE PARKING LIGHTS:
MODEL NO. 55, *STREAMLINER*
Designed c. 1950
Glass, chromium-plated steel
5.5 x 6.2 x 3.5 cm (each)
Produced by Electroline, Cleveland, Ohio
B172

155. Designer unknown
AUTOMOBILE CLEARANCE LAMPS:
MODEL NO. 410, *STREAMLINER*
Designed c. 1940
Chromium-plated steel, glass, rubber
7 x 20.5 x 7 cm (each)
Produced by Do-Ray Lamp Company,
Chicago, Illinois
 B189

Automobiles in the 1940s and 1950s were often streamlined both in their overall forms and in details. The details here are lighting devices that must be functional and beautiful at the same time; both employ the word "streamliner" in their brand names (fig. 180), and both are streamlined in their sleek, elongated forms, incorporating chromium-plated steel with colored glass. The parking lights are rounded ovals with lights at each end, suggestive of bullets, while the clearance lamps are dramatic sculptural teardrops, designed to allow easy judgment of their vehicle's distance from hazards such as low underpasses and high curbs.

Both accessories allowed drivers to update and upgrade their cars with a modest investment. They appear in this chapter, like the preceding train light and the posters following, because they conjure up the pleasures of travel and the aesthetic satisfactions of beautifully conceived accessories. These devices were the jewelry of automobiles, and their buyers could congratulate themselves on improving their vehicles in both appearance and function.

Cat. 154

Cat. 155

Fig. 180 Box for Do-Ray *Streamliner* clearance lamp.

156. John Vassos

TURNSTILE

Designed c. 1932
Iron, enameled and chromium-plated steel
96.5 x 72.4 x 61 cm
Produced by Perey Turnstiles Company,
Stamford, Connecticut
Montreal Museum of Fine Arts,
The Liliane and David M. Stewart Collection,
gift of David T. Owsley
D91.330.1

The turnstile may be most closely associated with stadium, cinema, and subway entrances, but this example was originally one of four in the Brooklyn Museum lobby, installed there in 1932 to control access and ticket payment. The lobby remodeling was designed by William Lescaze.[51] The following year the same model regulated entry to the Chicago World's Fair. In 1934 an article in *Fortune* on the economic benefits of new designs claimed that this conception by John Vassos had lowered the cost of the Perey product and increased sales by 25 percent.[52] Streamlining appears in the turnstile's rounded corners, its grooved, chromium-plated top, and the horizontal chromium bands that encircle its body. In the smooth green-enameled post is a window with a digital counter and a coin-catch drawer: the complex mechanics

for this and for the three-armed, rotating entry control remain safely hidden.

The founder of Perey Turnstiles, John Perey, and Conrad Trubenbach are credited with developing the three-armed, side-mounted mechanism around 1928 that is still used today. Perey was also prescient in hiring John Vassos to design this 1932 model: he was then best known for his set designs for Billy Rose's Broadway extravaganzas and his book illustrations, where his futuristic simplifications were first seen (fig. 181). The play in this illustration for the Vassos book, *Ultimo*[53] (1930), between curves and repeated horizontal lines appears distantly, in functional form, in his no-nonsense turnstile. His shiny design makes public traffic control look easy and efficient, rather than oppressive.

Fig. 181 John Vassos, "Caught in the ice . . .," from *Ultimo*, 1930.

A FLIGHT INTO THE FUTURE

The strange world depicted in this illustration likely doesn't look half as fantastic to you as our world today would look to residents on earth 100 years ago.

Many new products are in the offing. The versatile alloys—aluminum and magnesium—possessing lightness combined with great strength, will play an important part in these new developments. Bohn engineers would like to discuss with you the many advantages of these light metals in relation to the products you make.

BOHN ALUMINUM AND BRASS CORPORATION
GENERAL OFFICES—LAFAYETTE BLDG. — DETROIT 26, MICH.

Designers and Fabricators—ALUMINUM • MAGNESIUM • BRASS • AIRCRAFT-TYPE BEARINGS

BOHN

Cat. 157

157. Arthur Radebaugh

ADVERTISEMENT: "A FLIGHT INTO THE FUTURE"

Designed c. 1945

Photo-offset on paper

28.4 x 20.2 cm

Produced for Bohn Aluminum and Brass
Corporation, Detroit, Michigan

SLSLH 2003.11.6

158–166. Attributed to Arthur Radebaugh

ADVERTISEMENTS

Designed 1940–1945

Photo-offset on paper

Produced for Bohn Aluminum and Brass
Corporation, Detroit, Michigan

158. "Streamlined for Action!"

26.5 x 20.5 cm

SLSLH 2003.23.5

159. "When These Beauties Are
at Your Disposal!"

33 x 27 cm

SLSLH 2003.23.1

160. "Here Comes the Flying Bus"

28.2 x 20.4 cm

SLSLH 2003.11.2

161. "A New Transoceanic Treat"

28.3 x 20.7 cm

SLSLH 2003.11.5

162. "Future Commuter"

26.5 x 20.5 cm

SLSLH 2003.23.2

163. "Bohn Looks Ahead"

28.3 x 20.4 cm

SLSLH 2003.11.4

164. "Coming Lawnmowers"

26.5 x 20.5 cm

SLSLH 2003.23.3

165. "A Future Design!" (see p. 248)

33 x 27 cm

SLSLH 2003.23.4

166. "Bohn" (see fig. 23)

33 x 25.5 cm

SLSLH 2003.11.1

In 1889 the *Detroit Free Press* announced, "We believe the next age will be the aluminum age, with aluminum houses, boats, cars, bridges, flying ships," and was quoted in a 1939 *Aluminum News-Letter*.[54] For Bohn Aluminum and Brass Corporation, the prophecy was realized in *Buck Rogers*-style ads designed in the 1940s, both during and after the war. Bohn, founded in 1924, was not entertaining boys with futuristic fancies: aluminum had proved to be a miracle material in its lightness yet strength, corrosion resistance and near indestructibility, malleable form and silvery sheen. It can be cast, molded, extruded, and manufactured in sheet form. As a smooth, continuous, ultra-thin skin, it lent itself to aerodynamic designs like no other substance. The *Aluminum News-Letter* went on: "Nowhere are the economic advantages of light weight more evident than in the field of transportation. Everyone can observe the value of fast pick-up in trains and trolley cars; the extra payload in light buses and trucks; the special necessity for light weight materials in air transportation. . . . Strong aluminum alloys, properly specified and assembled, are being adopted universally in all branches of the transportation field for use when weight reduction is desired without reduction in strength." As they promoted the use of Bohn aluminum, the ads epitomized the glamour of streamline transportation in all its exhilarating variety, seemingly defying space, gravity, and time.

The Minuteman image and slogan "For Victory Buy War Bonds" at the bottom of some of these ads dates them to wartime, but the copy in most of them invites business people to plan for peace and to look to Bohn "in solving some of your manufacturing and selling problems" (cat. 163). After the Armistice, how would the aluminum industry cope with competition between companies and with rival metals? The Bohn ads imply that images of streamlined transportation could capture attention, that they still promised the future tomorrow. The primary illustrator for Bohn, Arthur Radebaugh, was prophetic in his visions: while there are no airplanes with four floors yet (cat. 157), the propeller-less, wedge-shaped plane in cat. 166 (see fig. 23) forecasts the Stealth bomber, and the wheel-less "flying bus" of cat. 160 foretells the Hovercraft. Nonetheless, his suavely airbrushed images are rooted in 1930s graphics: their bold diagonal compositions with drastic contrasts of scale and extreme vantage points recall the language of media from Alexander Rodchenko's photographs and Frank Lloyd Wright's imaginary city to Vassos's illustrations and outer-space comics.

Cat. 158

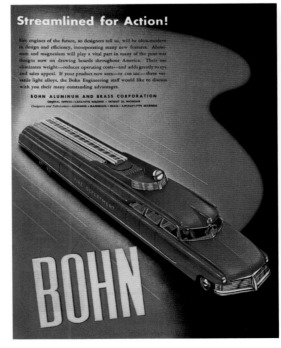

Cat. 159

COMING LAWNMOWERS

Power lawn-mowers of tomorrow will combine real beauty with utility. Lawn-mowers are only one of the products that will be made more attractive and useable through the use of light alloys in substitution for much heavier metals. Aluminum and magnesium alloys combine lightness with great strength and will supply the answer to many problems in design. Consider Bohn as the source for advice and assistance in helping plan your new products to meet post-war requirements.

BOHN ALUMINUM AND BRASS CORPORATION
GENERAL OFFICES—LAFAYETTE BUILDING • DETROIT 26, MICHIGAN
Designers and Fabricators
ALUMINUM • MAGNESIUM • BRASS • AIRCRAFT-TYPE BEARINGS

BOHN

Cat. 164

THE WORLD OF TOMORROW TODAY

Streamlining Now

6

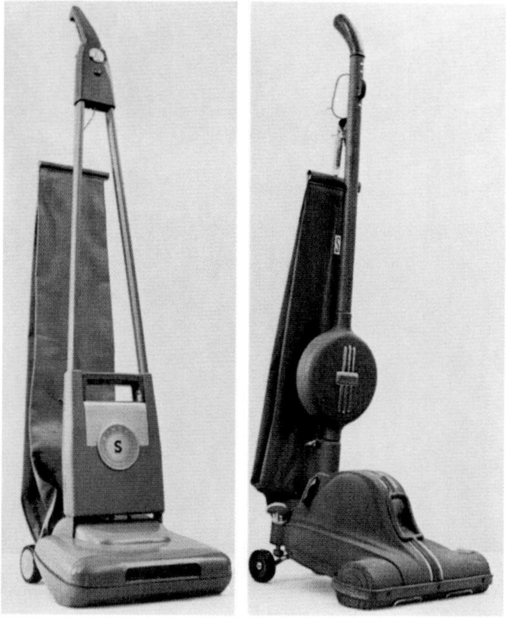

Fig. 182 Left: Raymond Loewy, vacuum cleaner for Singer Manufacturing Company, 1946. Right: Malcolm S. Park, vacuum cleaner for Singer Manufacturing Company, c. 1938. From Loewy, *Industrial Design*, 1979.

Although streamlining is synonymous in the United States with the 1930s and early 1940s, the style persisted into the 1950s and 1960s, as a number of product patent dates indicate, and it was also revived in the 1980s. Today it is selectively used both in campy quotations and admiring paraphrases. Despite the injunctions of puritanical modernists against streamlining, this appealing style proved to have a greater popularity and tenacity than had been thought.

Characteristic of postwar streamlining is the move from the sculptural forms of earlier designs to flatter, more two-dimensional creations. Looking back at the period before and just after World War II, Raymond Loewy compared two Singer vacuums (fig. 182) to demonstrate the superiority of his new, improved design of 1946, and in the process he illustrated the evolution of streamlining as it survived into the 1950s and 1960s. On the right is Malcolm S. Park's machine of 1938, and on the left Loewy's updated model. The earlier streamlined vacuum by Park is all curves: the humped motor housing, bisected by speed lines, contrasts with the disc on the handle and the cylinder shielding the front wheels. Loewy's appliance is boxier, however: the motor housing is a low flaring rectangle and the handle an open A-shape. Streamlining is restricted to the curved edges and corners of the slim appliance. In contrast to the darker colors of Park's machine, Loewy's product is in shades of pink and tan, reflecting the new postwar palette that a wider range of plastics made possible. Loewy described the need for a new model in practical terms: the old one "presented the housewife with problems in carrying and storing it; it also did not clean under sofas or low furniture because its casing was too high. We made it easy to transport; it could be hung in a closet, and the cleaning head was no higher than a cigarette pack, so it could clean under practically anything in the home."[1] The transition to a new type of streamlined aesthetic characterized by flattened, boxier, yet still aerodynamic forms is demonstrated by certain designs in each section of the book.

Does Loewy's vacuum of 1946 reflect a new sobriety among streamlined designers, chastened at last by the functional modernists? The latter had criticized the idiom from its inception. As early as 1934, a writer in *House & Garden* complained about "the current tendency to give every object that crawls, flies, creeps and has its being on this earth a long, low, soil-hugging figure."[2] This resistance to streamlining originated in the functionalist theories embodied in the teachings and designs of the Bauhaus, which did not tolerate design styling for what it considered mere marketing purposes. The Bauhaus influence was especially felt in America thanks to The Museum of

183

Modern Art. Reinforcing the values explicit in its epochal "International Style" show of 1932, it held an exhibition of Bauhaus architecture and design in 1938. In a brief article in the museum bulletin, John McAndrew, Curator of Architecture and Industrial Art, asserted that the Bauhaus had nothing to do with streamlining and noted that the famed school had closed in 1933 about the time that the streamlining mania had begun. Had it been in business, McAndrew concluded, "it would have rejected the streamlined form for objects such as cocktail shakers and fountain pens where its use is nonsense."[3]

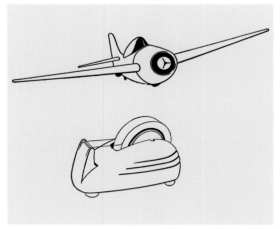

184

One notorious example of such nonfunctional "nonsense" was Loewy's 1944 model for a pencil sharpener of chromium-plated aerodynamic forms. In the catalogue of the 1944 MoMA exhibition *Art in Progress*, the pencil sharpener and an airplane were compared (fig. 183) with the comment: "The desire to make objects look 'up-to-date' by borrowing forms from unrelated modern machinery often leads to absurdities such as this pencil sharpener streamlined to resemble an airplane."[4] Even Henry Dreyfuss chimed in, illustrating the sharpener with huge bolts in its base as if to prevent its flight.[5] Loewy's design was never put into production, but it is now considered an icon of streamlining. The non-functional association is permitted and even celebrated today because we appreciate style as such more openly.

The Museum of Modern Art's condemnation of streamlining continued. In a 1950 exhibition catalogue for the museum, Edgar Kaufmann, jr. reinforced the museum's position in 1944 and criticized streamlining as "not good design." He juxtaposed line drawings of a tape dispenser and of the same plane (fig. 184), labeling the aircraft as efficient and the dispenser as imitation. The latter represented "the widespread and superficial kind of design known as streamlining used to style nearly any object from automobiles to toasters. Its theme is the magic of speed, expressed in teardrop shapes, fairings and a curious ornament of parallel lines—sometimes called *speed whiskers*. The continued misuse of these devices has spoiled them for most designers, though naturally engineers use teardrop shapes and fairings where they are efficient, on high-velocity objects."[6]

Perhaps the harshest criticism of the excesses of streamlining as "evils of style" appeared in a 1967 article in an English architectural periodical. It damned "the flashy 'modernistic' aesthetic adopted by commercial designers in the 1930s; the aesthetic of streamline refrigerators, super cinemas and cars that look like sucked lozenges. . . ."[7]

But earlier Dreyfuss had sought to define a conciliatory middle ground. In 1955 he wrote that:

> Some manufacturers still find that "streamlining" sells products, despite twenty years
> of scoffing by engineers and aesthetics. But out of the era of so-called streamlining,
> the designer learned a great deal about clean, graceful, unencumbered design. He
> learned to junk useless protuberances and ugly corners that not only spoiled good
> honest lines but interfered with efficient operation. Stand a 1929 toaster with its knobs

and knuckle-skinning corners and impossible-to-clean slits and overall ugliness next to today's model, and the difference is apparent. . . . Call it clean-lining instead of stream-lining, and you have an ideal that the designer today still tries to achieve.[8]

What Dreyfuss meant was hard to distinguish from the "Good Design" that Edgar Kaufmann, jr. espoused and displayed in a series of furnishings shows at The Museum of Modern Art held in collaboration with the Merchandise Mart of Chicago from 1952 to 1955. The works for sale were, for Kaufmann and his jurors, examples of "a thorough merging of form and function revealing a practical, uncomplicated beauty."[9] For today's viewers, certain mid-century works blessed by MoMA and designers such as Charles and Ray Eames and Eero Saarinen and by Scandinavian modernists could be called "clean-lined" for their graphic curvilinear silhouettes and organic metaphors. In the same period, streamlining designers including Loewy and Dreyfuss adjusted the aerodynamic contours of their products to the new rectilinear aesthetic.

It was in automobile design at mid-century that the streamlined style remained bold and ebullient. This is not surprising, given the sources of streamlining in "fast-going" transportation. Americans still wanted to move more rapidly and efficiently by car, train, or plane and to look chic while doing so. Indeed, with postwar prosperity and an ever-expanding network of highways, the American love affair with automobiles blossomed from its roots in the late 1920s, and the car became the country's A-1 status symbol. Amid the competitive styling changes of the 1950s, Harley Earl's 1954 Cadillac *La Espada* (fig. 185) gave streamlining a new extravagance of form and symbol-ism. Earl, head of design at General Motors from 1926 to 1959 (and personified in Buick television

Fig. 185 Harley Earl, interior of Cadillac *La Espada*, 1954.

Fig. 186 Roy Lichtenstein, *Times Square Mural*, 1990, fabricated 1994, installed 2002, Times Square Station. Commissioned and owned by Metropolitan Transportation Authority, Arts for Transit, New York.

ads since 2003), adapted the rocket-shaped cowlings and wrap-around windshields of fighter planes for his "insolent chariot," extending its already impressive length with tail fins and turning its front seat into a deluxe cockpit glistening with myriad chromium-plated dials. With a radio and cigarette lighter at his fingertips as well as high-speed technology, the driver in his two-toned bucket seat could feel like a potentate and a jet pilot simultaneously. Perhaps more than in the 1930s, such design sold an image of luxury, velocity, and power.[10]

In the 1960s, when serious design critics began to rehabilitate streamlining, they justified it on the grounds of the responsiveness of Detroit and particularly Earl to popular tastes. In his influential *Theory and Design in the First Machine Age*, Reyner Banham began by describing the shift in automobile design to streamlining in "the first genuinely stylist-designed car, Harley Earl's LaSalle of 1934 (see p. 15, left), whose aesthetics were conceived in terms of mass-production for a changing public market, not of an unchangeable type or norm."[11] Later Banham applauded the "streamlined ships, the tear-drop cars, those classic trains like the Burlington *Zephyr*—and finally a whole streamlined future expounded in a series of exhibitions culminating... [with] the New York World's Fair of 1939...."[12] In a 1976 article in the *Times Literary Supplement*, Banham cited Donald J. Bush's *The Streamlined Decade* of 1976 as contributing to the understanding of streamlining. What that book revealed, according to Banham, was that

> ... streamlining was not the opposite of European modern design but its logical continuation. . . . For, where the European modernists began to abandon those old Futurist mechanical analogies and engineering exegetics as soon as machinery ceased to resemble their own preferred abstract style . . . the Big Streamliners of American design tried to stay with machinery into the new age when it had ceased to look like architecture on casters, and had begun to turn low, organic and curvaceous.[13]

If streamlining was successful through the late twentieth century, it was because it evoked both modernism and American popular culture. Critics on the functional modernist side admitted that streamlining was suitable for transportation vehicles but considered it inappropriate for objects that did not move, such as Loewy's pencil sharpener. Those who were rebellious against strictly defined functional modernism championed the aspect of streamlining that reflected vital mass tastes and diverse stylistic inspirations. Streamlining, along with Art Nouveau and Art Deco, was incorporated into a new aesthetic that drew on aspects of both high art and mass culture.

The Pop Art movement was a major influence in the revival of interest in streamlining. The movement had begun in the late 1950s as artists in both England and America looked to mass culture, including streamlining, for inspiration. The sculptor Claes Oldenburg exaggerated the humanoid associations of certain older products in his soft, sewn constructions, and in his stuffed vinyl *Dormeyer Mixer*, 1966, he spoofed the sexual allusions of some streamlined household designs.[14] By the mid-1960s, the painter Roy Lichtenstein was incorporating images and motifs from American streamlining of the 1930s into his work.[15] His fascination continued into the 1980s and was given a public platform in 1989 when he was commissioned to create *Times Square Subway Mural* (fig. 186). Installed in 2002 in New York's Times Square subway station and made of enameled porcelain on steel, the immense work is fifty-three feet long and six feet high. A winged, spaceship-like, streamlined train dominates the composition, and the helmeted head of Buck Rogers appears at the far right. Placed at the crossroads of transport and entertainment in Manhattan, the mural looks wittily to the future as envisioned in the past. This is yesterday's world of tomorrow, given the Pop expression of today.

Fig. 187 Archizoom Associates, *Dream Bed*, 1967.
Fig. 188. Massimo Iosa Ghini, architectural drawing, c. 1985.

187

188

In part inspired by Pop Art, Italian design in the 1960s became a locus of protests against the elitism and conceptual strictness of modernism. An international influence on architecture and design was Robert Venturi's book *Complexity and Contradiction in Architecture*, published in 1966. Venturi scorned the formal Puritanism of the modernists and argued that historical styles and ornament and contemporary mass culture were appropriate, invigorating sources for architecture. Several groups were formed that criticized modernism and championed the sign language of the streets and other popular idioms. In 1966, Archizoom Associates was founded by Andrea Branzi and rebellious architectural students at the University of Florence, and their audacious work and happening-style shows helped usher in a design revolution. The *Dream Bed* of 1967 designed for exhibition by Archizoom (fig. 187) adapts streamlining forms and motifs in its curvaceous contours and the speed lines painted on its sides and down its middle. These decorations suggest movement for an object intended to be stationary—a conscious offense to the modernists.

The Italians' irreverent spirit and popular styles were revived in that country when another radical association, the Memphis group, began exhibiting in 1981. Ettore Sottsass articulated the group's differences with Bauhaus values: "Memphis, which allows the surface to send more sensorial information and tries to separate the object from its schematic idea of functionalism, is an ironic approach to the modern notion of philosophical pureness. In other words, a table may need four legs to function, but no one can tell me that the four legs have to look the same."[16]

The stylistic eclecticism and historicism of Memphis opened the door for yet another Italian radical group of the early 1980s. To promote the aesthetic of aerodynamics, Massimo Iosa Ghini co-founded the Bolidist design group in Milan in 1982 (from the Italian *bolide*, a fast-moving object). Iosa Ghini loved cartoons and drew his own, especially outer-space fantasies, and his futuristic architectural drawings reflected them in their swooping curves and megalomaniac scale (fig. 188). Though never intended for realization, these designs helped instill a taste for American streamlining of the 1930s among young Italian designers. In 1986, Roberto Semprini joined the Bolidist group and collaborated on interior designs with Iosa Ghini. Semprini's *Tatlin* sofa (fig. 189) can also be described as *bolidi*, emblematic of the group's fascination with shapes evocative of speed.[17] In openly quoting the spiral form of Vladimir Tatlin's *Monument to the Third International* of 1919–20, Semprini summoned up one of the original sources of streamlining.

Since the 1980s streamlining has thrived in both meanings of the word as it was used in the interwar years. Companies "streamline" their operations and workplaces for efficiency and cost-cutting. In product forms, the revivals of streamlining have stressed its inventive packaging and purely stylistic elements: our more prosperous decades have apparently seen no need for the low-cost innovations and lifestyle improvements that motivated 1930s design. In the 1990s, streamlining was revitalized with a new inspiration for its aerodynamic styling, and its commanding metaphor changed from the plane and train to the athlete's perfect body. A broad public of spectators was obsessed with competitive sports, and TV viewers including both bourgeois couch potatoes and street gangs bought professional-looking gear from running shoes (cat. 179) to baseball jackets and caps, making sportswear widely fashionable. Sporting goods designers, and the product designers they energized, incorporated the findings of motion and stress studies into their high-performance items, and they improved function and looks with new materials—light but strong alloys and the latest generation of plastics and synthetic fibers. As with many streamlined appliances of the 1930s, the recent designs seen here are eye-catching in their taut curves, whether or not they need aero-

Fig. 189. Mario Canazi and Roberto Semprini, Sofa, *Tatlin*, lacquered wood, chromium-plated steel, polyurethane foam, cotton velvet upholstery, 1989. The Montreal Museum of Fine Arts, The Liliane and David M. Stewart Collection.

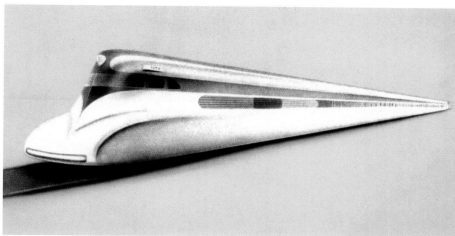

190

191

Fig. 190 Raymond Loewy, train of the future. From Cheney and Cheney, *Art and the Machine*, 1936.
Fig. 191 *Acela* train, Amtrak, c. 2000.
Fig. 192 Arlen Ness, *Smooth-Ness* Motorcycle, custom design for Harley-Davidson Motor Company, 1999.

nautical principles to perform well. The wet suit (cat. 178) gives the diver who wears it the comfort of a fish in the deep, whereas the *Go Chair* (cat. 173) suggests its owner is seated in the heel of a racing shoe. Unlike the critics of the 1930s, who set streamlining against modernism, today's design pundits are united in admiration for such formal and technical achievements as this chair.

In some current products, overt quotations of interwar streamlining flatter the knowing consumer (cat. 172) and build on the purposeful revivalism of past styles known as Retro Design. In Amtrak's *Acela* train of c. 2000 (fig. 191), streamlining improves velocity and "eye appeal" as it did in the "streamliners" of the 1930s. Indeed, the *Acela*—at least in its styling—realizes Raymond Loewy's 1936 visualization of a locomotive of the future (fig. 190), as the curve from its nose snakes back without interruption over its windshield and body. In Arlen Ness's 1999 custom-made motorcycle for Harley-Davidson (fig. 192), the swelling, forward-thrusting cowlings pay homage to the Bugatti cars of the 1930s. Such designs attest to the enduring popular appeal and romanticism of the idiom and its versatile applications. Streamlining—in its still fantastic yet somehow friendly pneumatic forms—now conveys both nostalgia for yesteryear and optimism about tomorrow.

192

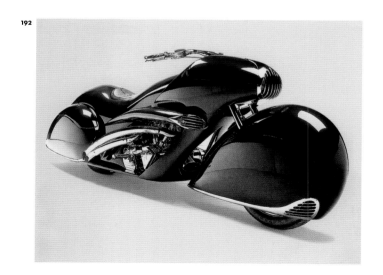

167. Massimo Iosa Ghini
BENCH: *VERTIGINE*
Designed 1989
Chromium-plated steel, ash, leather upholstery
65 x 224 x 110 cm
Produced by Moroso, Milan, Italy,
for Design Gallery Milano
The Montreal Museum of Fine Arts,
The Liliane and David M. Stewart Collection
D94.200.1

Inspired by American streamlining as well as Italian Futurist design and Fascist architecture, Massimo Iosa Ghini has created astonishing furnishing designs since the 1980s, as seen in this leather-upholstered bench. The notions of speed and simplification implied by streamlining are embodied by the splayed seat which swoops to the floor at the rear to replace back legs. The back rest attached to the seat is an opposed comma-like curve. These curves and the elongated teardrop shape are extensions of graphic strokes into the third dimension, thanks to computer-assisted factory technology; they are also elements of American streamlining which Iosa Ghini has transformed, without direct quotation, into this dramatic sculptural design.

Vertigine, which means "vertigo", was produced in a limited edition for an exhibition of Iosa Ghini's work organized by Design Gallery Milano in 1989 to coincide with the city's annual International Furniture Fair. The bench sums up the ideals of the designer's Bolidist design group (from *bolide*, a fast-moving object), which he founded in 1982.

According to Iosa Ghini, "The first step of this new trend is to break the right angle and the straight line . . . in order to find the sinuous curve, the volute, the spiral, and shapes that can be obtained from complex equations, because now we have the possibility to memorize and to use them."[1]

168. Massimo Iosa Ghini
TABLE LAMP: *FARO*
Designed 1988
Chromium-plated steel, aluminum, glass
40.5 x 22.5 x 16.5 cm
Produced for Memphis, Milan, Italy
The Liliane and David M. Stewart Collection,
promised gift of Dr. Michael Sze
SHLSL 2002.20

169. Massimo Iosa Ghini
PITCHER
Designed 1989
Silver-plated alpaca
32.5 x 20 x 11 cm
Produced for Design Gallery Milano, Milan, Italy
The Liliane and David M. Stewart Collection,
promised gift of Dr. Michael Sze
SHLSL 2002.27

170. Massimo Iosa Ghini
VASE: *EROTICO*
Designed 1989
Silver-plated alpaca
25.8 x 28.5 x 6.3 cm
Produced for Design Gallery Milano
The Liliane and David M. Stewart Collection,
promised gift of Dr. Michael Sze
SHLSL 2002.23

That a table lamp should be named *Faro*, or "lighthouse" in Italian, yet resemble a rocket launcher typifies Iosa Ghini's exuberant fancy. Images of speed obsess him. And with the Postmodern disregard for hierarchies of "high" and "low" art, he alludes here to American streamlining, Flash Gordon cartoons, Cape Canaveral illustrations, and costly moderne ornaments. Such amusing mélanges typify the work of this Bolognese designer, and in 1986 they led Ettore Sottsass to

invite him to join Memphis, the radical anti-Rationalist design group. Another attraction was Iosa Ghini's skill at cartooning, which he practiced from boyhood: its graphic conventions were popular and immediately readable, and thus delightful to Sottsass, who was seeking out new sign languages for expressive design. Iosa Ghini joined Memphis, which produced this lamp, and the alliance launched his career in industrial design.

The designer's reliance on drawing in generating his objects is obvious in *Faro*'s supports, one a fin and the others a pair of wire prongs where a matching fin might be expected. The vase, pitcher, and faucet illustrated here (cat. 169–171) are more completely gestural and witty. The cant of the pitcher is buttressed by two little legs, and the vase rests on tiny feet and a "tail"—the extension of its narrow body down to the table. Compared to the *Normandie* pitcher (cat. 98), this is anti-heroic, despite its streamlined body and silver-plated sheen.

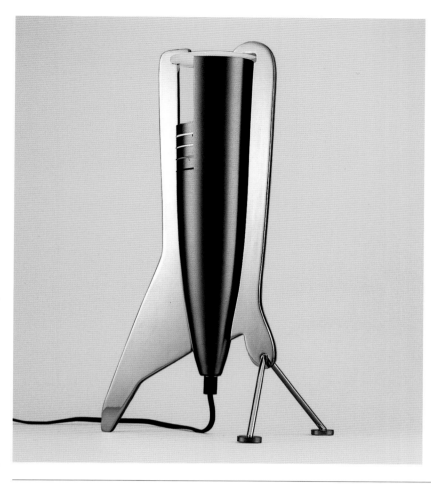

Cat. 169

Cat. 170

Cat. 168

171. Massimo Iosa Ghini

FAUCET

Designed 2000
Chromium-plated steel
14.5 x 18 x 6 cm
Produced by Dornbracht, Iserlohn, Germany
The Liliane and David M. Stewart Collection
SHLSL 2003.10

This faucet is almost purely linear, composed of two slashes of chromium-plated steel (the nozzle and control lever) cantilevered from a flaring base. It is part of Iosa Ghini's *Giorno* Collection, which includes sinks and tubs, and was inspired by the shapes of leaves and water, "the symbol of fluidity and movement," according to the manufacturer. Not surprisingly, the faucet resembles two spouts of cartoon water. It has no kinship to Dreyfuss's sober geometric faucet for Crane (cat. 79), suggesting the distance of Iosa Ghini's streamlining from functional modernism. Indeed, the appearance of function was only one of many styling possibilities for Postmodernists.

172. Jasper Morrison
The Thinking Man's Chair
Designed 1986
Painted steel
72 x 96 x 64 cm
Produced by Cappellini, Milan, Italy
The Liliane and David M. Stewart Collection,
gift of Cappellini
SHLSL 2004.8

First exhibited in Japan, this chair was originally produced by Aram Designers, London, before the adventurous manufacturer Giulio Cappellini saw it and took an interest in the then-emerging British designer. Produced by Cappellini, the chair continues in production today. Morrison described its inspiration: "For a long time after I noticed an antique chair with its seat missing outside a shop, I had the idea to do a chair consisting only of structural elements. Many sketches later I arrived at an approximation of the final shape, which included two small tables on the ends of the arms and an exotic assembly of curved metalwork."[2] The coaster-like "tables" gave the seating its first name, "The Drinking Man's Chair," which Morrison subsequently changed to "a more sophisticated title."

Typical of that sophistication are the chair's several allusions. R. Craig Miller, of the Denver Art Museum, writes that Morrison's preliminary sketches for the chair—with their elegant play of double curves—show that his initial inspiration may have been a modernist icon, such as the Basculant chair of 1928 by Le Corbusier, Pierre Jeanneret,

and Charlotte Perriand. Morrison whimsically layers more populist associations on the design by alluding to streamlined garden furniture of the 1930s through the S-curves of its extended, tubular steel arms-cum-legs and its seat of metal bands.[3]

Morrison, one of the generation of lively British designers who emerged in the 1980s, became a leading spokesman for the revival and

transformation of modernism in the 1990s. He acknowledges a wide range of influences on his conceptions, both the work of his contemporaries and of past modern masters, including the Italian designer Franco Albini and the American Buckminster Fuller.[4] His witty references to interwar design sources—both high and low—typify the arch historicism of much Postmodern art.

173. Ross Lovegrove
Go Chair
Designed 1999[5]
Magnesium-aluminum alloy, polycarbonate plastic
77.5 x 58.4 x 68.6 cm
Produced by Bernhardt Design, Lenoir, North Carolina
The Liliane and David M. Stewart Collection,
gift of Bernhardt Design
SHLSL 2004.6

This work was "For the Man Who Wants His Chair to Resemble a Race Car," according to *Esquire*

(October 2001). It was also the first seating to be mass-produced in injection-molded magnesium. The metal is lighter than aluminum yet equally strong, giving the chair its thin skeleton and aura of mobility and thus its name. Exploiting the high-tech material and molding process, the design has "go," evoking the streamlining of aerodynamic vehicles and sports equipment. The chair's front legs and back form a continuous swooping U-shape; its back legs and seat a similar one. The owner, poised on this work's taut slender legs and surprisingly comfortable in the molded, phosphorescently hued seat, could be sitting in a slingshot.

Asked what inspired the *Go Chair*, the designer Ross Lovegrove replied: "Body form, sensuality, anatomical base, high technology: [I] want to make things which can only exist today." He went on about his general goals: "I am an absolute committed futurist. I actually don't live in the time zone I stand in; I don't look back. I want to produce things that perhaps, when I'm dead and buried or whatever, people will say that guy really had a scintillating view of how life could be."[6]

Cat. 173

BAGEL

CANCEL

DEFROST

Cat. 175

174. Marc Berthier

LIGHTER: *PYROS*
Designed 1995
Anodized aluminum
6 x 10.5 x 3 cm
Produced by Lexon, Paris, France
The Liliane and David M. Stewart Collection
SHLSL 2003.22

Obvious echoes of 1930s streamlining appear in the elongated teardrop form of this tabletop lighter, in the fin-like thumb press that lights its fire, and the three perforated bands that aerate it as they wrap around its front like speed lines. The flawless finish of the lighter's body celebrates the beauty of the aluminum, a material especially beloved between the wars. Berthier's choice of anodized aluminum for this sophisticated smoking accessory reflects his aesthetic of "Lightness": it "is not only the cutting of weight" that he values, he says, but lightness also expresses "freedom, ecology, mobility/changeableness, economy, modernity, technology . . . lightness means heading towards [the] essential. . . ."[7] Berthier's sensuous minimalism appears in other consumer products he has designed for Lexon since 2000, including a prize-winning portable radio, a calculator, a fan in synthetic rubber, and a computer mouse in aluminum with polypropylene finger pads. The allure of these functionalist designs derives solely from their materials and refined silhouettes; they allude to modernist languages subtly, as the lighter does.

Berthier's connections to modernism can be traced to his work for the Italian architect and editor Gio Ponti in the 1960s, while his interests in synthetic materials and innovative manufacturing processes were catalyzed by that decade's explorations of plastic and inflatable furniture, especially among the young Italian vanguard. This history and Berthier's experience teaching, at the École Nationale Supérieure de Création Industrielle in Paris, help account for the assurance of his designs: they do not selfconsciously quote interwar styles as Postmodern products sometimes do, but evoke them where appropriate to an object's purpose.

175. Michael Graves

TOASTER: MODEL NO. TT 9275
Designed 2000
Stainless steel, rubber, plastic
20.5 x 31.5 x 20 cm
Produced in China for Rival, El Paso, Texas for Target, Minneapolis, Minnesota
The Liliane and David M. Stewart Collection
SHLSL 2003.9

Fig. 193 Michael Graves Design Group, Target Toaster Working Drawing, 1998.

In this mirror-bright stainless-steel toaster, Michael Graves has revived streamlining to engaging effect. The rounded form of this design and its bulging horizontal bands appear inspired by the streamlined toasters of the 1930s and 1940s. To this nostalgic plumpness Graves adds a blue handle and egg-shaped protrusions forming the feet: these simple spheroids have a childlike charm. Even if the consumer is too young or dim to recognize the period allusions, these delightful details combine with Graves's status-symbol signature on the side to attract sales through styling alone. At the same time, the toaster offers automatic shut-off, a slide-out crumb tray, and extra-wide slots for bagels. The producer Target claims: "Sensible and sublime, practical and whimsical, the objects envisioned by the world-renowned architect infuse our daily lives with joy." "Joy" was one of the unexpected contributions of Postmodern design. No longer was Good Design just good for you, as modernists seemed to imply in the interwar era: in addition, form followed fun.

Of the American Postmodernist architects to mine the past for inspiration, Graves has achieved the widest public recognition in his designs for Target, the mass-market consumer goods chain. His career in this area represents the latest chapter in the saga of the industrial designer and the branding of household products that began in the 1930s. In the early 1980s, the Italian housewares manufacturer Alessi commissioned vanguard architects including Graves to design for it, and that critical success led to further such alliances between art and industry. Just as industry wooed Bel Geddes from stage design and Teague from illustration in the 1930s, so current product manufacturers have lured creators from different fields with their now-intrinsic need for constant styling changes and technical innovation and their offer of fortune and fame.

176. Seymour Powell
(Richard Seymour and Dick Powell)
IRON: MODEL NO. 1830, *AVANTIS 130*

Designed 1999
Durilium, plastic
14 x 30 x 11.5 cm
Produced by T-Fal, West Orange, New Jersey
The Liliane and David M. Stewart Collection,
SHLSL 2004.4

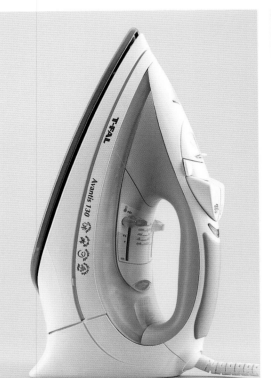 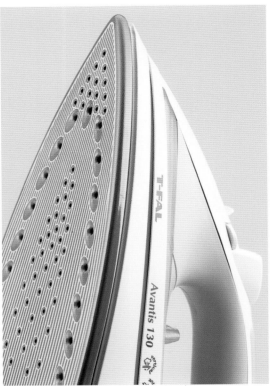

The base, handle, and controls of this iron are united in one swelling, almost uninterrupted teardrop shape, which reflects the forward, downward thrust of the user's gesture. This streamlined shape is outlined in a choice of pastels, which highlight the controls, while the pressing shoe of Durilium—a metal alloy that minimizes friction—is dramatized in a darker hue. An additional groove sweeping around the base of the iron further emphasizes its aerodynamic form.

The *Avantis* resembles irons of the 1930s in its twin references to flight and ocean liners cleaving the sea. But its plastics, which replace the chromium-plated steel of the past, make it lighter and therefore less tiring to use and easier to keep clean. The heel of the shoe is indented and raised so the iron can be tilted upward and rested, and the cord can be wrapped around the heel and neatly clipped when not in use. The iron's features include steam and spray for dampening laundry, with water tank and controls integrated at the front. These features—visible yet subordinate to the overall design—promise convenience, while the overall formal simplicity of the *Avantis* suggests that ironing can be almost effortless.

The manufacturer, T-Fal, is credited with inventing the nonstick frying pan in the 1950s, and its commission of this iron from the British team of Richard Seymour and Dick Powell typifies its combination of technical advances with striking designs in small appliances since then.

177. Seymour Powell
VACUUM CLEANER: *INFINIUM*

Designed 2000
Plastic, metal
40 x 33 x 45 cm
Produced by Rowenta, Germany
The Liliane and David M. Stewart Collection
SHLSL 2004.9

Teardrop in plan and form, the bagless *Infinium* vacuum recalls streamlined vacuums of the past, but is thoroughly contemporary in its compact unitary body and aerodynamic details. Its rear wheels continue its helmet-like contouring and its controls barely protrude from its face, where part of the motor is visible behind an oval window.

Three slanted perforations aerate the motor and evoke both speed lines and side vents of racing cars. (The Seymour Powell firm has designed for BMW, Ford, and Jaguar.) The smoothly integrated parts are differentiated by changes of color and finish (the cleaner comes in red, two tones of blue, and black and dark gray), and these variations dramatize the precise engineering of the body. Like a little Lunar Rover, the *Infinium* seems intended to vacuum up moon dust. Certainly it suggests that space-age design can lighten chores on earth.

ROWENTA
INFINIUM

178. Stephen Peart

WET SUIT: *ANIMAL*

Designed 1991
Neoprene, nylon
152 x 56 cm (widest diameter)
Produced by O'Neill, Inc., California,
for Vent Design, Campbell, California
Montreal Museum of Fine Arts
The Liliane and David M. Stewart Collection,
D92.121.1

Wet suits primarily retain the body heat of divers, who are almost always in water colder than human body temperature. Such suits must also allow free movement, survive salt water, dry easily, and, if possible, make the wearer look athletic. The *Animal* wet suit does all this and more: it is even flattering. Its Neoprene material is a stretchable synthetic fiber that assures heat retention, close fit, and easy care. For the user's maximum mobility, the garment is detailed with repeated ridges, like streamlines, in parabolic curves around the shoulders, arms, and thighs. According to the design curator R. Craig Miller, the *Animal* wet suit "expresses the muscular movement of the body and at the same time has the sculpted undulation of a pleated garment by Mariano Fortuny."[8] Made of a high-tech substance, this design combines performance and beauty—a beauty derived from aerodynamic athletic movement.

Other of Stephen Peart's designs include an adjustable computer keyboard for Apple Computers, Inc. and office accessories such as mouse pads and wrist and back rests for Knoll, Inc., the prestigious furnishings manufacturer identified with modernism from the late 1940s. These designs and the suit share a responsiveness to what Peart calls the "interface" of human use. He is interested, he says, in "people touching and feeling technology." It is the human's interface with the ocean that his suit facilitates.

179. Scott Patt

ATHLETIC SHOES: *AIR MAX CONTACT*

Designed 2001
Synthetic leather, mesh, tetrapolyurethane,
polyurethane, rubber
12.5 x 31 x 11 cm (each)
Produced in China for Nike, Beaverton, Oregon
The Liliane and David M. Stewart Collection,
SHLSL 2004.1

Since the 1970s Nike has been riding the popular obsession with sports and has come to dominate the design and manufacture of athletic shoes and clothing worldwide. Its trademark "swoosh"—a curved checkmark that springs up, forward, and to a point—witnesses the contemporary transformation of a streamlined form. This recognizable emblem, seen on the sides and soles of these shoes, is not Nike's only streamlined design. In fact, almost any pair of its athletic shoes is aeronautically styled in one or more of its features, and youths of all classes vie to wear the latest models.

The silver and black color scheme—which was a chic combination in the 1930s—demonstrates that popular fashion has ended the dominance of all-white dress in sports, which was required in almost all sports competitions into the 1990s.

180. John Larkin

BICYCLE HELMET: *LIMAR F-111*

Designed 2000

Plastic, polystyrene

15 x 26 x 21 cm

Produced by Limar, Costa di Mezzate, Italy

The Liliane and David M. Stewart Collection

SHLSL 2004.2

Biking helmets are essential safety equipment for competitive bicycle racing and highly recommended for amateur bikers, but few offer both the protection and panache of this product. It is as aerodynamic in form as a racing bike itself, and also extremely light, of plastics weighing only 290 grams. At the same time, its intricately perforated form, with thirty-six teardrop-shaped openings, shields the head while cooling it. The Italian-made helmet is available in "Red Ruby," "Electric Blue," gold, and orange; it was customized for use by the German team in the 2003 Tour de France. Its model name *F-111* recalls the American fighter plane of the 1960s.

It is not surprising that the designer, John Larkin, is both a biker and a former sculpture student (at the University of Idaho in Moscow, Idaho, where he now teaches). His designs of high-performance equipment for bikes and other "fit systems" are notable for their stylishly streamlined organicism and the protection offered by their engineering.

A Future Design!

The accumulation of new technical data, along with the great developments in the aluminum and magnesium fields, promise many new things for a post-war world. Among these is the building on a quantity production basis of motor launches in beautiful, intriguing and useful designs. Light alloys provide both sales appeal and great operating economy. If your product uses—or can use—aluminum or magnesium, the Bohn organization would be glad to discuss their many advantages with you.

BOHN ALUMINUM & BRASS CORPORATION

GENERAL OFFICES—LAFAYETTE BUILDING • DETROIT 26, MICHIGAN

Designers and Fabricators

ALUMINUM • MAGNESIUM • BRASS • AIRCRAFT-TYPE BEARINGS

BOHN

Cat. 165

Biographies of Designers

JOHN E. ALCOTT

(b. Chelsea, Massachusetts – d. Westwood, Massachusetts, August 1, 1899)

Alcott was raised in Everett, Massachusetts, and after high school enlisted in the military during World War I.[1] After his discharge, he entered the Massachusetts School of Art, graduated in 1922, and stayed on as an assistant teacher for a year. He then opened his own studio and became chief designer for Bird & Son, in Walpole, where he developed modern floor coverings. In 1927, he returned to the Massachusetts School of Art as head of Design and Manufacturing.

In 1935, he started his own industrial design company—Alcott, Thorner, and Marsh—and moved to Westwood where he opened his studio. His first major client was Dutchland Farms, an ice cream store, for which he designed everything from the building to the cups and plates. He was so successful that Howard Johnson asked him to design the logo for his new roadside businesses—the famous "Pieman." Alcott made each logo individually, cutting out the design, painting it, and then attaching it to each building and the sides of Howard Johnson trucks. In 1938 he designed a desk lamp for Polaroid (cat. 1). One of his most important projects was his design of the Massachusetts and Rhode Island buildings at the 1939 New York World's Fair. From 1941 to 1959, he was Professor of Industrial Design and Acting Dean at the Rhode Island School of Design.

EGMONT H. ARENS

(b. Cleveland, Ohio, December 15, 1887 – d. New York, New York, September 30, 1966)[2]

The son of Franz Xavier Arens, a well-known German-American composer, Egmont Arens spent his youth in New Mexico because of incipient tuberculosis before moving to New York in 1917. In 1918 he founded the Flying Stag Press to publish and print magazines, and he ran the firm until 1927. During the same period, from 1922 to 1923 he was Art Editor of *Vanity Fair* and from 1925 to 1927 Managing Editor of *Creative Arts Magazine*.[3] Experiments in designing lamps led to his second field of interest—industrial design—and in 1929 he became head of the industrial styling division of Calkins & Holden advertising agency where he remained until 1935. With Earnest Elmo Calkins, he is credited with initiating market research for design engineering as a profession. Arens's book *Consumer Engineering*, which he co-authored with Roy Sheldon in 1932, became a classic.[4]

In 1935, Arens founded his own industrial design firm. His merchandising plans and designs for packaging and store interiors were singled out by Sheldon and Martha Cheney.[5] His packaging included designs for Parliament and Philip Morris cigarettes, A&P's Eight O'Clock Coffee,

and Higgins ink. Among his most famous industrial designs were Hobart's meat slicer (cat. 51) and Kitchen Aid's mixer.

Arens's combination of intense creative vision and economic realism made him an astute prophet of future designs. In an article of 1931 he accurately foretold the appearance of a future train, and in 1956 he predicted that plastics technology would help conquer interplanetary space in ten years.[6] A founding member of the Society of Industrial Designers in 1944, he was elected President in 1949. In 1952 he was one of the twelve who established the Package Designers Council.

MARC BERTHIER

(b. Compiègne, France, 1935)

From 1955 to 1959, Berthier studied industrial design at l'École Nationale Supérieure des Arts Décoratifs, in Paris. In 1965, he designed furniture for the Paris department store Galeries Lafayette, and he introduced an innovative furnishings exhibitions program there. In 1967 he collaborated with the venerable Italian architect Gio Ponti and *Domus* to produce the first edition of *EuroDomus*. In 1971, he established his own firm, Design Plan Studio, in Paris. The cover of the March 20, 2000, issue of *Time* magazine pictured his rubber radio, headlined "The Rebirth of Design."

His early projects included work for Knoll Associates in the United States, a collaboration with the furniture manufacturer Magis in Italy, and designs for schoolroom furnishings for the French Centre de Création Industrielle. His clients include the French companies Lexon, Alcatel, and Group SEB; Guzzini (Italy); Fondation Cousteau; and Fujitsu and Index (Japan). A longtime teacher at Les Ateliers/Ensci (l'École Nationale Supérieure de Création Industrielle, Paris), he has also received many prizes for his designs, such as the Grand Prix National de la Création Industrielle from the French Ministry of Culture in 1986 and Italy's Premio Compasso d'Oro in 1991 and 1994.[7] In 2002, with Elise Berthier, Pierre Garner, and Frédérick Lintz, he redubbed his firm Elium Studio, dropping the *h* in helium to underline their commitment to lightness and mobility in their designs.

ARIETO (HARRY) BERTOIA

(b. San Lorenzo [Udine], Italy, March 10, 1915 – d. Bally, Pennsylvania, November 6, 1978)[8]

Bertoia is known as an industrial designer and a craftsman, a master of metalwork, a sculptor, and a printmaker. His wire chair designs for Knoll Associates, introduced in 1952, won him wide recognition.

Bertoia immigrated to the United States in 1930 and joined his brother in Detroit, graduating from Lewis Cass Technical High School in 1936. He attended the Art School of the Detroit Society of Arts and Crafts until 1937, when he received a scholarship to the Cranbrook Academy of Art, Bloomfield Hills, Michigan. He went on to work as a teacher at Cranbrook from 1938 to 1943, reopening their metal shop and producing some of his own designs, such as the coffee service seen in cat. 103–104. In 1943, when the metal shop closed because of the metal shortage during World War II, Bertoia taught in the graphics department.

In 1943, Bertoia moved to Southern California to work with Charles and Ray Eames as a furniture designer. He continued to make jewelry, which he had initiated at Cranbrook. In 1950, he relocated to Bally, Pennsylvania, setting up a studio near the Knoll Associates factory, for which he designed metal furniture. He also began making freestanding and architectural sculpture, some including movement and sound. His awards include the 1975 gold medal from The American Institute of Architects, and the 1975 Academy-Institute Award of the American Academy and Institute of Arts and Letters.

HERBERT E. BRIDGEWATER

(b. New York, September 27, 1878 – d. Pittsburgh, Pennsylvania, May 1970)[9]
To date, Herbert E. Bridgewater is known only through his patent applications, including his 1935 design (with John A. Zellers) of the *Streamliner* portable typewriter (cat. 3). Zellers and Bridgewater assigned their patent to Remington Rand Inc. of Buffalo, New York. Bridgewater was listed as a resident of Syracuse, New York.

THEODORE C. BROOKHART

(b. Celina, Ohio, May 8, 1898 – d. Sidney, Ohio, October 24, 1942)
Brookhart came to Sidney, Ohio, to work for the Hobart Manufacturing Co. in nearby Troy, where he was employed in the engineering department. He lived at 1018 East Franklin Street. [10] The patent specifications for the meat slicer (cat. 51) are signed by Brookhart and Hobart's consultant designer Egmont Arens, but the degree of Brookhart's participation in the design remains unknown.

ROBERT DAVOL BUDLONG

(b. Des Moines, Iowa, 1902 – d. Skokie, Illinois, February 13, 1955)
As a child in Des Moines, Budlong showed ability in art and he began formal studies at the Cummings School of Art at the age of eleven.[11] In 1922 he graduated with a degree in art from Grinnell College, Iowa. In his youth he entered advertising, but returned to his initial interest in art and studied at the Chicago Academy of Fine Arts and the American Academy of Art (Chicago). After completing his studies, he worked for a number of Chicago firms as a commercial artist and package designer. Around 1925 Budlong formed the advertising agency of Budlong and Eker. In 1930 he left to start his own industrial design consulting firm; his early commissions included designs for Montgomery Ward, Sunbeam, the Cory Co., and Chrysler Motors. Around 1935 he joined Zenith, where he was promoted by Eugene F. McDonald, Jr., the dynamic president of the company. Budlong became Zenith's leading and most prolific designer,[12] but he designed for other manufacturers as well, including the Chicago Musical Instrument Co. Its full-page advertisement of 1938 pictured Budlong and stated, "the exclusiveness of the modern streamlined design of Scandalli and Dallape accordions is . . . the work of one of America's foremost creative artists, Mr. Robert Davol Budlong of Chicago. . . ."[13]

CLARENCE M. BURROUGHS

(b. March 18, 1904 – d. Cathedral City, California, January 18, 1998)[14]
To date, Burroughs is known only through his patents, including his 1948

design for an ice water pitcher (cat. 72). The applications list him as a resident of Glendale, California. In a 1950 application for a saltshaker (D162,005), he submitted the patent on behalf of the Burroughs Manufacturing Corporation of Los Angeles, California. His subsequent patents for a batter bowl (1949), a breadbox (1952), and covered container (1955), all confirm that the inventor and manufacturer were one.

AILEEN BUSHNELL

(b. March 25, 1909 – d. Aurora, Illinois, April, 1987)[15]
Bushnell appeared in the city directories of Aurora as a resident of the Illinois town from 1939 through 1973.[16] In 1939 she is cited as a "screen artist" working for W. P. York, Inc.; Bushnell was her married name. In 1948–50, she took out patents for power tools assigned to the Independent Pneumatic Tool Co., Aurora, including the 1950 patent for the circular saw (cat. 43). Four years later she was still working for the company, then known as Thor Power Tool. Between 1961 and 1972 she was employed to draft for Fox Valley Engineering in Yorkville, Illinois.[17]

DAVID CHAPMAN

(b. January 30, 1909 – d. Chicago, Illinois, May 20, 1978)[18]
A graduate of Chicago's Armour Institute of Technology (later the Illinois Institute of Technology), Chapman was both an architect and an industrial designer.[19] In 1933 he worked on the design staff of the Chicago *Century of Progress Exposition*, and then joined Montgomery Ward, becoming head of product design. In 1936 he left the mail-order company to form his own firm, Dave Chapman Design, Inc., at 420 North Michigan Avenue in Chicago. An account of 1956 described Chapman as "an energetic spokesman for design both locally and nationally" who then had twenty-six employees. Among his clients were Parker Pen, International Harvester, Brunswick-Balke-Collender (school furniture), Felt Products Corp., and Scovill Manufacturing Co.[20]

Like many of his colleagues, Chapman joined the Society of Industrial Designers, succeeding Egmont Arens as president in 1950.[21] He was the only member to win its medal twice, once for his classroom furniture designs and once for rooms designed for educational television.[22] In 1954 he organized a subsidiary company, Design Research, Inc., to provide long-range planning for clients, and the following year he reorganized Montgomery Ward's Bureau of Design. The *New York Times* quoted him in 1955 as envisioning the house of the future without a kitchen, which he called a "dead dodo," replaced by a room where cleaning was done, while all other spaces were turned over to living.[23] Chapman retired from his firm in 1970.

THEODORE G. CLEMENT

(b. New York, January 6, 1903 – d. Sun City, Arizona, March 19, 1989)[24]
According to the 1947 patent specifications for a slide projector, Clement lived in Rochester, New York, and assigned his patent to the Eastman Kodak Company. The 1930 census lists him as a machinist and engineer at the Kodak factory in Rochester. A contemporary publication lists

Clement as the Head of Eastman Kodak Company's Styling Division and Walter Dorwin Teague as Consultant.[25]

JOHN S. COLDWELL

(b. Wisconsin, c. 1889)[26]

John S. Coldwell is known only through his patent applications, including his 1935 design (with John R. Morgan) of the *Flyaway Streamlined* roller skates (cat. 135), which was assigned to the Globe-Union Manufacturing Co., of Milwaukee, Wisconsin. Coldwell was listed as a resident of Milwaukee.

JACKSON D. COMSTOCK

(b. Illinois, March 26, 1890 – d. Las Vegas, Nevada, June 1973)[27]

To date, Jackson D. Comstock is known only through several of his patent applications, including his 1941 invention for a juice extractor, which he designed with Donald E. Grove. Comstock was listed as a resident of Los Angeles. The 1930 census lists him as a resident of Chicago and his occupation as inventor.

GEORGE R. COSS

(b. Ohio, January 31, 1885 – d. Rayland, Ohio, January 1973)[28]

According to the 1937 patent specifications for an electric roaster (cat. 56), Coss lived in Toledo, Ohio, and assigned his invention to The Swartzbaugh Manufacturing Company of the same city.

STEPHEN A. CROSBY

To date, Crosby is known only through his patents, which suggest he was employed between 1932 and 1939 by the Parrot Speed Fastener Corporation of Long Island City, New York. Parrot manufactured his stapler (cat. 15), designed in 1937 and stamped "Speed Products"; the company became Swingline in later years. Crosby's products of 1932–37 list him as a New York City resident; by 1939 he moved to Jackson Heights, New York. From 1940 to 1951 his patent applications locate him in Chicago, where he designed a power polisher for Sterling Tool Products Co. (1943) and a stapler for Vail Manufacturing Co. (1951).

DONALD EARL DAILEY

(b. Minneapolis, Minnesota, July 25, 1914 – d. Evansville, Indiana, April 22, 1997)[29]

As a child, Dailey attended art classes at The Minneapolis Institute of Arts, and in his teens he moved with his family to Cleveland. From 1934 to 1936 he studied at the Toledo Museum School of Design and took classes at The University of Toledo. In 1937 he began his career, with the designer Harold Van Doren in Toledo, and he helped prepare Van Doren's classic textbook, *Industrial Design*. In 1940, he moved to Philadelphia to head Van Doren's second office, which served Westinghouse and Philco, among other companies. Philco's military projects occupied Dailey during World War II, and in 1946 he opened his own firm, continuing to design refrigerators for the company, as well as small appliances for Proctor Electric Co.[30] Among Dailey's many patents was a two-temperature refrigerator of 1947 for Philco that improved the separation between the freezing compartment and the main food storage area.[31] In 1950, he became product manager at Servel, and then a vice president of the Product Planning Department. With thirty-seven patents, Dailey commented on creativity: "Turning out new models at regular intervals is as habit-forming as dope. The designer's only escape is to have new ideas first, and needle management with them."[32]

MICHAEL S. DESSER

(b. Youngstown, Ohio, September 8, 1906 – d. Toledo, Ohio, August 9, 1982)

Though not professionally trained as a glasswares designer, Desser functioned as one through his long experience in the business, having begun his career as a teenage office boy at Owens-Corning, Chicago. In the early 1920s, he moved to Toledo, Ohio, and worked for Owens-Illinois Glass Company, to which he assigned the 1936 patent for the condiment shakers (cat. 65). He was then a salesman for Owens-Illinois, according to the Toledo city directory. Around 1938 he transferred his family to Vineland, New Jersey, where he became merchandise manager at the Kimble Glass Company, in which Owens-Illinois had a part interest. His 1939 patent for a towel bar bracket was assigned to Kimble; and during World War II he was one of Kimble's employees who designed medical glasswares for the Armed Services, which used the company as its exclusive supplier. In 1948, after Owens-Illinois bought Kimble and made it a division, he returned to Toledo for a year at the parent firm. After quitting he spent the next three years as general manager of Geneva Pottery, in Lake Geneva, Wisconsin; he then returned to Toledo. Until his retirement in 1971 at age sixty-four, he was a sales representative for several housewares companies, including Autowyre of Waterbury, Connecticut, a manufacturer of bath fixtures.[33]

HENRY DREYFUSS

(b. New York, New York, March 2, 1904 – d. South Pasadena, California, October 5, 1972)

Dreyfuss was one of the most successful American industrial designers of the 1930s. After high school, he received a scholarship to the Ethical Culture Society's Arts High School in Manhattan, which he attended from 1920 to 1922. A second scholarship allowed him to study theater design in the New York studio of Norman Bel Geddes. After his apprenticeship to Bel Geddes, Dreyfuss spent the next five years designing sets, costumes, and lighting for the Strand Theater in New York and the RKO vaudeville theater chain. Seeing opportunities in the emerging field of industrial design, Dreyfuss opened his own firm, Henry Dreyfuss, in 1929. One of his first employees, Dora Marks, became his wife and business manager.

Dreyfuss's industrial designs were straightforward and seldom flashy, and relatively few of his industrial products were streamlined. Nevertheless, his *Twentieth Century Limited* for the New York Central Railroad (1938) and his interiors for Pan American Airlines became icons of the streamlined era. His early concern for ergonomics was one of his most important contributions to the field of design. His designs for Bell Telephone Laboratories and AT&T touched many lives: his model no. 300 desk phone set the standard between 1937 and 1949, and he replaced it with the classic model no. 500, and then the svelte *Trimline* phone in 1964. The Dreyfuss firm, which he headed until 1969, also designed for John Deere & Co.

(from 1937) and Polaroid (from 1961), and put its mark on products from alarm clocks and typewriters to magazines.[34]

In 1945, Dreyfuss opened a second office in Pasadena, California, continuing with the same longstanding corporate clients on both coasts. Renamed Henry Dreyfuss Associates in 1969, the firm continues to the present day.

ALBERT EDWIN EMMONS

(b. New York, May 9, 1913 – d. Victor, New York, April 4, 2002)[35]

To date, Albert Emmons is known only through several of his patent applications, including his 1946 design for an electric mower (cat. 38), submitted on behalf of Rumsey Products, Inc., of Seneca Falls, New York. Emmons was listed as a resident of Lockport, New York.

ARTHUR N. EMMONS

(b. New York, December 27, 1897 – d. Nedrow, New York, June 8, 1993)[36]

To date, Arthur N. Emmons is known only through his patent applications, including his 1951 design of the portable sander (cat. 45), which was patented with Peter Müller-Munk on behalf of the Porter-Cable Machine Co., Syracuse, New York. Emmons was listed as a resident of Nedrow, New York. The power tool was illustrated in the annual published by the Society of Industrial Designers, *U.S. Industrial Design* (1951), and credited to the Müller-Munk firm "in collaboration with the engineering department" of Porter-Cable. According to the 1930 census Emmons worked as a mechanical engineer for Porter-Cable.

RICHARD BUCKMINSTER FULLER

(b. Milton, Massachusetts, July 12, 1895 – d. Los Angeles, California, July 1, 1983)

Born to a well-to-do family of independent thinkers, Fuller graduated from Milton Academy in 1913, studied intermittently at Harvard University, and for three months at the United States Naval Academy, Annapolis, in 1918, following wartime service engaging his naval engineering skills. In the 1920s he sought to manufacture an innovative lightweight building material invented by his father-in-law, in a business whose failure did not dampen his concern with improving housing conditions. Fuller's c. 1929 *Dymaxion House* (a trademark associating "dynamic," "maximum," and "tension") was a circular aluminum and glass structure suspended from a mast containing stairs, power cables, and plumbing. Its concepts of mass production in die-stamped modern materials led to his development of fully equipped prefabricated bathroom units for American Standard (1930–32) and Phelps-Dodge (1936), and his design of the Wichita House, built in prototype by Beech Aircraft (1945–46), as the postwar aircraft industry was retooling for peacetime residential needs. In his second creative period, 1947–69,[37] Fuller concentrated on the construction techniques and building of his "geodesic" domes, hemispheres of triangles forming trusses secured by tension. Over 300,000 were erected in his lifetime, the largest the twenty-story, 250-foot-diameter U.S. Pavilion at *Expo 67*, the Montreal World's Fair. These elegant, rapidly assembled space frames became his trademark, while his dedication in the 1970s to saving what he called "Spaceship Earth"

through his prolific writings and lectures on behalf of rational technology and conservation inspired audiences worldwide.[38]

HAROLD R. GAMBLE

(b. Ohio, 1913)[39]

To date, Harold R. Gamble is known only through several of his patent applications, including his 1946 design for an air compressor unit (cat. 49), submitted in collaboration with Donald J. Peeps. Gamble was listed as a resident of Toledo, Ohio, at 2444 Oak Grove Place.

NORMAN BEL GEDDES

(b. Adrian, Michigan, 1893 – d. New York, New York, May 9, 1958)

One of the most inventive designers in the American streamlined style, Bel Geddes was known in his time more for his visionary projects than his executed products. With little formal education, he began work in 1913 as an advertising draftsman in Chicago and then Detroit.[40] After his marriage to Helen Belle Schneider in 1916, the two used the surname Bel-Geddes in their careers as theater designers and writers. Bel Geddes wrote plays and designed theater sets in New York and in c. 1916 collaborated with Frank Lloyd Wright on the children's theater for Aline Barnsdall in Los Angeles. Through his friendship with the German Expressionist architect Eric Mendelsohn, Bel Geddes was encouraged to enter the new field of industrial design, opening his own office in 1927. He created department store windows in New York (fig. 11) and furniture for the Simmons Co. In 1929 he designed products and buildings for the Toledo Scale Co.

Bel Geddes was a consultant to the Architectural Commission of the Chicago's *Century of Progress Exposition*, 1933, and he designed buildings for the 1939 New York World's Fair, including *Futurama* for General Motors (fig. 45). Although he conceived streamlined automobiles, airplanes, buses, and ocean liners, most of his visionary designs were never built. His books on design and urban planning, *Horizons* (1932) and *Magic Motorways* (1940), influenced contemporaries and a generation of industrial designers. Russel Wright, Henry Dreyfuss, and Eliot Noyes were among the notable designers who worked for his firm. An article at the time of his death summarized his contribution to the field of industrial design in "the ideas that never left the drawing board, the dreams that remained dreams . . . but somehow got into the air and were absorbed by hundreds of other designers, who drew inspiration . . . from a man they may never have known."[41]

MASSIMO IOSA GHINI

(b. Bologna, Italy, June 18, 1959)

Although Massimo Iosa Ghini began his architectural studies in Florence, he graduated from the Polytechnic Institute in Milan. In 1981 he joined the group Zak-Art. In 1982 he was one of the founding members of the Bolidist group (from *bolide*, for fast-moving object). In 1985 he moved to Milan and began a collaboration with the RAI network which led him to design a number of television sets. In that year Moroso produced his first piece of furniture, the *Numero Uno* armchair. In 1986 Iosa Ghini was invited by Ettore Sottsass to join the Memphis group, which launched his activity in industrial design and would lead to his work with international furniture manufacturers.[42]

As an architect Iosa Ghini has designed exhibit areas and retail chains internationally; in product design, his firm has developed projects for Ferrari, Maserati, Omnitel, and Infostrade. Additional clients have included Yamagiwa Lighting (Japan), Duravit, Dornbracht and Hoesch (Germany), Roche-Bobois (France), and Moroso, Poltrona Frau, and Cassina, among others (Italy). The Iosa Ghini offices, located in Bologna and Milan, offer services from market research to branding.[43]

MICHAEL GRAVES

(b. Indianapolis, Indiana, July 9, 1934)

Graves received a BA in architecture from The University of Cincinnati in 1958 and a master's degree in architecture from Harvard University in 1959. From 1962 to 1964 he worked in the design office of the modernist George Nelson in New York City. In 1964, he started his own architecture and design firm, which continues to the present in Princeton, New Jersey.[44] He also has an office in New York City.

By the late 1970s Graves was one of the most publicized architects in America, helping to popularize Postmodernism in mainstream America. In addition, he is known as an educator, primarily through his long career of teaching at Princeton University, from 1962 to the present. His first designs for household articles date to the 1980s: deluxe lines for Alessi in Milan and Swid Powell in New York City. He has also designed carpeting for Vorwerk, furniture for SunarHauserman, and fixtures for Duravit, among other companies. In recent years, his designs for moderately priced consumer products for Target, such as the toaster (cat. 175), have broadened his celebrity status. His most celebrated architectural designs include the Public Services Building, Portland, Oregon, 1980; the Humana Building, Louisville, Kentucky, 1982; the Swan and Dolphin hotels, Orlando, Florida, 1987; and the Denver Central Library, 1985. A trustee of the American Academy in Rome, Graves was a fellow there in 1960–62. He holds a dozen honorary degrees and has received ten AIA awards (American Institute of Architects), including its 2001 Gold Medal.

DONALD E. GROVE

To date, Donald E. Grove is known only through his patent applications, including his 1941 design for the Hollywood Liquefier juice extractor (cat. 77), which he assigned to the Hollywood Liquefier Corporation, Los Angeles. Grove was listed on the patent as a resident of West Los Angeles.

LURELLE VAN ARSDALE GUILD

(b. Syracuse, New York, August 19, 1898[45] – d. Darien, Connecticut, March 4, 1985)[46]

In 1936 Forbes magazine listed Guild as one of the five foremost industrial designers in the United States, alongside Dreyfuss, Bel Geddes, Teague, and Loewy. Although best known for his aluminum wares for the Kensington Division of Alcoa, Guild was an industrial designer in many fields, conceiving coaches for the New Haven Railroad, refrigerators for Norge, washing machines for General Electric and Montgomery Ward, air

conditioners for Carrier, typewriters for Underwood-Elliott-Fisher, and building materials for Johns-Manville. His best-known design may be his 1937 Electrolux vacuum cleaner (cat. 34).[47]

While at Syracuse University Guild studied painting and sold freelance designs to different companies. In 1920 he moved to New York where he illustrated interiors for House & Garden and pursued his fascination with the manufacturing techniques and craftsmanship of American and English eighteenth-century furniture. This study led him to the new field of industrial design in 1927 and within three years he established his own firm—Lurelle Guild Associates—with a staff of eight. He also operated Dale Decorators, which sold the firm's wallpapers, curtains, and carpeting door-to-door.[48] Guild's work for Alcoa, which began in 1927, transcended the usual designer-client relation and he became the design voice of the company in the 1930s. In 1935 he designed the aluminum "museum" at Alcoa's New York offices at 230 Park Avenue (figs. 64–65). In 1942 he also produced a series of streamlined drawings, featuring a train, bus, airplane, washing machine, cooker, and weekend cottage for Alcoa, forecasting the postwar "shape of aluminum things to come."[49] His work for the company continued after the war, but tapered off in the 1950s as Alcoa sought new talent.

WAYNE A. GUSTAFSON

(b. Minnesota, January 9, 1921—d. Fennimore, Wisconsin, December 11, 1999)[50]

According to the 1946 patent specifications for a portable electric space heater (cat. 117), Gustafson lived in Minneapolis and assigned his design invention to M. S. Aviation Co. of the same city.

WILLIAM H. HARSTICK

(b. Iowa, c. 1872)[51]

To date, William H. Harstick is known only through several of his patent applications, including his 1939 invention for a cream separator (cat. 53), which he designed with Albert W. Scarratt and Raymond Loewy. Harstick was listed as a resident of Kenilworth, Illinois. The 1930 census lists his residence as Savanna, Illinois, and his occupation as engineer.

ROBERT HELLER

(b. New Jersey, January 14, 1899 – d. Cleveland, Ohio, January 1973)[52]

Heller was a well-known figure in the design world of the 1930s and 1940s, both as an industrial designer and interior architect, and his work was often published. His 1933 design for the WCAU broadcasting station and theater in Philadelphia was an Art Deco monument with a façade of blue cement and zigzag stainless steel trim, celebrating the glamour of radio. According to an article of 1934, Heller also designed the furniture for New York's Bonwit Teller store and the Samuel Paley house in Chestnut Hill, Pennsylvania. He was quoted as saying he was interested in industrial design in addition to "commercial styling."[53]

In 1948 Heller converted a townhouse at 161 East 61st Street, New York City, into living quarters and new offices for his business, tearing down almost all nonbearing walls (which impressed a New York Times reporter).[54]

Among a number of his interior designs in the modern style published in magazines was the apartment in beige with ebony furnishings for D. H. Silberberg in New York.[55] His fan for A. C. Gilbert is his best-known product design (cat. 114). Other designs for A. C. Gilbert included an electric humidifier (1935), a percolator and a toaster (1936), an electric fan (1937), and an electric mixer (1938). In 1952 he patented a series of patterned carpet designs for C. H. Masland & Sons, Carlisle, Pennsylvania.

EDWARD C. HOFFMANN

In his 1939 patent specifications for an electric pencil sharpener (cat. 21), Edward C. Hoffmann was listed as a resident of University City, Missouri, a suburb of St. Louis.

SAMUEL N. HOPE

(b. Fond du Lac, Wisconsin, February 24, 1887 – d. Milwaukee, Wisconsin, October 1969)[56]
In 1908 Hope graduated from the University of Wisconsin with a degree in engineering and moved to Milwaukee to work for the AO Smith Co., which manufactured frames for automobiles. During World War I he served in Europe as captain in the Army Corps of Engineers. After the war he returned to Milwaukee and joined the Briggs and Stratton Corporation, where he became chief engineer. In 1922 he and Raymond Griffith left the firm to start the Griffith-Hope Co., which manufactured metal-stamping equipment. Through Hope's friendship with a paper company founder, Griffith-Hope soon specialized in designing and manufacturing dispensers for paper products. From 1922 until his death in 1969, Hope was awarded over forty patents, primarily for such dispensers.[57] In the 1940 patent specifications for a cup dispensing cabinet (cat. 24), he assigned the patent to the Lily-Tulip Cup Corporation. His other clients included the Fort Howard Paper and Marathon Paper companies, now both part of Georgia-Pacific Corporation.

ALFONSO IANNELLI

(b. Andretta, Italy, February 17, 1888 – d. March 1965)[58]
Born in poverty in rural Italy, Iannelli immigrated with his family to the United States in 1898 and settled in Newark, New Jersey. At thirteen Iannelli was forced to leave school because of the family's economic hardships and was apprenticed to a jeweler. Then in 1900 he was apprenticed to Gutzon Borglum, a well-known sculptor of the time. Throughout his life Iannelli would be known primarily as a sculptor, though his role as an industrial designer was equally important.[59]

In 1908 Iannelli left Newark and moved to Cincinnati to work as chief designer for a lithograph company. In 1910 he moved to Los Angeles, working as a graphic designer and as a sculptor. His first work was in stained glass and then posters for a local theater. His best-known commission came in 1914, when he was twenty-six, for a project in Chicago to create stylized decorative figures for Frank Lloyd Wright's Midway Gardens. Wright did not give Iannelli artistic credit, and the sculptor deeply resented Wright for this oversight. Nevertheless, Iannelli moved to Chicago, establishing a studio in Park Ridge while teaching industrial design at Hull

House and The Art Institute of Chicago. His sculptural commissions were often for churches in the Chicago area, and he designed stained glass as well. Although he refused to collaborate with Wright again, he worked for other Prairie School architects such as Purcell & Elmslie and Barry Byrne.

For Chicago's 1933 World's Fair, Iannelli designed a number of exhibits and the streamlined façade for Raymond Hood's Electrical Group pavilion. His clients for consumer products included Sunbeam, Eversharp, Parker, and Oster, among others. Although Iannelli's sculpture and graphic designs tended toward angular cubistic compositions, his industrial designs adhered to the tenets of streamlining.

HERBERT C. JOHNSON

To date, the only information available about Herbert C. Johnson derives from the 1946 patent application for the *Juice King* juice extractor (cat. 66). The application cites him as the inventor and a resident of Wilmette, Illinois.

CLARENCE KARSTADT

(b. New York, New York, August 18, 1902 – d. Santa Monica, California, October 1968)[60]
Karstadt was the youngest of eight children born to John Karstadt, a painter and decorator, and Regina Weber, both German émigrés.[61] In 1934 Clarence took out a design patent for a streamlined automobile hood ornament and listed his residence as 757 Covington Drive, Detroit. He was still in Detroit in 1936 when he took out two additional patents, for a water closet and another streamlined hood ornament. Known for his designs of household products for Sears, Roebuck and Co., Karstadt is listed on the patent specifications for the 1938 *Silvertone Rocket* radio (cat. 125) as residing in Chicago. By 1939 he had moved to Glen Ellyn, Illinois, a prosperous Chicago suburb. This was his address on the patent applications he filed in 1945 for a handsomely streamlined upright vacuum cleaner (D145,215). He continued to design appliances, including a portable vacuum in 1948 and a food mixer in 1950. Although listed in the city directories in 1952 as still living in Glen Ellyn, his patent application for a humidifier in 1951 listed his residence as Santa Barbara, as did a patent application in 1952. By 1960 he had moved to Pacific Palisades, California.

RUSSELL KATZ

(b. March 22, 1898 – d. Butler, Ohio, January 1966)[62]
To date Russell Katz is known only through several of his patent applications including his 1938 design for a casing for an autographic register (cat. 10). Katz was listed as resident of Hamilton, Ohio.

WILLIS A. KROPP

(b. Illinois, July 16, 1906 – d. Deland, Florida, August 23, 1999)[63]
Kropp is listed as a resident of Chicago in a 1939 patent application for his design for an adding machine (cat. 5), which he assigned to the Victor Adding Machine Co. A 1946 design patent for a comma-shaped bottle opener lists him as living in Summit, New Jersey. Kropp subsequently resided in Stamford, Connecticut, according to a 1966 utility patent; a 1967 utility patent for a gas-dispensing device refers to him in Duxbury,

Massachusetts; and a 1972 utility patent for an inhalation-activated aerosol dispenser puts him in Warner, New Hampshire.

RALPH E. KRUCK

(b. April 20, 1906 – d. Clinton, Connecticut, March 20, 1994)[64]
Kruck's streamlined containers (cat. 69–70) were designed in 1939 for The Hall China Company and produced as giveaways accompanying refrigerators by Westinghouse. With such a close collaboration between companies, it is not surprising that in 1943 Kruck left Hall China to work for Westinghouse as Manager of the Product Design Department of the Appliance Division. For Westinghouse, according to a contemporary article, Kruck would be responsible for "appearance designing" of "electric ranges, automatic laundering machines and all other appliances. . . ."[65] It is unknown how long he was employed by the company. In 1941 he had patented a vacuum cleaner and an electric fan for Westinghouse; both applications cite him as a resident of Springfield, Massachusetts. In a 1946 utility patent for a lipstick container, his address changed to Longmeadow, Massachusetts, and in a 1949 patent for a kitchen range, he was listed as a resident of Clinton, Connecticut. Kruck's later patents were primarily for cosmetic devices such as rouge applicators and aerosol sprays, the last application in 1975 when he was living in Waterbury, Connecticut.

PETER W. LAHR

(b. Wisconsin, October 26, 1893 – d. Racine, Wisconsin, April 1983)[66]
To date, Peter W. Lahr is known only through his patent applications, including one from 1950 for a floor polisher (cat. 36). Lahr was listed as a resident of Racine, Wisconsin, and assigned his patent to S. C. Johnson & Son, Inc., the manufacturer of the polisher.

JOHN LARKIN

(b. Zaragoza, Spain, December 19, 1960)
Born in Spain to American parents in the Foreign Service, Larkin grew up in Germany, Turkey, and Japan.[67] He came to the United States at the age of seventeen to study at the University of Idaho, where he graduated with a BFA in sculpture in 1984. Larkin remained in Moscow, Idaho, and in 1985 started his own industrial design firm called Machine Language, which continues to the present. His clients include Nike, Trek, Burton Snowboards, Marvin Windows, and Limar, for which he designed the *F-111* helmet (cat. 180). His specialty is sports equipment, and he has enjoyed national recognition for his work. He received design awards from *I.D. Magazine* in 1995 and *Consumer Reports* in 1999, among others. He teaches industrial design at the University of Idaho.

HENRY DE SEGUR LAUVE

(b. Montclair, New Jersey, September 3, 1910 – d. Grosse Pointe, Michigan, September 1, 1998)[68]
A cum laude graduate of the University of Paris, Lauve also earned a degree in philosophy from the Sorbonne and then studied design at the Kunstgewerbeschule in Vienna.[69] His first job was in New York, working in advertising and commercial art, but in 1939 he was recruited by Harley Earl to work for General Motors and he moved to Detroit as a bilingual designer for the company. He would spend seventeen years at GM, rising to become chief designer for the Buick division and for interiors in all divisions. Among his stylish contributions to automotive designs were the 1948 Buick *Roadmaster* convertible and the first Corvette, produced in 1953. When he was passed over for the position of design chief, Lauve left GM in 1957 to work independently. His design for a scale for Fairbanks, Morse (cat. 82), patented in 1961, is an example of his work in independent practice. He also designed electrical appliances, including toasters and lawnmowers, and a few buildings in Israel and Mexico. In 1972, as a design consultant to Citroën-Maserati, he designed the car of the year, the *SM*; and in 1985 he conceived the prototype *Silver Volt*, a luxury, six-passenger, battery-powered sedan, for the Electric Car Co.

WAYNE LESER

(b. August 1, 1892 – d. Rosedale, New York, October 1985)[70]
To date, Wayne Leser is known only through his 1941 patent specifications for an "air finned smoking pipe" (cat. 111). He was listed as a resident of South Ozone Park, New York.

LEW W. LESSLER

(b. Wisconsin, c. 1901)[71]
To date, Lew W. Lessler is known only through his utility patent application for the construction of the *Flash Champion* camera (cat. 143), which he assigned to General Aniline & Film Corporation, New York, New York. Lessler was listed as a resident of Johnson City, New York. According to the 1930 census, Lessler was a resident of Binghamton, New York, and his occupation was listed as a mechanical engineer in the field of "camera works."

RAYMOND LOEWY

(b. Paris, France, November 5, 1893 – d. Monte Carlo, July 14, 1986)
"Raymond started industrial design and the streamlining movement," said the architect Philip Johnson about Raymond Loewy.[72] This versatile, prolific, and flamboyant designer epitomized the new profession from the late 1920s. In his lengthy and active career, his clients included Westinghouse Electric, Hupp Motor, Studebaker, Coca-Cola, United Airlines, Shell Oil, Exxon Oil, International Business Machines, and the National Aeronautics and Space Administration.[73]

Loewy attended the University of Paris from 1910 to 1912, and after serving in the French Army Corps of Engineering in World War I, received a degree in engineering from the École de Laneau in 1918. In 1919 he moved to New York City where he worked as a freelance window designer for Saks Fifth Avenue and Bonwit Teller as well as a fashion illustrator for *Vogue*, *Vanity Fair*, and *Harper's Bazaar*. He opened his own industrial design firm in 1929. His greatest successes include the Gestetner duplicating machine housing (1929), the *Hupmobile* car (1932), the *Coldspot* refrigerator for Sears, Roebuck (1934), and the Pennsylvania Railroad *S-1* locomotive (1937). By 1944, when he formed Raymond Loewy Associates with four partners, he was a design consultant to over one hundred companies, and had offices in New York, Chicago, London, São Paulo, and South Bend, Indiana.

Loewy's Lucky Strike cigarette package of 1942 indicates his mastery of corporate packaging and branding, fields that flourished from the 1950s. His postwar clients, many in the oil business, included British Petroleum, Shell, Standard Oil, and Esso, the last of which became recognizable as Exxon with his design supervision. Among his U.S. government projects were the design of Air Force One for President John F. Kennedy and the interiors of the Skylab orbiting space stations for NASA. His autobiography, *Never Leave Well Enough Alone* (1950), was reissued in 2002.

ROSS LOVEGROVE

(b. Cardiff, Wales, August 16, 1958)[74]

The designer of the *Go Chair*, cat. 173, Lovegrove graduated from Manchester Polytechnic (England) in 1980 with a BA in industrial design, and received a master's degree from the Royal College of Art, London, in 1983. He was first employed by Allied International Designers, London, and the widely acclaimed consultancy frog design inc. of Altensteig, Germany, where he worked on the Sony *Walkman* and Apple Computer designs. In 1984 in Paris, he became in-house designer for Knoll International and a member of the Atelier de Nîmes, a group of designers including Philippe Starck, Jean Nouvel, Martine Bedin, and Gérard Barrau. At the Atelier, his clients included Louis Vuitton, Cacharel, DuPont, and Hermès. In 1986, Lovegrove returned to London and, with Julian Brown, cofounded Lovegrove and Brown Design Studio; in 1990 he established his own industrial design practice, Studio X. International clients for his firm have since included Sony, British Airways, Kartell, Cappellini, Phillips, TAG Heuer, Driade, Luceplan, Herman Miller, and Apple. In 1993 he curated the first permanent collection at the Design Museum, London. Since 1997 solo exhibitions of his work have been held in Cologne, Copenhagen, Stockholm, and Tokyo. In 2001 the magazine *Architektur & Wohnen* named him designer of the year.

JOSEPH M. MAJEWSKI, JR.

(b. Missouri, c. 1887)[75]

To date, Majewski is known only through his patent applications, including his 1937 design for a "fruit press" (cat. 67) submitted on behalf of the Rival Manufacturing Co., Kansas City, Missouri. The designer is cited there as a resident of Kansas City. According to the 1930 census, Majewski was the proprietor of a pattern and model shop in that city. Between 1936 and 1946 Majewski took out a number of patents for kitchen products, most of them assigned to John C. Hockery, Foster L. Talge, and Henry J. Talge of Rival Manufacturing. The majority were designs for juice extraction, one of which used the same principles in an ice crusher; and there were also applications for an electric broiler and an insulated liquid dispenser intended to prevent spills when used on airplanes.

ROLAND A. MANNING

(b. April 18, 1906 – d. Sheboygan, Wisconsin, April 23, 1993)[76]

Manning, the designer of the air compressor (cat. 48) appears only twice in directories for Milwaukee, Wisconsin, where he was living when he assigned his 1938 patent to The Electric Sprayit Co. He was listed in the 1937 Milwaukee City Directory with his wife, Helen, and identified as an industrial designer. In the following year he and his wife were still living at the same address, but his occupation was then listed as designer at Moe-Bridges Co., a company that began as a manufacturer of lighting fixtures in 1919. Moe-Bridges continued in operation until 1943, after which it disappeared from the city directories.[77]

CASPER J. MILLER

To date, Casper J. Miller is known only through his 1951 utility patent for the *Relax-it* Massager (cat. 87). He was listed as a resident of Los Angeles, California.

JOHN (JACK) RICHARD MORGAN

(b. Canada, 1903 – d. 1986)

After attending the Detroit Technical Institute, Morgan joined the styling section of General Motors in 1928, where he was responsible for conceiving the first automobile bumper to be integrated into the overall car design. In 1934 he became chief product designer at Sears, Roebuck and Company where he designed appliances. In the patent specifications for his 1935 design for a roller skate (cat. 135), Morgan listed himself as a citizen of Great Britain, residing in Oak Park, Illinois. In the patent specifications for his 1938 design for the *Silvertone Rocket* radio for Sears, Morgan listed himself as a citizen of Guatemala, again residing in Oak Park, Illinois. In 1944 he opened his own office, Jack Morgan Associates, at 919 North Michigan Avenue in Chicago, designing small and large appliances, and working for such firms as Dormeyer, Hotpoint, Magic Chef, RCA, Camfield, and Webcor. His associates included Harry Giambrone, John Defner, and Burton Kelly.[78] Three of Morgan's designs were illustrated in Harold Van Doren's 1940 book *Industrial Design: A Practical Guide*, including his streamlined skates for Sears.

JASPER MORRISON

(b. London, England, 1959)

In 1982 Morrison graduated with a degree in design from the Kingston Polytechnic Design School, London, and in 1984 he studied for a year on scholarship at the Hochschule der Kunste, Berlin.[79] In 1985 he received a master's degree in design from the Royal College of Art, London. In 1986 he set up his design office in London, which continues today. He first drew significant attention at Documenta 8 in Kassel, Germany, in 1987, for which he designed the Reuters News Center.

In 1992, in collaboration with James Irvine, he organized *Progetto Ogetto*, a collection of household objects for Cappellini that he conceived together with a group of young European designers. In 1995 his office was commissioned to design trains for Hanover, Germany, said to be the largest light-rail production contract to that date in Europe. The first vehicle, presented in 1997, won awards in transportation design and ecology. He has exhibited at "Interieur '94," Belgium; Bordeaux's Arc en Rêve Centre d'Architecture, 1995; the Axis Gallery and Yamagiwa Center, Tokyo; and as designer of the year at the 2000 Paris Design Fair. Some of Morrison's most important early furniture was produced by the London firm of SCP.

Recent projects include the 1998 design of the London restaurant Pharmacy with artist Damien Hirst and graphic designer Jonathan Barnbrook; furniture for the Tate Modern Gallery, London; and kitchen appliances for Rowenta. In 2002, he worked with publisher Lars Müller to produce *Everything But the Walls*, a summary of his work to date. Morrison's clients have included Alessi, Alias, Canon (camera division), Cappellini, Magis, Rosenthal, Samsung, Sony, and Vitra.

PETER MÜLLER-MUNK

(b. Berlin, Germany, June 25, 1904–d. Pittsburgh, Pennsylvania, March 13, 1967)
Müller-Munk received a degree in the humanities from the Friedrich-Wilhelms Universität, Berlin, and was trained at the Kunstgewerbeschule in Berlin with Waldemar Raemisch, a noted German silversmith. That Müller-Munk learned the precepts of the modern movement in early twentieth-century German design is reflected in the simple geometric shapes and restrained ornament of his wares. After immigrating to the United States in 1926, he worked for three years designing silver for Tiffany & Co. before establishing his own studios, first in New York and Chicago, and then in 1935 in Pittsburgh.[80] In the early 1930s, he moved from producing handcrafted, made-to-order pieces of silver to designing mass-produced objects. The latter, as a contemporary critic noted, "reflect his lifelong precision and refinement of form [acquired] from his early study in Berlin of languages and silversmithing (with a sideline in history). . . ." [81]

Müller-Munk was also deeply committed to the development of the industrial design profession. In 1935 he was a founder of the country's first degree-granting industrial design program, at Pittsburgh's Carnegie Institute of Technology.[82] He resigned from teaching in 1945 to form Peter Müller-Munk Associates, devoted to product design,[83] and he was president of the Society of Industrial Designers in 1954–55 and a founder and the first president of the International Council of that society (1957–59). Among his firm's clients were Westinghouse, U.S. Steel, and Bell & Howell. His 1948 design for a streamlined blender for the Waring Mixer Corporation was widely published. After Müller-Munk's death, his firm continued until 1983.

ISAMU NOGUCHI

(b. Los Angeles, California, November 17, 1904 – d. New York, New York, December 30, 1988)[84]
Of Japanese-American descent, this celebrated artist united aspects of Asian sensibility and Western modernism in a sixty-four year career. Spanning genres from sculpture, painting, furnishings, and product design to stage sets, fountains, playgrounds, and sculpture gardens, his work is marked by its sensuous organic forms and sensitivity to the qualities of materials.

After growing up in Japan, Noguchi returned to the United States in 1918 for high school and attended Columbia University in 1922–24. In 1924 he decided to devote himself to sculpture, and had his first sculpture exhibition. In 1927 he went to Paris on a Guggenheim travel fellowship, where he worked as Constantin Brancusi's assistant for six months. Then followed travels in 1930–32 to Berlin, Moscow, and the Far East, where he studied brush painting in Beijing and ceramics and Zen gardens in Japan. The 1930s brought him recognition: sculpture purchases by the Whitney and Metropolitan museums in New York, 1931–32; first large public monuments, 1933; first stage designs for modern dancer Martha Graham (he would conceive sets for thirteen of her seasons); first mass-produced object, *Radio Nurse*, 1937 (cat. 109); and first fountain design, 1938, for Ford Motors at the 1939 New York World's Fair.

Noguchi's first furniture, of 1939, was biomorphic in form, growing out of his contemporary sculpture; and his coffee table of 1944, manufactured by Herman Miller, and his lamps of c. 1945 and 1954, for Knoll Associates, were widely imitated. In the 1950s his early interest in public monuments and sculpture gardens began to bear fruit in realized projects. Among his best known are the sunken garden for the Beinecke Rare Books Library, Yale University, 1960–64; the Billy Rose Sculpture Garden at Jerusalem's Israel Museum, 1960–65; and the climax of this development, the Isamu Noguchi Garden Museum in Long Island City, New York, 1981–85. In 1986 Noguchi represented the United States at the Venice Biennale; the following year he won the National Medal of Arts; and the year of his death he was named a Sacred Treasure by the Japanese government.

JOSEPH PALMA, JR.

(b. Illinois, c. 1909)[85]
Palma graduated from Chicago's Armour Institute in 1932, worked on the city's *Century of Progress Exposition*, and then took a job at Montgomery Ward's Bureau of Design. According to the patent application for the *Amplicall* intercom (cat. 22), he was a resident of Berwyn, Illinois, and assigned his invention to the Rauland Corporation, Chicago, Illinois, in 1947. This was the year that he and J. Gordon Knapp formed their design partnership, Palma-Knapp Associates, Chicago. Earlier Knapp had studied engineering at Northwestern University, and then pursued manufacturing and business administration. In the 1950s Palma-Knapp had thirteen employees and was known for its designs of business and home equipment.[86] Berwyn, Illinois, directories list Palma through 1953.[87]

MALCOLM S. PARK

(b. Scotland, October 13, 1905 – d. December 5, 1991)[88]
According to his 1938 patent specifications, Park was a resident of Mount Kisco, New York, and assigned his invention for a vacuum cleaner (cat. 33) to the Singer Manufacturing Co., Elizabeth, New Jersey.

SCOTT PATT

(b. Allentown, Pennsylvania, May 20, 1971)
After receiving a BA in graphic design from The Pennsylvania State

University in 1993, Patt studied classical painting, design, and color theory in conjunction with the golden section principles of design at Barnestone Studios, Coplay, Pennsylvania. Patt's first jobs were in graphic design, first at Suzuki Design, Falls Church, Virginia (1994), then with the Giorgio Armani company, New York City (1995–97), where he created monthly national boutique displays and print ads. In 1997 he started working for Nike in Portland, Oregon, first in the Team Sports division (1997–98), then as a senior designer for Nike Image Design (1998–2000), and as a level II designer in Cross Training (2000–03), responsible for product engineering, development, and marketing. In 2003 he became senior designer for Active Life at Nike, where his position is the first at Nike to combine graphic design and footwear design.

Patt's combined interest in the fine arts and design is reflected in ongoing exhibitions of his artwork from 1993 to the present. Among the venues displaying his canvases, and selling his related silk-screened shirts and posters, was the Portland Art Museum Contemporary Arts Biennial in the summer of 2003.[89]

WORTHEN PAXTON
(b. July 31, 1905 – d. New York, New York, June 25, 1977)[90]

A graduate from Yale University, he was one of the few U.S. industrial designers trained as an architect. Paxton first worked for Norman Bel Geddes, ultimately becoming president of the firm. In *Magic Motorways* Bel Geddes acknowledged Paxton's contribution to the firm,[91] and in the design of the 1938 *Soda King* Syphon Bottle (cat. 100), Paxton's contribution is evident as his name appears on the patent specifications. He worked on the Pan Am *China Clipper* in 1934 and eight major exhibitions for the Bel Geddes firm at the 1939 New York World's Fair, including the General Motors Building.[92]

During World War II, Paxton served as art editor and assistant managing editor of *Life* magazine, after which he established his own firm, Paxton, Kreugger & Associates Industrial Design.

WALTER B. PAYNE
(b. Virginia, September 27, 1881 – d. Penfield, New York, February 1975)[93]

To date, Walter B. Payne is known only through his patent applications, including his 1940 design with Henry Dreyfuss for a casing for a check-writing machine (cat. 6). According to the 1930 census, Payne was a resident of Rochester, New York, and worked as a mechanical engineer for the Protectograph Mfg. Co.

STEPHEN PEART
(b. Durham, England, June 25, 1958)

Peart was educated at the Sheffield City Polytechnic, where he earned a first class BA degree with honors in industrial design, and at the Royal College of Art, London, where he received a master's degree in the field. He began his career in London, then went on to work for frog design inc. in Germany, and then as a design director in California. In 1987, he established Vent, his own design firm, in Campbell, California. His

Animal wet suit for O'Neill (cat. 178) and adjustable keyboard for Apple Computer both reflect his interest in interfaces between people and their environments, whether natural or technological. His clients also include Nike, Herman Miller, the Knoll Group, Compaq, and Plantronics.

DONALD J. PEEPS
(b. August 26, 1907 – d. Toledo, Ohio, February 1983)[94]

To date, Peeps is known only through his patents for spraying machines, including his 1946 design of an air compressor (cat. 49) with Harold R. Gamble and the Sundberg-Ferrar Company. The application lists Peeps as a resident of Toledo, Ohio. Since most of his patents were assigned to the DeVilbiss Company, he was probably an employee of the Toledo manufacturer. By 1957 he moved to Rossford, Ohio. His last patent, assigned to Champion Spark Plug Co., was granted in 1971 for a safety device for a steam vaporizer.

GLENN W. PERIMAN
(b. Oklahoma, November 5, 1912 – d. Santa Monica, California, September 15, 1983)[95]

To date, Periman is known only through his patent applications, including his 1948 design for a toy racer (cat. 139). His 1947 design for a file box for business cards was also streamlined. His other patents of the 1940s were for clamps and pliers, the first of which was assigned to Aircraft Tools, Inc., of Los Angeles, California. All Periman's applications identify him as a resident of Los Angeles.

WILLIAM B. PETZOLD
(b. Missouri, June 21, 1898 – d. Hamilton, Ohio, August 1983)[96]

Petzold came to Pittsfield, Massachusetts, in 1938 to work as a designer-engineer for the plastics division of General Electric, but he also designed plastic products for other companies, including Autopoint in Chicago. In 1946 he designed an office for himself utilizing plastic or blends of plastic with other materials at 1 Plastics Avenue, Pittsfield. A contemporary description in an article in *The New York Times Magazine* described his all-plastic residence with Lucite drawer pulls, a sofa with synthetic foam rubber cushions covered with black vinylite, a clock with Lucite knobs, and a wall covered with a synthetic resin paint.[97] With his close association with plastic products, it is not surprising that J. H. DuBois would include his work in his classic book *Plastics* for which Petzold designed the cover.[98] Two of his designs were illustrated—the postcard addressing machine (cat. 7) and the "Calendaire" (cat. 13). A lamp designed by Petzold was included in *Plastics History USA*, and a novel radio cabinet was illustrated in General Electric's *Chemical Works News* of November 16, 1951 where it was noted that he was a member of the Society of Industrial Engineers.

ALBERT E. POLLOCK
(b. September 21, 1914 – d. Peace Dale, Rhode Island, May 31, 1992)[99]

According to the 1938 patent specifications for a list finder (cat. 8), Pollock was a resident of New York City.

HARRY S. PREBLE, JR.

(b. October 20, 1911 – d. Centerville, Massachusetts, February 1982)[100]
In 1944 Preble opened a studio at 104 East 40th Street in New York City for the design and development of both commercial and industrial products.[101] This was the same year he applied for a patent for his hairdryer (cat. 83). In 1958 Preble designed a collection of steel pantryware for Heller Hostess-Ware featuring footed bases and a choice of copper or chrome finish. Part of the line included a "step-on garbage can and a music box ice bucket."[102]

ARTHUR RADEBAUGH

(b. 1906 – d. Grand Rapids, Michigan, 1974)
A product of The School of the Art Institute of Chicago, Radebaugh began his career as an illustrator in 1935 and became known for his futuristic designs for such periodicals as *Esquire*, *Fortune*, and *Motor Magazine* and his advertisements for Bohn Aluminum and Brass Corporation of Detroit.[103] He pioneered in the use of airbrush and fluorescent paints, and during World War II developed a method of illuminating Army vehicle instrument panels with blacklight paints, concealing them from enemy detection. After the war, he settled in Detroit and designed the symbol of the city's jubilee as car capital of the world, a woman waving an atom-smashing wand. In addition to Bohn Aluminum (cat. 157–166), his commercial clients included Dodge in the 1930s, Coca-Cola in the late 1940s, and Chrysler in the 1950s. Introduced in 1958, his nationally syndicated cartoon strip, *Closer Than We Think*, ran for four years and inspired futurist fantasy designs by others. In 1962, he retired from illustrating for health reasons.

JAMES H. REICHART

(b. Kentucky, September 8, 1889—d. Detroit, Michigan, September 1973)[104]
To date, James H. Reichart is known only through his patent applications, including his 1944 design for a whistling water kettle (cat. 63). Reichart was listed as a resident of Muncie, Indiana.

JEAN OTIS REINECKE

(b. Bourbon County, Kansas, July 9, 1909 – d. Seal Beach, California, December 8, 1987)[105]
Jean Reinecke attended Kansas State Teachers College and Washington University's art school. In 1930 he opened an office in Chicago to build exhibition displays for the 1933 Chicago *Century of Progress Exposition*. In 1934 Reinecke and Jim Barnes established an industrial design and engineering firm in Chicago. During World War II the Reinecke and Barnes partnership provided an extensive engineering service.[106] The firm rapidly grew to become one of the Midwest's largest and most influential design firms, with 375 employees during the war years.[107] Reinecke is perhaps best known for his tape dispensers for the Minnesota Mining and Manufacturing Company, for which he worked from 1937 to the 1970s. One of the earliest, of 1938, is seen in cat. 18 and a late example, of 1952, appears in cat. 19. In 1948, Reinecke sold his interest in the larger consulting business and began Reinecke Associates, which was devoted to industrial design. Among their many products was the *Toastmaster* for McGraw-Edison, the top-selling toaster of the 1940s and 1950s. In 1952, Reinecke was elected president of the Society of Industrial Designers.[108] He was influential as a teacher, especially as an instructor at the New Bauhaus in Chicago and as a lecturer and advisor throughout the country.

FREDERICK HURTEN RHEAD

(b. Hanley, Staffordshire, England, August 29, 1880 – d. New York, New York, November 2, 1942)
From a family of artists and potters for many generations, Rhead attended the Wedgwood Institute in Burslem and the Stoke-on-Trent Government Art School. For three years he was an instructor in design at the Government Art School at Longton. He received diplomas in design, modeling, geometry, perspective, and painting. For five years, he was apprenticed at Brownfields, Burslem, Staffordshire, and for three years he was art director of the Wardle Art Pottery, Hanley, Staffordshire. After coming to the United States in 1902, he served as art director at the Roseville Pottery, Zanesville, Ohio, for six years. For three years he was associated with Taxile Doat as an instructor in pottery at Peoples University, University City, St. Louis, Missouri.[109] From 1937 until his death in 1942, he was art director for the Homer Laughlin China Co., Newell, West Virginia, where he created his most famous line—*Fiestaware*.[110]

JOHN GORDON RIDEOUT

(b. St. Paul, Minnesota, 1898 – d. Cleveland, Ohio, 1951)[111]
Rideout studied architecture at the University of Washington before working as a graphic designer in Chicago in the 1920s. In 1931 he moved to Toledo to become the partner with Harold Van Doren in Van Doren and Rideout, one of the first of the emerging industrial design firms in the Midwest. In 1935 Rideout left the partnership and moved to Cleveland where he established his own Company, John Gordon Rideout and Staff.[112] The firm designed products and packaging for Air-King Radio, Easy Washing Machine Corporation, American National Company, DeVilbiss, Swartzbaugh Manufacturing Company, and Toledo Scale.

A contemporary article on new materials in design highlighted Van Doren and Rideout's midget radio for the Air-King Radio in the 1933 exhibition organized by the National Alliance of Art and Industry. The design was "molded into its small form from a new material called Plaskon, its lines suggesting the modern style of architecture."[113]

GILBERT ROHDE

(b. New York, New York, 1894 – d. New York, New York, 1944)[114]
Among the most versatile and prolific furniture designers working in the 1930s and early 1940s, Rohde began his career as a political cartoonist and furniture illustrator. The son of a German-born cabinetmaker, he studied at the Art Students League and Grand Central School of Art in New York, and in 1927 he traveled to France and Germany. Inspired by the modern movement, he opened his own office in the same year to design and produce custom furniture. He designed furniture and showrooms for Troy Sunshade in Ohio, Kroehler, Heywood-Wakefield, and the Herman Miller Furniture Company. In 1932, he was appointed director of design

at Herman Miller and produced furniture and clocks for the "Design for Living House" for the *Century of Progress Exposition*. He also served on the committee of architects and designers that developed the general plan for the 1939 New York World's Fair.

Rohde was also an educator. From 1936 to 1938 he directed the Design Laboratory School established in New York by the Works Progress Administration to train designers, and he headed the industrial design department at New York University School of Architecture from 1939 to 1943. His work was included in the 1932 *Design for the Machine* exhibition in Philadelphia and the 1934 *Machine Art* exhibition at The Museum of Modern Art. In 1940 he exhibited in the *Contemporary American Industrial Art* exhibition at The Metropolitan Museum of Art.[115]

HENRY RUSKIN

(b. August 27, 1908 – d. Cranford, New Jersey, March 2, 1997)[116]
To date Henry Ruskin is known only through several of his patent applications, including his 1940 design for a stapler (cat. 16), which he assigned to the Metal Specialties Manufacturing Co., Chicago, Illinois. Ruskin was listed as a resident of Chicago.

HAROLD S. RYDEN

(b. August 6, 1906—d. Anaheim, California, June 1987)[117]
According to the 1955 patent specifications for his vacuum cleaner (cat. 35), Ryden lived in Anaheim, California, and assigned his vacuum cleaner design to Interstate Precision Products Corporation in the same city.

ABE O. SAMUELS

(b. Ohio, March 30, 1899—d. Westport, Connecticut, May 1966)[118]
To date, Abe O. Samuels is known only through his patent applications, including his 1937 design for an iron (cat. 27), which he assigned to the Samson-United Corporation, Rochester, New York. Samuels was listed as a resident of Rochester.

ROLPH SCARLETT

(b. Guelph, Ontario, Canada, June 13, 1889 – d. Kingston, New York, August 7, 1984)[119]
Product and stage design and Kandinsky-inspired abstract painting occupied this prolific artist, sometimes simultaneously, through his long career. He showed a gift for drawing as a boy, and first pursued a career in the jewelry business in New York and Toronto before and after World War I. In 1923 in Geneva, on a business trip for the Swiss Omega Watch Company, he met the painter Paul Klee by chance, and was encouraged to pursue a career as an artist and stage designer. Between 1926 and 1932 he lived in Toledo, Ohio, Hollywood (where he designed film sets), and his birthplace, Guelph. He began winning prizes for his paintings, works that would bring him a Guggenheim Foundation scholarship and a position as a lecturer at the Museum of Non-Objective Painting (now the Solomon R. Guggenheim Museum) after he returned to New York in 1933. There in 1934-39 he was also a freelance product designer of domestic goods, from bar wares and game boards to light fixtures and furniture. Over 800

of his carefully rendered designs, made as proposals, survive and are held in the Stewart Collection at the Montreal Museum of Fine Arts (cat. 101-102). In 1935-37 Scarlett also designed sets for Radio City Music Hall. Uniting his skills in product and stage design was his display for the Bakelite Company in the Industrial Science Building at the 1939 New York World's Fair. In 1941-62 Scarlett worked for the Swivelier Company, designing swivel-mounted light fixtures for commercial use, while exhibiting his paintings. After his retirement, he painted full-time until his death at age ninety-five.

ALBERT W. SCARRATT

(b. St. Paul, Minnesota, April 16, 1886 – d. Elgin, Illinois, January 5, 1966)[120]
In the patent specifications for the cream separator (cat. 53), Scarratt is listed along with Raymond Loewy and William H. Harstick as inventors. According to the 1930 census, he lived in Evanston, Illinois, at that date; and in Kenilworth, Illinois, from 1932 to 1969, according to that city's directories. Scarratt was a vice-president of International Harvester and a member of the Society of Automotive Engineers.[121]

DR. PETER SCHLUMBOHM

(b. Kiel, Germany, 1896 – d. New York, New York, November 6, 1962)
Famous for his many inventions, Peter Schlumbohm, the son of a chemical manufacturer, graduated from Berlin University with a doctorate in chemistry. In 1931, despite the Depression in the United States, Schlumbohn moved to New York, "attracted by U.S. patent laws, which he found the world's best from an inventor's viewpoint."[122] Among his first inventions in the United States were vacuum-bottle designs for The American Thermos Bottle Co. In his loft studio at 41 Murray Street, "he devised the Minnehaha, a device that mixes and aerates cocktails . . . a frying pan that never needs to be washed, and a lidless hot water kettle."[123]

His most famous and successful invention was the *Chemex*, an hourglass-shaped Pyrex coffee maker designed for use with paper filters. According to Schlumbohm, filtered coffee was a better and healthier drink than coffee made by other methods because the "vile mixture of some 50 different chemicals are eliminated by filtering."[124] He held over three hundred patents for his many designs. Schlumbohm insisted that "no design was viable unless it was rooted in invention. . . ."[125] Archives for Schlumbohm are located in the Hagley Museum and Library.

VIKTOR SCHRECKENGOST

(b. Sebring, Ohio, June 26, 1906)
Best known as a ceramist, Schreckengost is also notable for his wide-ranging invention and his vitality: though he retired from his industrial design practice in 1972, he continued teaching the subject at the Cleveland Museum of Art into his nineties.

Schreckengost learned clay modeling from his father, a commercial potter, and studied at the Cleveland School of Art (now The Cleveland Institute of Art) in 1924-29.[126] In 1930 he traveled to Austria to attend Vienna's progressive Kunstgewerbeschule. He returned to Ohio a year later and began winning awards in ceramics and exhibiting his designs nationally. His most coveted work is the Art Deco *Jazz* punchbowl of 1931, commissioned by Eleanor Roosevelt and executed by the Cowan Pottery Co., Rocky River, Ohio. The Cowan Co. closed that year, defeated by the Depression, but Schreckengost diversified: in the mid-1930s he designed the first modern dinnerware for mass production in the United States, by American Limoges; the first cab-over-engine truck, with the engineer Ray Spiller, for the White Motor Co.; and the first *Mercury* bicycle, for Murray Bicycles, Murray, Ohio, beginning a relation that helped make Murray the largest bike manufacturer in the world. During this fertile period, he designed the streamlined Jiffy Ware pitcher (cat. 71).

During World War II, Schreckengost developed a radar recognition system for the Navy; subsequently he returned to industrial design with clients including Sears, Roebuck and Co., GE, Salem China, and Harris Printing. His products ranged from flashlights to refrigerators and broadcast equipment, but he never gave up ceramics. In 1947 he exhibited "hewn clay" forms, carved rather than wheel-thrown objects, in a process later identified with ceramists such as Peter Voulkos. Schreckengost has lived long enough to celebrate his retrospective at the Cleveland Museum of Art in 2000.

EDWARD P. SCHREYER

(b. Romania, April 22, 1896 – d. Boca Raton, Florida, July 1981)
To date, Edward P. Schreyer is known only through his patent applications, including his 1941 design for the *Petipoint* iron (cat. 29), where he is listed, along with Clifford Brooks Stevens, as inventor. Since Stevens assigned the patent to Schreyer, it is likely that Schreyer worked for the manufacturer, Waverly Tool Company, Sandusky, Ohio. Schreyer was listed as a resident of Milwaukee, Wisconsin. According to the 1930 census, Schreyer came to the U. S. in 1901 with his brother. At the time of the census, they were living in Brooklyn, and Edward was working in bankruptcy sales.

BARTON T. SETCHELL

(b. Minnesota, November 6, 1907 – d. Boynton Beach, Florida, November 1, 1995)[127]
To date, Barton T. Setchell is known only through his patent applications, including his 1946 design for a table radio (cat. 129), presumably submitted on behalf of his own company, Setchell-Carlson, Inc. Setchell was listed as a resident of St. Paul, Minnesota. According to the 1930 census, Setchell was a proprietor of a retail radio shop.

ARTHUR W. SEYFRIED

(b. Germany, January 14, 1898 – d. Cleveland, Ohio, September 1984)[128]
According to the 1952 patent specifications for the drink mixer (cat. 52), Arthur W. Seyfried was a resident of Racine, Wisconsin. According to the 1930 census, he previously resided in Cleveland, Ohio and was a superintendent at an electrical manufacturing company.

SEYMOUR POWELL

Richard Seymour (b. Scarborough, England, May 1, 1953)
Dick Powell (b. Great Kingshill, England, December 26, 1951)

The son of one of Europe's leading product designers, Richard Seymour received a master's degree in graphic and interdisciplinary studies from the Royal College of Art, London, in 1976, and became a freelance art director the following year.[129] As creative director of Blazelynn Advertising in 1979–82, he won awards for book and record cover designs, interests that evolved into work on commercials for books and new products and on film production designs through 1984. In that year he joined Dick Powell to form the London design firm Seymour Powell.

Dick Powell graduated with a BA in industrial design from Manchester Polytechnic in 1973 and received his master's degree in the field from the Royal College in 1976, the year he won his second Burton Award. In 1980–83 he was a freelance designer and part-time lecturer on industrial and car design, and won a Mamiya competition to design a camera of the future.

Clients of the Seymour Powell firm have included BMW, Jaguar, Renault, and Ford, as well as Nokia, Casio, Dell, T-Fal, and Hewlett-Packard. Around forty percent of the partners' consultancies and awards are in transportation design. They are also known for their design commentaries on television and radio programs; Seymour writes regularly on the subject. Seymour Powell's research team, SP Foresight, explores future products and services; their *Better by Design* series on British television has rethought such products as the bra, the bathroom, the kitchen cabinet, and the economy airline seat.

PHILMORE F. SPERRY

(b. Missouri, February 23, 1890 – d. April 1942)[130]
According to the 1939 patent application for a design for a motion picture projector (cat. 145), Sperry was a resident of Chicago and assigned his patent to the Revere Camera Company of that city. According to the 1930 census, Sperry was a resident of Chicago and was a mechanical engineer at Radiator Co.

CLIFFORD BROOKS STEVENS

(b. Milwaukee, Wisconsin, June 7, 1911 – d. Thiensville, Wisconsin, January 4, 1995)[131]
Brooks Stevens attended local schools in Milwaukee and when he contracted polio, his father encouraged him to develop his talent for drawing while bedridden. He studied architecture at Cornell University from 1929 to 1933.[132] As the Depression curtailed new construction and the opportunity for architectural commissions, Stevens returned to Milwaukee without graduating to work as a package designer at Jewett and Sherman. In 1934 Stevens opened his own design office and began to develop staff and find clients through his family's social connections in the Milwaukee area. His business grew and its prodigious output included products for hundreds of clients. His firm designed household appliances, farm machinery, motorcycles, buses, trucks, powerboats, trains, snowmobiles, and aircraft. One of the founders of the Society of Industrial Designers in 1944, he retired from business in 1983, and taught at the Milwaukee Institute of Art & Design.[133]

CHARLES P. STRITE

To date, Charles P. Strite is known only through his patent applications, including his 1926 design for a bread toaster for Waters-Genter Company, Minneapolis, Minnesota (cat. 57). Strite was listed as a resident of Minneapolis.

SUNDBERG-FERAR COMPANY

Carl W. Sundberg (b. Calumet, Michigan, March 11, 1910 – d. Boynton Beach, Florida, March 1982)[134]

Montgomery Ferar (b. Boston, Massachusetts, April 14, 1909[135] – d. Lutz, Florida, March 1982)[136]

Carl Sundberg graduated from Northern High School and attended Wicker Art School in Detroit. He began his career in 1927 designing custom car bodies for the Dietrich Body Co.; subsequently he worked as a body designer and model supervisor at the General Motors Corporation where he met Montgomery Ferar. In 1934 the two established the Sundberg-Ferar firm.

Montgomery Ferar graduated from MIT in 1932 with a master's degree in architecture, and in 1933 he traveled in France, Germany, and the Scandinavian countries. Soon after his return he and Sundberg became partners. By 1936, the firm was known for designing business machines, refrigerator parts, automobile accessories, and small products, as well as heavy industrial equipment.[137] The firm continues in business today, and asserts that "Sundberg-Ferar is in the business of tomorrow, and we have been in the business of tomorrow since 1934."[138]

JOHN B. SUOMALA

(b. Fitchburg, Massachusetts, July 8, 1896 – d. Moorestown, New Jersey, June 1, 1985)[139]

Born of Finnish immigrants to Fitchburg, Massachusetts, Suomala gained mechanical proficiency from his father who worked at the Marshall Orchard and designed machinery for handling and processing its fruit. While attending Fitchburg High School, John Suomala was enrolled in a cooperative education program in industry, and he learned precision grinding at the Bath Grinder Company. After his graduation in 1914, he continued working there. Later he moved to Erie, Pennsylvania, to work as a machinist for the American Brake Shoe and Foundry Company, and became expert with high-speed steel-cutting tools. A position at West Electric Company took Suomala to Cleveland for a brief period where he developed machines to cut and form women's hair clips from spring steel. He married; the couple then settled near Philadelphia, and he began employment at the Victor Talking Machine Co. in Camden, New Jersey. In 1929 the firm was bought by the Radio Corporation of America, and during the transition he worked at Stearns Motor Car and Leeds & Northrup in Philadelphia, before resuming what would be a long career as an engineer at RCA.

Sometime after 1931 the family moved to Camden, and in 1936, to Haddonfield, New Jersey.[140] Suomala's early inventions for RCA were related to record players, record changers, and associated devices. In 1932 the company experimented with 33 1/3 rpm records, and he designed a ball bearing planetary speed reducer that would allow playing 33 1/3 records on the same turntable as 78 rpm discs. He also invented a pull-out turntable drawer for record player cabinets, replacing the old top-access model; and low-cost turntables connected to AM radios, intended to promote the sale of RCA records. He took out six U.S. patents,[141] including a 1939 patent application for a record player (cat. 122). During World War II he helped develop magnetic anomaly detection equipment to locate submerged submarines; and afterwards he was an engineer at RCA's Home Instruments Division. He retired in 1961.

WALTER DORWIN TEAGUE

(b. Decatur, Indiana, December 18, 1883 – d. Flemington, New Jersey, December 5, 1960)

Like many of his colleagues Teague began in advertising, and he went on to become one of the first industrial designers in America and an early advocate of streamlining.[142] His first work was pictorial: in 1903–1907 he studied at New York's Art Students League, and he created typographical designs and illustrations for mail-order catalogues, becoming known for his decorative borders framing ads. After working for Calkins & Holden and another New York advertising agency, he opened his own office in 1910, and catered to a clientele primarily of advertising agencies and publishers. Teague dated his conversion to industrial design to 1926, when he studied the work of Le Corbusier in Europe. From then on he championed the new field of industrial design and distinguished himself by the functionalism and sober elegance of his product conceptions. He expressed his theories in *Design This Day: The Technique of Order in the Machine Age*, published in 1940.

Although Teague worked for many major corporations—Ford, U.S. Steel, Corning Glass, and National Cash Register—he is most identified with his designs for his lifelong client Eastman Kodak Company. A "progressive conservative,"[143] as the Cheneys described him, he was known for his straightforward designs for domestic objects, which by mid-century included Scripto pens and Schaefer beer cans. In 1940 he was the founder and first president of the American Society of Industrial Designers, and in 1951–53 he served as president of the American Institute of Graphic Arts. His New York firm was incorporated in 1967 and continues to the present.

RICHARD TEN EYCK

(b. Marseilles, Illinois, 1920)

After studying industrial design at the University of Illinois, Urbana, in the 1930s, Ten Eyck was employed by several factories in Chicago and Aurora, Illinois. During World War II he worked on product designs for Montgomery Ward in the Chicago office of Dave Chapman. In 1945 he moved to Wichita, Kansas, to design the Bonanza airplane and an experimental automobile for Beech Aircraft. He opened his own office in 1948, and counted Cessna Aircraft Company among his clients, serving as chief consulting designer to the aircraft manufacturer. Around 1948 he designed the Vornado fan (cat. 116). In 1996 Ten Eyck closed his Wichita office and retired to Orlando, Florida, where he still resides.[144]

JOSEPH PALIN THORLEY

(b. England, June 4, 1892 – d. Lightfoot, Virginia, February 1987)[145]
After serving in World War I, Thorley worked as an apprentice for seven years at the Wedgwood factory, and moved to the United States in 1929. He was employed by several ceramic manufacturers, and in c. 1940 became art director of The Hall China Company, East Liverpool, Ohio. A book on decorative art included an example of his work, which *The New York Times* cited in its 1931 review as an "excellent dinner service."[146]

HAROLD LIVINGSTON VAN DOREN

(b. Chicago, Illinois, March 2, 1895 – d. Philadelphia, Pennsylvania, February 3, 1957)[147]
A native of the Midwest, Van Doren finished high school in New Jersey, graduated from Williams College in 1917, and served in the Army during World War I. From 1920 to 1921 he studied at the Art Students League, New York. He then went to Paris for two years (1922–24) with a fellowship in the history of art and worked as a lecturer at the Louvre, an artist for the *Chicago Tribune*'s Paris edition, an actor in a Jean Renoir film, and a translator of books on Cézanne and Renoir. He returned to the United States to become assistant director at the The Minneapolis Institute of Arts (1927–30).

Credited with introducing industrial design to the Midwest, Van Doren formed a design partnership in 1931 in Toledo, Ohio, with John Gordon Rideout. According to the Cheneys, "Van Doren was the first man we know of in America to go extensively into experiments with new synthetic materials (known under the group name of 'the Plastics') with the purpose of applying to them the scientific principles of modern color, as the artist understands them, and the principles of color standardization as required in modern merchandising practice. . ."[148]

RUSSELL E. VANDERHOFF

(b. Wisconsin, April 24, 1897 – d. Oak Lawn, Illinois, September 1982)[149]
According to the 1933 patent application, Vanderhoff was a resident of Chicago and assigned his invention to the Health-O-Meter Company of that city. According to the 1930 census, Vanderhoff resided in Chicago and was a factory supervisor with Scale Works.

JOHN VASSOS

(b. Bucharest, Romania, October 23, 1898 – d. Norwalk, Connecticut, December 6, 1985)[150]
Born John Vassacopoulos, of Greek parents living in Constantinople, Vassos studied from 1912 to 1914 at Robert College, an American-run private academy in Constantinople.[151] In 1919 he immigrated to the United States, first to Boston, where he studied with John Singer Sargent, then to New York, attending the Art Students League from 1921 to 1922 and then the New York School of Design in 1923. He worked as an assistant staff designer to Joseph Urban, before turning to industrial design and illustration. His graphic design career included work for books written by his wife, Ruth Carriere Vassos, including *Contempo* (1929), *Ultimo* (1930), and *Humanities* (1935).

Among his most important designs were radios and televisions for RCA, where in 1932 he began a thirty-eight-year consultancy. Vassos recalled:

"My first job was the elimination of the wooden tombstone radio, which had dominated the market-place since its introduction. In 1934 we introduced the first plastic radio, which met with great public acceptance. At the same time, although a survey indicated a preference for either six or four legs for console radios, I designed the first console to the floor."[152] Other clients for his display designs included *Harper's Bazaar*, Macy's, Saks Fifth Avenue, and Lord & Taylor. Other industrial design clients were Waterman, Remington, and DuPont. His description of an industrial designer for an educational film sums up his own life: "Leonardo da Vinci was the first industrial designer—he could paint pictures, design tools, guns, fortifications, water systems, air-planes, even clothes for his patrons. The perfect example of the renaissance man and the industrial designer."[153]

LOUIS VAVRIK

(b. Straznice, Czechoslovakia, August 5, 1904 – d. Rossford, Ohio, January 10, 1995)[154]
After graduating from high school, Vavrik attended Prague Technical Engineering School and the Fine Arts Institute of Prague. In 1923, he immigrated to the United States, following his father and older brother who had already moved to the Toledo area to work for the Edward Ford Plate Glass Co. of Rossford, Ohio.[155] In Ohio Louis attended night school for English and American citizenship and took courses in industrial design and art at the Toledo Museum of Art.

He began his career as a glass cutter at the Ford Glass Co. (1923–25); then he joined the art department of the DeVilbiss Co. (1925–27), and started designing in 1928 with car control panels. In the 1930s he worked for the Conklin Pen Co., Toledo, and the Buick division of General Motors, among others. In 1943 he launched his firm called Louis Vavrik Industrial Design. His best-known client was Sears, Roebuck and Co., for which he designed the *Craftsman* line of power home-improvement tools (cat. 37 and 44). An industrial designer for over sixty years, he held numerous patents for his furniture and specialized machinery designs.[156]

CHAUNCEY E. WALTMAN

(b. Indiana, January 18, 1897 – d. Lexington, Kentucky, December 1975)[157]
To date, Chauncey E. Waltman is known only through his patent applications, including his 1939 design for an electric mixer (cat. 73), which he assigned to the A. F. Dormeyer Manufacturing Co., Chicago, Illinois. Waltman was listed as a resident of Chicago.

KARL EMANUEL MARTIN (KEM) WEBER[158]

(b. Berlin, Germany, November 14, 1889 – d. Santa Barbara, California, January 31, 1963)
A major contributor to the success of streamlined architecture and design on the West Coast, Weber brought the tenets of German modernism with him when he came to California in 1914. He had trained as a cabinetmaker under Eduard Schultz, a royal cabinetmaker in Potsdam, and in 1908 entered the Unterichtanstalt des Kunstgewerbemuseums (School of the Decorative Arts Museum) in Berlin, where he studied with the functionalist designer Bruno Paul. Even before his graduation in 1912, he worked on Paul's projects and thereafter continued in his studio, assisting on the

construction of the German part in the Brussels World's Fair of 1910. With Paul's recommendation, he designed Germany's contribution to the Panama-Pacific International Exposition held in San Francisco, and was there on site overseeing construction when war broke out. He was unable to return to Germany.

After the war Weber moved to Santa Barbara, where he taught art and opened a design studio. His architectural concepts echoed the Mayan and Egyptian sources that also appealed to Frank Lloyd Wright in the early 1920s, and he too executed furniture and interior designs. From 1922 to 1927 in Los Angeles he was art director for the furnishings store, Barker Brothers, where his work reflected the cubistic modernity he saw at the 1925 "Art Deco" exposition in Paris. In 1927 he opened his own industrial design studio in Hollywood, and the following year he was part of Macy's second *International Exposition of Art in Industry,* which established his national stature. His work included architectural projects, furniture for Lloyd Manufacturing of Michigan, and clocks for Lawson of Los Angeles, as well as silver accessories for Friedman Silver of New York (cat. 94), all in the streamlined style. His 1934–35 project for a new building for the Los Angeles Art Center School (where he taught in 1931–41) echoes Eric Mendelsohn's aerodynamic façade designs. In the late 1930s he concentrated on interior design and architecture, in 1939–40 designing the Walt Disney Studios in Burbank—from which came a version of his best known work, the *Airline* chair (cat. 91). In 1945 Weber moved back to Santa Barbara and worked from a studio in his home, concentrating on architectural projects.

WILLIAM ZAISER

(b. New York, New York, December 21, 1891 – d. Rockville Center, New York, 1985)

William Zaiser is best known for his designs for the Rudolph Wurlitzer Co., Cincinnati, Ohio.[159] One of his outstanding commissions was for the Wurlitzer organs at Radio City Music Hall, which opened in 1932. Although he did much work for the Wurlitzer Co., he had his own industrial design firm in New York City, renting space in the Wurlitzer Building on 42nd Street. He established a partnership with Joseph Johnson[160] for a short period around 1940, which is credited in a contemporary periodical with the design of the accordion (cat. 131).[161] A resident of Rockville Center, Long Island, from 1924, Zaiser moved his business there in the 1960s.

PETER ZASADNY

(b. Poland, June 18, 1911 – d. Oak Park, Illinois, September 18, 1988)[162]

To date, Peter Zasadny is known only through his patent applications, including his 1946 design with Stephen A. Crosby for the *Speedmatic* electric sander/polisher (cat. 47), which was assigned to the Sterling Tool Products Co., Chicago, Illinois. According to the 1930 census, Zasadny was a resident of Chicago, and his occupation was draftsman.

JOHN ADAM ZELLERS

(b. Lebanon, Pennsylvania, 1873 – d. New York, New York, April 29, 1954)

After Zellers attended William Jewell College in Liberty, Missouri, he took his first job as a bank clerk. What would become a forty-five year career in the typewriter business began in 1904 when he became a salesman for the Smith-Premier Company in Kansas City, Missouri. He then joined the Remington Typewriter Company, where he was a branch sales manager in Kansas City, St. Louis, and New York. In 1927 he became vice president of Remington Rand Inc., successor to the Remington Typewriter Company. He also served as the president of the Advertising Club of New York,[163] which reflected the ongoing relationship between industrial design and advertising. He retired in 1949.

Although his name appears on the patent specifications as one of the two inventors of the 1935 *Streamliner* portable typewriter made by Remington Rand, there is no evidence that Zellers was trained as a designer. It is not surprising that he would have been involved in the design, since he knew the product intimately and worked cooperatively with Remington Rand staff and consultants to manufacture and market it, using the team design approach for complex consumer products that became widespread in the late 1930s. The more advanced the technology of the product, the more experts were required for the final design.

ROY H. ZINKIL

(b. Illinois, May 10, 1890 – d. Oak Park, Illinois, April 1968)[164]

To date, Roy H. Zinkil is known only through his patent applications, including his 1936 design with Henry Dreyfuss for the *Neuvogue* sink (cat. 80), which was assigned to the Crane Co., Chicago, Illinois. Zinkil was listed as a resident of Oak Park, Illinois, where he lived as early as 1930, according to the 1930 census, which cited his occupation as a plumbing company manager.

Appendix

U.S. patents have recently become available on line, simplifying the once cumbersome process of obtaining patent records. The United States Patent and Trademark Office has a Web site (www.uspto.gov) through which patent drawings and specifications from 1836 to the present can be accessed by number or by product type. The design patents are of the greater interest for the purposes of this book, but utility patents often have information about mechanical inventions incorporated into the design.

The patent documentation is crucial in dating designs and identifying designers or inventors who would otherwise remain unknown. Since the patent specifications list the location of the designer at the time of the application, it is possible to obtain biographical information from local historical societies in the respective cities, thus filling in a picture of the individuals responsible for streamlined designs in America. Sometimes the patent holder is not a designer but a salesman or an officer in the firm, such as John A. Zellers (cat. 3), whose familiarity with his company products and customers gave him insights leading to improvements in the product design. In other instances, two or more individuals are cited in patents, shedding light on how designs were generated. For the soda siphon (cat. 100), for example, the patent was held by Worthen Paxton, but Bel Geddes, whose fame and firm were foremost in marketing the design, signed the object itself. In exploring the biographical data for Paxton, we know that he worked in the Bel Geddes office: he was probably the designer of the soda siphon and Bel Geddes may have only approved the design that bears his signature. On the other hand, the two could have collaborated in this work. While we can only speculate on specific details, the patent information gives us an idea of the cooperative nature of the design process in a world of increasingly complex technology and marketing.

Utility patents give insight into mechanical inventions and the degree to which patented objects are new in minute parts or entire designs. A radio patent, for example, might list many individual patents for various tubes and other mechanical parts. In our entries, such a product is dated no earlier than the latest of these patents. When the utility patent illustrates the overall design, the exterior design can be attributed to the holder of that utility patent.

The result of the exploration of patent records is that most product designs can now be accurately dated and attributed and the complex process of twentieth-century design can be more fully understood.[1]

Notes

Preface and Acknowledgments

1. The Stewart Program is an outgrowth of the activities of the Montreal Museum of Decorative Arts, which was founded in 1979 and merged with the Montreal Museum of Fine Arts in 2000.
2. On accessing U.S. patent drawings, which have provided illustrations and essential design information for our entries, see Appendix, p. 265.
3. Donald J. Bush, *The Streamlined Decade* (New York: George Braziller, 1975); Jeffrey Meikle, *Twentieth Century Limited: Industrial Design in America, 1925–1939* (Philadelphia: Temple University Press, 1979; revd. 2002).
4. John Perreault, *Streamline Design: How the Future Was*, exh. cat. (Queens, N.Y.: Queens Museum, 1984); *Streamlining America*, exh. cat. (Dearborn, Mich.: Henry Ford Museum, 1987); Reyer Kras, *Streamline: The Dawn of Tomorrow, American Design '30–'55*, exh. cat. (Amsterdam: Stedelijk Museum, 2002).
5. Richard Guy Wilson, et al., *The Machine Age in America, 1918–1941* (New York: Brooklyn Museum in association with Harry N. Abrams, 1986); Martin Eidelberg, ed., *Design 1935–1965: What Modern Was* (New York: Harry N. Abrams, 1991; repr. 2001).
6. Bevis Hillier, *Art Deco of the 20s and 30s* (New York: E. P. Dutton, 1968).
7. Charlotte Benton, Tim Benton, and Ghislaine Wood, eds., *Art Deco, 1910–1939* (London: V&A Publications, 2003).
8. Edgar Kaufmann, jr., "Borax, or the Chromium-Plated Calf," *Architectural Review* 104, no. 6 (August 1948): 89. Kaufmann was then director of the Department of Industrial Design at MoMA.

Introduction

1. Sheldon Cheney and Martha Cheney, *Art and the Machine* (New York: Whittlesey House, McGraw-Hill, 1936), 97–98.
2. These observations are made in the designer Norman Bel Geddes's article, "Streamlining," in *Atlantic Monthly* 154, no. 5 (November 1934): 553–563. Also see chapter 12, "Streamlining," 137–152, in the designer Harold Van Doren's *Industrial Design: A Practical Guide* (New York and London: McGraw-Hill, 1940). Both texts typify 1930s efforts to define and promote streamlining.
3. Walter Dorwin Teague, "Plastics and Design" (condensed from an address before the National Conference on Plastics. . . , December 12, 1939), *Architectural Forum* 72 (February 1940): 94.
4. A Danish-born silversmith, Magnussen (1884–1960) immigrated to New York City in 1925 and became artistic director for Gorham Silver Company, for which he designed this coffeepot and its accompanying service; Charles H. Carpenter, Jr., *Gorham Silver 1831–1981* (New York: Dodd, Mead & Company, 1982), 256–264.
5. The Romanian-born Lobel (1899–1983) probably saw Le Corbusier's Pavillon de l'Esprit Nouveau when he visited the 1925 Paris Exposition. He designed this teapot and its service for the 1934 exhibition *Contemporary American Industrial Art* at The Metropolitan Museum of Art; J. Stewart Johnson, *American Modern* (New York: Harry N. Abrams, 2000), 179.
6. Teague, "Plastics and Design," 94.
7. Van Doren, *Industrial Design*, 137.

8. Philip Johnson, "Machine Art," *Bulletin of The Museum of Modern Art* 3 (November 1933): 2. In his delight in U.S. silos and factories as vernacular functionalist design sources, Johnson was preceded by Le Corbusier, whose *Vers une architecture* illustrating them was translated into English in 1927 and widely read.
9. Philip Johnson, *Machine Art*, exh. cat. (New York: The Museum of Modern Art, 1934; new ed. 1994), n.p.
10. The museum's antagonism toward streamlining became more overt in later exhibitions and catalogues. See, e.g., John McAndrew, "'Modernistic' and 'Streamlined,'" *Bulletin of The Museum of Modern Art* 5, no. 6 (December 1938): n.p.
11. Some 34 million men, women, and children were without any income at all—28 percent of the population. Paul Johnson, *Modern Times: The World from the Twenties to the Eighties* (New York: Harper & Row, 1983), 246–247.
12. Symptomatic was Ford's introduction of the Model A in 1927, under the pressure of competition from style-savvy General Motors. Previously Ford had relied on the steadily decreasing cost of cars alone to assure market dominance, allowing him to tell customers for the Model T that they could "have it in any color, as long as it's black."
13. Anon., "Art in Industry," *Tide* 7, no. 5 (May 1934): 18.
14. That a number of Art Nouveau designers were also painters, and that Bauhaus applied arts were created under the aegis of architecture and engineering sheds light on their respective styles.
15. Phil Patton, *Made in USA* (New York: Grove Weidenfeld, 1992), 235.
16. Egmont Arens, quoted in Meikle, *Twentieth Century Limited*, 164.
17. See Donna R. Braden, "Selling the Dream and Buying the Dream," in *Streamlining America*, exh. cat. (Dearborn, Mich.: Henry Ford Museum, 1987), 37–69.
18. Arthur Marwick, "Modernity and History," in *Art Deco, 1910–1939*, 32.
19. Glenn Porter, *Raymond Loewy: Designs for a Consumer Culture* (Wilmington: Hagley Museum and Library, 2002), 40, 84.
20. Carlton Atherton, "Henry Dreyfuss: Designer," *Design* 36, no. 7 (January 1935): 7.
21. Edgar Kaufmann, jr., "A Century of Modern Design," *Arts & Architecture* 74, no. 8 (September 1957): 24.
22. David Gebhard and Harriette Von Breton, *Kem Weber: The Moderne in Southern California, 1920 through 1941*, exh. cat. (Santa Barbara: The Art Galleries, University of California, 1969), 37–38.
23. Sheldon Cheney, *The New World Architecture* (New York: Longmans, Green, 1930), 97.
24. Meikle, *Twentieth Century Limited*, 49.
25. Oskar Beyer, *Eric Mendelsohn, Letters of an Architect* (London: Abelard-Schuman, 1967), 772.
26. Quoted in Russell Lynes, *The Tastemakers* (New York: Harper & Brothers, 1949), 244.
27. "A Department Store Builds a New Warehouse Designed for the Hecht Company, Washington, D.C.," *Architectural Record* 81, no. 6 (June 1937): 79.
28. David Gebhard and Harriette Von Breton, *Los Angeles in the Thirties: 1931–1941* (Los Angeles: Hennessey & Ingalls, 1989), 76.

FACING PAGE
Designer unknown, advertisement for Burlington Northern Railroad, c. 1941–45. The Liliane and David M. Stewart Program Archives.

29. In the realm of unbuilt streamlined designs, Norman Bel Geddes's 1931 House of Tomorrow exploits curves in every direction; see *Design 1935–1965: What Modern Was*, 73.

30. Cheney and Cheney, *Art and the Machine*, 173.

31. Quoted in Kathleen Church Plummer, "The Streamlined Moderne," *Art in America* 62, no. 1 (January–February 1974): 46–54.

32. Van Doren, *Industrial Design*, 152.

33. Advertisement in *Creative Design* 1, no. 1 (Fall 1934): 23.

34. "Post-War Monel," *Tide* 6, no. 4 (April 1932): 13.

35. According to the exhibition catalogue, the "Streamline Monel metal sink" was lent by the International Nickel Co.; *Machine Art*, exh. cat. (New York: The Museum of Modern Art, 1934), n.p.

36. Cheney and Cheney, *Art and the Machine*, 86. See J. H. DuBois, *Plastics* (Chicago: American Technical Society, 1946), and Jeffrey L. Meikle, *American Plastic: A Cultural History* (New Brunswick, N. J.: Rutgers University Press, 1995).

37. Cheney and Cheney, *Art and the Machine*, 86.

38. Siegfried Giedion, *Mechanization Takes Command* (New York: Oxford University Press, 1948), 607.

39. "New Trains," *The Architectural Forum* 69, no. 3 (September 1938): 175.

40. Meikle, *Twentieth Century Limited*, 158.

41. Cheney and Cheney, *Art and the Machine*, 43.

42. See Paul Atterbury, "Travel, Transport, and Art Deco," in *Art Deco, 1910–1939*, 315.

43. Bush, *The Streamlined Decade*, 38.

44. Le Corbusier, *Aircraft* (London: The Studio Ltd., 1935), 13.

45. Kenneth Reid, "Norman Bel Geddes, Master of Design," *Pencil Points* 18, no. 1 (January 1937): 2.

46. Advertisement for "New Airflow Chrysler," *House & Garden* 65, no. 3 (March 1934): 22.

47. Bush, *The Streamlined Decade*, 105.

48. Advertisement in Pryor Dodge, *The Bicycle* (Paris: Flammarion, 1996), 176.

49. Design patent filed December 13, 1938; granted February 28, 1939 (D113,584).

50. Arens to Kieth [sic] Morgan, Nov. 27, 1934, box 27, *Arens* (George Arents Research Library at Syracuse University), as quoted in Meikle, *Twentieth Century Limited*, 165. Arens was promoting a "Better Homes Caravan" to the Federal Industries Sales Committee, a fleet of trucks intended to tour the nation selling kitchen appliances and home furnishings.

51. Meikle, *Twentieth Century Limited*, 160.

The Brill Collection and The Richard H. Mandel House

1. E-mails from Eric Brill to David A. Hanks, spring 2002. Eric Brill has generously shared his recollections, and has made scholarly contributions to this catalogue as well. See also Mary Anne Hunting, "Living with Antiques: The Richard H. Mandel House in Bedford Hills, New York," *The Magazine Antiques* 160 (July 2001): 72–83, for a thorough consideration of the house.

2. The Malevich painting was purchased in 1992 by Howard Schickler, the New York dealer in Russian Modernism, from the private collection in Moscow of Nikolai Khardzhiev, a noted art critic, historian, collector, and friend of Malevich. Schickler sold the painting to Eric Brill in 2001.

3. E-mail from Eric Brill to David A. Hanks, June 2002.

4. In an advertisement in the September 1935 issue of *The Architectural Forum*, Versen illustrated the living room in the Mandel house with text proclaiming, "The Lighting . . . throughout the residence of Mr. R. H. Mandel at Mt. Kisco. A typical example of our design and engineering service . . . in collaboration with E. D. Stone and D. Deskey" [ellipses in original text].

5. See Edward Durell Stone, *The Evolution of an Architect* (New York: Horizon Press, 1962), 32.

6. Ibid.

7. See David A. Hanks and Jennifer Toher, *Donald Deskey: Decorative Designs and Interiors* (New York: E. P. Dutton, 1987), 100–19.

8. Compare Deskey's Cubist designs of c. 1926–27 with his textile designs of c. 1930–31 (illus. Hanks and Toher, *Donald Deskey*, 9, 18, 67–70).

9. This was Deskey's recollection; see Hanks and Toher, *Donald Deskey*, 85. Dominique was founded in 1922 by André Domin (1883–1967) and Marcel Genevrière (1885–1967). Their furniture is characterized by the use of geometric forms in exotic woods without carved ornament. Contributors to the decoration of the deluxe ships *Normandie* and *Rouen*, the firm was also represented at the Paris exhibitions of 1925 and 1937. See *Dictionnaire international des arts appliqués et du design* (Paris: Editions du Regard, 1996), 170–71.

10. These are the recollections and suppositions of Mandel's son Steven, communicated to David A. Hanks in May 2002. Hunting, "Living with Antiques," 81 n. 9, points out that the earliest documentation of a professional association between Mandel and Deskey appears in "Off the Record" in the October 1935 issue of *Fortune*.

11. Alfred H. Barr, Jr. in Henry-Russell Hitchcock and Philip Johnson, *The International Style* (1932; New York: W. W. Norton, 1966), 13.

12. In an interview with Donald Deskey by David A. Hanks, June 15, 1984, Deskey stated that he designed the Mandel house, claiming he used Stone only to draft and sign the drawings. See Stone, however, *The Evolution of an Architect*, 30.

13. Eric Brill (e-mail to David A. Hanks, June 2002) reports that, according to Steven Mandel, the hill was extensively dynamited to create a relatively level site for the sizeable building.

14. In his informative essay "Edward Durell Stone and the International Style in America: Houses of the 1930s," *American Art Journal* 20, no. 3 (1988): 49–73, Dominic Ricciotti remarks that Le Corbusier's ideas were popular at Harvard University when Stone studied there in 1925–27; the young architect would also have noted the Frenchman's influence when he subsequently studied in Paris on scholarship and traveled in Europe in 1927–29.

15. "The House of Richard Mandel," *The Architectural Forum* 63 (August 1935): 79.

16. *Vogue*, May 15, 1935: 70–71.

17. For Eric Brill's lively account of the restoration of the house, see his "Caretakers, Owners, and Admirers: The Richard Mandel House," *do.co.mo.mo. Journal* 22 (May 2000): 46–49.

18. "The House of Richard H. Mandel," 80.

CHAPTER 1 ■ INTRODUCTION
"To Grace the Finest Desk":
Streamlining the Commercial World

1. This mockup was famous in its day and published widely. For example, see *Arts and Decoration* 42, no. 3 (December 1934).

2. Other rooms included in The Metropolitan Museum's exhibition were Eliel Saarinen's "Room for a Lady" and a living room designed by William Lescaze, both of which also emphasized streamlining. For illustrations of these rooms, see R. Craig Miller, *Modern Design in The Metropolitan Museum of Art, 1890–1990* (New York: Harry N. Abrams, 1990), 27–28.

3. "The Showroom as a Design Problem," *Architectural Record* 82, no. 1 (July 1938): 75.

4. Ibid.

5. "Ford Show Room," *The Architectural Forum* 68, no. 4 (April 1938): 329.

6. *Contempo: The American Tempo* (New York: E. P. Dutton, 1929).

7. "Norman Bel Geddes Design," *Pencil Points* 18, no. 1 (January 1937): 10–13.

8. Lorraine B. Diehl and Marianne Hardart, *The Automat* (New York: Clarkson Potter, 2002), 28–33. In 1912 the newly patented American-made machine was introduced.

9. "Cafeteria Uses New Mechanical Food Server to Complete Food Service System," *Architectural Record* 83, no. 4 (April 1938): 70.

10. See Richard J. S. Gutman and Elliott Kaufman, *American Diner* (New York: Harper & Row, 1979).

11. Frederick W. Taylor, *The Principles of Scientific Management* (1911; reprint, New York: W. W. Norton, 1967), 24–25.

12. David A. Hanks, *The Decorative Designs of Frank Lloyd Wright* (1979; reprint, New York: Dover, 1999), 84.

13. William S. Miller, "Apply Factory Technique to Office Planning," *Architectural Record* 82, no. 6 (December 1937): 113.

14. Then and now the S. C. Johnson Building housed the administrative offices for a business specializing in floor and furniture polishes.

15. Hanks, *The Decorative Designs*, 148.

16. Donald Albrecht and Chrysanthe B. Broikos, eds., *On the Job: Design and the American Office* (New York: Princeton Architectural Press, 2000), 17–18.

17. Few decorative objects clearly identified with the streamlined restaurants, bars, automats, and diners of the 1930s seem to have survived, but these icons are known through period photographs, and in some instances the structures still exist.

CHAPTER 1 ■ CATALOGUE
"To Grace the Finest Desk":
Streamlining the Commercial World

1. Design patent filed March 15, 1938; granted May 24, 1938 (D109, 838).

2. Production dates are provided where available throughout this catalogue. Eric Brill's donations to the Stewart Program for Modern Design, noted by B followed by the inventory number, were made through the American Friends of Canada.

3. A contemporary article explained the process: "The selective action of this unit passes only those waves which vibrate in a vertical plane, since these penetrate paper and ink when they meet the reading surface and make visible color, message, and detail. Horizontal waves, vibrating in the same beam, strike the surface horizontally and glance off, producing glare. Use of Polaroid lenses completely shuts off these latter. . . ." From "Polarized Light Now Available for Desks," *Architectural Record* 82, no. 6 (June 1938): 70.

4. Advertisement for Bullock's Department Store, Los Angeles, *California Arts & Architecture* 59, no. 3 (September 1938): 9.

5. *Fortune* 18, no. 5 (November 1938): 169.

6. For more on Teague's lamp, see *What Modern Was*, 80.

7. Cheney and Cheney, *Art and the Machine*, 74.

8. Design patent filed December 6, 1935; granted January 1, 1937 (D102,734).

9. www.officemuseum.com

10. This streamlined portable was illustrated in the 1937 company sales literature, which claimed the Remington line of portable typewriters was the most complete in the world (Acc. 1825. Remington Rand Archives, Hagley Museum and Library, Wilmington, Delaware).

11. Design patent filed October 24, 1939; granted February 27, 1940 (D119,204).

12. Impressed markings under the removable lid give the manufacturer's name and address: "The Stenotype Co./ Michigan Avenue at 41st Street/ Chicago." The machine is accompanied by its original carrying case.

13. www.ncraoline.org

14. Anon., "The Eyes Have It," *Business Week*, January 29, 1930.

15. Design patent filed June 30, 1939; granted March 26, 1940 (D119,624).

16. James Redin, "A Brief History of Mechanical Calculators," www.dotpoint.com.

17. www.victortech.com

18. Design patent filed March 8, 1940; granted May 14, 1940 (D120,529).

19. Cheney and Cheney, *Art and the Machine*, 89.

20. Design patent filed November 1, 1940; granted March, 11, 1941 (D125,784).

21. J. H. DuBois, citing the manufacturer and designer, illustrated this machine and commented that it was noteworthy for its distinctive raised letters. See *Plastics* (Chicago: American Technical Society, 1943), 232.

22. www.kevinlaurence.net

23. Design patent filed April 2, 1938; granted June 7, 1938 (D110, 007).

24. Design patent filed April 20, 1934; granted July 10, 1934 (D92,699).

25. Design patent filed August 16, 1938; granted December 13, 1938 (D112,576).

26. Design patent filed June 15, 1946; granted October 7, 1947 (D147, 626).

27. collections.ic.gc.ca

28. Design patent filed March 26, 1940; granted July 9, 1940 (D121,424).

29. Design patent filed November 27, 1940; granted February 11, 1941 (D125,093).

30. Meikle, *American Plastic*, 50–55.

31. Utility patent filed April 30, 1934; granted July 21, 1936 (2,048,415). This patent covered only the mechanism for the calendar.

32. Design patents filed April 26, 1937; granted August 9, 1938 (D110, 796–D110, 800).

33. Design patent filed March 25, 1940; granted June 4, 1940 (D120,898).

34. www.officemuseum.com

35. Letter to David A. Hanks from Ken W. Sayers, IBM Corporate Archives, May 28, 2003.

36. Design patent filed March 29, 1938; granted May 31, 1938 (D109,930).

37. Design patent filed January 24, 1952; granted July 7, 1953 (D169,989).

38. Design patent filed January 20, 1942; granted June 16, 1942 (D132,802).

39. Society of Industrial Designers, New York, *U.S. Industrial Design* (New York: The Studio Publications and Thomas Y. Crowell, 1951), 104.

40. Society of Industrial Designers, *U.S. Industrial Design 1949-1950* (New York: The Studio Publications, 1949), 98.

41. Ibid.

42. Design patent filed April 13, 1939; granted December 5, 1939 (D117,901).

43. *The Alliance of Art and Industry*, 141.

44. Design patent filed October 20, 1947; granted March 8, 1949 (D153,012).

45. An earlier model in the Brill Collection (2105) is marked with Rauland Corporation as the manufacturer.

46. There is no design patent for this object, but Dixie Cup Company was a longtime client of Lurelle Guild (Lurelle Guild papers, University of Syracuse Library).

47. Design patent filed July 22, 1940; granted November 5, 1940 (D123,402).

48. The cone-shaped cup, made of one piece of paper, was not selected for manufacture. His second cup, the classic *Dixie* cup, made with two pieces of paper (one forming the sides and lip of the cup, one forming the bottom), was chosen and is still made today.

49. www.lafayette.edu. "Dixie Cup Company History," Special Collections, Lafayette College Libraries, Easton, Pennsylvania.

50. Henry Dreyfuss, *A Record of Industrial Design by Henry Dreyfuss, 1929 Through 1946* (New York: Henry Dreyfuss, 1947), unpaged.

51. Dreyfuss was referring to a typewriter, but his point is pertinent to the pitcher. Henry Dreyfuss, *Designing for People* (New York: Paragraphic Books, 1955), 57-58.

52. Ibid., 58

53. *What Modern Was*, 82.

CHAPTER 2 ■ INTRODUCTION
"Power at Your Fingertips": Streamlining Manual Labor

1. Ronald C. Tobey, *Technology as Freedom: The New Deal and the Electrical Modernization of the American Home* (Berkeley: University of California Press, 1996), 108.

2. Cheney and Cheney, *Art and the Machine*, 230.

3. Since the 1980s gender scholars have explored the "social construction of housework." See, among others, Ruth S. Cowan, *More Work for Mother: The Ironies of Household Technology from the Open Hearth to the Microwave* (New York: Basic Books, 1983), which asserts that the middle-class homemaker in fact gained no new leisure through buying labor-saving devices, for in many cases they replaced paid labor, whether commercial laundries or hired help.

4. Anon., "Model T Appliances," *Business Week*, June 16, 1934: 11. The author was specifically praising

General Electric's $74.50 refrigerator, costing 20 percent less than its nearest competitor, but the point applies to other domestic durables.

5. "Maintenance Dept.," *House & Garden* 77, no. 1 (January 1940): 36.

6. "Planning the Postwar House II," *The Architectural Forum* 80, no. 2 (February 1944): 70.

7. "Ten Who Work for Their Hobbies," *House & Garden* 82, no. 1 (July 1942): 74.

8. "Garden Gadgets," *House & Garden* 75, no. 4 (April 1939): 63.

9. "Modern Educational Standards Require New Facilities for Industrial Arts Training," *Architectural Record* 87, no. 4 (April 1940): 88.

10. Cheney and Cheney, *Art and the Machine*, 271.

11. Tobey, *Technology as Freedom*, 115, notes that of course a longer repayment schedule allows consumers with lower incomes to buy on time.

12. See Meikle, *Twentieth Century Limited*, 109, for the benefits seen by the Ex-Cell-O Aircraft and Tool Corporation in Teague's designs for them.

13. Teague, *Design This Day*, 49.

CHAPTER 2 ■ CATALOGUE
"Power at Your Fingertips": Streamlining Manual Labor

1. Design patent filed April 24, 1936; granted December 22, 1936 (D102,448).

2. Design patents filed May 19, 1941; granted July 15, 1941 (D128,268 and D128,269).

3. According to a July 2, 2003 conversation with Glenn Adamson, the *Petipoint* iron was first produced in 1941 for the Edmilton Company, a small shop in Milwaukee. In 1942, rights to produce the iron were sold to Waverly Tool Company, which discontinued production after one year owing to the war. See Glenn Adamson, *Industrial Strength Design: How Brooks Stevens Shaped Your World*, exh. cat. (Milwaukee: MIT Press for the Milwaukee Art Museum, 2003), 12-14.

4. Giedion, *Mechanization Takes Command*, 571.

5. Cheney and Cheney, *Art and the Machine*, 43.

6. For further discussion of the *Petipoint* iron, see Adamson, *Industrial Strength Design*, 12-13.

7. The original instruction brochure accompanies this iron. Stewart Program Archives, Montreal.

8. The original operating instruction brochure accompanies this machine.

9. Design patent filed January 16, 1936; granted July 27, 1937 (D105,399).

10. Arthur J. Pulos, *American Design Ethic: A History of Industrial Design* (Cambridge, Mass.: MIT Press, 1983), 165.

11. Design patent for casing filed November 23, 1935; granted December 31, 1935 (D97,990).

12. Design patent filed May 28, 1937; granted August 3, 1937 (D105,493-D105,495).

13. Design patent for protective covering for casing filed August 17, 1938; granted November 15, 1938 (D112,236).

14. Design patent filed March 25, 1937; granted October 26, 1937 (D106,662).

15. The Lurelle Guild archives at the Syracuse University Library have a drawing for the Electrolux vacuum, as well as photographs of prototypes that led to the now familiar design. This vacuum is accompanied by its original box and instruction brochure describing its multiple uses.

16. Jay Doblin, *One Hundred Great Product*

Designs (New York: Van Nostrand Reinhold, 1970), 32.

17. Design patent filed March 7, 1955; granted October 18, 1955 (D175,857).

18. Design patent filed June 12, 1948; granted February 14, 1950 (D157,268).

19. Advertisement, *Better Homes & Gardens* 8, no. 10 (June 1930), 6.

20. Sears, Roebuck and Company, 1948-49 Fall/Winter catalogue, 1167.

21. Design patent filed May 28, 1945; granted September 25, 1945 (D142,452).

22. Design patent filed December 18, 1946; granted June 14, 1949 (D154,108).

23. www.oldlawnmowerclub.co.uk

24. Advertisement for *Eclipse* power mower, *Better Homes & Gardens* 16, no. 9 (May 1938): 68.

25. Tobey, *Technology and Freedom*, 33, states that New Deal requirements led to the modernization of wiring in two thirds of American homes to permit the use of appliances, especially refrigerators. This doubled the amount of such wiring over the 1920s.

26. The first listing of the product was in the Sears, Roebuck and Company 1948/49 Fall/Winter catalogue, 1168.

27. This drill first appears in the Sears, Roebuck catalogue for 1948-49 Fall/Winter, 1153, selling for $13.50.

28. "Annual Design Review" *Industrial Design* 1, no. 6 (December 1954): 83.

29. Sandor Nagyszalanczy, *Power Tools* (Newtown, Conn.: Taunton Press, 2001), 88. Duncan Black and Alonso Decker, Sr. founded Black & Decker in 1910.

30. Design patent filed August 2, 1949; granted June 20, 1950 (D159,043).

31. Design patent filed March 26, 1945; granted August 21, 1945 (D142,235).

32. One summary of the concern is given in chap. 2 of Henry Dreyfuss's *Designing for People* (New York: Simon & Schuster, 1955).

33. Design patent filed January 27, 1951; granted March 11, 1952 (D166,148).

34. This sander first appears in the Sears, Roebuck catalogue for Fall/Winter 1955-56, selling for $27.95.

35. Design patent filed September 28, 1946; granted November 4, 1947 (D147,783).

36. Design patent filed September 29, 1943; granted August 22, 1944 (D138,567).

37. Design patent filed September 2, 1938; granted February 21, 1939 (D113,427).

38. Design patent filed November 9, 1946; granted May 11, 1948 (D149,545).

39. DeVilbiss advertisement, "Stanley Hanks, noted painting contractor, states his case for spray painting," *Business Week*, no. 1359 (September 17, 1955): 58-59.

40. Society of Industrial Designers, New York, *51 U.S. Industrial Design* (New York: Studio Publications, 1951), 132. The patent specifications were under the names of Gamble and Peeps of Toledo, Ohio, who probably worked for the DeVilbiss Company in collaboration with the consultant industrial designers.

41. Ibid.

42. Design patent filed August 22, 1942; granted June 1, 1943 (D135,739).

43. Design patent filed December 6, 1952; granted June 9, 1953 (D169,829); design patent

for mixing blade filed October 30, 1939; granted December 26, 1939 (D118,249).

44. Utility patent for a drink mixer filed by Thomas B. Myers, Racine, Wisconsin, April 17, 1940; granted September 2, 1941 (2,254,236).

45. Design patent filed December 30, 1939; granted September 3, 1940 (D122,277).

46. Loewy, *Industrial Design*, 121.

47. Loewy, *Never Leave Well Enough Alone*, 208.

48. In the October 1940 issue of *The Architectural Forum*, Loewy was referred to as the "consultant designer," and in the design patent specifications, Loewy is listed second, after Scarratt.

CHAPTER 3 ■ INTRODUCTION
"Amazing Appliances": Streamlining the Kitchen and Bath

1. Victoria Kasuba Martranga, *America at Home* (Rosemont, Ill.: National Housewares Manufacturers Association, 1977), 14.

2. Ellen Lupton and J. Abbott Miller, *The Bathroom, the Kitchen, and the Aesthetics of Waste* (Cambridge, Mass.: MIT List Visual Arts Center, 1992), 23.

3. Tobey, *Technology as Freedom*, 33.

4. Ibid.

5. N. W. Ayer and Sons advertisement, *Saturday Evening Post*, March 24, 1928, 53.

6. General Electric advertisement, *Saturday Evening Post*, August 11, 1934, 44-45. For a cultural exploration of U.S. mass advertising, see in particular Roland Marchand, *Advertising the American Dream: Making Way for Modernity, 1920-1940* (Berkeley, Los Angeles, London: University of California Press, 1986).

7. *Housekeeping with Efficiency*, 1913, quoted in Giedion, *Mechanization Takes Command*, 521.

8. Jeannine Fiedler and Peter Feierband, eds., *Bauhaus* (Cologne: Könemann, 1999), 57.

9. "The Electric Kitchen and What It Costs," *House Beautiful* 78, no. 2 (February 1936): 47.

10. Cheney and Cheney, *Art and the Machine*, 175.

11. Advertisement for General Electric Unit Kitchen, *Pencil Points* 18, no. 1 (January 1937): 25.

12. "Culinary Color News," *House & Garden* 63, no. 5 (November 1935): 71.

13. Advertisement for Crane Co. in *The Architectural Forum* 73, no. 6 (December 1940): 9.

14. See Tobey, *Technology as Freedom*, 14, 116.

15. Ibid., 122-23.

16. Article in *Forbes* (April 1, 1934): 13.

17. "The Richard Mutt Case," *The Blind Man* no. 2 (May 1917): 5. In 1925 the California camera artist Edward Weston followed with a photograph of a toilet, which he titled *Excusado*.

18. Cheney and Cheney, *Art and the Machine*, 209.

19. Advertisement for bathroom fixtures of c. 1935, quoted in Gail Caskey Winkler, *The Well-Appointed Bath* (Washington, D.C.: The Preservation Press, 1989), 12.

20. In *Advertising the American Dream*, Roland Marchand points to Hollywood bathing scenes as giving the bathroom a sense of opulence and sensuality (p. 124). The streamlined bath in fig. 116 also indicates that the sensual user is up-to-date.

21. Both quotes from Walter Dorwin Teague, *Design This Day* (New York: Harcourt, Brace, 1940), 61.

CHAPTER 3 ▪ CATALOGUE
"Amazing Appliances":
Streamlining the Kitchen and Bath

1. Design patent filed March 22, 1937; granted June 15, 1937 (D104,914).
2. Brochure for *Everhot* by the Swartzbaugh Mfg. Co., c. 1937, Collection David A. Hanks & Associates.
3. Ibid., n.p.
4. Design patent filed April 14, 1947; granted June 15, 1948 (D149,937).
5. Utility patent filed by Raymond L. Barton of Los Angeles, January 19, 1935; granted October 26, 1937 (2,096,726); utility patent also filed by Barton, January 19, 1935; granted September 20, 1936 (2,130,533).
6. Design patent filed November 23, 1944; granted April 3, 1945 (D140,754).
7. Van Doren, *Industrial Design*, 108.
8. Harold Van Doren, "The Private Life of a New Model," *Saturday Evening Post* 219, no. 8 (August 3, 1946): 17.
9. Doordan, *The Alliance of Art and Industry*, 61.
10. A version of this kettle with a metal band around the center and a different wooden handle was illustrated in "For the Well-Run House, New Equipment and Utensils," *House & Garden*, Section II, 78, no. 4 (October 1940): 33. This provides an approximate date for our kettle.
11. Design patent filed June 1, 1936; granted August 4, 1936 (D100,663).
12. Design patent filed January 8, 1946; granted November 26, 1946 (D145,978).
13. Design patent filed July 20, 1937; granted June 5, 1937 (D105,335).
14. "Window Shopping, *House Beautiful* 80, no. 9 (September 1938): 8.
15. Design patent filed January 10, 1939; granted July 25, 1939 (D115,833).
16. In 1984, in the decade when nostalgic Postmodern design flourished, Hall reintroduced this pitcher as part of its American line. Margaret and Kenn Whitmyer, *Collector's Encyclopedia of Hall China* (Paducah, Ky.: Collector Books, 2001), 212.
17. Ibid.
18. See Martin Eidelberg, *Eva Zeisel: Designer for Industry* (Montreal: Montreal Museum of Decorative Arts, 1984), 19.
19. Henry Adams, *Viktor Schreckengost and 20th-Century Design* (Cleveland: The Cleveland Museum of Art, 2000), 107. See the illustration of containers and additional pieces of the set.
20. Design patent filed March 1, 1948; granted September 20, 1949 (D155,269).
21. Design patent filed December 21, 1939; granted July 7, 1942 (D132,968). This mixer is attributed to Waltman on the basis of its close but not exact similarity to the image in the patent drawing assigned by the inventor to Dormeyer.
22. Penny Sparke, *Electrical Appliances: Twentieth-Century Design* (New York: E. P. Dutton, 1987), 73.
23. Design patent filed November 22, 1950; granted April 10, 1951 (D162,833).
24. The *Osterett* is accompanied by its original box, manufacturer's guarantee and brochure, and the original bill of sale, dated "January 24,6" (probably 1956), from Dayton's in Minneapolis. It cost $8.48.
25. Design patent filed April 1, 1941; granted June 16,

1942 (D132,762). The blender was illustrated in the August 1950 issue of *Modern Plastics*. This reference was pointed out to us by Jean Bernard Hebey. Utility patent filed by Don E. Grove and Jackson D. Comstock, April 1, 1941; granted August 31, 1943 (2,328,526). Although the generic term "blender" is used here, the design and utility patents refer to it as a "juice extractor."
26. Utility patent filed May 12, 1938; granted November 5, 1940 (2,220,482)
27. Joachim Krausse and Claude Lichtenstein, eds., *Your Private Sky: R. Buckminster Fuller: The Art of Design Science* (Baden, Switzerland: Lars Müller Publishers, 1999), 209.
28. Design patents filed May 15, 1936; granted October 6, 1936 (D101,442–D101,443). Both patents are marked underneath the porcelain bowl of the *Neuvogue* sink with the stamp "India Ivory."
29. Design patent filed May 15, 1936; granted October 6, 1936 (D101,445).
30. Russell Flinchum, *Henry Dreyfuss, Industrial Designer: The Man in the Brown Suit* (New York: Rizzoli, 1997), 80.
31. Compare Gropius's nickel-plated door handles of c. 1925, illustrated in Phillips, de Pury & Luxembourg, *20th-21st Century Designs*, auction catalogue, December 8, 2003, 39.
32. Design patent filed October 25, 1933; granted December 26, 1933 (D91,255).
33. Design patent filed December 16, 1960; granted July 18, 1961 (D190,928).
34. "Bathrooms," *House & Garden* 69, no. 6 (June 1936): 69.
35. Design patent filed March 29, 1944; granted June 6, 1944 (D138,044).
36. Design patent filed December 14, 1937; granted February 8, 1938 (D108,381). The hair dryer closely resembles the drawing in Donald F. McCarron's design patent filed September 24, 1949; granted May 30, 1950 (D158,779). However, the object is marked with the earlier patent number.
37. Utility patent filed by Casper J. Miller, October 13, 1951; granted January 6, 1953 (2,624,335). Because no design patent was filed and the utility patent image is identical to the manufactured object, one may conclude that Miller was responsible for both the works and the casing of this device.
38. A service brochure accompanies the massager with its original box. It states that it was inspected January 1, 1951. The utility patent was filed by Alfred C. Gilbert on December 27, 1921; granted May 1, 1928 (1,668,364).
39. Bruce Watson, *The Man Who Changed How Boys and Toys Were Made* (New York: Viking Penguin, 2002), 78–81.
40. Design patent filed January 29, 1942; granted April 7, 1942 (D131,928).

CHAPTER 4 ▪ INTRODUCTION
"Flash-and-Gleam Beauty":
Streamlining the Living Space

1. "Design Today," *House & Garden* 81, no. 5 (May 1942): 27.
2. "Dominating Colonial," *House & Garden* 46, no. 3 (September 1934): 25.
3. Anon., "Contrast in Design," *Creative Design* 3, no. 7 (September 1938): 31.
4. The low mantel planned in the rendering is much higher as executed, because it had to cover

an existing fireplace. A rectangular coffee table replaces the round one shown in the rendering, and the corner sofa is less circular.
5. Anon., "Decorator's Scrap Book," *House & Garden* 70, no. 4 (October 1936): 86.
6. *House & Garden* 76, no. 1 (August 1939): 25.
7. *House & Garden* 79, no. 3 (March 1941): 76.
8. Paul T. Frankl, *Space for Living* (New York: Doubleday, Doran, 1938), 14–16.
9. "A Twentieth Anniversary in Modernism Shows how Tastes Change with the Years," *House & Garden* 66, no. 1 (July 1934): 53.
10. Paul T. Frankl, "The Apartment of Roger Wolfe Kahn, by Paul T. Frankl," *House & Garden* 66, no. 1 (July 1934): 54.
11. "Apartment of Roger Wolfe Kahn," 54.
12. Walter Rendell Storey, "Kem Weber," *The Studio* 117 (1939): 264.
13. In Los Angeles, Richard Neutra's homes of the 1930s, especially the aluminum-clad residence for Hollywood director Josef von Sternberg, 1935, blend streamlining and the International Style to dramatic effect. See Thomas S. Hines, *Richard Neutra and the Search for Modern Architecture: A Biography and History* (New York and Oxford: Oxford University Press, 1982), 132–38.
14. "Curves for Contrast," *House & Garden* 73, no. 6 (June 1938): 49.
15. "Apartment of Roger Wolfe Kahn," 54.
16. See Gail Cooper, *Air-Conditioning America: Engineers and the Controlled Environment, 1900–1960* (Baltimore and London: Johns Hopkins University Press, 1998).
17. "Work and Recreation," *House & Garden*, Section II, 76, no. 3 (September 1939): 30–31.
18. Quoted in "Interiors and Furniture," *30s & 40s Decorative Arts: A Source Book*, ed. Charlotte and Peter Fiell (Cologne: Taschen, 2000), 233.
19. Vicki Goldberg, *Margaret Bourke-White: A Biography* (Reading, Pa.: Addison-Wesley, 1987), 130. For additional views of the studio, see Stephen Bennett Phillips, *Margaret Bourke-White: The Photography of Design 1927–1936* (New York: Rizzoli, 2002), 48–49.
20. "Prophetic Panorama," *House &Garden* 76, no. 1 (July 1939): 25.
21. Myrtle Fahsbender, *Residential Lighting* (New York: D. Van Nostrand, 1947), 108.
22. "Interiors and Furniture," *30s & 40s Decorative Arts*, 288.
23. Ralph Bennett and T. J. Maloney, "Technical News and Research: Paint—A Partner in Illumination," *Architectural Record* 77, no. 4 (April 1935): 300.
24. We have found few period color illustrations of streamlined interiors. In any case, color reproduction in magazines of the 1930s was not widespread and the printing technology softened saturation and contrast. That color was used apparently only for more conventional interiors suggests the power of conservative tastes among U.S. readers.

CHAPTER 4 ▪ CATALOGUE
"Flash-and-Gleam Beauty":
Streamlining the Living Space

1. William Muschenheim, "Furnishing the Interior: Airline Chair of Wood by Kem Weber," *The Architectural Record* 77, no. 5 (May 1935): 311.

2. *Creative Design* 1, no. 4 (Summer, 1935): 27.
3. Entry by Christopher Wilk, *What Modern Was*, 77.
4. Biographical entry by Martin Eidelberg, *What Modern Was*, 404–405.
5. See *Kem Weber: The Moderne in Southern California 1920–1941*, 80–81.
6. Derek Ostergaard and David A. Hanks, "Gilbert Rohde and the Evolution of Modern Design, 1927–1941," *Arts Magazine* 56 (October 1981): 103.
7. Catalogue, *Troy Streamline Metal* (Troy, Ohio: The Troy Sunshade Company, Fall 1935), 28, Archives, David A. Hanks & Associates, New York.
8. The chair, which retains its original brown vinyl upholstery, has the manufacturer's paper label attached to the bottom: "TROY/STREAMLINE/METAL/"
9. A photograph in the Weber archives describes this piece as "Silver Style."
10. Quoted in Cheney and Cheney, *Art and the Machine*, 192.
11. Martin Eidelberg, in correspondence with David A. Hanks office, December, 2003.
12. David Gebhard and Harriette Von Breton, *Kem Weber and the Moderne in Southern California 1920–1941* (Santa Barbara: University of California, 1969), 40.
13. www.storage.fiestafanatic.com
14. Ibid.
15. Design patent filed January 16, 1937; granted April 6, 1937 (D 103,967).
16. Design patent filed October 11, 1934; granted May 7, 1935 (D95,505).
17. Penny Sparke, "Cookware to Cocktail Shakers: The Domestication of Aluminum in the United States, 1900–1939," in Sarah Nichols, *Aluminum by Design* (Pittsburgh: Carnegie Museum of Art, 2000), 137.
18. Advertisement for Kensington, *House & Garden* 66, no. 5 (November 1934): 74.
19. A drawing for the bowl is in the Guild archives at the University of Syracuse Library.
20. Advertisement quoted in Paula Ockner and Leslie Pina, *Art Deco Aluminum Kensington* (Atglen, Pa.: Schiffer Publishing, 1997), 35.
21. Ibid., 45
22. *Fortune* 9, no. 2 (February, 1934), 43.
23. Revere Copper and Brass Company catalogue of 1936, n.p., Stewart Program Archives.
24. Christopher Wilk, *Normandie* pitcher, *What Modern Was*, 81.
25. Design patent filed December 11, 1940; granted March 4, 1941 (D125,632).
26. Design patent filed May 18, 1938; granted December 13, 1938 (D112,535).
27. Norman Bel Geddes, *Horizons* (Boston: Little, Brown & Co., 1932), 45.
28. Brochure, "Won't You Have Fun with Your Sparklet Syphon," Sparklet Devices Inc., Division of Knapp-Monarch Co., St. Louis, Mo., n.d. (1942), n.p.
29. Toni Lesser Wolf, *What Modern Was*, 85–86, noted that French designer Jean Puiforcat may have inspired Bertoia's decision to attach the handle to the coffeepot at just two small points, and his contrast of circular body and rectangular spout. The Bertoia service includes a sugar bowl, reproduced in *What Modern Was* on p. 85.
30. Design patent filed February 9, 1937; granted March 23, 1937 (D103,749).

31. The patent number on the brass plaque attached to the back (1,990,645) is for the mechanism for the digital movement, filed by Frederick A Greenwatt on March 10, 1933, and received on February 12, 1935.

32. Design patent filed February 9, 1937; granted March 23, 1937 (D103,748).

33. Weber's building designs of 1934–36 suggest admiration for the German Expressionist architect: see David Gebhard and Harriette Von Breton, *Los Angeles in the Thirties: 1931–1941* (Los Angeles: Hennessey & Ingalls, 1989), 74.

34. *Tide* 6, no. 4 (April 1933): 46–47.

35. Advertisement for Warren Telechron, *House & Garden* 65, no. 4 (April 1934): 26.

36. Patented by Loewy for Westinghouse in 1931; see Glenn Porter, *Raymond Loewy: Designs for a Consumer Culture* (Wilmington, Del.: Hagley Museum, 2002), 33.

37. *Tide* 5, no. 1 (February 1931): 22.

38. Ibid., 23.

39. Design patent filed December 31, 1937; granted March 15, 1938 (D108,837).

40. Harold N. Cones, John H. Bryant, Martin Blakinship, *Zenith: The Glory Years, 1936–1945, History and Products* (Atglen, Pa.: Schiffer Publishing, 2003), 89.

41. Anon., "Safe at Home," *House & Garden* 79, no. 3 (March 1941): 34.

42. *Streamliner* is stamped on the stem of this pipe.

43. Design patent filed January 30, 1941; granted May 20, 1941 (D127,324).

44. See Christina Cogdell, "Products or Bodies? Streamline Design and Eugenics as Applied Biology," *Design Issues* 19, no. 1 (Winter 2003): 36–37, 42.

45. Joanne Dubbs Ball, *Costume Jewelers* (Atglen, Pa.: Schiffer Ltd., 1990, rev. ed., 1997), 147–150.

46. Fahsbender, *Residential Lighting*, 135.

47. Design patents filed January 13, 1937; granted April 27, 1937 (fan: D104,259; base: D104,260; motor unit: D104,261).

48. Design patent filed August 27, 1936; granted April 13, 1937 (D104,060).

49. Utility patent filed by Ralph K. Odor and Kern Dodge, July 26, 1940; granted June 30, 1942 (2,287,822); filed by Ralph K. Odor, July 6, 1939; granted March 23, 1943 (2,314,510); filed by Ralph K. Odor and Kern Dodge, September 10, 1938; granted October 5, 1943 (2,330,907).

50. About Robert Heller's *Airstream* fan of 1936, also for The A. C. Gilbert Company, a contemporary account read: this fan "takes its inspiration from the airplane. The streamlined base suggests the wings of a plane and the blade is a miniature propeller" (Anon., *Creative Design* 1, no. 7 [Spring 1936]: 31).

51. "Products and Practice: 'Airflow Electric Fan,'" *The Architectural Forum* 66, no. 3 (March 1937): 200.

52. *The Architectural Forum* 66, no. 6 (June 1937): 512.

53. Interview with the designer, November 2002. Ten Eyck designed only the cowling, while Ralph K. Oder, of Edmond, Oklahoma, and Kern Dodge of Philadelphia filed the utility patents for the cones of the "blower."

54. www.wichita.bizjournals.com.

55. Design patent filed July 5, 1946; granted April 13, 1948 (D149,266).

56. Design patent filed September 11, 1948; granted March 14, 1950 (D157,659).

57. Promotional brochure, papers of Mark Harrison (Acc. 2193), Hagley Museum and Library, Wilmington, Delaware.

58. Utility patent filed April 13, 1939; granted May 6, 1941 (2,241,368).

CHAPTER 5 ■ INTRODUCTION
"Won't You Have Fun": Streamlining Recreation

1. A 1937 article, "Recreation Has a Room of Its Own," in *Architectural Record* puts the term in quotation marks (82, no.3 [September 1937]: 116). There were doubtless earlier uses of "rumpus room" in the media.

2. Kenneth Day, "Basement Game Room," *Architectural Record* 89, no. 2 (February 1941): 72.

3. "Recreation Has a Room of Its Own," 116.

4. Kurt Helfrich, *Designing the Moderne: Kem Weber's Bixby House*, exh. brochure, University Art Museum, University of California at Santa Barbara, November 29, 2000–February 11, 2001, n.p.

5. Vincent Abbott, "Game Rooms," *House & Garden* 67, no. 5 (May 1935): 27.

6. Cheney and Cheney, *Art and the Machine*, 225.

7. "Recreation Has a Room of Its Own," 117.

8. Tobey, *Technology as Freedom*, 22–23.

9. "Illustrated News Radio Sets Outnumber Telephones," *Architectural Record* 77, no. 1 (January 1935): 18.

10. See Ghislaine Wood, "Art Deco and the Hollywood Film," in *Art Deco*, 325–333. Wood calls *Grand Hotel* "the quintessential streamlined Art Deco movie" (p. 329) and sees in the sets of Fred Astaire and Ginger Rogers musicals of 1933–36 "the increasingly widespread acceptance of streamlining as a contemporary design idiom and metaphor of modernity" (p. 332).

11. www.mediahistory.umn.edu/time/1930s

12. "Pittsburgh Glass Institute Competition, 1937. Winning Entries. Commercial Theatre," *Architectural Forum* 67, no. 2 (August 1937): 108.

13. "Restaurant Longchamps, New York City," *American Architect and Architecture* 149, no. 2652 (December 1936): 65. The Longchamps Restaurant at 253 Broadway designed by Ely Jacques Kahn also had a streamlined bar. See *Architectural Forum* 69, no. 4 (October 1938): 266. Interior decoration was also by Winold Reiss. Fabricoid was a leather-like, water-resistant fabric used in upholstery.

14. George D. Butler, "Planning for Recreation," *Architectural Record* 81 (June 1937): 113.

15. Robert Moses, "Municipal Recreation," *American Architect and Architecture* 149, no. 2651 (November 1936): 21.

16. Ibid., 22.

17. On Moses' impact on New York City and state, see Robert A. Caro, *The Power Broker: Robert Moses and the Fall of New York* (New York: Alfred A. Knopf, 1974).

18. "Sports Buildings," *Architectural Record* 89, no. 2 (February 1941): 72. The building was converted to a maritime museum in 1951.

19. See Maurice Culot and Anne-Marie Pirlot, *Antoine Courtens, Createur Art Deco* (Brussels: Archives d'Architecture Moderne, 2002), 64–83.

CHAPTER 5 ■ CATALOGUE
"Won't You Have Fun": Streamlining Recreation

1. www.history-of-rock.com

2. For an illustration of this model and further information, see Christine W. Laidlaw, *What Modern Was*, 78–79.

3. An observation made by Laidlaw in *What Modern Was*, 79.

4. Design patent filed April 29, 1939; granted July 9, 1940 (D121,427).

5. Design patent filed November 18, 1938; granted January 24, 1939 (D113,004).

6. Design patent filed September 19, 1940; granted December 3, 1940 (D123,839).

7. Utility patent numbers on the bottom help to date this radio, which came in various color combinations.

8. Design patent filed April 24, 1946; granted August 17, 1948 (D150,660).

9. Meikle, *Twentieth Century Limited*, 17.

10. Catalogue of Sears, Roebuck and Co., 1939, microfilm, Science, Industry & Business Library, New York Public Library.

11. Meikle, *Twentieth Century Limited*, 9.

12. Utility patent filed by C. Lindeberg, October 19, 1938; granted January 2, 1940 (2,185,984). Utility patent filed by C. Lindeberg, March 9, 1939; granted January 23, 1940 (2,188,085).

13. The utility patent protected the improved construction of various parts of the accordion. The purpose was "to simplify the same, improve the appearance, reduce the weight and at the same time permit of its manufacture at lower cost."

14. www.wurlitzer-jukebox.com

15. "Design Decade," *Architectural Forum* 73, no. 4 (October 1940): 244.

16. Design patent filed for April 1, 1939; granted August 8, 1939 (D116,069).

17. "Fabrique en Allemagne/Made in Germany" in capital letters is stamped on both sides and on the aluminum banding, and impressed in the plastic.

18. "A Brief History of the Harmonica," www.eharmonica.net. The company's German founder, Matthias Hohner, had turned from clock making to manufacturing harmonicas in 1857. In 1862 he began exporting his product to North America, and by 1930 the firm was selling more than 25 million instruments annually. Located in Richmond, Virginia, the American branch of Hohner continues in business today.

19. "A Brief History."

20. Design patent filed October 27, 1933; granted December 26, 1933 (D91,256).

21. Doordan, *The Alliance of Art and Industry*, 88.

22. "Design Decade. Recreation," *The Architectural Forum* 73, no. 4 (October 1940): 244.

23. Ibid., 242.

24. For illustrations of these other vehicles for children, see *The Alliance of Art and Industry*, 85–88.

25. Design patent filed January 15, 1934; granted March 20, 1934 (D91,796).

26. Van Doren, *Industrial Design*, 32.

27. Utility patent filed January 29, 1934; granted May 26, 1936 (2,041,982).

28. Design patent filed February 23, 1935; granted May 28, 1935 (D95,773). The leather straps that are an integral part of the skates survive but are not shown in this photograph.

29. www.ilsa.org

30. Bush, *The Streamlined Decade*, 88–89.

31. Loewy, *Industrial Design*, 79.

32. Lionel advertisement in *Saturday Evening Post*, December 3, 1932, 75.

33. The utility patent no. 1,860,251 is painted on the front of the trolley. Utility patent filed by Harry T. Kingsbury, July 28, 1931; granted May 24, 1932.

34. Founded by Fred Lundahl, the Buddy L Company was named after the founder's son; its first line was introduced in 1921.

35. Design patent filed March 18, 1948; granted December 26, 1950 (D161,367).

36. The original directions that accompany the airplane kit are marked copyright 1947.

37. Design patent filed June 24, 1933; granted August 29, 1933 (D90,602).

38. Design patent filed February 20, 1937; granted March 23, 1937 (D103,700).

39. Utility patent filed March 18, 1939; granted July 23, 1940 (2,208,799).

40. Archives, Stewart Program for Modern Design, Montreal.

41. Lloyd's brochure, reprinted from *U.S. Camera*, March, 1956. Archives, Stewart Program for Modern Design, Montreal, acquired separately from the camera.

42. Design patent filed June 3, 1939; granted July 18, 1939 (D115,771).

43. Design patent filed February 24, 1947; granted February 24, 1948 (D148,764).

44. Designed with Kodak Styling Division and Camera Works engineering department.

45. Society of Industrial Designers, *51 U.S. Industrial Design* (New York: The Studio Publications and Thomas Y. Crowell, 1951), 83.

46. Design patent filed July 30, 1937; granted May 2, 1939 (D114,597); design patent for fuel tank structure filed July 30, 1937; granted November 1, 1938 (D111,987).

47. Sears, Roebuck catalogue for Spring/Summer, 1936.

48. "Boating World Creates a New Industry," *Industrial Design* 4, no. 5 (May 1957): 60.

49. Promotional brochure, *Twentieth Century Limited*, Henry Dreyfuss Archive, Cooper-Hewitt, National Design Museum, Smithsonian Institution.

50. "Train of Trains," brochure, Henry Dreyfuss Archive, Library, Cooper-Hewitt, National Design Museum, Smithsonian Institution.

51. Correspondence with Deborah Wythe, Archivist, Special Library Collections, Brooklyn Museum of Art, July 30, 2003.

52. *The Machine Age in America*, 83.

53. John Vassos, *Ultimo* (New York: Dover, 1930), 29.

54. Quoted in Anon., "A Brave Prediction," *Aluminum News-Letter*, February 1939: 2. Department of Special Collections, Syracuse University, Syracuse, New York.

CHAPTER 6 ■ INTRODUCTION
The World of Tomorrow Today: Streamlining Now

1. Loewy, *Industrial Design*, 128.

2. "Streamline Satiety," *House & Garden* 64, no. 4 (April 1934): 33.

3. "Modernistic and Streamlined," *Bulletin of The Museum of Modern Art* 5, no. 6 (December 1938), n.p.

4. Serge Chermayeff and René d'Harnoncourt, "Design for Use," *Art in Progress*, exh. cat. (New York: The Museum of Modern Art, 1944), 195.

5. Henry Dreyfuss, *Designing for People* (New York: Simon & Schuster, 1955), 77.

6. Edgar Kaufmann, jr., *What is Modern Design?* (New York: The Museum of Modern Art, 1950), 8.

7. Justin De Syllas, "Streamform Images of Speed and Greed from the Thirties," *Architectural Association Quarterly* 1, no. 2 (April 1967): 32.

8. Dreyfuss, *Designing for People*, 77

9. Kaufmann, *What is Modern Design?* 9.

10. Anne Massey, *Interior Design of the 20th Century* (London: Thames & Hudson, 1990), 150.

11. Reyner Banham, *Theory and Design in the First Machine Age* (1960; reprint, Cambridge, Mass.: MIT Press, 1980), 329.

12. Quoted in Nigel Whiteley, *Reyner Banham, Historian of the Immediate Future* (Cambridge, Mass.: MIT Press, 2002), 68.

13. Ibid., 67.

14. Compare p. 239 in Claes Oldenburg, *Claes Oldenburg: An Anthology*, (New York: Solomon R. Guggenheim Museum, 1995), with cat. 75 here.

15. See Diane Waldman, *Roy Lichtenstein* (New York: Solomon R. Guggenheim Foundation, 1993). In chapter 8, "Art Deco and Modern, 1966–70," 166–178, Waldman discusses several paintings that demonstrate the influence of streamlined design.

16. Ettore Sottsass, as quoted in Joe Dolce, "Profiles: Four Designers," *I.D., The International Design Magazine* 36 (January/February, 1989): 56.

17. David A. Hanks and Anne Hoy, *Design for Living: Furniture and Lighting, 1950–2000* (Paris: Flammarion, 2000): 169.

CHAPTER 6 ■ ENTRIES
The World of Tomorrow Today: Streamlining Now

1. Quoted in *Design for Living*, 168.

2. Jasper Morrison, *Everything but the Walls* (Baden, Switzerland: Lars Müller Publishers, 2000), 7.

3. Correspondence with David A. Hanks and Associates, December 2003.

4. Charles Arthur Boyer and Federica Zanco, *Jasper Morrison* (Paris: Editions du Voir, 1999), 45.

5. Design patent filed April 17, 2000; granted August 28, 2001 (D446,960).

6. Interview with Ross Lovegrove, July 2001 on www.design-engine.com

7. www.designzinc.com

8. R. Craig Miller, *U.S. Design 1975–2000* (Munich: Prestel Verlag, 2001), 161.

BIOGRAPHIES OF DESIGNERS

1. Information was supplied by the designer's son David Alcott, to Joan Swann and Libby Johnson, co-curators of the Westwood Historical Society.

2. Date of birth from Social Security Death Index.

3. Obituary, *The New York Times*, Sunday, October 2, 1966, 87.

4. Roy Sheldon and Egmont Arens, *Consumer Engineering: A New Technique for Prosperity* (New York: Harper and Bros., 1932).

5. Cheney and Cheney, *Art and the Machine*, 259.

6. Obituary, *New York Times*, October 2, 1966, 87.

7. Information from correspondence with Marc Berthier, March 8, 2004, and *Dictionnaire International des Arts Appliqués et du Design*,74.

8. Information based on Toni Lesser Wolf, Bertoia biographical entry, *What Modern Was*, 363.

9. From Social Security Death Index and 1930 United States Federal Census records.

10. Obituary, *The Miami Union*, October 29, 1942.

11. Harold Cones, et al., *Zenith: The Glory Years, 1936–1945* (Atglen, Pennsylvania: Schiffer Publishing Ltd., 2003), 42–43. Correspondence with Harold Cones, March 17, 2004, who provided photocopies of obituaries and other data to document the life of Budlong.

12. Cones, *Zenith: The Glory Years*, 42–43.

13. "Accordions by Robert Davol Budlong," *The Music Trades* (September 1938): n.p.

14. From Social Security Death Index.

15. From Social Security Death Index.

16. Information from correspondence with Dennis Buck, Curator, Aurora Historical Society, December 17, 2003.

17. Thor Power Tool operated independently until 1967 when Stewart-Warner purchased it, and in 1980 it moved its operation to Johnson City, Tennessee. Steve Lord, "City Landmark Bites the Dust," *Aurora Beacon News*, December 24, 1989, n.p.

18. From Social Security Death Index and 1930 United States Federal Census records.

19. Carroll Grantz, *100 Years of Design—A Chronology 1895-1995*. © 2002, Industrial Designers Society of America excerpts at www.idsa.org.

20. "Supply and Design: They Strike a Balance in the Chicago Area," *Industrial Design* 3, no. 5 (October 1956): 115. Obituary, *The New York Times*, May 22, 1978, 10.

21. "New President Elected by Industrial Designers," *The New York Times*, October 2, 1950.

22. Fred M. Hechinger, "Video is Altering Shape of Schools," *The New York Times*, April 25, 1960, 31–32.

23. Betty Pepis, "Big Changes in Kitchens Seen on Way," *The New York Times*, October 11, 1955, 46.

24. From Social Security Death Index and 1930 United States Federal Census records.

25. Index, *U.S.I.D.*, 1949, p. 172.

26. From 1930 United States Federal Census records.

27. From Social Security Death Index and 1930 United States Federal Census records.

28. From Social Security Death Index and 1930 United States Federal Census records.

29. From Social Security Death Index and 1930 United States Federal Census records.

30. Victoria K. Matranga, "Biographies of Designers," *The Alliance of Art and Industry*, 195–196.

31. Winifred Mallon, "New Refrigerator is Among Patents," *The New York Times*, November 15, 1947, 21.

32. "A Talk with Donald Dailey," *Industrial Design* 1, no. 3 (June 1954): 95.

33. Obituary, *The Blade*, August 9, 1982. Also telephone conversations with William Desser, the designer's son, December 2, 2003, and March 17, 2004; correspondence of December 2, 2003, with Greg Miller, Librarian, Toledo-Lucas County Historical Society.

34. Russell Flinchum, *Henry Dreyfuss, Industrial Designer*.

35. From Social Security Death Index and 1930 United States Federal Census records.

36. From Social Security Death Index and 1930 United States Federal Census records.

37. Alice Hoogenborne, in *American National Biography*, ed. John A. Garraty and Mark C. Carnes (New York: Oxford University Press, 1999), 560.

38. The latest significant book on Fuller is: Joachim Krauss and Claude Lichtenstein, eds., *Your Private Sky: R. Buckminster Fuller; The Art of Design Science*, (Baden-Baden, Switzerland: Lars Müller / Zurich, Switzerland: Museum für Gestaltung Zürich, 1999).

39. From 1930 United States Federal Census records.

40. Biographical information from *The Alliance of Art and Industry*, 201–202; and Jennifer Davis Roberts, *Norman Bel Geddes: An Exhibition of Theatrical and Industrial Designs* (Austin: College of Fine Arts and the Humanities Research Center, University of Texas at Austin, 1979).

41. "Norman Bel Geddes 1893–1958," *Industrial Design* 5, no. 6 (June 1958), 48.

42. *Massimo Iosa Ghini: 15 Years of Projects* (Milan: Electa, 2001), 15.

43. Karrie Jacobs, "When is a Chair not a Chair?" *Metropolis*, June 1988.

44. See Vincent Scully, *Michael Graves, Buildings and Projects, 1966–1981* (New York: Rizzoli, 1982); and *The Master Architects Series III: Michael Graves; Selected and Current Works* (Mulgrave, Victoria, Australia: Images Publishing, 1999).

45. Obituary, *The New York Times*, March 10, 1985, 36.

46. From Social Security Death Index and 1930 United States Federal Census records.

47. Cheney and Cheney, *Art and the Machine*, 232.

48. Ockner and Pina, *Art Deco Aluminum Kensington*, 13.

49. Sarah Nichols, *Aluminum by Design* (Pittsburgh: Carnegie Museum of Art, 2000), 228.

50. From Social Security Death Index and 1930 United States Federal Census records.

51. From 1930 United States Federal Census records.

52. From Social Security Death Index and 1930 United States Federal Census records.

53. "A Directory of Contemporary Designers," *Creative Design* 1, no. 1 (Fall 1934): 26.

54. "Designer Converts House into Offices," *The New York Times*, October 22, 1948, 33.

55. "Two Apartments in Masculine Taste Present the Extremes of Decoration," *House & Garden* 66, no. 3 (September 1934): 35.

56. From Social Security Death Index and 1930 United States Federal Census records.

57. Information from correspondence with Sam Hope, the designer's grandson, December 19, 2003, courtesy of the Wauwatosa Historical Society, Wauwatosa, Wisconsin.

58. From Social Security Death Index.

59. Biographical information based on Joseph Griggs, "Alfonso Iannelli, The Prairie Spirit in Sculpture," *Prairie School Review* 2, no. 4 (Fourth Quarter, 1965): 5–23.

60. From Social Security Death Index.

61. Information based on correspondence with Judy Johnson, Glen Ellyn Historical Society, Glen Ellyn, Illinois, November 14, 2003.

62. From Social Security Death Index.

63. From Social Security Death Index and 1930

36. From Social Security Death Index and 1930 United States Federal Census records.

United States Federal Census records.

64. From Social Security Death Index.

65. "Directs Appliance Design of the Westinghouse Co.," *The New York Times*, October 16, 1943, 23.

66. From Social Security Death Index and 1930 United States Federal Census records.

67. Correspondence with the designer, March 10, 2004, and "Head Case," *Industrial Design Magazine* (January/February, 2004): 64.

68. From Social Security Death Index and 1930 United States Federal Census records.

69. Obituary, *Detroit Free Press*, April 7, 1998, 7A. Biographical information from correspondence with the Grosse Pointe Historical Society, August 19, 2003, and with John Lauve, the designer's son.

70. From Social Security Death Index.

71. From 1930 United States Federal Census records.

72. Obituary, *The New York Times*, July 15, 1986.

73. Ann Lee Morgan, ed., *Contemporary Designers* (London: St. James Press, 1985), 500.

74. Information from correspondence with the office of Ross Lovegrove, March 19, 2004.

75. From 1930 United States Federal Census records.

76. From Social Security Death Index.

77. Information from correspondence with Steve Daily, Milwaukee County Historical Society, October 21, 2003.

78. "Chicago Design Directory," *Industrial Design* 3, no. 5 (October, 1956): 117.

79. Information from correspondence with the office of the designer, March 2004.

80. *Who's Who in American Art*, 1947 and Lenore Newman, *What Modern Was*, 388.

81. "Peter Müller-Munk: Product Design Offices of a One-time Silversmith," *Interiors* 113, no. 11 (June 1954): 95.

82. Ann Lee Morgan, ed., *Contemporary Designers* (London: St. James Press, 1985), 441.

83. Obituary, *The New York Times*, March 14, 1967, 35.

84. Biographical information is based on Bruce Altschuler, *Noguchi* (New York: Abbeville Press, 1994).

85. From 1930 United States Federal Census records.

86. Correspondence with Berwyn Historical Society, December 9, 2003.

87. "Supply and Design: They Strike a Balance in the Chicago Area", *Industrial Design* 3, no. 5 (October 1956): 117.

88. From Social Security Death Index and 1930 United States Federal Census records.

89. Information from conversations and correspondence with the designer, March 2004, and resumé.

90. From Social Security Death Index.

91. Norman Bel Geddes, *Magic Motorways* (New York: Random House, 1940), n.p.

92. Obituary, *The New York Times*, July 1, 1977, A21.

93. From Social Security Death Index and 1930 United States Federal Census records.

94. From Social Security Death Index.

95. From Social Security Death Index and 1930 United States Federal Census records.

96. From Social Security Death Index and 1930 United States Federal Census records.

97. Mary Roche, "New Ideas and Inventions," *The New York Times Magazine* (November 10, 1946): 42.

98. J. H. DuBois, *Plastics*, iii.

99. From Social Security Death Index.

100. From Social Security Death Index.

101. "Business Notes," *The New York Times* (August 16, 1944): 27.

102. "Pantryware Collection Features Footed Bases," *The New York Times* (July 3, 1958): 16.

103. www.palaceofculture.org, also www.inliquid.com/gallery/lostHighways

104. From Social Security Death Index and 1930 United States Federal Census records.

105. From Social Security Death Index.

106. "Supply and Design: They Strike a Balance in the Chicago Area," *ID* 3, no. 5 (October 1956): 115.

107. *Toledo Designs for a Modern America*, 208.

108. "Selected for Presidency of Industrial Designers," *The New York Times*, (October 4, 1952): 26.

109. "Frederick Hurten Rhead," *The Bulletin of the American Ceramic Society* 21, no. 12 (December 15, 1942): 306.

110. Sharon Dale, *Frederick Hurten Rhead: An English Potter in America* (Erie, Pennsylvania: Erie Art Museum, 1986).

111. Date and place of birth confirmed in 1930 United States Federal Census records.

112. *The Alliance of Art and Industry Toledo Designs for a Modern America*, (Toledo, Ohio: Toledo Museum of Art, 2002), 208-209.

113. Walter Rendell Storey, "New Materials in the Decorative Arts," *The New York Times Magazine* (January 29, 1933): 12.

114. Date and place of birth confirmed in 1930 United States Federal Census records.

115. Biographical information from *The Alliance of Art and Industry*, 210.

116. From Social Security Death Index.

117. From Social Security Death Index.

118. From Social Security Death Index and 1930 United States Federal Census records.

119. The following biographical information is derived from Judith Nasby's unpublished manuscript, "Rolf Scarlett: Art, Design and Jewelry," David A. Hanks & Associates Archives, n.d.

120. From Social Security Death Index.

121. Correspondence November 13, 2003, with Karen Miller, Reference Librarian, Wilmette Public Library who supplied a copy of the designer's obituary.

122. Obituary, *The New York Times*, November 7, 1962, 39.

123. *"Time,"* November 25, 1946, 96-97

124. "Peter Schlumbohm," *Industrial Design* 9, no. 12 (September 1962): 14.

125. Ralph Caplan, "Cross Section," *Industrial Design* 9, no. 12 (December 1962): 121.

126. Information from Henry Adams, *Viktor Schreckengost and 20ᵗʰ Century Design* (Cleveland: Cleveland Museum of Art, 2000), 1-29.

127. From Social Security Death Index and 1930 United States Federal Census records.

128. From Social Security Death Index and 1930 United States Federal Census records.

129. Biographical information from the office of Seymour Powell, March 15, 2004.

130. From Social Security Death Index and 1930 United States Federal Census records.

131. From Social Security Death Index, listed as "Brooks Stevens."

132. See Glenn Adamson, *Industrial Strength Design* (Milwaukee: MIT Press for the Milwaukee Art Museum, 2003), 1-8.

133. John Holusha, Obituary, *The New York Times*, January 7, 1995, 30.

134. From Social Security Death Index.

135. Biographical information derived in part from *The Alliance of Art and Industry*, 212-13.

136. From Social Security Death Index.

137. Cheney and Cheney, *Art and the Machine*, 82.

138. http//www.shapetomorrow.com

139. Information from "Remembering Father," a biographical manuscript of 2004 by the designer's son Robert A. Suomala, on deposit at the Haddonfield Historical Society, Haddonfield, New Jersey.

140. Obituary, *Haddon Gazette*, June 6, 1985, 7; courtesy of Kathy Tassini, Librarian, Haddonfield Historical Society, New Jersey.

141. 2,051,799; 2,094,246; 2,106,733; 2,229,358; 2,295,368; D121,427.

142. See biographical entry by Frederica T. Harlow in *What Modern Was*, 401.

143. Cheney and Cheney, *Art and the Machine*, 69.

144. Annemarie Van Roessel, "Oral History of Richard Ten Eyck," Chicago Architects Oral History Project, Ernest R. Graham Study Center for Architectural Drawings, Department of Architecture, Art Institute of Chicago, 2003. Telephone conversation between David A. Hanks and Richard Ten Eyck, November 2002.

145. From Social Security Death Index and 1930 United States Federal Census records.

146. Walter Randell Storry, "Modern Decorative Art Here and Abroad," *The New York Times*, May 31, 1931, 19.

147. Date and place of birth confirmed in the Social Security Death Index.

148. Cheney and Cheney, *Art and the Machine*, 86.

149. From Social Security Death Index and 1930 United States Federal Census records.

150. From Social Security Death Index.

151. *Contemporary Designers*, 857.

152. *Industrial Design* 18, January–June, 1971, 46.

153. *Contemporary Designers*, 859.

154. Date of birth from Social Security Death Index.

155. Conversation with Milan Vavrik, the designer's son, November 5, 2003, and resumé written by Milan Vavrik.

156. Obituary, *Rossford Record Journal* (January 19, 1995).

157. From Social Security Death Index and 1930 United States Federal Census records, which has the first name incorrectly transposed from the handwritten record as "Chuncey."

158. Biographical information is derived from entry by Martin Eidelberg in *What Modern Was*, 404, and Kathryn Hiesinger and George H. Marcus, *Landmarks of Twentieth-Century Design: An Illustrated Handbook* (New York, 1993), 396.

159. Obituary, *Rossford Record Journal*, January, 19, 1995.

160. Joseph Johnson is listed in the Manhattan Classified Telephone Directory for the Fall-Winter of 1939 at 55 West 42ⁿᵈ Street.

161. "Design Decade," *Architectural Forum* 73, no. 4 (October 1940): 244.

162. From Social Security Death Index and 1930 United States Federal Census records.

163. Obituary, *The New York Times*, April 31, 1954, 24.

164. From Social Security Death Index and 1930 United States Federal Census records.

APPENDIX

1. For specific instructions on accessing patents, especially those before 1927, see Brian Pennington, "Patent Searches: Step-by-Step," *Chronicle of the Early American Industries Association* 55, no. 4 (December 2002), 160-165. We are grateful to Eric Brill for his research into patents, which uncovered the majority of those cited here for the dating of products and the identification of their designers.

Selected Bibliography

The following cites the sources that informed our introduction and chapter essays. For more specific scholarship, see the sources cited in the endnotes and in the designers' biographies.

PERIOD SOURCES

ATHERTON, Carlton. "Henry Dreyfuss Designer." *Design* 36, no. 7 (January 1935): 7.

CHENEY, Sheldon. *The New World Architecture.* New York, New York: Longmans, Green, 1930.

CHENEY, Sheldon, and Martha Candler Cheney. *Art and the Machine: An Account of Industrial Design in 20th-Century America.* New York, New York: Whittlesey House / McGraw-Hill, 1936, reprint, 1992.

DUBOIS, J. H. *Plastics: A Simplified Presentation of the Important Plastics Materials and Products with Tables of Their Properties and the Basic Design Information Required by Engineers and Designers.* 3rd ed. Chicago, Illinois: American Technical Society, 1946.

FRANKL, Paul T. *Space for Living: Creative Interior Decoration and Design.* New York, New York: Doubleday, Doran, 1938.

GEDDES, Norman Bel. *Horizons.* Boston, Massachusetts: Little, Brown, 1932, reprint, 1977.

———. "The House of Tomorrow." *Ladies' Home Journal* 48, no. 4 (April 1931): 12–13, 162.

———. "Streamlining." *Atlantic Monthly* 154, no. 5 (November 1934): 553–563.

GIEDION, Siegfried. *Mechanization Takes Command: A Contribution to Anonymous History.* New York, New York: Oxford University Press, 1948, reprint, 1969.

HITCHCOCK, Henry-Russell, and Philip Johnson. *The International Style: Architecture Since 1922.* New York, New York: W. W. Norton, 1932, reprint, *The International Style,* 1966.

KAUFMANN, Edgar, jr. "Borax, or the Chromium-Plated Calf." *Architectural Review* 104, no. 6 (August 1948): 89.

LOEWY, Raymond. *The Locomotive.* New York, New York: Universe Books, 1937, reprint 1988.

———. *Never Leave Well Enough Alone.* New York, New York: Simon & Schuster, 1951, reprint, Baltimore and London: Johns Hopkins University Press, 2002.

MCANDREW, John. "'Modernistic' and 'Streamlined.'" *Bulletin of the Museum of Modern Art* 5, no. 6 (December 1938).

MUMFORD, Lewis. *Technics and Civilization.* New York, New York: Harcourt, Brace, 1934, reprint, 1963.

REID, Kenneth. "Norman Bel Geddes, Master of Design." *Pencil Points* 18, no. 1 (January 1937): 1–32.

SHELDON, Roy, and Egmont Arens. *Consumer Engineering: A New Technique for Prosperity.* New York, New York: Harper, 1932, reprint, 1976.

TEAGUE, Walter Dorwin. *Design This Day: The Technique of Order in the Machine Age.* New York, New York: Harcourt, Brace, 1940.

VAN DOREN, Harold. *Industrial Design: A Practical Guide.* New York, New York: McGraw-Hill, 1940. 2nd ed., *Industrial Design: A Practical Guide to Product Design and Development,* 1954.

CONTEMPORARY SOURCES

ADAMS, Henry. *Viktor Schreckengost and 20th-Century Design.* Cleveland, Ohio: The Cleveland Museum of Art, 2000.

BENTON, Charlotte, Tim Benton, and Ghislaine Wood, eds. *Art Deco: 1910–1939.* Boston, Massachusetts: Bulfinch Press / AOL Time Warner; London, England: V&A Publications, 2003.

BRADEN, Donna R. "Selling the Dream and Buying the Dream." In *Streamlining America.* Dearborn, Michigan: Henry Ford Museum, 1987.

BUSH, Donald J. *The Streamlined Decade.* New York, New York: George Braziller, 1975.

COGDELL, Christina. *Eugenic Design: Streamlining America in the 1930s.* Philadelphia, Pennsylvania: University of Pennsylvania Press, 2004.

COHEN, Jean-Louis. *Scenes of the World to Come: European Architecture and the American Challenge, 1893–1960.* Paris, France: Flammarion for Canadian Centre for Architecture, 1995.

DOORDAN, Dennis P., et al. *The Alliance of Art and Industry: Toledo Designs for a Modern America.* Toledo, Ohio: Toledo Museum of Art, 2002.

EIDELBERG, Martin, ed. *Design 1935–1965: What Modern Was; Selections from the Liliane and David M. Stewart Collection.* Montréal, Québec: Musée des Arts Décoratifs de Montréal; New York, New York: Harry N. Abrams, 1991, reprint, 2001.

FLINCHUM, Russell. *Henry Dreyfuss, Industrial Designer: The Man in the Brown Suit.* New York, New York: Cooper-Hewitt, National Design Museum, Smithsonian Institution / Rizzoli, 1997.

GEBHARD, David, and Harriette Von Breton. *Kem Weber: The Moderne in Southern California, 1920 Through 1941.* 2nd ed. Santa Barbara, California: Standard Printing, 1976.

———. *Los Angeles in the Thirties, 1931–1941.* 2nd ed. Los Angeles, California: Hennessey & Ingalls, 1989.

GREIF, Martin. *Depression Modern: The Thirties Style in America.* New York, New York: Universe Books, 1975.

HANKS, David A., and Jennifer Toher. *Donald Deskey: Decorative Designs and Interiors.* New York, New York: E. P. Dutton, 1987.

HESKETT, John. *Industrial Design*. New York, New York: Oxford University Press, 1980.

JOHNSON, J. Stewart. *American Modern, 1925-1940: Design for a New Age*. New York, New York: Harry N. Abrams; New York, New York: American Federation of Arts, 2000.

KAPLAN, Wendy, ed. *Designing Modernity: The Arts of Reform and Persuasion, 1885-1945; Selections from the Wolfsonian*. New York, New York: Thames and Hudson; Miami Beach, Florida: The Wolfsonian, 1995.

KRAS, Reyer. *Streamline: The Dawn of Tomorrow; American Design, '30-'55*. Amsterdam, Netherlands: Stedelijk Museum, 2002.

KRAUSSE, Joachim, and Claude Lichtenstein, eds. *Your Private Sky: R. Buckminster Fuller; The Art of Design Science*. Baden-Baden, Switzerland: Lars Müller / Zurich, Switzerland: Museum für Gestaltung Zürich, 1999.

LICHTENSTEIN, Claude, and Franz Engler, eds. *Streamlined: A Metaphor for Progress; The Esthetics of Minimized Drag*. Baden-Baden, Switzerland: Lars Müller, 1995.

LUPTON, Ellen, and J. Abbott Miller. *The Bathroom, the Kitchen, and the Aesthetics of Waste: A Process of Elimination*. Cambridge, Massachusetts: MIT List Visual Arts Center, 1992.

MARCHAND, Roland. *Advertising the American Dream: Making Way for Modernity, 1920-1940*. Berkeley and Los Angeles, California: University of California Press, 1985.

MEIKLE, Jeffrey L. *American Plastic: A Cultural History*. New Brunswick, New Jersey: Rutgers University Press, 1995.

——. *Twentieth Century Limited: Industrial Design in America, 1925-1939*. Philadelphia, Pennsylvania: Temple University Press, 1979, reprint, 2001.

MORSHED, Adnan. "The Aesthetics of Ascension in Norman Bel Geddes's Futurama." *Journal of the Society of Architectural Historians* 63, no. 1 (March 2004): 74-99.

NICHOLS, Sarah. *Aluminum by Design*. Pittsburgh, Pennsylvania: Carnegie Museum of Art, 2000.

OCKNER, Paula, and Leslie Piña. *Art Deco Aluminum: Kensington*. Atglen, Pennsylvania: Schiffer, 1997.

PERREAULT, John. *Streamline Design: How the Future Was*. Flushing, New York: Queens Museum, 1984.

PHILLIPS, Stephen Bennett. *Margaret Bourke-White: The Photography of Design, 1927-1936*. Washington, D. C.: The Phillips Collection; New York, New York: Rizzoli, 2002.

PLUMMER, Kathleen Church. "The Streamlined Moderne," *Art in America* 62 (January–February 1974): 46-54.

PORTER, Glenn. *Raymond Loewy: Designs for a Consumer Culture*. Wilmington, Delaware: Hagley Museum and Library, 2002.

PULOS, Arthur J. *The American Design Adventure, 1940-1975*. Cambridge, Massachusetts: MIT Press, 1988.

——. *American Design Ethic: A History of Industrial Design to 1940*. Cambridge, Massachusetts: MIT Press, 1983.

QUEENS MUSEUM. *Dawn of a New Day: The New York World's Fair, 1939/40*. Flushing, New York: Queens Museum; New York, New York: New York University Press, 1980.

REED, Robert C. *The Streamline Era*. San Marino, California: Golden West Books, 1975.

SCHÖNBERGER, Angela, ed. *Raymond Loewy: Pioneer of American Industrial Design*. Munich, Germany: Prestel, 1990.

SMITH, Terry. *Making the Modern: Industry, Art, and Design in America*. Chicago, Illinois: University of Chicago Press, 1993.

SPARKE, Penny. *Electrical Appliances: Twentieth-Century Design*. New York, New York: E. P. Dutton, 1987.

TOBEY, Ronald C. *Technology as Freedom: The New Deal and the Electrical Modernization of the American Home*. Berkeley, California: University of California Press, 1996.

WILSON, Kristina. *Livable Modernism: Interior Decoration and Design During the Great Depression*. New Haven, Connecticut: Yale University Press, 2004.

WILSON, Richard Guy, Dianne H. Pilgrim, and Dickran Tashjian. *The Machine Age in America, 1918-1941*. Brooklyn, New York: Brooklyn Museum; New York, New York: Harry N. Abrams, 1986.

WURTS, Richard, et al. *The New York World's Fair, 1939/1940*. New York, New York: Dover Publications, 1977.

ZIMMERMANN, Karl R. *20th Century Limited*. St. Paul, Minnesota: MBI Publishing, 2002.

Several archival sources have been helpful in the research that was done for this catalogue. The Syracuse University Library's Department of Special Collections, established by Arthur J. Pulos, holds the archival collections of many important designers, including Egmont Arens, Lurelle Guild, Walter Dorwin Teague, and John Vassos. The Hagley Museum and Library in Wilmington, Delaware, holds company records of firms such as Remington-Rand, as well as the archives of individual designers such as Raymond Loewy. The Harry Ransom Humanities Research Center at the University of Texas, Austin, is the foremost collector of material related to Norman Bel Geddes. Other sources of archival material on twentieth-century American industrial designers are The Art Institute of Chicago, The Chicago Athenaeum, The Wolfsonian-Florida International University in Miami, and the Architecture & Design Collection of the University Art Museum at the University of California, Santa Barbara.

Index

Numbers in italic refer to illustrations.
Designers' biographies are not indexed.

Photographic credits

The authors and publisher wish to thank the following photographers, institutions, companies, and collectors who have graciously granted permission to reproduce their photographs. All catalogue objects photographed by Denis Farley except where noted.

Airstream, Inc., Jackson Center, Ohio: fig. 42.

Amtrak, Washington, D.C., and White & Baldacci, Herndon, Virginia: fig. 191.

Bauhaus-Archiv, Museum für Gestaltung, Berlin: fig. 104.

Bourke-White Estate, Okemos, Michigan: p. 2; p. 6; p. 14, right; p. 15, left; fig. 140.

Eric Brill, Bedford Hills, New York: p. 7; fig. 49.

Burlington Northern and Santa Fe Railway, Fort Worth, Texas: fig. 118.

Butler Manufacturing Company, Kansas City, Missouri: fig. 130.

Centre Georges-Pompidou, Bibliothèque Kandinsky, Fonds Archizoom, Paris: fig. 187.

Collection Centre Canadien d'Architecture/Canadian Centre for Architecture, Montreal, Quebec: p. 280; figs. 12, 14, 25, 28, 53, 61, 62, 63, 74, 102, 105, 107, 114, 129, 136, 137, 139, 151, 152, 159, 160, 161, 164, 168.

Vogue © The Condé Nast Publications, Inc., photo by Edward Steichen: fig. 54; photo by Anton Bruehl, fig. 150.

Coolstock.com Collection, Austin, Texas: fig. 67.

Cooper-Hewitt, National Design Museum, Smithsonian Institution, New York, New York: fig. 22, used by permission of the New York Central System Historical Society; fig. 26, gift of Henry Dreyfuss, 1972; figs. 50, 56, 134, 135, Donald Deskey Collection; fig. 179, gift of Henry Dreyfuss, 1972.

Denis Farley, Montreal, Quebec: figs. 77, 84, 86, 157, 170, 173, 180.

General Motors Corporation. Used with permission, GM Media Archives, Detroit, Michigan: fig. 185.

Michael Graves Design Group Target Toaster Working Drawing, 1998. Princeton, New Jersey: fig. 193.

Greyhound Lines, Inc., Dallas, Texas: fig. 39.

Diner Archives of Richard J. S. Gutman, West Roxbury, Massachusetts: fig. 69.

Hagley Museum and Library, Wilmington, Delaware: p. 15, left, and figs. 25, 32, 46, used by permission of Laurence Loewy.

Sharon and Bob Huxford, Covington, Indiana: fig. 145.

IBM Corporation Archives, Somers, New York: figs. 73, 76.

Library of Congress, Prints & Photographs Division, HABS, Reproduction number: CAL,19-LOSAN-41-1: fig. 17; HABS, Reproduction number: WIS,51-RACI,5-24: fig. 71; HABS, Reproduction number: CAL,38-SANFRA,157-1: fig. 163.

Lockheed Martin Corporation, Bethesda, Maryland: fig. 174.

Laurence Loewy, Marietta, Georgia: figs. 27, 28, 29, 34, 35, 36, 39, 101, 182, 190.

Maidenform, Inc., Bayonne, New Jersey: fig. 8.

Shirley Manning, Shirley's Hall China Reference Pages, http://home.att.net/~hallchina/index.htm: figs. 109, 123.

The Metropolitan Museum of Art, New York, New York: fig. 6, gift of M. H. Lobel and C. H. Lobel, 1983 (1983.493.1–.4); fig. 60.

By artist Roy Lichtenstein, designed 1990, fabricated 1994, installed 2002. Commissioned and owned by Metropolitan Transportation Authority Arts for Transit, New York, New York. Photo by Rob Wilson: fig. 186.

Missouri Historical Society, St. Louis, Missouri: fig. 117.

The Montreal Museum of Fine Arts, Montreal, Quebec: fig. 141, used by permission of The Huntington Library, San Marino, California, photo by Maynard Parker; fig. 142, used by permission of University of California, Santa Barbara, California, Architectural Drawing Collection, University Art Museum; fig. 166, photo by Cervin Robinson, New York; fig. 189, photo by Denis Farley; cat. 101, 102, used by permission of the Rolph Scarlett Estate, Bearsville, New York; cat. 104, © 2005 Estate of Harry Bertoia / Artists Rights Society (ARS), New York.

Installation view of the exhibition "Machine Art," The Museum of Modern Art, New York. March 5, 1934 through April 29, 1934. Photograph by Wurts Brothers, Digital Image Courtesy The Museum of Modern Art, New York: fig. 7; illustration 65 from Johnson, Philip: *Machine Art*. New York: The Museum of Modern Art, 1934. Offset lithograph, printed in black, page size: 10 x 7" (25.4 x 19.1 cm). The Museum of Modern Art Library, The Museum of Modern Art, New York. Digital Image ©2004 The Museum of Modern Art, New York: fig. 24.

National Motorcycle Museum & Hall of Fame, Anamosa, Iowa: fig. 41.

Arlen Ness Enterprises, Dublin, California: fig. 192.

The New-York Historical Society: fig. 133.

Photofestnyc.com, New York, New York: fig. 19.

Queens Museum of Art, Queens, New York: fig. 47.

Harry Ransom Research Center, The University of Texas at Austin: figs. 11, 52; figs. 31, 83, used by permission of the Bel Geddes Estate.

Museum of Art, Rhode Island School of Design; Gift of Textron, Inc. Photography by Cathy Carver: fig. 5.

The Victor Schreckengost Foundation, Cleveland Heights, Ohio, object from the Paul Schreckengost collection, photography by Gary Kirchenbauer: fig. 4.

Staatliche Museen zu Berlin, Bildarchiv Preussischer Kulturbesitz, Berlin, Germany, through Art Resource, New York: fig. 13.

Studio Iosa Ghini, Bologna, Italy: fig. 188.

Courtesy of Syracuse University Library, Department of Special Collections, Syracuse, New York: p. 2, p. 6, p. 14, right, p. 15, left, and fig. 140, used by permission of the Bourke-White Estate, Okemos, Michigan; figs. 15, 16, 64, 65, 93, 158.

United States Patent and Trademark Office website, http://www.uspto.gov: figs. 40, 78, 79, 80, 82, 92, 94, 95, 96, 97, 98, 99, 100, 120, 121, 122, 124, 125, 126, 127, 128, 132, 147, 148, 149, 153, 165, 169, 177, 178.

History & Cultures Project, University of California, Davis, California: fig. 10.

University of California, Santa Barbara, Kem Weber Collection, Architecture & Design Collection, University Art Museum, Santa Barbara, California: figs. 144, 154, 155.

Richard Wurts, *The General Motors Building, 1939 World's Fair*, Museum of the City of New York, The Wurts Collection: fig. 44.

FOLLOWING PAGE
Anon., photograph of the *Twentieth Century Limited*, 1937, by Henry Dreyfuss. From *Architectural Forum*, September 1938. Brill Collection.